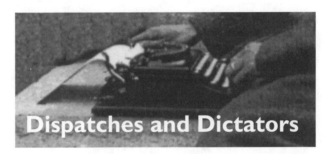

Dispatches and Dictators

Dispatches and Dictators:
Ralph Barnes for the Herald Tribune

By Barbara S. Mahoney

Oregon State University Press
Corvallis

Substantial gifts from the following donors helped make publication of this book possible. The Oregon State University Press is grateful for their support.

Suzanne & Robert Morrison and Joan & Gerald Kelly
Ancil H. Payne

The paper in this book meets the guidelines for permanence and durability of the Committee on Production Guidelines for Book Longevity of the Council on Library Resources and the minimum requirements of the American National Standard for Permanence of Paper for Printed Library Materials Z39.48-1984.

Library of Congress Cataloging-in-Publication Data
Mahoney, Barbara S.
  Dispatches and dictators : Ralph Barnes for the Herald Tribune / by
Barbara S. Mahoney.— 1st ed.
     p. cm.
Includes bibliographical references and index.
  ISBN 0-87071-546-1 (alk. paper)
  1. Barnes, Ralph, 1899-1940. 2. Journalists—United
States—Biography. 3. Foreign correspondents—United
States—Biography. I. Title.
  PN4874.B326 M34 2002
  070.4'332'092—dc21

                                    2002003765

Oregon State University Press
101 Waldo Hall
Corvallis OR 97331-6407
OREGON STATE   541-737-3166 • fax 541-737-3170
UNIVERSITY   http://oregonstate.edu/dept/press

Contents

Acknowledgments

Many people made this book possible. My greatest debt of gratitude is to Suzanne Barnes Morrison and Joan Barnes Kelly, who entrusted their father's clipping books, correspondence and other papers to me and had faith in this project from the beginning. They also shared memories of their father and the stories their mother had passed along.

I could not have tackled this book without the background of my graduate studies at St. Louis University. There I was privileged to know Kurt von Schuschnigg, an experience that heightened my interest in this period of history. There too I benefitted from the guidance of Professor José M. Sanchez. Many years later, Joe kindly read this manuscript and contributed many helpful observations.

John McMillan, then publisher of the Salem *Statesman Journal,* answered many questions about American journalism and its history. He also passed along relevant books and articles as he encountered them in his reading. Robert Notson, Ralph's childhood friend and the longtime publisher of the Portland *Oregonian,* contributed stories of Ralph from his high school and college days. Ruth Rhoten provided details about the time spent at Harvard.

Through the long process of researching and writing this book, friends and colleagues at Willamette University provided encouragement and inspiration. Mike Bennett, Pat Alley, Roger Hull, and the late Larry Cress took a particular interest. Sheri Martin tackled the task of preparing the manuscript to be sent out. David Worrix did wonderful work in restoring the photographs for publication. Willamette's president, Jerry Hudson, gave this effort the same generous support he has given other aspects of my career. Ken McCormick with his wife Anne, Ancil Payne, Bill MacDougall, and Greg Nokes, among other Willamette alumni, assisted me through their vast experience in the field of communications.

The photographs in the book were provided to me by Suzanne Morrison, and the source of many of them is unclear. The photograph of the Barnes family home was probably a family snapshot, but could have been by the Cronise Studio in Salem, which closed in the 1920s. The photograph of Esther and Karl Radek appeared in the *Saturday Evening Post,* April 29, 1939. The photograph of the Barnes children with a lion cub was taken by a photographer at the Berlin Zoo. The photograph of the Liberty Ship may have appeared in the *Oregonian.*

I am grateful to the staff at Oregon State University Press for their professionalism and their enthusiasm.

Finally and most importantly, I thank my children Michael, Brian, Ellen and Colin, and especially my husband Tim, without whose love and tolerance this would never have come about.

Introduction

Ralph Barnes flew from Germany to the United States in 1936 as one of the few reporters on the maiden voyage of the airship *Hindenburg*. While in New York, he talked to publishers about his proposed book, *Under Three Dictatorships*. Among the journalistic community of his day, he was uniquely qualified to write it. After three years of apprenticeship on the Paris *Herald*, Barnes had served as the correspondent of the *New York Herald Tribune* in Rome for over a year, and in Moscow for more than four years. By the time he visited New York, he had been head of the Berlin bureau of the *Herald Tribune* for nine months and had already reported on the internal workings of the Nazi regime, its anti-Semitism, its treatment of Protestant dissenters, and the crisis that ensued when Hitler sent his troops into the Rhineland.

As Europe rushed toward war, however, Ralph Barnes never found time to write *Under Three Dictatorships*. On his return to Germany, he chronicled the power struggles between Hitler and the High Command of the German Army, the annexation of Austria, the Munich Conference, and *Kristallnacht*. Transferred to London in the spring of 1939, he returned to Berlin in April, 1940. As a correspondent, he followed the German Army as it swept west through the Low Countries and into France. Germany's quick successes led him to report on a cooling of relations with the Soviet Union and to predict that the East would be the next object of Nazi conquest. The reaction of the German government was swift; Barnes was immediately expelled. He spent the next few months covering the Balkans and the Mediterranean. When he flew from Athens with a British bombing mission, the plane crashed in Yugoslavia on November 18, 1940, killing all aboard. Barnes was forty-one years old.

Despite the efforts of Ralph Barnes's friends and colleagues, his story was nearly lost. It came to me through serendipity when I was working as a teacher and administrator at his alma mater, Willamette University in Salem, Oregon. In 1985, I read about the death of his widow, who had returned to Salem and later remarried. Her obituary introduced me to Barnes himself and led me to his daughters, Suzanne Barnes Morrison and Joan Barnes Kelly, who generously shared with me the family correspondence and the clipping books containing all of his reporting. For a student of history, it was a windfall. I was attracted by the untouched quality of the material, by the chance to look at a significant period of our century in a new way. As I studied the material, several threads emerged. Perhaps the least obvious, but in many ways the most engaging, is the sense of Ralph Barnes as a son, a husband, a father, a reporter, and a friend. His ambition, his insecurity, his humanity, even his depression, are all revealed. Along the same lines, the letters recorded one family's experience with the maelstrom that was Europe in the 1930s. To me this thread is an integral part of the story. It is good to be reminded that, even in troubled times, people find solace in their marriages and joy in their children, that concerns about health or finances often eclipse great events.

Ralph Barnes's day-to-day exposition of occurrences provides a new perspective for the historian who normally goes back after the fact and discerns order, progression, and often inevitability. Barnes did not know what was coming next. His work gives us the opportunity to isolate happenings as they were experienced. It also enables the reader to explore the question of what was "knowable" by an able and thorough reporter. Under the best of circumstances, daily journalism is a challenging and competitive enterprise. Even an open society is adept at keeping its secrets. Working under a deadline while competing for a newspaper's limited space often weighs against thoughtful analysis; yet the best reporters strive to understand the events and personalities they cover, to provide some context to their stories. They seek to illuminate complex issues without sacrificing nuance. They work to develop sources to present a broader, truer picture. For foreign correspondents, each of these challenges is heightened by the need to master another language, unfamiliar customs, and a new historical framework. In much of the world, they encounter governments for whom a free press is an alien concept.

Too often, it seems to me, we do not study the work of journalists first hand. For example, I am struck by the degree to which the recent Library of America anthology, *Reporting World War II*, relies on diaries, memoirs, and later accounts rather than the actual reporting at the time of the event. The record of Ralph Barnes's journalism lies solely in what he filed day by day in the *Herald Tribune*. Other correspondents later published books about the period and had the opportunity for revision. They could, and did, say, "I knew it all along!" Ralph Barnes never had that chance. Yet the body of his work stands up remarkably well.

In a time when newspapers were too often obedient or ideological or sensational, Barnes's reporting was none of these. For most of his career, he worked under repressive regimes whose methods of dealing with the press were at once sophisticated and brutal. Getting at the facts amidst the constant barrage of propaganda was a trial. Developing reliable sources in societies ridden by fear was nearly impossible. Like other correspondents before and since, he struggled to report the truth in a way that would not result in his expulsion by the government he was assigned to cover. His paper was supportive but it, and Barnes, labored under the shadow of their major competitor, the *New York Times*. William Stoneman, who worked in Rome, Moscow and Berlin when Barnes did, once observed: "At the other end of the line was the *New York Times* which was pro-Fascist in Italy, pro-Commie in Russia and pro-Nazi or at least not anti-Nazi in Germany. Since the *New York Times* had a blown-up reputation it was very difficult for Ralph to be as independent as he was."[1] When Barnes was expelled from Germany in June of 1940, William Shirer in his diary attributed his expulsion to "the Nazi hate of the *Herald Tribune*'s editorial policy and its insistence on maintaining fearlessly independent correspondents here [in Berlin]—the only New York paper that does."[2]

Nor was Barnes ever sensational in his reporting. He was scrupulous about checking his facts, careful not to let his opinions intrude. It mattered. Through the 1930s, with radio news still in its infancy, the American people relied almost exclusively on their newspapers to find out what was going on. At home, the Depression, the Roosevelt administration, the New Deal, and the Huey Longs, Father Coughlins, Upton Sinclairs with their varied solutions to the country's problems captured attention. In Asia, the Japanese Empire pressed against its neighbors. From Europe, reports about Italian Fascism, Soviet Communism, and German National Socialism provided an education for the American people. Many were horrified, but each of those regimes also had its admirers in the United States. As a foreign correspondent for the *Herald Tribune*, Ralph Barnes saw his role as providing the best possible information about events and their background and, just as important, about the lives of the people in the various countries where he worked. He did not wait for stories to come to him but sought them out; he was unstinting in his energetic pursuit of information.

As the succession of crises leading to World War II mounted, most Americans thought their country could remain secure behind its protecting oceans. Ultimately Pearl Harbor decided the question, but even before December 1941, President Franklin Roosevelt managed to signal the support for the British war effort that sustained Winston Churchill and his people through the dark days of 1940. That Roosevelt did so in the midst of a political campaign, and won the election, suggests that the American people had come to some understanding of their country's wider responsibilities and to some sense of the threat the dictatorships represented. John Lukacs has pointed to the significance of the fact that the Republican candidate in the 1940 presidential campaign was Wendell Willkie rather than Robert Taft. Even as late as January 1941, Taft still rejected the idea that Hitler's defeat was in any way vital to American interests. That Willkie's views on the international situation were similar to Roosevelt's enabled the President to act on Britain's behalf without its becoming a campaign issue. Lukacs ascribes Willkie's nomination in part to the internationalist readers of the *New York Herald Tribune,* who exercised greater influence at the Republican convention than the isolationist readers of the *Chicago Tribune.*[3] From September of 1935 through March of 1939, the preponderance of news from Germany that appeared in the *Herald Tribune* came from Ralph Barnes's typewriter.

Barnes respected his readers. He assumed that they wanted as full and complete a chronicle as he could provide, that they appreciated the importance of nuance and context, that they were, in short, intelligent people eager to understand the questions of their time. He was idealistic about his profession and at the same time determined to make the front page. He lived and reported in an era unsurpassed for its complexity and peril. His story is also its story.

Part I. Oregon to Rome:

June 1899—March 1931

From Mussolini's Italy, Stalin's Russia and Hitler's Germany, Ralph Waldo Barnes reported on the events of the 1930s for the readers of the *New York Herald Tribune*. For his efforts, he was confined to Moscow by Stalin and kicked out of Germany by Hitler. In pursuit of a story, he went along on a British bombing mission in the Mediterranean in 1940 and was killed when the plane crashed.

Barnes had many friends and most of them, like him, earned their living by reporting. At his death, and for the rest of their lives, they wrote about him with warmth and respect. To Al Laney, who first knew him as a novice on the Paris *Herald,* Ralph Barnes was "one of the greatest reporters that ever lived and the Paris *Herald*'s finest contribution to the profession of journalism." In 1987, the hundredth anniversary edition of the *International Herald Tribune* saluted Ralph Barnes as "a quintessential foreign correspondent, eternally curious and incurably active."[1]

Leland Stowe, a Pulitzer Prize-winning correspondent for the *New York Herald Tribune* and later for the *Chicago Daily News,* described Barnes as "an Oregonian, tall and big and contagiously western in his outspokenness. His earnestness and high intelligence always impressed people, while his boyish spontaneity and good nature always won him friends."[2]

His colleagues and competitors recognized the qualities that made him an outstanding reporter. William Stoneman of the *Chicago Daily News* worked with Barnes in Rome and Moscow and found him "full of guts in dealing with the authorities wherever we were."[3] To Maurice Hindus, his collaborator in Moscow, Barnes was "one of the great newspapermen of our times—he always got his story and got it out, and neither GPU nor Gestapo could stop him." William

Henry Chamberlin, another Moscow contemporary, thought Barnes deserved a Pulitzer Prize for his coverage of the Soviet famine in 1932-33. William Shirer, then with CBS radio in Berlin, wrote of trying to console Barnes when he was expelled from Germany and of Barnes "not quite realizing that his going was proof that he had more integrity than any of us who were allowed to stay."[4]

Stowe recorded the comment of a younger journalist who served with Barnes in Egypt: "Ralph always wanted to know everything about everything. He had to see for himself. He had to know how they load the bombs and how the gunners operate. He always asked more questions than all the rest of us put together. Out on the desert he got interested in the stars, so he bought several books on astronomy as soon as we got back to Cairo. Of course, he was a veteran and we were lots younger than he. But we could never get over his enthusiasm. He had been through everything and covered all of Europe for fourteen years, but you know how he was. He still had more enthusiasm than most cub reporters ever have."[5] To "pack in background," as Barnes put it, he read extensively: Bismarck's memoirs, biographies of Napoleon and Cromwell, *All Quiet on the Western Front, Mein Kampf, The Arab Awakening, Lawrence of Arabia,* among many other books and journals. He learned languages and immersed himself in each new culture he encountered.

The Barnes family home at Capitol and Chemeketa in Salem.

Courage, intelligence, curiosity, integrity, perseverance. These characteristics emerge very early in his life, natural results of his makeup and his upbringing. After he had embarked on his career, Ralph Barnes came home only once, but the house at the corner of Capitol and Chemeketa Streets in Salem, Oregon, was always his base. Like all real homes, it was both an anchor and a launching pad. From Moscow at Christmas in 1934, Barnes wrote his mother, "Don't forget to light the candles in my room," as if the lighted candles somehow made him present, a part of the celebration. Built around 1890 for a jeweler and his family, the house had nine commodious rooms on two stories, with a large attic and a stone-walled basement. Its half-acre lot was dotted with trees, many of them planted by the Barnes family who moved there in 1906 when Ralph was seven years old.[6] That the house was grand by Salem standards was not an important consideration for Ralph. He took the comfort of his youth rather for granted, but perhaps that comfort and security made the later sacrifices bearable.

Ralph Barnes grew up in a world that was safe and insular. The house's grandeur and its location at the center of Oregon's capital city reflected the position his father had built in the community. Like so many Oregonians of that time and since, Ralph's father, Edward Talbot Barnes, was born elsewhere. His family had come originally to Virginia from England, then moved on to Ohio, to Missouri where Edward was born in 1872, and then to Kansas where he grew up in a German community. His father, James, had been a Union soldier during the Civil War and was wounded at the Battle of Lookout Mountain in 1863. When depression hit Kansas in 1891, James traveled through the Pacific Northwest "to find a place for Edward's store." For Edward was destined by his family to be a merchant, even though his own aspirations tended to more intellectual pursuits.

James Barnes settled on the little community of Salem: "I like the city and its surroundings quite well. If all things are favorable I think I would as soon stop here as anywhere I have seen. There are two stores such as we have thought of but one of them is selling out and there is room for one more." He dismissed the fabled Oregon rain with assurances both practical and enticing: "This has been a clear day without rain and it has been pleasant. The sun has been shining most of the day but the sky has not been entirely clear of clouds. They float around in a dim hazy way."[7]

Salem had grown from the vision of a small band of Methodist missionaries who came in 1834 to bring Christianity to the natives, but stayed to establish an American presence in the Pacific Northwest against the encroaching British of the Hudson's Bay Company. The economic potential of the Willamette Valley was not lost on the clergymen who fostered such enterprises as banking, forestry, agriculture, cattle ranching and cloth making.[8] Their success opened the territory for the great migration over the Oregon Trail that began in 1841 and continued for two decades, bringing more than two hundred thousand people to Oregon along its 2,170-mile route from Missouri. By the 1890s, with the population of the entire state totaling just over three hundred thousand, Salem had a population of 2,617.

James and Mary Barnes moved to Salem and opened the Barnes Racquet Store, later the Barnes Cash Store, on Commercial Street downtown, close to the Willamette River. Although Edward was only twenty-one when the store opened, he assumed responsibility long before his father's death in 1908. Edward Barnes was, it seemed to his granddaughters, a somewhat difficult man; but perhaps that was only later in life when he had become embittered by the loss of his fortune and his son. Ralph's childhood friends remembered his father for his store and the family's large home, and as a pillar of the First Methodist Church. Indeed, the store was sufficiently profitable for Edward to marry in 1894. His new wife, Mabel Nancy Baker, was born in Ohio in 1871 and had come to Salem in 1890. They met when he stayed in her family's boarding house on his arrival in Salem. Mabel Baker Barnes was "a precise and able person ... always carefully dressed and coifed."[9] Her family and the Methodist Church were the centers of her life. Adapting well to the social standing thrust on her, she was hospitable and kind.

By the time of Ralph's birth, June 14, 1899, the store afforded the family a comfortable living. They moved from their first house on Liberty Street to State Street and finally to Capitol and Chemeketa. When Ralph's daughter Joan lived there later, it brought back many memories: "I wish so much that I could see Joannie playing within the fence which Uncle Joe and you, Dad, put up for her. I have a vague recollection of some such arrangement on Liberty Street; but don't seem to figure out just exactly what it was. My memories of that home are rather confused anyhow. I remember quite a good deal about the place on State Street; but most of all, of course, about the Chemeketa Street home. Every nook and corner of that house and yard is familiar and very dear."[10]

Mabel Baker Barnes
with Ralph and Ruth

After the death of a second baby in June 1900, Ralph was joined in the nursery by his sister Ruth in 1901. As young children, they attended Garfield School five blocks away. Their parents' interest in the arts led to private instruction in painting and music, and for a time, Ralph saw his future as an artist. In eighth grade, he wrote and illustrated a "newspaper" that included his renderings of animals, insects, and the battleship *Oregon,* "the leader of the Panama Canal fleet in 1915." The paper also suggested his later consuming interest in international affairs. The April 1914 edition included his editorial on Mexico where the great revolution that shaped the country was taking place. Apparently basing his opinions on the photographs accompanying an article he had read in the *Literary Digest,* he concluded that Venustiano Carranza "would be the most suited for the office of President of Mexico" because he appeared "calm and placid" in contrast to Pancho Villa who "had a villainous look in his eye." Villa's death, in an ambush perhaps instigated by Carranza, settled the question.

The family went on vacation trips and outings to the nearby mountains and to the Oregon coast, and once to Hawaii, sailing from

San Francisco after seeing the sights of that city. In that era, even sixty-mile trips were undertakings, as Barnes recalled in writing his mother in 1931: "I enjoyed your description of the trip to the coast, Mother. How the journey has changed! Do you remember how we were accustomed to make the rail trip to Albany the night before, in order to catch an early train for the coast, the following morning? Now you speak of a trip over and back in one day, and a walk on the beach included."[11]

Driving the twenty miles from Salem to Silvercreek Falls took more than two hours in the early years of the twentieth century, and their first automobile trip to the Oregon Coast involved fording streams and climbing very steep grades. On another such trip, to Odell Lake in the Cascade Mountains in 1914, the wider world intruded into Ralph's comfortable childhood. The family Rambler broke down, stranding them for a time at the mountain lake. Friends arrived with word of the outbreak of World War I. The Barnes family refused to believe the news until they were shown the *Oregonian's* headlines.[12]

~

Salem High School provided the usual outlets for the teenaged Ralph Barnes. He led the debate team to the state championship and was president of the senior class. He played a newspaper reporter in the senior play and his acting was judged "very satisfactory." In student government, when he was a junior, he met Esther Parounagian. Born December 18, 1901, in Pittsfield, Vermont, Esther was a year behind Ralph in school. Her mother Clemma Centennia Mathews was a Vermonter and her father Marcus Parounagian was Armenian, born in Caesaria in the Turkish Empire. He came in 1887 to the United States, where he attended New Jersey's Drew Theological Seminary to become a Methodist minister. Marcus and Clemma led the itinerant life common to preachers' families of the period; he held pastorates in Vermont and Indiana before coming to Oregon in 1907. There he served at Estacada, Gresham and Brownsville. When Ralph met Esther, Parounagian was the district Sunday School superintendent in Salem.

Esther was beautiful, bright and charming.[13] She was a class officer, played on the girls' basketball team, sang in the chorus, acted in the plays, and reported for the school newspaper. Ralph was immediately taken with her and remained her devoted admirer all his life. A prophecy in the school yearbook, *The Clarion,* referred to her as "Mrs. Barnes" although a notation accompanying Ralph's picture said that his hobby was "trying to get a steady." His parents were not particularly keen on Ralph's continuing infatuation with Esther Parounagian, especially when he used the new family car to teach her to drive. But Esther later remembered them as always kind to her as a young girl. No doubt her Methodist background helped.

World War I did much to shape the Europe of the 1930s and therefore Ralph's life and career, but it only slowly insinuated itself into his Salem existence. When the United States entered the war in 1917, a reserve training unit was established at Salem High School with Ralph as captain of the Company. The unit drilled in the morning before classes. Recruits were often late and it was Ralph's responsibility to deal with the tardy. He had a sign painted that read: "Awkward Squad—the clock runs too fast for us." Latecomers followed the company as it drilled on city streets near the school, bearing the sign. Predictably, the day came when Ralph himself was tardy and carried the "Awkward Squad" sign throughout the drill period, to the considerable delight of his fellows.[14]

During the summer after graduation, he went off to military training at St. John's Military Academy, Delafield, Wisconsin. His letters to Esther are the only record of the period, the tentative writings of a young lover: "Remember that this is the first letter I have written to a girl other than my sister for about five years. I'll bet it is crude all right. I'll try to do better next time. ... Montana is still wet. It looks funny to see the saloons. I had to take a picture of some of them." He pleaded: "When you write, please say 'Boy,' or something like that once in a while, also tell me how often I may write to you and how long the letters should be. I sure will jump when I see any letters addressed back-hand."[15]

Although military service loomed, Ralph began college in the fall of 1918 at Willamette University, just two blocks south of his home. Established by Methodist missionaries in 1842, Willamette offered a classical liberal arts education in a setting respectful of the tenets of the church. The catalog made it clear: "In directing the student life, appeal is made to reason and conscience; and principles of Christian honor and courtesy are emphasized. The regulations are such as everywhere govern the conduct of ladies and gentlemen of high ideals and serious purposes. The student is required to abstain from the use of intoxicants and cigarettes at all times, and of tobacco in any form on the campus. Undue attendance at social functions or forms of amusement is discouraged. The University wishes to devote itself to students who are earnest and not triflers, who are of high morals and not idlers."[16]

Ralph had hardly settled in when his reserve unit was called up and ordered to proceed to Fort McArthur in Waco, Texas, for officers' training. Again, his letters to Esther give a picture of the experience, including the escapades of his traveling companions: "Anybody who didn't know us would sure think we were a bunch of ruffians come out of the west." But they were not terribly wild. A fellow recruit from Willamette wrote home that of the group "not a one smokes, chews, drinks, gambles or does anything worse than play cards."[17] En route to Fort McArthur, Ralph visited San Antonio and wrote of seeing the Alamo and of how "southern" Texas was. He noted the "compartments on the street cars for Negroes."[18]

Although the Armistice came on November 11 soon after their arrival in Texas, the troops were held there. Ralph did not write Esther much about the discomforts of Army life but a companion wrote home to describe the "Battle of Waco":

> Our camp is on a perfectly level place of black ground and this mixed with almost continual rain has made a mire all about the tent. As I look out from my tent I can see a street of mirey black mud, sticky with water, and stirred up by continual formations, and at these formations, we stand in mud up to our ankles and occasionally fall head long into the slop. ... We have had neither raincoats or overcoats until yesterday, ice cold water for dinner and supper, water shut off from the toilet for two days preventing shaves, baths, and other things essential to a soldier's health. Our mess is truly a mess and all canteens are shut down preventing us from substituting our scanty rations. I have received no wages for two months and very little mail. ... We have to carry our wood nearly half a mile and wash our dishes in water so greasy that it is next to impossible to get them clean.[19]

When, at last, the unit was discharged, Ralph took the opportunity to tour the East, visiting New Orleans, Atlanta, Vicksburg, Washington, D.C., Columbus, Chicago, Minneapolis, and Denver before returning to Oregon.

~

His college records suggest that Ralph was only an average student, although he did attend summer school in order to graduate with his classmates. His best grades came in history and economics. He got a "Satisfactory" in Newswriting, described in the catalog as "a general course in the writing of newspaper articles, news story, feature story, the editorial and other forms common to newspaper practice; copy reading, proof reading and problems of reporting." A history major, he also took a number of classes dealing with contemporary social and economic issues, as well as Spanish and French.

Ralph's yearbooks picture him as active and tenacious, whether on the football field or in his courtship of Esther Parounagian who had also come to Willamette. Their romance is a recurring theme. In a parody of the daily chapel readings, Ralph was assigned the verse: "And he walked every day before the court of the women's house, to know how Esther did, and what should become of her." (Esther 2:10) She on the other hand was described as a "rare combination of beauty and brains, originality and wit. To think that one mere man should have a corner on such a girl!" Ralph recorded that on March 27, 1920, he kissed Esther: "She is the finest girl going." Things moved quickly; on April 5, he wrote "Esther and I were engaged today. I am mighty happy. I only hope I will be worthy of her. I know she loves me and I certainly love her."

The earnestness and resolution so often noted by later colleagues and rivals were demonstrated on the Willamette football field: "If real stubbornness counts, Ralph wins. Eighty-eight bulldogs in as many fights cannot produce a greater display of tenacity than Barnes does in one grid battle. He has never been known to give up and argues in just the way he plays. This trait, with his lengthy proportions and solid bulk, goes toward wrecking the best of interference."[20] Ralph's decision to play football at Willamette was the source of considerable discord with his father. He had played on his class team during his senior year in high school. As a college junior he took the game up again and played, against his father's wishes, until he was injured in his senior year. For the rest of his life he attributed his fitness to having played. As sons do, he seemed to enjoy renewing the argument even ten years later: "that crushed cheek didn't disfigure me for life at all. I hardly ever think about it. My hair, it is true, is becoming thinner. Do you think that some of the hair nerves were injured in the course of my football experience?"[21]

Through high school and college, Ralph worked the usual summer jobs then available to youngsters in the Willamette Valley. In a later resumé, he noted: "Have had considerable experience at unskilled jobs. Two summers harvesting, one summer with surveying crew, one summer in construction work in paper mill, and varied experience in lumber yards, etc. Business experience very slight."

He graduated on June 7, 1922, with seventy-three classmates. His interest in the labor movement led him to pursue graduate studies in economics at Harvard. He went off to Cambridge, where he roomed with a college friend, Truman Collins, and with his father, who had sold the store and come east to study astronomy. Before Ralph left Salem, he gave Esther an engagement ring. She remained at Willamette to graduate the next year. To Ralph's delight, "I feel like I was some lowly peasant going to marry into the nobility," she was May Queen in 1923. After graduation, and a summer when both were in Salem, she went to teach at the tiny high school in Klaber, Washington, a small and now defunct lumber town in the Cascade Mountains.

A letter from Esther, about a discussion among her friends at the school in Klaber, occasioned a response from Ralph that gives a sense of his attitudes toward the role of women and marriage. As for "woman's place," he wrote: "I have an idea that when the opportunity comes you will want to help me, or work for something outside the home. I certainly hope that you will not feel tied down to routine in the home so much that you will not feel free to be active in things outside when you want to." His concern was a deeper one: "Frankly, as you know, I have worried about our interests. What I mean is that when we have been together, which has been for long periods at a stretch, as you know, it has meant an almost complete dropping of our respective interests." In summary, he stressed: "I'm 20th century to the degree that I am opposed to: 1. Women spending 3/4 of their time at teas, in entertaining, dressing, etc. 2. Women so tied down to household details that they are unable to know what the world is like and unable to keep on a par intellectually with their running mates." Finally he recognized "that my girl has a perfect right to disagree with me and that I haven't a right to attempt to dominate the household in question."[22]

Despite their separation, the time in Cambridge passed quickly. Ralph assured his Willamette friends that he had managed to avoid

New England habits and did not pronounce "idea" with an r at the end or Harvard without any r's or wear golf socks and bloomers.[23] After he received his Master's degree in economics, decisions about his future loomed. He envisioned two or three years' work in the East, with an eventual return to the West Coast, and hoped to follow the interest in the labor movement he had developed in college and pursued at Harvard.[24] The first order of business was his marriage to Esther on October 11, 1924, at Salem's First Methodist Church. After a wedding trip to the Oregon coast, they headed to New York in November. Ralph expected to do social service work in a settlement house, but found the position taken. They took an apartment at 318 W. 108th Street. Through the Harvard employment bureau, Ralph made several applications. Some months later he was offered two jobs, one with the Standard Oil Company in its Industrial Relations department and the other with the Carnegie Foundation as assistant in a planned survey of college athletics. But by that time, he had found his calling.[25]

At the end of 1924 Ralph Barnes went to work for the *Brooklyn Daily Eagle,* a venerable newspaper established in 1841 and edited briefly by Walt Whitman. It once ranked "next to the Bible in dependability and respectability" but by 1924 was in decline.[26] In fact, New York was not a hospitable place for would-be journalists, no matter how ambitious. Frank Munsey was buying up newspapers only to shut them down or merge them with papers he already owned. In the process New York had lost five or six dailies, and many experienced reporters were out of work. Barnes's job was a good deal less grand than he let on to friends back home. The *Eagle,* an afternoon paper with a full daytime staff, hired novices to cover evening events. They were paid only for what the newspaper printed.

Esther's chance to "work for something outside the home" came quickly; she got a job at the New York Public Library. Her intermittent journal gives a sense of their life. New Year's Day, 1925, with Ralph working, was a "lonesome, busy day. Today I don't think I like New York." Starting work the next day, she was sent through the snow to the Mott Haven Library in a part of the Bronx then largely populated by new immigrants. She appreciated the kindness of the other librarians and was touched by those she encountered: "Little forlorn boy wanted to join the library today. His father couldn't write or make cross X. His mother was dead but his grandmother knew how to make a cross. Poor youngster."

Until Esther began to receive a paycheck, money was a problem. "Ralph forgot to get his check. Will have to be hungry today." "There was nothing to eat and I had 20 cents which I was saving for tomorrow. Don't know where Ralph is. ... Ralph just called and is bringing something home to eat. He got some money. Hurrah." Her paycheck was a little more than half what she had earned teaching, but she was studying to become a grade I librarian, and that would mean a raise. She occasionally covered a meeting or event when Ralph had a scheduling conflict: "I went to Salem Church to cover Urban Club for him. All negroes, nicely dressed. Interesting meeting. Harlem." New York was an adjustment: "There seems to be a certain fascination about New York but still one just goes, goes, goes. It is no place to sit down and live and enjoy life. I wouldn't want to live here when I am old. It's a place for youth and lots of excess pep to keep above the crowds. Something stirring at every moment of the day. Never a lull." On balance, Esther was a happy bride: "Married life is much more wonderful than I thought it would be. The companionship is so much deeper. Ralph and I seem to get along so much better. We are dependent on each other and I love him more each day."[27]

Esther's support, both emotional and financial, meant everything. Ralph was not making enough money to provide for them, but he found newspaper work "the most fascinating thing I have ever done."[28] The night editor of the *Eagle,* Fletcher Snapp, was demanding but willing to spend time with his young reporters, particularly those who were "promising." Barnes was a slow and labored writer. His newswriting class in college had not prepared him for the routines of the news room. Moreover, his experience in life was limited. He wrote his Willamette classmates late in the spring of 1925: "The night editor is exactly my age, is not a college graduate, but has had a lot of experience with life in his three years with the newspaper. ... I have been forcibly struck with the fact that he is able to present a multitude of actual happenings to support his ideas, while I am able only to put forth what some Ph.D. has said in his latest book. If it were to come to a debate I wouldn't stand one chance in a thousand."[29]

Despite the drawbacks of his job, Barnes had found in newspaper work his lifetime vocation. After his promotion from night beat to editor of the *Eagle*'s feature page, his responsibilities included getting out a camp directory. He got a byline for a two-page feature article on Margery, the Boston medium then capturing the attention of the popular press. With the thoroughness that became typical of his reporting, Barnes attended three séances and meticulously researched other published reports of the phenomenon, including those in the *Atlantic Monthly* and *Scientific America*.[30] He stayed with the *Eagle* through all of 1925, but by the end of the year he was eager to make a move. Armed with letters of recommendation from his editor, L. M. Pasquin, he made the rounds of the other newspapers. For the benefit of the colleagues to whom he addressed the letters, Pasquin described Ralph Barnes as "steady, conscientious, and a glutton for punishment." "He's cutting loose from us of his own free will and without rancor on either side. He's a good honest worker, steady and can be depended on to do the usual day's work and then eat up a little more for good measure. He has other qualifications which he can be persuaded to give personally."[31]

Since they are still in Ralph's files, it is not clear that the letters were ever used. Al Laney, night editor at the Paris *Herald* during Ralph's time, provided the most complete account of Barnes's New York period in his book *Paris Herald: The Incredible Newspaper,* which is dedicated to Ralph Barnes. Laney wrote that Barnes heard at the *Eagle* of an opening on the *Evening World* copy desk and asked to be sent over—to the great amusement of his *Eagle* colleagues. The *Evening World* was considered the fastest desk in New York, and even experienced reporters wanted nothing to do with it. They explained that he would not last five minutes. But Barnes figured they would have to keep him for a time and that he could learn something there. His persistence was such that the head of the *Eagle* desk finally agreed and sent him over to the *Evening World.* On his recommendation, Barnes got the job and, as predicted, lasted five minutes. Told to pick up a week's pay at the cashier's window and get out, Ralph refused. He convinced the head of the copy desk to let him stay and learn. They gave him two weeks and even paid him while he asked a hundred questions and absorbed everything he could.

According to Laney, during this time Barnes wrote Laurence Hills, the editor of the Paris *Herald,* using *Evening World* stationery. Saying he had been a reporter on the *Eagle* and was now on the desk of the *Evening World,* he asked for a job on the *Herald.* With no details or dates specified, the *Evening World* association proved decisive. Hills wrote that if he wanted to pay his own way to Paris, there might be a job for him. Barnes's next stop was the *New York Herald Tribune,* where he argued that since he was going to work for the Paris *Herald* he ought to get a feel for the home office by working there. In fact, he needed a job to earn passage for himself and Esther.[32]

~

The *Herald Tribune* was a relatively new blend of two great newspaper traditions, the *New York Herald* of James Gordon Bennett and Horace Greeley's *Tribune*. Bennett's *Herald* had fallen upon hard times before his death without heirs in 1918. Frank Munsey bought it and merged another of his papers, the *Morning Sun*, into it as a part of the twenty-four year process by which he reduced by six the number of New York newspapers. His activities earned the scorn of William Allen White, who wrote that Munsey brought to journalism "the talent of a meatpacker, the morals of a money-changer and the manners of an undertaker."[33] Horace Greeley had founded the *New York Tribune* and edited it until his death in 1872, when it became the property of longtime staff member Whitelaw Reid. After the first few years, Reid was something of an absentee owner. His close relations with President James A. Garfield led to diplomatic assignments in France and Great Britain, while his marriage to the heiress Elisabeth Mills freed him of concern about the profitability of his paper.[34] Their son, Ogden Mills Reid, was groomed for succession as a reporter on the paper until his father's death in 1912, when he became editor and publisher. In 1924, he and his family bought the *Herald* from Munsey after a series of negotiations initiated when Munsey attempted to acquire the *Tribune*.

Ostensibly headed by the charming, benevolent and increasingly alcoholic Ogden Reid, the new company was actually dominated by his mother, Elisabeth Mills Reid, and his wife, Helen Rogers Reid. Elisabeth Reid was willing to spend great sums of her own inherited wealth to support the paper as a memorial to her husband. Helen Reid was a tiny, immensely capable person of modest background who had served as Elisabeth Reid's secretary and then married her son. The advertising side of the company was almost entirely in her able hands. Editorially, the paper reflected and promoted the business-oriented, conservative Republicanism of its owners. In his first, brief contact with the *Herald Tribune,* Barnes did not impress the editors, but he was allowed to work long enough to buy tickets to Europe. He and Esther sailed in April 1926.

2

" Just one sandwich and a half, and a half glass of
water." Thus Charles Lindbergh, the sandy-haired
American youth who couldn't do it, but did,
summarized his total consumption of food and drink
during thirty-three and one half hours of grueling
flying without stop, in fog, sleet, and rain, across the
Atlantic. The ruddy-faced stripling, following ten hours
and thirty-five minutes of peaceful slumber, continued
the discussion in the United States Embassy yesterday
afternoon of his history-making air venture.

Ralph Barnes, Paris *Herald*, May 27, 1923)

Arriving in Paris on April 13, 1926, Ralph and Esther Barnes were
met at the Gare du Nord by several Willamette classmates there on a
world tour. With their friends, *New York Times* reporter Lawrence
Davies and his wife Edna, they set off immediately on a ten-day
cycling trip through the Loire Valley. Returning to Paris, they found
lodging at 159 Boulevard du Montparnasse. Barnes went to work at
the Paris *Herald* and Esther adapted to what was in the beginning a
rather lonely life. But she took French lessons from an elderly baron
who wished to improve his English, and soon began to enjoy Paris,
visiting the markets, frequenting the American Library and making
friends among the newspaper community. Special friends were
Leland and Rida Stowe. A graduate of Wesleyan University, Stowe
began his newspaper career in Worcester, Massachusetts, then moved
on to the *Herald* shortly before it merged with the *Tribune*. Stowe
had also come to Paris in 1926, as assistant to the *Herald Tribune*
bureau chief, Wilbur Forrest.

The paper Barnes joined was still in many ways the creature of
its founder, the legendary James Gordon Bennett, Jr. In self-imposed

exile in Europe, the owner of the great New York *Herald* established the Paris *Herald* in 1887 as a newspaper for English-speaking, particularly American, tourists. For years he did not require the paper to turn a profit but poured into it vast amounts of money from his other enterprises and his personal fortune. He put the stamp of his personality on it from the beginning, focusing on news from New York and London, on advertising, and on society notes. His idiosyncrasies shaped its content and its editorial policies: "If a nation is friendly to America, I wish the *Herald* to be friendly to that nation, but if a nation shows an unfriendly policy, I wish the paper to adopt an unfriendly tone." His antipathies toward Theodore Roosevelt and William Randolph Hearst meant that neither man's name could be mentioned in the *Herald* even when one was running for President of the United States and the other for governor of New York.[1]

His prolonged absences from Paris made Bennett's management of the *Herald* generally erratic except during World War I, when he made sure that the paper never missed an issue, even when the German army was at the city's gates. His paper first reported the story of General Joseph Gallieni's army that was rushed to the front in taxis to help turn the tide at the First Battle of the Marne in 1914. With the coming of the American army, the *Herald* at last became profitable. Despite the collapse of his financial empire, Bennett ignored these profits that were deposited in a Paris bank account. At Bennett's death in 1918, the New York *Herald,* along with the Paris *Herald,* was sold to Frank Munsey whose usual pattern was to merge or close papers he acquired. The million dollars in its bank account saved the Paris *Herald.*

The four years of Munsey ownership saw the Paris *Herald* establish itself as the number of Americans resident in Paris grew to over twenty thousand. Paris became a magnet to high society, celebrities, and other tourists attracted by a very favorable exchange rate and the prospect of respite from the restrictions that Prohibition imposed on the United States in 1919. Munsey brought in Laurence Hills, formerly chief of the Washington bureau of the New York *Evening Sun,* to manage the newspaper. In 1924, when the paper was acquired by the Reid family as part of its purchase of the New York *Herald* to form the new *Herald Tribune,* Hills stayed to manage the paper for Ogden Reid. He was an owner's, not a reporter's, manager; Ralph Barnes fought many battles with him, both in Hills' capacity as manager of the Paris *Herald* and later when Hills became European manager for the *Herald Tribune*'s foreign service.

Laney judged the paper Ralph joined in 1926 harshly: "a poor paper, badly produced and unconcerned with giving even a reasonably complete picture of the day's news." He characterized its staff at the time as men who "saw nothing of what was going on in the world and cared nothing, whatever they may have said later when events of which they were a part had crystallized and taken on some meaning." As the guest of the French government, the Paris *Herald* presented "only the bright side of life, American and French. It would offend no one, offer no criticism of any phase of life and would be passionately devoted to the proposition that making money and international amity are wonderful things." Charles Robertson, in his study of the Paris *Herald,* went so far as to write that the *Herald* "never took a strong editorial stand in the interwar years, except on the matter of dog droppings on Paris sidewalks." The flourishing arts and culture of the Left Bank, to which so many Americans contributed, were given short shrift.

What news did appear in the Paris *Herald* came largely from two sources. The first was the ticker from London, where the paper's correspondent Bob Champion assiduously read the London newspapers and transmitted the news through a "system of abbreviation and skeletonizing which produced a weird language undecipherable by the uninitiated."[2] News from the second source, New York, was also sent along in the cryptic language of the cable. It took the skill and imagination of the *Herald*'s copywriters to make something coherent, and more or less factual, out of these bits and pieces. During this period, local, that is, continental, news was confined to society gossip and sports. One redeeming quality of the Paris *Herald* was its independence from the great French news agency Havas. Laney described Havas as "ostensibly an impartial news service but actually a huge and worldwide advertising agency and the greatest handicap to a free press in France."[3] The international news that Havas distributed was much less reliable than the news in the *Herald* despite its limited cable service.

Later observers have accepted Laney's assertion that change began on the Paris *Herald* when Barnes joined its staff as a copy writer. Certainly Ralph's size, his awkwardness, his hyperactivity, his utter Americanness, brought chaos to the copyroom. But his presence had a greater impact than the merely physical. A long way from an experienced newspaperman, Barnes, during his apprenticeship on the Paris *Herald,* "learned much and taught a great deal more."[4]

In the twenties, American tourists in Europe, like Americans at home, were interested less in the background of international events than in the exploits of those heroes of the era, athletes and aviators. Moving from the copy desk to reporting, Barnes had his opportunity to cover both and distinguished himself in the effort.[5] His first big assignment was Gertrude Ederle's swim of the English Channel in August 1926. A newspaper picture captured him in the background as Ederle was being prepared to enter the water in her second attempt to conquer the channel. Following along with other reporters in the tugboat as she crossed, Barnes was violently ill with seasickness. Because of the high seas, the tug could not dock when Ederle landed. Determined to file his story and calculating that the Channel would not be deep so close to shore, he jumped in but found himself over his head. He struggled ashore and went in search of a telephone. He found nothing but darkness and an empty village whose inhabitants had gone to see Ederle land. Eventually an old man with a motorboat agreed to take him to the nearest available telephone but that meant going out again on the choppy waters.

His seasickness notwithstanding, Barnes filed his story for the *Herald* and the *Herald Tribune*. For his readers, he captured the day, the athlete and the accomplishment vividly. Starting at seven in the morning after three weeks of seemingly endless waiting for good weather, Ederle swam to the leeward side of a tugboat from which her coach, her father and sister, and other supporters encouraged her by cheering, playing phonograph records and singing. Occasionally someone from the boat dove in to swim along and pace her. Her trainer tried to keep her from swimming too fast and wearing herself out but she responded, "If I go any slower, I'll sink." In the course of the day, the tides swept her down the Channel and then back up. The calm seas she had entered in the morning turned to "a boiling mass of rain-swept water, making the tug deck almost untenable and wearing out all of the plucky American girl's pacemakers long before the finish of the swim."[6]

Barnes made both Ederle and her achievement real to his readers: "Considering the adverse conditions, Miss Ederle's was the greatest swimming feat ever performed, and few feats of such endurance and grit have been recorded in any field." He quoted her statement at the finish: "I am overjoyed at my success. It was the ambition of my life and I coveted no other prize. I was nervous before I started, but once I got going all fear left me and I felt in perfect form. I didn't mind the buffeting of the waves, which troubled me far less than I had expected, and at no time did I feel inclined to give up. I am particularly pleased because I have brought honor to America." As Laney noted, Ederle's triumph was in many ways Ralph Barnes's baptism: "He had been in competition with the best reporters in Europe and none had a better story."[7]

The $25,000 prize offered by French-American hotelman Raymond Orteig for the first nonstop flight between New York and Paris set off a contest that captured the public imagination in France and the United States. Before its end, the competition took the lives of at least two aviators, the Frenchmen Charles Eugene Jules Marie Nungesser, a wartime hero, and Francois Coli. Their flight was erroneously reported as successful, setting off wild celebrations in Paris. As time passed and no confirmation of a safe landing came, the joy of Paris turned to anger and then sorrow. The plane was lost.

Charles Lindbergh's attempt came shortly thereafter. The Paris *Herald* geared up for the story but its reporters were mainly expected to assist Wilbur Forrest, the head of the Paris bureau of the *Herald Tribune*. Considered too inexperienced even for such a support assignment, Barnes had no role. The *Herald Tribune* was already laboring under the handicap of an exclusive contract Lindbergh had signed with the rival *New York Times*.

When Lindbergh landed on May 21, 1927, hundreds of thousands of people mobbed the plane. Fearing for his safety, several French fliers spirited him away before the press was able to talk to him. Forrest sent out the report of his safe landing but there was little else to say. Reporters searched all over Paris for the aviator and then gave up and headed for the bar at the Hotel Continental. Barnes listened to their tales and became convinced that, despite denials, Lindbergh was at the American Embassy. He badgered the night editor of the *Herald,* Al Laney, for taxi money to pursue his idea. Less out of confidence in his plan than out of weariness in the face of his determination, Laney provided the money. Barnes made his way to the Embassy, the other reporters following. His insistence forced Ambassador Myron T. Herrick to speak to the press and finally to admit that Lindbergh was sleeping upstairs. It was after three o'clock in the morning. Despite Barnes's objections, the reporters were agreeing with the Ambassador's suggestion that Lindbergh be allowed his night's sleep when word came downstairs that the aviator would see the press.

After the interview, Ralph rushed back to the *Herald* offices where, under pressure, he put his story on paper, each paragraph sent to the composing room as he finished it. It was the turning point, said Laney, "in the career of one of the greatest correspondents of all time." When, in his later memoirs, Wilbur Forrest claimed the story as his own, Laney and others were quick to correct that distortion.[8]

Barnes noted Lindbergh's response to the questions of the reporters gathered around his bed:

> *"The weather was better than I had anticipated over Nova Scotia and Newfoundland—better than the Weather Bureau had expected," the youth sitting at the edge of the bed answered. He looked young enough to be preparing to receive a high school diploma. "And then out on the open sea," he continued, "I ran into fog. I had 1,000 miles of it. I couldn't get over it, and I couldn't dive in under it, so I had to go right through it a good deal of the time. Sometimes I was within ten feet of the water, just skimming above the surface. Sometimes I was 10,000 feet above it. I saw the lights of one vessel at night on the open ocean. That was all. I didn't sight a single ship in the daytime. I understand, though, that one liner caught sight of my monoplane. One time there was considerable sleet and ice on the bow of the plane and I was a little concerned. But that cleared up."*

Ambassador Herrick, standing by proudly during Lindbergh's interview, told the reporters that when he met Lindbergh at his plane and asked him to come to the embassy to spend the night, the aviator responded, "I should like a lot to go with you, but I really ought to see about the windows of the plane first. They won't know how to close them." From his description of Lindbergh as "the sandy haired American youth who couldn't do it but did," through the aviator's response to a question about the most dangerous part of the trip, "when the crowd pressed around the plane at Le Bourget," Ralph Barnes recorded the event with all its nuances. Lindbergh expressed his sadness to his French hosts at the loss of Nungesser and Coli and graciously received the congratulations of a veteran French aviator blinded during World War I. Asked about the future of aviation, he predicted commercial flights across the Atlantic within four or five years, "as soon as an organization appears willing to back such a venture with sufficient funds."[9]

By the time of the Lindbergh flight, Barnes and his difficulty in letting go of a story while it could still be improved had become the butt of jokes around the *Herald* newsroom. His interest in China occasioned more teasing. Convinced of the importance of the Chinese revolution, he immersed himself in the background of events there. According to Laney, he came to understand the complex situation "better than some of the correspondents on the spot." "He forced it into the paper by his relentless pounding and thus forced it upon the consciousness of a lot of people who might not otherwise have taken note of it."[10] The ongoing China story was an early indication of Barnes's style as a foreign correspondent. His earnestness, intensity and focus, as well as his determination to understand the complexities of an event or issue, made him a good reporter, a worthy competitor, and sometimes difficult to live with at home.

Ralph and, to a lesser degree, Esther were becoming acclimated to the life they had chosen, as strangers in strange lands. Both were interested in the history and culture of the countries where they lived. When they did not already know it, they made an effort to learn the language. Both read the important works of literature. When time permitted, they traveled outside the capitals where Ralph was assigned, making it a point to know the countryside and smaller towns. In 1928, they took a trip down the Rhine River and spent several weeks with a German family. The following year, they bicycled through Switzerland and Italy, and Esther undertook a trip through Brittany without Ralph.

Still, there was an undeniable gulf. Ralph wrote to Willamette classmates: "That it is almost impossible for a Frenchman and an American to understand each other is one of the chief impressions I have gained from eleven months in Paris and vicinity. A few fortunates in each of the two national groups, through long contact and well-developed sympathies, are able to comprehend, but a real understanding is not for the great majority." One adjustment reflected his temperance background: "To the great majority of French people wine is about as common as bread. No moral significance is attached to imbibing. Prohibition would mix with this country about as oil does with water." Observation progressed to experience as Esther recorded a visit to the Café Select where she had drunk, and enjoyed, her first champagne cocktail.[11]

For Esther, the best part of these early years in Paris was the opportunity to travel, taking advantage of the favorable exchange rates to see much of Europe. Their most ambitious undertaking was a month-long journey in 1927 through Germany, Czechoslovakia, Denmark, Sweden, and Finland, finally reaching the Soviet Union, a trip that greatly influenced Ralph's career and aspirations. In the ten years since the overthrow of the Czar and the subsequent takeover by the Bolsheviks, the Russian Revolution had passed through its romantic phase. The civil war was over; Lenin had died; his attempt to rebuild the economy along the lines of free enterprise, known as the New Economic Policy or NEP, was being reversed. Although the fact was not yet completely evident to outsiders, Josef Stalin was firmly in control. Leon Trotsky represented a dissident force, but was steadily losing adherents. In the United States, the virulent Red Scare of the period immediately after World War I had abated. But there was still uneasiness about the regime, and the Soviet government had not been recognized by the stolidly Republican administrations of the 1920s, making it even more attractive to those with leftist leanings. Visiting the young Soviet Union was Ralph's clear objective for their trip, but Esther, fearful and anxious about what they would encounter there, was much less enthusiastic. Their travel journals reflect their differing responses to the experience. On the ship crossing from Sweden to Finland, Esther wrote, "Ralph spied an old boat in the harbor flying a red flag and he became very excited over the fact while my heart sank. I felt exactly like I was going to my doom."[12]

On the train from Helsingfors in Finland to Leningrad, they passed through Russian customs with only minor inconvenience. They shared their compartment with the English-speaking Polish consul at Leningrad who provided some orientation, even lending them Russian currency to get to their hotel. He warned them to be careful about what they wrote and said, thus reinforcing Esther's conviction that she would be followed throughout the trip. They found their hotel in Leningrad and bargained down the price of the room but concluded it was worth even less when Ralph was attacked by bedbugs during the night. Venturing out the next morning, they were reminded of "a city to which the inhabitants have just returned after a great disaster. A great many of the buildings are unpainted and are generally in a dilapidated condition. The pavements are badly worn and in urgent need of repair. Many streets are extremely dusty and some, in the places less used by traffic, are covered with grass." On the other hand, "the population appeared to us to be comparatively buoyant and light-hearted."[13]

They explored the usual tourist attractions in and around Leningrad and made the acquaintance of other Americans there to study the Soviet regime. Ralph recorded the conclusions they shared: "The Soviet system is working and working ever more smoothly; the enemies of the regime, for the time at least, have been subdued; all this has been brought about in part through a tyranny which permits virtually no individual liberty; the men in power know what they are about in the matter of retaining their power ... plan is to consolidate their position and thus be in such a position ten years hence as to be able to thumb noses at rest of world."

Invited to watch the filming of *October*, Ralph had the opportunity to interview Sergei Eisenstein. The soon-to-be-legendary director was more than willing to discuss his ideas and techniques. Still relatively new to film work, Eisenstein had begun as a director in theater. He told Ralph that he preferred not to use professional actors for films, but instead picked particular people for particular parts wherever he was able to find them. The commander of the women's battalion in *October*, for example, was a policeman he had noticed in the street. He searched for four months for the person to play Alexander Kerensky, the first premier of post-Czarist Russia. His favorite actors, he said, were peasants, who never looked at the camera and were always serious. Working with amateurs made the process much slower, but the result, in Eisenstein's view, was better. By the time Ralph met him in August 1927, Eisenstein had been at work on the film for four months, sometimes for thirty hours at a stretch. He hoped to have it ready for a screening in Berlin in November. Nevertheless, Ralph found him calm and unruffled, smiling most of the time as he worked.

Barnes's journal of the trip reflects the endless curiosity that became one of Ralph's greatest assets as a reporter. He meticulously recorded all that they found in the Soviet Union, from the prevailing theory that the displayed body of Lenin was actually wax down to the price of two peaches he bought in a Moscow store. Although he spoke no Russian at the time, he plied everyone he could talk to with questions.

One of the people Barnes met during this trip was his future rival, Walter Duranty, the correspondent of the *New York Times*. A letter of introduction from the press office in hand, Ralph found Duranty at his apartment, suitcases packed, irritated because a delay in securing his exit visa had prevented his departure on the afternoon train. For Ralph, it was a piece of good luck. In this, their first encounter, there was no evidence of the controversy that later swirled around Duranty, who has come to be viewed by many as an apologist for Stalin. Barnes approached him respectfully. He was already nearly a veteran, in his fourth year of reporting from Moscow after serving as a correspondent in Paris during the war. Ralph first asked him about Soviet relations with China and their role in the troubles there. In Duranty's view, there had been a split between the Soviet administration, which he identified with Stalin, and the opposition, specifically Karl Radek and Leon Trotsky. The administration had stayed with the Kuomintang as opposed to the true Communists. Then Chiang Kai-Shek had crushed the Bolshevik elements in the Kuomintang, leaving the Soviets with only the agrarian and labor movements. Both were, in Duranty's view, vague and weak. He thought the Bolsheviks had little chance in China under current conditions.

Speaking of the Soviet situation, Duranty told Barnes of a "terror" two months before that resulted in the killing of perhaps twenty to thirty people and the imprisonment of five thousand. One of Duranty's sources had been among those shot, probably because he was perceived as having too close a relationship with the British. Duranty said that he had little trouble reporting from Moscow. He had a good relationship with the censors; when they had objected to his story referring to the "terror," he readily agreed to change his wording to the "so-called terror." Barnes invited Duranty to dinner, Dutch treat. They rounded up Esther and Percy Knauth of the United Press.[14] Over caviar and borscht at the Ermitage, Duranty expounded on his conviction that war between Russia and Turkey was imminent. Behind the war was Britain's determination to crush Bolshevism. Turkey would be the British avenue into the Soviet Union.

Both Duranty and Knauth saw the regime as much less threatened from within than without. They agreed that the recent terror was a show of power rather than a sign of weakness. It was effective, Duranty said, because while Russians were not afraid of death, they did fear "the preliminaries." Both correspondents emphasized what they termed the "oriental" qualities of the Russians. They thought the current regime the best possible system for Russia under the circumstances, and expected substantial economic development if there was no interference from the outside. The major impediment to development was the bureaucracy that had grown up. The corruption of the period of Lenin's New Economic Policy had formed an endless cycle that Barnes recorded as: "B checked A, C checks A and B, and D checks A, B, and C." In their view, the mass of the people were much better off than under the old regime. The Orthodox Church continued to be a powerful force; the government-inspired anti-religious demonstrations had been stopped because of their unpopularity.

After listening to Duranty and Knauth, Barnes set out to gather his own impressions, with particular emphasis on the labor movement. He spoke to local labor leaders, including the chairman of the Moscow Province Trade Union Congress, and visited several Moscow factories. He interviewed Bill Haywood, the leader of the Industrial Workers of the World, who had been sentenced to prison in the United States for his opposition to American involvement in World War I. He had jumped bail to come to Moscow. Ill and nearing the end of his life, Haywood was deeply pessimistic about the American labor movement, but hopeful about Russia. When Barnes asked him about individual rights and freedom of the press, Haywood said he saw no reason to encourage the development of a capitalist press in the Soviet Union. He had a low opinion of the American press, even the labor press. He supported the Soviet administration and dismissed the opposition.

Also visiting Moscow at the time of the Barneses' visit was Anne O'Hare McCormick, a member of the *New York Times* European staff since 1922. An insightful observer who had early foreseen Mussolini's rise, she traveled about Europe interviewing political leaders and studying governments. At their meeting in Moscow, she and Barnes must have found common ground, because in their later correspondence both Esther and Ralph referred to visits from her. Eventually she became the first woman to serve on the editorial board of the *Times*. She wrote a regular column from Europe, beginning in 1937 when she won the Pulitzer Prize for foreign correspondence.[15]

Ralph and Esther also made the acquaintance of Albert Rhys Williams, one of the first American socialists to come to Russia following the 1917 Revolution. A Congregational minister from Boston, he became a reporter for the New York *Evening Post* and with John Reed edited *The Russian Revolution in Pictures,* a weekly propaganda magazine directed at the German and Austrian troops fighting on the Eastern Front during World War I.[16] "Out of the clear sky," as Esther put it, he invited the Barneses to spend the night at his home in a little village on the Moscow River. Because they spoke no Russian, a young man at the tourist bureau wrote down for them the three sentences they would need to get to Williams's village.

The trip proved an undertaking, but they made it to Kolomna, a provincial Russian town without a restaurant in which they had the courage to eat. Waiting for the train, they entertained one another telling "of the things we would have our mothers cook for us if we were only home." The interior of the train smelled so bad that they stood on the back platform throughout their short trip to Voskrensk, a little village with a hog wallowing in the center of the square. From there they hired a drosky and, riding on the straw, were taken to a place on the river where the driver pointed to a small boat and made them understand that they were to row themselves across. Despite the darkness and the rain, they made it. They knocked on doors in the village until someone understood them and took them to the Williams house. The welcome of Williams and his wife Lucita Squire was warm, the soup was hot and good, and Esther recorded that "we were soon thinking that our trip had been most thrilling and that we wouldn't have missed it for anything." Before long they were sleeping soundly "in the first good bed we had had in Russia."

The Williamses rented part of the most substantial home in the village of eighty houses, the only one without a thatched roof. After a "real American breakfast," Lucita Squire took Ralph and Esther to see the kitchen with its open oven. Over the oven was a small cubby hole where the peasant family of three slept "with little regard for air or sanitation, seeking only warmth during the long cold winter." Walking through the village and the surrounding countryside, Ralph and Esther got a sense of Russian peasant life as yet largely unchanged by the Soviet regime. They photographed the local Orthodox priest who lamented that the Soviets had taken the best icons from his small church's collection.

After taking leave of the Williamses, they returned to Moscow only to set out again for a trip down the Volga to Nizhni Novgorod, the city famous since medieval times for its fair. Ralph found the fair manager interested in establishing other fairs around Russia to display Soviet products. He was also anxious to secure American financial aid, but said that commercial relations had to be accompanied by diplomatic recognition. For the most part, Ralph found the regime still relatively relaxed toward foreigners. He toured a number of factories, talking freely with the workers, although always through interpreters. Barnes also visited a prison where he interviewed two political prisoners among its population of common criminals. The first was a former Czarist officer who had been a prisoner of war in Germany. When he returned in 1919 he had joined the Red Army because his home was still occupied by the Germans. Mistrusted because of his Czarist background, he was discharged but instead went to the Polish Russian border where he joined in the rebellion against the Soviet government. After several years of counterrevolutionary activities, he returned home and tried to live quietly. Found out, he was tried and sentenced to ten years and "stringent treatment." He chafed at being in prison, but thought the prison officials reasonable. When one of the visitors spoke favorably of the Soviet government, the former officer replied that "the streets may be clean, but the soul is dirty." He said he was not able to speak freely but "if we knew what he knew, [we] would have different opinion of the regime."

The second prisoner Ralph interviewed was a sixty-two year old man named Zelonoff, who said he was being detained only because he had served the old regime for more than thirty years. He said the authorities might just as well imprison a man who had used a plow in the old days because tractors were in use now. He appeared satisfied with prison treatment and mentioned that his wife came to see him every two weeks. His record showed that he had been a secret agent for the Czarist police. The court had concluded that his activities were directed against workers and peasants and ordered him imprisoned for ten years. Still he told Ralph that he was not opposed to the present government.

Barnes's contacts indicated that the Russian people had some sense of the struggle that had gone on between Stalin and Trotsky for control of the Communist party. Repeatedly he heard references to Trotsky, occasionally approving, but mostly critical, with one mechanic saying he was an anti-Communist like Chiang Kai-Shek. A unionist said that Trotsky was wrong, but "not consciously anti-Communist."

After postponing their departure twice and "paying and paying," Ralph and Esther were finally able to get their exit visas and leave the Soviet Union, Esther with Ralph's notebook under her clothes to secure it against confiscation. They went on to Warsaw, Vienna, Budapest, Salzburg, and Munich before returning to Paris "dirty, broke and happy."

~

Back in Paris, Ralph continued his work on the Paris *Herald,* where he was known as "Insert" Barnes in the composing room because he was always adding to the stories he was working on. His energy and earnestness often tried the patience of the more experienced members of the staff, but he was viewed with real affection and, according to Laney, growing regard.[17]

In 1929, the representatives of seven nations met in Paris to deal with one of the problems left over from World War I, the question of war reparations and debts. The Treaty of Versailles had focused full responsibility for the war on the German Empire and had therefore required the new German government to pay substantial reparations to the Allies. The British and French had in fact financed their war effort on one overriding premise: "The Hun will pay." The logic of saddling a new, and democratic, government with this burden was troubling to many, particularly President Woodrow Wilson, who had therefore not included the United States in the list of those countries to receive reparations. The great British economist, John Maynard Keynes, had seen in the required payments a tremendous impediment to Germany's recovery and to the restoration of a viable international economy. In 1923, the French had occupied the foremost industrial area of Germany, the Ruhr Valley, in order to force the German government to comply with its obligation.

Through the 1920s when several historians with access to the archives published new works on the subject, scholarly opinion regarding responsibility for the war had become less focused on Germany.[18] Nevertheless, the victorious allies still demanded payment. Although it did not participate in the reparations, the United States played a role because it expected repayment of the war debts incurred by Great Britain, France, and other countries. Finally an international conference was convened in Paris to create the framework for a more orderly, and perhaps less exigent, way of dealing with these various international obligations.

Barnes was assigned to cover the meeting for the *Herald,* along with Lee Stowe, by then Paris bureau chief for the *Herald Tribune.* It was a compatible partnership. Stowe later recalled: "No bureau chief ever had a more eager and indefatigable assistant than he, nor a more loyal friend." Even then, Stowe thought Barnes had "all the instincts of an exceptionally great reporter."[19]Already Ralph had earned the sobriquet "Ambulating Kiosk," for his habit of carrying around books and periodicals related to the stories he was working on, in this case books on the reparations controversy, the most recent issue of *The Economist,* and several other financial periodicals. Barnes's preparation for his work impressed Stowe then and later: "He read constantly and voraciously concerning every country and subject which he covered ... literally volumes ... politics, history, sociology, military science ... all that built solid, perceptive factual background."[20]

For four months, Stowe and Barnes worked together to cover the conference, although they each wrote their stories separately. They developed sources to provide inside information about the proceedings. Stowe later boasted that they had achieved twenty-three scoops. One brought a confrontation between Barnes and Thomas W. Lamont, a New York financier and member of the American delegation, who had identified a particular member of the German delegation as the source for one of the Stowe/Barnes stories, when in fact that had not been the case. Stowe listened with awe and amusement as the young reporter berated the J. P. Morgan partner for damaging their relations with the German representatives. As it turned out, Lamont held no grudge. Just before leaving for America, he wrote Stowe and Barnes expressing his appreciation for their coverage of the conference and assuring them that "the latch-string would always be out" when they came to New York. He and Ralph crossed paths a number of times during Ralph's career, and he was always cordial and helpful.[21]

The best contact for Barnes and Stowe proved to be a member of the Japanese delegation who gave them a copy of the conference final document before it had been officially released. Named the "Young Plan," for the leader of the American delegation, Owen D. Young of the General Electric Company, it called for the creation of a bank of international settlement and afforded Germany a less onerous schedule of reparations payments. Stowe and Barnes copied the document through the night in order to be able to return it to their source. Each then filed his story, Stowe for the *Herald Tribune*, Barnes for the Paris *Herald*. Stowe later earned the 1930 Pulitzer Prize for his coverage of the conference. Although by Stowe's own account Ralph deserved a great deal of the credit but received no such recognition, he was among the first to write Stowe a congratulatory letter. But Barnes's achievement did not go unnoticed. He was shortly named by the *Herald Tribune* to head the paper's Rome bureau. He had, as Laney noted, outgrown the Paris *Herald*.[22]

Mussolini is convinced that Italy must be a world
power, capable of defending herself against all comers,
and prepared to battle successfully for world markets.
It has been his view in the past—and presumably he
has not changed his mind—that these two objects can
be attained by Italy only through perfect discipline
within. Italy, it is pointed out, must make up in
national discipline for what she lacks in coal, iron, oil,
fertile soil and, perhaps, in experience as a unitary
national state. Liberty is a luxury, it has been said,
that Italy cannot afford.

Ralph Barnes, *Herald Tribune*, March 4, 1931, from Rome

The appointment to Rome was a welcome promotion. Since their
marriage in 1924, Esther and Ralph had consciously postponed
having children. Now Esther was pregnant with their first child.
The move came, however, at a time when the personal costs of the
career Ralph had chosen were particularly painful. Esther's beloved
father, Marcus Parounagian, died of a heart attack on October 23,
1929, while running to catch a trolley. Esther was unable to return
to Oregon to be with her family. Her parents had settled in Portland
when her father retired. Her mother and sister Mary continued to
live there, with Mary teaching at Grant High School. Aside from
Ralph's articles, the only available record of the Barneses' time in
Italy is what has been saved of Esther's correspondence with her
mother and Mary.

When Barnes arrived in Rome, Benito Mussolini's regime was
nearly eight years old. Mussolini had spent his early years as the
editor of *Avanti,* the Socialist newspaper in Milan, and had emerged

as a leader of the proletarian movement in Italy. At first opposed to Italian entry into World War I, he came to favor it and broke with the Socialist Party over the issue. His detractors later suggested that loans from French sources to support his new paper, *Il Popolo d'Italia*, had influenced his thinking. Serving briefly in the military, he was wounded when a mortar exploded accidentally.

Italy's participation in the war proved a disappointment because of the poor performance of its armies and its failure to achieve its aims at the peace table. A matured Mussolini returned from the war to found a new political organization that developed into the Fascist Party. A perception of national humiliation in the war combined with intractable economic problems to produce widespread discontent. The traditional political parties and their corrupt parliament proved helpless in dealing with repeated strikes and poor public services.[1] Many were attracted to the Fascist Party because it seemed committed to action, even though its program was vague. The key was Mussolini's leadership and his ability to play to the fears and disillusionment of the people. He presented himself and his party as both the alternative to Communism and the antidote to the impotence of the traditional parliamentary parties. Through a combination of instigated street violence and behind-the-scenes political maneuvering, Mussolini soon emerged as the only man who could save Italy. The King invited him to form a government in late October 1922. With the full force of the state behind him, Mussolini transformed Italy into a dictatorship and himself into the *Duce*. He tolerated the monarchy as long as the king, Victor Emmanuel, understood his place. Otherwise he concentrated power in his own hands and routed his enemies. Observers abroad mostly seemed accepting, and occasionally admiring.[2]

In its earliest days, Mussolini's government treated foreign correspondents with special favors, free railroad passes and guided tours, and even for a short time an arrangement involving tax exemptions and rebates to the correspondent personally for telegraph and cable transmission. Clearly an attempt at bribery, this last was for the most part resisted and soon dropped. Mussolini made himself available for the private interviews at which he was a master. Many correspondents responded by lauding Mussolini and his alternative path even as they decried the repression his regime practiced. But just enough criticism appeared in foreign newspapers to change the government's pro-press attitude, and the job of the journalist became more difficult. Access dried up. Italians became less willing to talk to members of the foreign press. George Seldes of the *Chicago Tribune* was expelled in 1925, the only expulsion of a correspondent from Italy until 1935.

Although the regime denied that censorship existed before 1934, reporters found that government control of communications meant that cables were delayed, sometimes altered, sometimes never sent. In the face of cable office apologies and denials, it proved impossible to stage effective protests. When items considered "unfavorable" were published in their papers, reporters were subject to pressure, beginning with a chiding by the press office and escalating to withdrawal of privileges, warnings, and subtle threats. If these proved unsuccessful in changing a reporter's tone, the Italian government would have its consul take up the matter with the paper's home office, perhaps with references to an impact on advertising revenue, and finally make a formal protest to the United States ambassador or to the State Department. After his expulsion, Seldes wrote: "All correspondents are lectured when their Paris or London colleagues send news unfavorable to Fascism: [Foreign Minister Dino] Grandi and Mussolini not only control the reports from Italy but try to affect the news regarding Italy sent from other countries."[3]

The Rome assignment brought the first of Ralph Barnes's many experiences of government interference with his reporting. He made his objections felt, yet retained his relationships. Stowe later wrote: "It was almost impossible for them not to like the man, and those who tried to budge him learned to their sorrow it was wasted effort. Sometimes his lack of humour and intense earnestness simply paralysed the totalitarian press gods, as when he wrathfully informed a Fascist censor in Rome one day: 'You can censor what you want—but I won't have you interfering with my objectivity!' Small wonder that the Italian press chief, after Barnes's departure, resignedly confessed to Joseph Phillips that he felt as though an earthquake had passed."[4]

~

In Paris, Barnes had covered the stories he was assigned to. In Italy, an important part of his job was to determine what was news. His year in Rome—January 1930 through February 1931—saw few "big stories." Nevertheless, he averaged four or five articles of varying length each week in the *Herald Tribune*. His first story from Rome described a royal wedding, a topic then as now of inexplicably consuming interest to the American people. Accompanied by her parents Queen Astrid and King Albert, a hero for his resistance to the Germans during the war, Princess Marie José of Belgium was coming to Italy to marry Crown Prince Umberto. Over the course of a week, Barnes described the pomp and pageantry of the festivities, the royal wedding guests, the elaborate gifts. He reported that people found the princess prettier than her pictures made her seem. He noted that President Herbert Hoover's gift of ten Alaskan sealskins was "the more appreciated because it is considered typically American." He wrote that the Pauline Chapel, where the wedding took place, was of special significance because papal elections had traditionally been held there until it was seized from the Papacy at the time of the unification of Italy in 1870. Its use now was an expression of the reconciliation between the Catholic Church and the Italian State, effected in the Lateran Treaty of the previous year.[5]

In the eyes of many, Italians and foreigners, the Lateran Treaty was Mussolini's greatest accomplishment. Until 1859, the pope was the temporal sovereign of the Papal States, 16,000 square miles of territory, mostly in the central part of the Italian peninsula, inhabited by more than 3,000,000 people. The Papal States were considered the greatest obstacle to the unification of all of Italy under one government, an outcome long sought by Italian nationalists. Gradually the papal territories were absorbed into the Kingdom of Italy until the final step, the 1870 takeover of Rome itself. Italian statehood left the pope as "the prisoner of the Vatican," unwilling to acknowledge the legitimacy of the Italian government.

This situation persisted until 1929 when Mussolini's government negotiated the Lateran Treaty, in which the Pope recognized the Kingdom of Italy with its capital in Rome. The government of Italy in its turn recognized the Holy See and its sovereignty over the Vatican. The most difficult provisions of the agreement, both to negotiate and to live with in practice, were those dealing with education and marriage. The Lateran Treaty did not meet the expectations of either contracting party, but in the end neither wished to overturn the treaty, and it has survived through subsequent Italian governments. Mussolini even went so far as to change the Italian national day from the date of the 1870 capitulation of Rome to Italian troops to the date of the Lateran Treaty.

The ups and downs of the opportunistic relationship between the Fascist regime and the Papacy provided Barnes with considerable material. One early story reported, briefly and without comment, that two works had been placed on the Index, a listing of books that Catholics were forbidden to read. One was *Render Unto Caesar,* a study of the Roman Question and the Lateran Treaty by an Italian journalist, Mario Missiroli. The other was a work on the Fascist theory of education. In his piece on the elevation of Eugenio Pacelli, later

Pope Pius XII, to cardinal and papal secretary of state, Barnes noted Pacelli's role in negotiating concordats with Bavaria while papal nuncio to Munich and with Prussia while nuncio to Berlin. He suggested that Pacelli's appointment foreshadowed efforts to reach a new *rapprochement* with the Italian government after months of controversy "over the respective spheres of Church and State in education."[6]

The Roman Catholic Church and the Papacy were concepts alien to Ralph Barnes's Methodist upbringing and education in Oregon. Nevertheless, it fell to him to cover the canonization of saints, the appointment of cardinals, and the edicts of the pope and of the Sacred Congregation. One edict reflected papal reaction to "those styles of modern feminine dress which not only fail to be ornamental but which may prove to be 'what is very much worse—the spiritual ruin' of women who indulge in them." On another occasion, Pius XI exhorted parents to fulfill their disciplinary responsibilities: "The modern parent, the Pope stated, has abdicated before the exigencies of the present-day child, and in many cases exercises little or no surveillance over his offspring. As an example, the Pope cited the fact that it is customary for modern youth to seek out whatever company it prefers and to go about at all hours without parental supervision."[7]

A major papal encyclical on Christian marriage condemned contemporary evils such as divorce, adultery and contraception, calling the latter "a foul stain on the nuptial union." Barnes characterized the encyclical as "one of the most significant Vatican documents of modern times." It was printed in its entirety in the *Herald Tribune*.[8]

Pius XI was also concerned about Protestant proselytizing in Rome itself, and about the degree to which such efforts had government protection. But such tensions between Church and State did not prevent the Church's participation in the celebrations marking the anniversary of the March on Rome, the beginning of Fascist rule in Italy. In fact, Barnes reported that Cardinal Sincero in his invocation said: "Let God send his benediction on our Chief of Government and Duce, and maintain him in vigor and power entirely dedicated to the welfare of Italy."[9]

～

Through his thirteen months in Italy, Barnes wrote about not only religion but also foreign policy, the internal workings of the regime, economics, art, music, and everyday life. He seems to have set his own assignments although he wrote his father of the *Herald Tribune*'s preferences: "Recently I have been spending most of my time on non-political stories—aeronautics, archeology, and the like. The New York office is anxious that I shall not give them too big a proportion of economics and politics, and they are quite justified. I like writing the other kind of thing, anyway."[10]

Barnes's attention was frequently drawn to the rich cultural life of Italy, especially when there was an American tie, such as the Italian tour of Arturo Toscanini and the New York Philharmonic Orchestra. Barnes noted that the critic of *Il Popolo d'Italia*, a newspaper edited by Mussolini's brother, wrote: "With this orchestra America is revealed—to those who would revile her for materialism and mechanical civilization—as a musical power of the first order." When for the first time a woman was appointed to head Milan's renowned La Scala Opera, Barnes wrote that Anita Colombo was seen as "not only a first-class musician, but also an intelligent, energetic business woman, fitted to cope with the serious financial problems which now face La Scala."[11]

What Barnes had called "the other kind of thing" in his letter to his father was what we might today call "style" or "living" coverage. Such coverage was something of a hallmark of the *Herald Tribune,* its niche in contrast to the *New York Times.* In Italy, his first experience of competing head-to-head with the *Times,* Barnes was acutely conscious of the contest. While the *Times,* intent on being the "newspaper of record" for the United States, was more sober and serious than the *Herald Tribune,* its management was also far more willing to commit resources to international news coverage. Its eminence gave it a certain cachet in foreign capitals, while the *Herald Tribune* struggled for respect. The competition was a challenge to Ralph's initiative and independence through most of his career. Still Barnes was remarkably independent, particularly considering that this was his first real assignment as a foreign correspondent. His success depended on his ability to get his story, please his bosses in New York, and not offend too greatly the Fascist government. Like most correspondents during the period, Ralph Barnes never had assurance that, should he be expelled for some offense against the host government, another job would be waiting.

From Esther's letters, and the one or two of Ralph's that survive, it is clear that the Great Depression was making itself felt at the *Herald Tribune.* Ralph wrote: "The best information I can get from Paris is to the effect that I will have difficulty securing a raise in the near future, simply because the paper is having a tough time. Almost everything in New York is hit by the depression, and the press has not escaped." Ralph and Esther borrowed money from their parents to get by and struggled to repay it: "We are sending another $50 to you for the insurance tomorrow, and hope to send another $50 ten days later. A third installment will be forthcoming as soon as we can scrape the money together."[12]

The birth of their first child, Joan, in May 1930, after six years of marriage, involved some adjustments. While Esther could no longer accompany Ralph on working trips, she found rewards in being with her daughter: "She was certainly perfect while Ralph was gone and caused me no trouble at all. I am going to have to watch myself or I will be wanting to be with her all the time." Like many couples who have delayed parenthood, they were determined to avoid the excesses they had witnessed in their friends, but Joan worked her magic. Her mother wrote: "How I wish you could see her. We get more in love with her every day. Now here I am raving about our baby when I swore I would never do that." Ralph made a discovery familiar to fathers everywhere: "Really I had no idea a child could be so fascinating before it had learned to talk."[13]

Reporting at a time when there was considerable foreign admiration for the accomplishments of the Fascist government and for Mussolini himself, Barnes explored the nature of the regime. The government moved to control the universities, "centers," as Barnes put it, "of a certain amount of stubborn, though not always manifest, opposition to the present regime." When resistance surfaced, it was dealt with harshly, but opposition was not well developed.[14]

His domestic front secure, Mussolini began to claim what he considered to be Italy's, and his, rightful place in international affairs and in the colonial arena. Convinced that France stood in his way, he encouraged attacks in his controlled press: "Another French ministerial crisis of a series which is now long. Since 1922 Italy has had one single government and one single line of policy, a policy carried forward with a single method. How many governments have there been in France since 1922? More than ten. That is the parliamentary regime, the thing called democracy, the thing which gives continued proof of decadence."[15]

With the memory of World War I vivid, statesmen labored to set in place structures to contain European rivalries. But when the French Foreign Minister Aristide Briand proposed a European Union to secure the peace, the Italian press dismissed the idea in light of France's elaborate system of military alliances.[16] Another major dispute between the two powers was the London Naval Conference, one of several inter-war attempts to limit the military and naval competition perceived retrospectively as a cause of World War I. Although the United States, Great Britain and Japan were able to reach agreement, the conference broke down in May when France refused to be put on a par with Italy. After months of negotiations, agreement was finally reached in February 1931, as Barnes reported in one of his last dispatches from Rome.

By that time, another set of negotiations was being completed, one that would have a more personal and profound effect on Ralph and Esther. The *Herald Tribune* had offered Ralph the assignment of his dreams: Moscow. Although torn by the knowledge that Esther and Joan would not accompany him and concerned about financial arrangements, Ralph was elated. In a letter to Esther's family, he explained the circumstances that had led to the offer:

> *Before we left Paris, I wrote to both London and New York, saying that if at anytime they should decide to open a Moscow bureau, I would like to be considered for the post. At that time there was no thought whatever of such a bureau because of the expense. There is no change in the expense item—unless it is for the worse—but the New York Times has been having ever more news from its correspondent in Moscow and thus the Herald Tribune has been feeling the competition from that quarter. You will probably have noted that recently the New York World went out of existence. That development left the Times and the Herald Tribune alone in the dignified morning field, and of course has strengthened both papers. The final decision to open a Moscow bureau came within forty-eight hours after the last issue of the World had been published, and I believe there was a causal relationship between the two developments. Presumably because the H.T. is now in a stronger position than hitherto, the home office was more generous with us in respect to salary and expenses than I had expected them to be. If they had not been, we would have been under the necessity of refusing the offer.[17]*

Although she was again pregnant, Esther was supportive, writing home: "The fact that I will have to spend most of the time in Paris alone will be hard but the experience Ralph will have in Russia and the results it will no doubt have on his future will justify it."[18]

His coming transfer provided Barnes with the rationale and the freedom to do a series on conditions in Italy. A part of a larger series exploring several European countries, it involved the longer, more thoughtful mail pieces that he enjoyed doing even though they were a strain.[19] Coincidentally, the *New York Times* published a series of articles on the outlook of the "average man" in Italy, the United States, France, Germany and Great Britain. Anne O'Hare McCormick wrote a decidedly positive piece on Italy that concluded with a number of observations: "My own impression is that the Fascist regime is actively supported by more people who do not like it—to put the case mildly—than any other existing government. The average Italian is for Mussolini because he thinks that Mussolini is good for the country." She saw the effects of the reconciliation between Italians and their Church: "These same young men crowd into the churches on Sunday morning, though once they assumed the same superior attitude toward religion affected by young men everywhere. Religious practice is also now the fashion in Italy. In this popular effect on the new entente between Church and State, you see how artificial was the old conflict in a country more than 90 per cent Catholic. Perhaps, indeed, the success of this revolution is due to the fact that it is not a revolution at all. It is a restoration, the Italian returning to his own gods and to his natural ways."

In a Depression-ridden world, McCormick saw Mussolini as protecting his people from the negative effects of industrialization: "Italy is not an industrial country. Comparatively few countries are highly industrialized; what makes Italy different is that there is no furious drive to make her industrial. Almost alone among modern statesmen, Mussolini bends all his energies not only to keep his country as agrarian as it is but to make it more so. Land reclamation and a redistribution of the population in new farming areas are among his fundamental policies." As a result, the average Italian "remains more his man under a dictatorship than the average American or the average German can be in a democracy. For all his curtailed political rights, he retains more individual independence. He does not easily prosper in the modern world, but neither does he starve. There are no bread lines in Italy. He is at the mercy of forces outside himself, but not completely. If not more secure, he is at least on familiar ground, master of his tools. His life, like his landscape, is adjusted to the human scale. Is that what makes him seem more at home in his world than we are in ours?"[20]

McCormick's rather elegiac mode does not stand up well in historical perspective. In contrast, Barnes's six long articles, published between February 28 and March 5, explored Italy's political, economic and social outlook as well as its aspirations in the international arena. The pieces reflect his development as a correspondent. His conclusions have been confirmed by later historians who have enjoyed the advantages inherent in the passage of time and full access to archival materials.

The first article disabused its readers of the notion that Mussolini's government was in jeopardy. Opposition to the regime certainly existed in and outside of Italy but there was "no sign that discontent among the masses or among the intellectuals [would] crystallize soon into anything resembling an effective force" despite the economic problems the country was suffering. Barnes reviewed and dismissed two possible foci of opposition: the industrialists who feared that "to destroy Fascism would be to invite chaos and Communism," a fear assiduously fostered by the Fascists, and the universities which had "failed to develop a vigorous liberal tradition." Significantly, and understandably in light of so many of the articles he had written over the past year, he did not address the possibility of the Catholic Church acting against the regime. As for the population as a whole, they had, he noted, been exposed to democratic institutions for a period too brief "to have acquired a deep-seated attachment for them."

Reminding his readers of Italy's history of foreign domination and delayed national unification, Barnes pointed to a kind of national inferiority complex. The disillusionment resulting from Italy's lackluster performance in World War I and its lack of rewards at the peace table heightened the defensive nationalism left over from the *Risorgimento*. Out of the combination had grown the Fascist movement. Fascism, Barnes said, displayed "some of the characteristics of a precocious adolescent," pointing to "the chip on its shoulder" and its "awkwardness" in dealing with its contemporaries.

Despite its detractors Fascism was not, in Barnes's view, in any particular danger, for the "crucial factor" was Benito Mussolini, who still enjoyed the "personal allegiance" of many Italians. The current economic situation would not bring about the fall of the regime, but "an unsuccessful war" might, and certainly Mussolini's death would.[21] In this observation, he disagreed with Henry Kittredge Norton who in an earlier *New York Times* article attributed the strength of the regime specifically to its foundation in a political party. Norton wrote that, Italy's "mature" democracy required that the dictatorship have "a party instead of a personal basis" and saw Fascism as having "a much firmer grasp on the political forces of the nation than would be possible for any personal dictatorship."[22]

On March 1, in the second article of the series, Barnes analyzed Italy's economic outlook as it was being hit by the full force of the world economic depression. Observing that "when the natural resources which form the basis of modern industrial civilization were distributed, Italy was overlooked," he further reported that the country was handicapped by "obsolete industrial, commercial and financial practices." Mussolini's extensive public works program employed a great many people who would otherwise be unemployed. In addition, the Fascist government forced industrialists to "maintain inflated payrolls in slack times to minimize unemployment," a burdensome practice but one that avoided "the distress and turbulence which almost certainly would attend rising unemployment."

The regime was contending with the results of its policies: overtaxation and a budget deficit. It had recently imposed a 12 percent wage reduction affecting nearly 1,000,000 persons employed directly or indirectly by the government. In an effort to increase the competitiveness of Italian products in foreign markets, the government successfully "sponsored a move for a reduction of from 5 to 25 percent in the wages of industrial, commercial and agricultural workers and simultaneously campaigned for the reduction of prices and rents." Barnes recognized the advantages of being able "to follow a definite economic policy through the elimination of parliamentary bickering," noting that it was "doubtful whether a liberal, democratic regime of the type which existed in Italy before 1922 would have brought the country through the economic stress of the last eight years so well." This journalistic judgment, he emphasized, was limited to economic matters. Even in that arena, he questioned "whether, other things being equal, a national economy thrives better in the long run under a regime of rigid governmental control than under a regime of laissez-faire."[23]

In the third article of the series, Barnes attempted to give his readers a sense of the achievements of the Fascist regime. He emphasized its opportunistic nature, pointing out that a movement that had espoused republicanism and anti-clericalism was now "closely aligned with the monarchy and Church." It had brought discipline and order to Italy, admittedly at a price. Many intellectuals and industrialists, he observed, who now felt that "Fascist discipline had become an overdose, supported the regime at the outset because the regime stood for vigorous methods to maintain order."

Clearly, to foreign and domestic observers alike, the greatest achievement of the eight-year-old regime was the Lateran Treaty. Some, like historian Arnold Toynbee, questioned whether the settlement would survive. Barnes's own judgment, confirmed by time, was that while there would certainly be future modifications in the agreement, "it is inconceivable that either the papacy or the Italian government—this one or its successor—will ever be so foolish as to risk the loss of the substantial benefits accruing to both sides from the conciliation."

Barnes found less agreement about the success of the economic structure known as "integral syndicalism" by which all those in any occupation were grouped "into economic associations, so-called syndicates, which form the cells of the new state." In contrast to Marxism, Fascist syndicalism accepted capitalism, regarded all classes as productive and sought to substitute "class cooperation for class strife." In practice, however, the system had not advanced "beyond an embryonic stage." More difficult to convey was the sense of energy and renewal which the Fascist regime sought to instill in the Italian people through the encouragement of the social, recreational and cultural aspects of life. Public works and social welfare institutions tangibly benefitted the population. Special emphasis was placed on the young, although much of that effort appeared to have militaristic goals. Barnes closed the article by quoting the Duce's speech to a youth group: "You are the dawn of life. You are the hope of the country. You are, above all, the army of tomorrow."[24]

The next article portrayed the dark side of the regime. Because it was printed when Barnes was no longer in Italy, he was freer in discussing the suppression of opposition and the censorship that prevailed throughout the country. Recently a perceived relaxation of the police system had given rise to more open criticism of the government. "Suddenly there were reports that this or that ex-Liberal in Milan or Rome had been arrested. People who had believed before that they were free from surveillance found that their mail was being examined. The reports of arrests multiplied and finally came the laconic communiques, listing the names of those persons taken into custody."

While the government claimed there was no censorship, each editor was well aware that "were he to publish an article really distasteful to the regime, the issue would be confiscated, and he would lose his standing." Among the foreign press, Americans were particularly handicapped because all cable and radio messages went to the Ministry of the Interior before transmission, often resulting in great delays even if the story was undisturbed. The European reporters avoided this problem by using the long distance telephone.

Restoration of civil liberties, Barnes concluded in the fifth part of the series, was unlikely in Mussolini's Italy. Fascism exalted the state over the individual. Mussolini's personal beliefs came from Machiavelli whom he often quoted: "it is necessary for him who has the directing of a republic and who has the ordering of its laws to presuppose all men to be bad and to exploit the evil qualities in their minds whenever suitable occasion offers. Men never affect good actions save from necessity; but where freedom abounds and where license can come about everything is filled immediately with confusion and disorder." Just as important, Mussolini was well aware of existing resentment against his government and feared that any relaxation of repression would unleash that resentment, to the peril of his regime. Moreover Mussolini was convinced that only through rigorous internal discipline could Italy overcome its natural handicaps and assume its proper position among nations.

Nevertheless, Barnes emphasized again that the opportunistic nature of the regime made it difficult to predict what the future would hold. He cited as an example Italy's postwar experience in foreign policy. Italy's traditional enmity toward Austria, historically the major impediment to Italian unification, was heightened after the war when Italy was given control of the Alto Adige, an area on the border between the two states but largely populated by German-speaking people. Italy immediately inaugurated an aggressive Italianization policy limiting the use of German in schools and in all official transactions. Tensions between Italy and Austria nearly reached the point of a rupture of diplomatic relations. Yet recent negotiations had led to a treaty with Austria and substantial amelioration of the conditions in the Alto Adige. Mussolini was strong enough to change his mind.[25]

In the final article of the series, Barnes identified a limitation on Mussolini's power that was to plague him for the remainder of his career: while Italians, even those who were anti-Fascist domestically, in general supported him in his foreign policy moves, that support lasted only as long as he stopped short of "war or rumors of war." Currently France was the "arch-opponent," with the Italians determined to resist French efforts to shore up the postwar status quo, to the detriment of those nations, including Italy, that saw themselves as betrayed by the Peace of Versailles. Italians rallied to the anti-French cause, particularly in the Balkans, where each country had its client states, but many faded away when war seemed a real possibility. This attitude proved to be Mussolini's greatest frustration.[26]

Barnes's final official task before leaving Italy was a meeting with Mussolini. He later wrote his parents of the experience: "I had an interesting fifteen minutes with him; but because of my having to rush off to Paris, and because of a mix-up at the Foreign Ministry, the details of which I am not quite clear about, I was not in a position to publish the results. However, it was a worthwhile experience, and may be of use later. Perhaps you will understand how, in the not distant future, I might be able to compare some rather prominent personalities as I have experienced them. I have very vivid impressions of the big man in Italy. We talked in French, for my Italian was not equal to the occasion."[27]

The year in Italy provided Ralph Barnes with valuable experience, testing him with the challenge of covering an entire country on his own. He operated there as in most of his career largely independent of direction or, for that matter, reaction from his editors and managers in New York. The body of his work showed a breadth apparently encouraged by the *Herald Tribune* but also reflected his own interests and preferences. It was a formula he took along to Moscow.

Part II. Moscow:
March 1931—August 1935

Here in the center of the black soil belt, 450 miles southeast of Moscow, it is not hard to understand the observation of certain keen students of the Soviet experiment that, as a result of the changes of the last two years, rural Russia has felt the revolution more even than urban Russia. Nor it is difficult here to believe, as it has been asserted, that the movement which has thrown perhaps 70,000,000 peasants into collective farms within the brief span of twenty-four months is one of three or four of the most significant social and economic upheavals in history.

Ralph Barnes, *Herald Tribune*,
August 16, 1931, Rossach, U.S.S.R.

When Barnes took up his Moscow assignment in the spring of 1931, the Great Experiment of the Russian Revolution had been under way for fourteen years. In the midst of World War I, the dilapidated government of the czars had collapsed, to be replaced temporarily by a constitutional regime. Its leader, Alexander Kerensky, was determined to continue the war against the German Empire. Desperate to secure their eastern conquests in the face of increasing pressure from the west where the United States had entered the war against them, the Germans facilitated the return to Russia of the exiled V. I. Lenin. From his refuge in Switzerland, the leader of the Bolshevik wing of the Communist Party had ardently opposed Russia's involvement in the war. In October 1917, the Bolsheviks overthrew the constitutional government and inherited the vast country with its huge population, its backwardness, and its gaping social, economic, and ethnic divisions. After prolonged negotiations and renewed fighting, on March 3, 1918 the Soviet government finally accepted German demands and withdrew from the war under the stringent provisions of the Treaty of Brest-Litovsk. The pact left the German army in control of vast stretches of formerly Russian territory. Meanwhile the Bolsheviks' move to suppress all rivals brought civil war lasting nearly three years. Millions died in the fighting, in the cycle of atrocity and revenge, and from hunger and disease.[1] As the leader of the Red Army, Lenin's former rival Leon Trotsky proved himself a brilliant, if ruthless, organizer and tactician.

Shortly after the civil war ended in 1920, Lenin inaugurated his New Economic Policy in response to the failure of reality to correspond to Marxist theory. Russia at the time of the 1917 revolution was still a largely pre-industrial society. When revolutions in western Europe did not inevitably follow that in Russia, Lenin found himself isolated in a country whose economy, shocked by the stringencies of civil war and forced procurement, had ceased to function. Production, especially of food, had fallen to 13 percent of prewar figures. Since any surplus the peasants accumulated was confiscated by the government, they stopped planting. Under Lenin's new policy, private trade was allowed internally, a progressive grain tax replaced the requisitions, compulsory labor was abolished, currency and taxation were restored, and small industries were returned to their pre-revolutionary owners. The program brought comparative prosperity as well as the inevitable return of a class structure to Soviet society, so that many in the hierarchy saw it as a threat to their power.

Meanwhile, Lenin's stroke in 1922 had opened the question of succession. Although Leon Trotsky, because of his intellectual capacity and his organizational ability, was the obvious choice, Lenin thought him too idealistic and sought to balance him with someone more practical, a qualification Josef Stalin fulfilled. While Lenin saw Stalin as power hungry, he thought he could be controlled in a triumvirate that included Trotsky. In a secret will, Lenin warned against the power Stalin was accumulating through his control of the bureaucracy. At Lenin's death in 1924, Stalin moved to consolidate his power, first allying himself with the Right within the party in order to isolate Trotsky. Against Trotsky's cry for permanent revolution, Stalin advocated "socialism in one country," a turning inward that many saw as promising a period of relaxation after the strain of war and revolution. Trotsky was dismissed from the war ministry in 1925 and quietly exiled to Soviet Central Asia in January 1928. He eventually left the Soviet Union, never to return, but his specter haunted Stalin until 1940, when Stalin ordered him assassinated in Mexico.

Trotsky was hardly gone from Moscow before Stalin convinced the Central Committee to adopt "administrative measures" toward the peasants who were withholding grain from the market because of artificially low prices. Stalin was now intent on drastic change that included collectivization, an end to private trade, and the acceleration of industrialization regardless of the cost. Barnes had returned to the Soviet Union in the midst of this process. He would chronicle its fortunes.

~

The opening of a Moscow bureau, no small investment as the full force of the Depression was hitting the United States, indicated that the *Herald Tribune* itself had entered a decidedly dynamic phase. In 1931, the United States had not yet recognized the Soviet government and had no diplomatic representation in Russia. As Barnes noted in his correspondence, the *Herald Tribune*'s decision to have a regular correspondent there reflected its determination to compete with the *New York Times* in that arena as in all others, especially since the demise of the *Evening World* left the two as the clear rivals for the more serious New York readership.[2] Another bellwether of the *Herald Tribune*'s dynamism was Helen Reid's luring the celebrated liberal commentator Walter Lippmann to its staff a few months later. Given his own political leanings, Barnes welcomed any sign that his paper was broadening its perspective. He took the hiring of Lippmann to be "one more sign of the movement of the *Herald Tribune* toward the left; I mean away from rigid hide-bound Republicanism." A year later, he felt that, as he had predicted, the addition of Lippmann had "increased the prestige of the *Herald Tribune* tremendously."[3]

Whatever the *Herald Tribune*'s editorial policy, Barnes found his journalistic freedom unfettered: "I have not been told by the New York office whether I should oppose or favor Fascism, or whether I should oppose or favor Bolshevism. Presumably, I was in Paris and Rome, and am now in Moscow, to send my paper the facts, as I find them."[4]

Barnes moved to Moscow to take up his new assignment in April 1931, after settling Esther and Joan in Paris to await the birth of their second child. Staying at first with the Stowes, Esther eventually found an apartment on rue Joseph-Bara. They would not be together again until Christmas, a reunion much anticipated in Ralph's correspondence. They soon fell into the habit of exchanging five letters a week, as Ralph described it: "I ask questions about Joan, and she spends most of her letters answering them. How tremendously attached I became to our daughter in those ten months in Rome!"[5]

In Paris and Berlin, he had gathered the equipment and supplies necessary to set up an office, fearing they would not be available in Moscow. He also brought a supply of canned goods purchased at Wertheim's department store in Berlin. His first letter from Moscow confirmed reports of a food shortage, although he added that "the average person that you meet in the street appears to be standing up under the strain." For a time, he settled in the Metropole Hotel. He immediately hired a Russian woman to spend a few hours each day reviewing the Soviet newspapers and arranging his appointments. His routine included Russian lessons from a former army colonel. He wrote his parents that his tutor had him reading Pushkin's "Queen of Spades" and that he was making progress in the everyday essentials of the language.[6]

While Esther, who was making the greatest sacrifice, remained enthusiastic about Ralph's Moscow posting, his father was opposed. Fortunately, despite his unhappiness with the Moscow move, Edward Barnes began in 1931 to transcribe and save Ralph and Esther's letters and to keep clipping books of Ralph's articles. At the time, letters took fifteen to twenty days to reach Oregon from Moscow. By reading the *Herald Tribune* they received by mail, Ralph's parents had some idea of their son's activities within five days of their happening.

Only Ralph's side of his correspondence with his parents survives, but the reader concludes that Edward Barnes's opposition to the Moscow move was based partly on his antipathy toward the Soviet regime and partly on his assessment of what would be advantageous to Ralph's career. His objections elicited a strong response from his son: "Dad, I hope that you are a bit more reconciled about this Russian experience. In any case, I hope that you don't write any more epistles like the one you typed off after receiving my first letter." Ralph's own estimation of the assignment was clear: "Both of you must realize how important this may be for us. In Rome or Paris I am just one of many correspondents. Here I am one of a few observers of what is undoubtedly the most important experiment of this century; and perhaps for several centuries; either for good or bad. I know that it would be difficult to convince you that it would conceivably be anything but bad, bad, bad; but try to be a bit philosophical about it, or at least objective."[7]

The early letters suggest Barnes's growing fascination with Russia, and his conviction that the move was worth its price: "You will think that I am crazy; but if someone were to offer me the headship of our European service in exchange for the Moscow post, I would wish to keep the Moscow post for professional reasons. Of course, the matter of Esther and Joan might decide me to go to London; but I am convinced that there is more of a future for me here than there is in London." After all, he wrote in another letter, "It is not often that one finds himself in a job he would want to be in more than any other." He was encouraged to learn that "when the *Herald Tribune* decided it must have a Moscow bureau, it set out to find some one for the post who 'would be as good as Duranty of the *New York Times.*' " He added a disclaimer: "Of course, they don't expect any such thing during the first two months; but, presumably, they believe I will be able to do it later."[8]

In the earliest years of the Soviet regime, western reporters had not been permitted. They were the enemy, representatives of the imperialist world the Bolsheviks sought to overthrow. For a time, the West got its information on the new Soviet Union through the Latvian city of Riga, a hotbed of rumor that was then packaged as news and shipped to the West. Unfortunately, most of the rumors proved to be untrue, as Walter Lippmann and Charles Merz documented in an article on the *New York Times* coverage that was published in the *New Republic* in 1920. Finally, in August of 1921, the Soviets relented and allowed western journalists to enter the country, under conditions carefully calculated to limit their potential to damage Soviet interests. The Press Department of the Commissariat of Foreign Affairs had the responsibility for censorship, while the secret police, the O.G.P.U., kept an eye on the correspondents themselves.[9]

Under these limitations, the correspondents' routine was well established when Barnes arrived a decade later. Information already published in the Soviet press was "safe" and could therefore be used by foreign journalists. Thus the correspondents devoted a tremendous amount of energy to the "drab and monotonous" Soviet press searching for nuances that might suggest what was really happening. The other official source for news was the communique, from this or that body of Soviet government. For reasons that were never clear, the communiques invariably came late at night. Ralph's letters, and later Esther's, referred over and over again to the annoyance.[10] All too often, the communiques were of little interest to editors back in the United States, so that the correspondents' late nights were frequently futile. Even without the disabilities of censorship and travel restrictions, the correspondents based in Moscow faced a formidable challenge in covering a country that spanned eleven time zones and had a population of 176 million people. The editors of the *Herald Tribune* were willing to devote more space to news from the Soviet Union than from Italy, providing Barnes with more opportunity and more work. His output was prodigious.

When Barnes arrived in Moscow, only four other American newspapers, the *New York Times,* the *Christian Science Monitor,* the *Chicago Daily News,* and the *New York Sun,* and four wire services, the Associated Press, the United Press, Universal and International, had regular correspondents there.[11] Other papers sent reporters in for short periods from time to time. Barnes's major competitor was Walter Duranty of the *New York Times,* the old Moscow hand whom Ralph and Esther had met during their 1927 visit. Duranty had all the advantages. He had been in Moscow for ten years and he worked for a more prestigious newspaper. His 1932 Pulitzer Prize lauded the "scholarship, profundity, impartiality, sound judgment and exceptional clarity" of his dispatches. The later debate about Duranty's rather selective reporting and the motives behind it is not reflected in Barnes's correspondence. He viewed Duranty as "an excellent correspondent and a highly cultured person" and respected him as a competitor: "I have had to keep going even to begin to compete with him. It will be a long time before I can touch him."[12]

In a review of Duranty's articles during the first half of 1931, several themes recur. The idea Duranty had expressed to Barnes in their 1927 conversation figures prominently: The Soviet regime was the best one for the Russians, who were different from other people, so that governing them required different measures. The government was constantly forced to fight the

> *ignorance and inertia of the masses. ... One might almost suggest that behind the practical advantages of rural collectivization, in producing more grain and promoting socialism among the peasants, there exists—not clearly formulated but wholly real—this terrific urge to stir the people up, force new ideas into their heads and make them talk and think and learn despite themselves. The word that expresses it best is 'ferment'—something that will keep the whole mass seething and*

*fizzing and bubbling—uncomfortable, no doubt, but at least in
movement and not inert. To this end the Kremlin is devoting every
device and art of government known to man—reward and
punishment, cajolery and pressure, oratory and written or pictured
propaganda, the bogey of hostile invasion and the hope of an
attainable millennium. … The whole purpose of the plan is to get the
Russians going—that is, to make a nation of eager, conscious workers
out of a nation that was a lump of sodden, driven slaves. … Russia
and Russians and Russian logic are different, but the fact that they are
different does not necessarily mean they are wrong.*

In fact, Duranty wrote,

*Stalin is giving the Russian people—the Russian masses, not
Westernized landlords, industrialists, bankers and intellectuals, but
Russia's 150,000,000 peasants and workers—what they really want,
namely joint effort, communal effort. And communal life is as
acceptable to them as it is repugnant to a Westerner. This is one of the
reasons why Russian Bolshevism will never succeed in the United
States, Great Britain, France or other parts west of the Rhine.*

*Stalinism, too, has done what Lenin only attempted. It has
reestablished the semi-divine, supreme autocracy of the imperial idea
and has placed itself on the Kremlin throne as a ruler whose lightest
word is all in all and whose frown spells death. Try that on free-born
Americans, or the British with their tough loyalty to old things, or on
France's consciousness of self. But it suits the Russians and is as
familiar, natural and right to the Russian mind as it is abominable
and wrong to Western nations.*

The results of Soviet efforts were manifest in the healthy children
he saw in the streets and in a new spirit: "In the towns and cities the
public has borne unusual hardship with comparative equanimity,
at least without evidence of discouragement or exhaustion. From
the top to the bottom of Soviet society there is a feeling that the
worst is past and it is possible to sense the first swell of a gigantic
surge of national energy which indicates that the 'dark' millions of
the Russian plains are beginning to see the light and grow conscious
of their new strength and cohesion."

Class distinctions were being abolished with the former upper
classes "melted in the hot fire of exile and labor into the proletarian
mass." The minority problem was being solved: "Stalinism has
already achieved a marked degree of transmutation of petty
nationalism into a great Pan-Sovietism." Even the censorship of
foreign correspondents was "usually applied with intelligence and

moderation." The Soviet censors were "always willing to discuss matters with a correspondent before a cable message is sent and meet him half way in modifying a sentence so as not to break the thread of his message or even to convey in more moderate form the item disapproved."

Duranty recorded Stalin's development as a leader:

Henceforth his own entity, with the qualms and doubts he has repressed and conquered by sheer force of will, is submerged and ceases to trouble him, because of this fresh discovery that he is no longer Joseph Stalin but the mouthpiece of the word, Lenin's word. He is not the dictator of all the Russias, nor the arrogant ruler of the Communist party, but an instrument, a chosen vessel, to express the will of the party along the lines laid down by Lenin, its founder. I admit this comes dangerously close to metaphysics and the elusive doctrine of predestination, but Stalin after all is no Slav fatalist but a Caucasian, who can hold fast to the thread of his own free will in the labyrinth where Slavs are lost. That he senses and follows "the party line" (that mysterious Holy Ghost of the Communist religion) is true as death. That he forms and inspires it is no less true.

Duranty did have misgivings about the Soviet bureaucracy: "Stalin has created a great Frankenstein monster, of which, as I said earlier, he has become an integral part, made up of comparatively insignificant and mediocre individuals, but whose mass desires, aims and appetites have an enormous and irresistible power. I believe it is not true, and I devoutly hope so, but it haunts me unpleasantly. And perhaps haunts Stalin."[13]

Throughout his time in Moscow, Barnes felt the challenge of Duranty with his prestige and his access keenly. With journalists other than Duranty, his relations were cordial and often cooperative.[14] Stanley Richardson became a collaborator and a friend, even to providing facilities lacking in Barnes's rather primitive hotel room: "I shave with an enameled cup full of hot water, and take most of my baths in a washpan—except when I pay a friendly visit for that purpose at the apartment of the Associated Press correspondent Richardson." Barnes became particularly close to William Henry Chamberlin of the *Christian Science Monitor*. Chamberlin and his wife Sonya, a Russian émigrée, came to the Soviet Union in 1922 out of revolutionary conviction. They soon became disenchanted, but remained in Moscow. Along with his journalism, Chamberlin was doing research for a history of the Russian Revolution. In one of his first letters Barnes noted that the Chamberlins did not "exactly fit in with the American newspaper colony here; but I think that is to their credit."[15]

For many in the depression-ravaged West, the highly publicized progress of the U.S.S.R. under the Five-year Plans confirmed its claims that communism was superior to capitalism. In their ideological fervor, western supporters paid little attention to the human costs of this "progress" or to the increasingly repressive nature of Stalin's regime. Barnes consistently explored these issues. At the same time, he wrote of day-to-day events, the political, economic, diplomatic and military happenings of the period. Further, he attempted to give his readers a picture of everyday life in the Soviet Union and an introduction to the Soviet people as individuals not very different from themselves.

Understandably Barnes's earliest articles from the U.S.S.R. reflected the government-controlled press and official communiques, but he gradually developed the sources necessary to provide a more balanced picture. More than most of his colleagues, he made an effort to get out of the city, to find out what was going on in the rest of the country. He read books about the Five-year Plans and about the state of Russian agriculture, recognizing that the government programs for industrialization and collectivization were the central forces operating in the country at the time. Careful study of his articles provides a picture largely confirmed by the recently opened archives of the Soviet Union. The problems were clear to the informed observer.

Indeed, Barnes's first story with a Moscow dateline, which ran in the *Herald Tribune* on April 24, 1931, reported a campaign in the Soviet press "for a general tightening of the belt and quickening of pace to meet the stern exactions of the Five-year Plan." He quoted *Izvestia, Pravda,* and *Economic Life* as each attempted to prod Soviet workers into greater productivity and decried the failure of the Stalingrad tractor plant to meet its goals. Workers in Leningrad wrote to reproach their Stalingrad comrades: "One hundred thousand peasants' collective farms are awaiting tractors and still you delay."[16] Barnes was hardly settled before the *Herald Tribune* was advertising his coverage of the Second Five-year Plan, the Soviet initiative designed to modernize agriculture in order to transfer millions in the rural work force to industry. He noted that the planners assumed the total success of the First Five-year Plan by its scheduled completion date of December 30, 1932, "despite serious difficulties being experienced."[17]

The early stories highlighted the competitive nature of the Soviet endeavor, with Barnes comparing Russian interest in the Stalingrad tractor plant's "box scores" to the American fixation on the World Series. Improvements were cheered, while failings brought "a flood of letters from widely scattered labor groups condemning the Stalingrad workers and factory officials for their failure to produce and pleading with them to change their ways so as not to deal a body blow to the Five-Year-Plan." Forecasts for the 1931 harvest were optimistic and avidly reported in the Soviet press. The prediction that the Second Five-year Plan would enable the Soviet Union to "catch up with and surpass the United States" by 1938 foreshadowed Nikita Khrushchev's 1959 boast "We will bury you."[18]

In their attempt to diversify Russia's economic base, the Soviets employed American engineers and advisors. The general technical advisor to the Soviet government for its massive industrial construction projects was John K. Calder of Detroit. Barnes's 1931 interview with Calder found him enthusiastic and optimistic, with no indication of the disillusionment that later caused him to leave the Soviet Union: "There is no reason in the world, it appears to me, why the plan can not and will not be realized." As for the Russian worker, "you won't find better anywhere."[19]

Even in 1931, Barnes found other points of view emerging. Following a six- month study, the American engineering firm Stuart, James & Cook, Inc. issued its report on the coal industry in the Soviet Union, pointing to the fact that "the daily average production of a man in the United States is fully 400 per cent higher than that in Russia." The catalog of problems that Stuart, James & Cook found would seem familiar to later observers of Soviet industry in general:

lack of supplies at some mines and excess at others; delays in receiving supplies; many plans providing for improvements and alterations never reach the mine office; mining machinery of the same type not properly concentrated in the same mining districts, with resulting high repair costs; delays in repair work, keeping machines unnecessarily idle; voluminous statistics, instead of recording simple vital facts related to those factors which go to produce coal; accounting and clerical forces too numerous; antagonism between the head office and mine officials, which cannot but exist when mines officials are being pressed for production and when not receiving proper co-operation; lack of co-ordination among the head office, district office and mine offices; jealousy and petty politics which cannot fail to exist under the present

*system of functioning, and lack of enthusiasm for rationalization
work.*[20]

The Soviet Union recognized its need for technical expertise but
American engineers complained that they were able to "make only
a fraction use of their knowledge, abilities and experience." The
government passed decree after decree to remove obstacles from their
paths.[21] More problematic from an ideological perspective was the
question of the "technicians of the Old Order," engineers and others
from the Czarist regime. Barnes reported that Stalin himself ruled
that "it is our task to change our attitude toward the technical and
engineering forces of the older school, to pay more attention to them,
to take better care of them, and to encourage them to show more
initiative in their work." This had not previously been possible,
Stalin explained, because many of that class were infected with "the
illness called sabotage," but now Soviet progress had changed their
attitude. By government decree, engineers and technicians received
food cards that gave them access to the same supplies as their working
class counterparts. Their children were now assured the same access
to education, "one more move," Barnes wrote, "toward the
elimination of much of the class antagonism to which many outside
observers have taken exception." He called the development
"encouraging to those persons who are watching intensively the
human side of the Soviet experiment." [22] The darker side, the role of
the OGPU and of the forced labor of the *Gulag*, was less readily
evident to a reporter in Moscow in 1931. Repression became an
economic apparatus providing an endless supply of workers for
whatever project the leadership envisioned.[23]

Some of the Moscow journalistic contingent, such as Chamberlin
and Eugene Lyons, had come to further the cause of socialism.
Experience in the Soviet Union led to almost immediate disillusionment. Lyons, a leftist long active in New York radical circles,
recounted his surprise when "casual table talk among the
newspapermen treated as matters of common knowledge facts which
I had vehemently denied for so many years—facts for which I had
helped consign friends to the garbage-heap of 'renegacy.' "
Chamberlin detailed the inhumanity of the first Five-year Plan: "the
uncounted executions, the institution of virtual slavery for millions
of people, the fraudulent sabotage trials, the espionage and terror,
both ten times worse than during the first years which I had spent
in Russia, the consequent degradation of the human personality."[24]

Despite his later cynicism, Malcolm Muggeridge, who came to
Moscow in 1932 for the *Manchester Guardian,* also arrived wide-eyed

and eager. One of his first experiences was the government-sponsored tour of Dnieprostroy. Lyons pictured him as "among the most gullible on this journey, having only just arrived from London, with all the preconceptions about Russia fostered by the paper he represented and other well-meaning liberal publications."[25] Certainly Barnes did not come to Russia as an opponent of the Soviet regime, but he did come as a reporter, a responsibility about which he remained idealistic throughout his life. He was quite sure of the importance of the Soviet experiment.

With his paper's encouragement and following his own instincts, Barnes made the human side of Russian life an important focus of his reporting. He urged his father to "ask all the questions you want to" for then he would "know more about what people in America are interested in. It is difficult for me already to look in on Russia from an outside standpoint." He turned to Albert Rhys Williams, whom he and Esther had known during their 1927 trip to the Soviet Union. Once an ardent revolutionary, Rhys Williams's devotion to the cause of Socialism had been severely tried. By the 1930s, Eugene Lyons described Rhys Williams as "one of the small band of Americans which witnessed the Bolshevik revolution and championed it ardently in its first romantic years, [who] now sought, with a determined and melancholy mien, for traces of the dream and blew conscientiously upon the embers of his ardor."[26]

Perhaps it was his background in the ministry but, even as a revolutionary, Rhys Williams retained a sympathy for the remnants of the Russian Orthodox Church and its followers. On Easter weekend, 1931, he took Barnes on visits to Moscow churches, including those of the "Old Believers." Barnes found the Old Believers, so long accustomed to hardship and persecution, to have survived better under the pressure of the Soviet government than the Orthodox Church that had enjoyed such a favorable position during Czarist times. The visit to the Old Believers' congregation resulted in a mail article that appeared in the *Herald Tribune* several weeks later. Barnes closed it with the observation: "Perhaps religion is dying in Russia, but it is not yet dead."[27]

Rhys Williams also afforded an opportunity increasingly rare in Moscow at the time, a visit to the home of a Russian writer, where they dined on "Russian salad, with several kinds of vegetables, including green peas; two kinds of fish, both tasty; black bread, two varieties of wine, vodka, and afterwards tea and wafers." After being entertained with Russian folk music played by another guest, they went on to a writers' club where they remained until three in the morning.[28]

Russian life interested Barnes, and he was convinced it interested his readers. During his first months in Moscow, he wrote stories on the cabmen in the streets, the clothing of ordinary people, the lunchroom in the Moscow railway station, women working on streetcars and as police on the beat, and the popularity of western sports.[29] His editors clearly supported his choice of material. Still, there were occasional aggravations. The New York office asked for mail material, the longer, more in-depth pieces that Barnes enjoyed working on, then did not always print them. They cut his articles and interfered with the flow of the story; placement in the paper was not always what he would have liked; occasionally they made erroneous changes or additions. Usually Barnes passed these complaints off, but sometimes the errors had more serious implications: "The short item in the May 11th issue, relative to a new steel plant in Leningrad, was *not* mine. It should not have had a 'bureau' line on it, and I am sending in a complaint. Of course, that particular story was innocuous; but, in view of the strict censorship, I do not desire to be held accountable here for stories that I don't send in."[30]

Early in his Russian sojourn, Barnes experienced that phenomenon so dear to the hearts of the Moscow correspondents, the "distinguished visitor," described by Muggeridge as "our best—almost our only—comic relief." He added: "They are unquestionably one of the wonders of the age, and I shall treasure till I die as a blessed memory the spectacle of them travelling with radiant optimism through a famished countryside, wandering in happy bands about squalid, over-crowded towns, listening with unshakeable faith to the fatuous patter of carefully trained and indoctrinated guides, repeating like schoolchildren a multiplication table, the bogus statistics and mindless slogans endlessly intoned to them."[31]

During the 1930s, visitors came in increasing numbers and went away "experts" on the Soviet experiment after a week or two. Probably the most famous was the playwright George Bernard Shaw. Accompanied by Lord and Lady Astor and the Marquess of Lothian, he arrived for a nine-day visit on July 21, 1931, encouraging his hosts with the admonition: "It is for you to carry out your lead to an absolutely triumphal conclusion which will make it impossible for other countries not to follow you." Contrary to warnings about conditions in the Soviet Union, he said he found such plenty that his party threw away the provisions brought for the trip. Ralph wrote his parents that the "Shaw-Astor party kept me going day and night. ... I have talked to Lady Astor ten or fifteen times in the course of her visit; and also have been able to converse a bit with Shaw. He is rather shy of newspapermen; perhaps because he knows something of journalism himself."[32]

The Shaw visit took on extra drama when Professor Dmitri P. Krynine of Yale University appealed to the visitors for help in securing permission for his wife to leave the Soviet Union. Two years before, the Soviet government had sent Krynine to study road building in the United States where his son was a student. Krynine declined to return, whereupon the Soviet government refused to allow his wife to join him. Lady Astor presented the petition to Maxim Litvinov, only to be told that "the matter was quite outside his province." Other efforts on her part came to nothing.[33]

Working with Stanley Richardson of the Associated Press, Barnes found Madame Krynine in the two-room apartment she now shared with another family. Their interview attracted a good deal of attention when it appeared in the *Herald Tribune* and went out on the Associated Press wire. Mme. Krynine asked only to be reunited with her family and stated, "Never have I been bothered by anyone, and if I were to be permitted to leave I would not on my arrival in America have any charges to make."[34] Duranty and the *New York Times* did not cover the Krynine story. It was Barnes's first Moscow scoop and occasioned his first substantive struggle with the censor. He reported to his father that he was unable to fulfill a number of follow-up requests from New York because of the censorship. After he and Richardson spent one long day producing a story, the censor turned them down. Only after another day of argument and considerable toning down were they finally able to send the article. "There are a good many details which cannot yet be told. Perhaps they will come out later." Barnes referred cryptically to having a "trump card" but there is no indication of it in later articles or correspondence. Three years later, he reported that Madame Krynine had been exiled from Moscow "somewhere in the Soviet provinces" where she was "not imprisoned but confined to a certain provincial district."[35]

Censorship was a daily battle, sometimes annoying just because of its inefficiency. In Stalin's Soviet Union, all outgoing dispatches were screened by censors before transmission. Muggeridge likened it to "taking an essay to one's tutor at Cambridge; watching anxiously as they were read over for any frowns or hesitations, dreading to see a pencil picked up to slash something out." The face-to-face process required negotiation skills. There were ways other than the wire to get a story out but the Soviets read the foreign press and, if an unfavorable story could be traced to a Moscow correspondent, held him responsible.[36] As oppression heightened during the 1930s, the situation worsened because the censors became more and more fearful of the consequences to themselves of any adverse reporting.

Barnes's contemporaries described the pressures, subtle and otherwise, to conform: restriction of access, delays at the border upon re-entry or perhaps denial of re-entry visas, travel restrictions within the country, and the ultimate threat of expulsion. Lyons wrote later: "Whether in Moscow or Berlin, Tokyo or Rome, all the temptations for the practicing foreign reporter are in the direction of conformity. It is more comfortable and in the long run more profitable to soft-pedal a dispatch for readers thousands of miles away than to face an irate censor and closed official doors." The threat of expulsion in a depression-ridden world was particularly potent, because often "loss of the visa meant loss of the job."[37]

The Shaw visit and the Krynine drama were side trips in Barnes's pursuit of the story of the collectivization of agriculture, well under way when he arrived in the Soviet Union. The hunger of the Russian peasant for land had given impetus to the Russian Revolution of 1917 when the peasants seized the land they farmed from their landlords. Since the Revolution, the government's agriculture policy had lurched from peasant ownership of the land, to forced requisition of grain during the Civil War with the consequent steep decline in the amount harvested, to the relative freedom and improved agricultural production of the New Economic Policy.

But like the greater freedom in the commercial and industrial sectors which the N.E.P. promoted, economic freedom in the countryside was viewed with suspicion by the Soviet hierarchy. Further, the conviction arose that only through the collectivization of agriculture could the resources, human and economic, be found to industrialize the country. All agricultural land, along with the people who farmed it, was to be gathered into large collective farms to be run along industrial lines. The policy called for complete collectivization by the autumn of 1932, with the most important agricultural areas to be brought into the system by the autumn of 1931.[38] It envisioned a countryside mechanized and modernized by the resources gained through the confiscation of the possessions of the *kulaks*, the so-called "rich peasants" who had prospered under the New Economic Policy. They were to be stripped of their land

and other possessions and deported to remote parts of the Soviet Union as obstacles to the success of collectivization.

But by any reasonable definition the *kulaks* represented only four percent of the population of the countryside. Their resources were not sufficient to provide for the needs of the collective farms. The peasants were thrown into a system for which they were unprepared and which was not ready to receive them. In protest, they destroyed their livestock rather than turn it over to the State. Opposition to collectivization was not confined to the small part of the population who could truly be classified as *kulaks;* it included the vast majority of the peasantry. Faced with massive resistance, the government relented and Stalin himself wrote an article on March 2, 1930, criticizing the overzealousness of party operatives in the countryside. But *Pravda* shortly indicated that the change of policy was only temporary: "Again we are dividing the land into individual farms for those who do not wish to farm collectively, and then once more we will socialize and rebuild until kulak resistance has been broken once for all."[39]

Divining the realities of collectivization was an immediate, and elusive, goal for Barnes. Reports were contradictory; he was determined to get to the countryside, writing home that he "would rather see something of the collectives than of any other part of Russia." After many postponements, he finally succeeded in early August. His guide was Maurice Hindus, who had served the same function for the Shaw party. Barnes, and others, considered Hindus to be the authority on rural Russia. He assured his father that Hindus was not "by any means a communist" but "finds many bad points as well as good points" in collectivization. Born in Russia, Hindus had migrated to the United States as a child, but returned to make himself a recognized authority on rural Russia with his books *Red Bread* and *Humanity Uprooted.* In a passage parhaps more revealing of his father's prejudices than of Hindus, Barnes wrote E. T. Barnes that Hindus "is a good travelling companion; and, of course, he knows the Russian village about as well as any person living; or at least as well as any person who knows the English language. He is a Jew, but appears to have escaped a good many of the characteristics which sometimes make members of his race disagreeable."[40]

The trip to the collective farms near Rossach, 450 miles southeast of Moscow, was a difficult one. The trains offered few amenities and the villages were infested with insects: "Bed bugs and fleas were the principal pests during our jaunt into the villages; and they were well seconded by great swarms of flies. Several nights we slept hardly a wink before daylight, because of the great swarms of insects which seemed to be set upon devouring us." Nevertheless for Barnes the trip was "a glorious experience, the best I have had since coming to Russia."[41] Years later, Hindus remembered these trips and Ralph Barnes: "So eager was he to be with the common folk of Russia that he never would travel in the luxurious sleeping cars, but always insisted on going 'hard,' in a third-class carriage, with only a bare bench on which to stretch out in the night and no chance to undress or to enjoy the least privacy. I never had known a foreigner in Russia who could make himself so easily understood to Russians with monosyllables, with unfinished phrases, above all with his ringing laugh, his merry eyes, and his boundless humanity."[42]

Barnes found the scope of collectivization overwhelming: "The movement which has thrown perhaps 70,000,000 peasants into collective farms within the brief span of twenty-four months is one of three or four of the most significant social and economic upheavals in history."[43] Problems quickly emerged. The government was unable to provide the necessary technical expertise or the requisite equipment, buildings and supplies. Nor were the day-to-day needs of the peasants being met; in one of Russia's richest agricultural regions, food supplies were inadequate while the government predicted the largest crop in history. Striking to Ralph's western eyes was the threatened collapse of home life, with the advent of communal kitchens, nurseries, and even living quarters. "A ferment among the peasants is beginning," he predicted.[44] To ensure the regime's future in the countryside, the government turned to means employed in the cities, an indoctrination effort focused on children and teenagers who were "expected to use their influence to bring uncertain parents into line with the new order."[45]

Conditions inside and outside the Soviet Union caused planners to make adjustments to the Five-year Plan. Even the five-day week was short-lived as the Soviets went to a five-day-on, one-day-off schedule.[46] The worldwide depression meant that markets for Soviet products, never substantial, shrunk further. Incentives proved necessary to encourage production and to promote consumption. Such abandonment of some of the most basic premises of Marxist theory caused the editorial writers of the *Herald Tribune* to observe that Russia had returned to capitalism, in a special form with its own distinctive characteristics: "perhaps in the long run what it offers is less a menace than a question. Will it ever come to serve the people who must live by it any better than the older forms would serve them? It is not doing so now, and it is hard to believe that it ever will. If it does, other nations can adopt it for themselves; if it doesn't it will not survive. A year ago the Five-year Plan was still causing alarm; today it seems a pretty empty bogey."[47] This rather cool editorial contrasted sharply with both the Red Scare hysteria of the day and the exaggerated claims many on the left were making. It reflected, perhaps, the changing mindset that eventually led to United States recognition of the Soviet government.

Barnes showed that the country was not without its social issues. In a long article on the *bezprisorni*, he recounted Soviet efforts to deal with the problem of as many as 750,000 homeless, roaming children. Through efforts to confine the children to institutions around the country, the numbers had been reduced to 4,500, according to government figures. About 2,000 of these were in Moscow, where Barnes wrote of encountering a small group late at night. Ranging in age from eight to thirteen, they were clothed in rags and gathered around a fire on a work site for what little warmth they could find. The authorities repeatedly blamed misappropriation of funds for the failure to deal with the problem.[48]

Meanwhile, a new challenge emerged. While the international atmosphere had certainly not been friendly, the young Soviet Union had for a decade been free from foreign threats to its territory. The Japanese invasion of the Chinese province of Manchuria in September ended this fortuitous circumstance. At least since the Russo-Japanese War of 1905, Manchuria, ostensibly controlled by the Chinese, had been subject to Russian economic penetration, particularly in its railways. While the Soviet government clearly preferred to have a weak and divided China on its eastern border, it quickly tried to distance itself officially from the strife in Manchuria while at the same time taking measures to secure both its interest in the railway and the integrity of its territory.[49] The question of Japan's aggressive designs affected Soviet policy throughout the 1930s and afforded Stalin a rationale for increasingly repressive measures.

❧

Through the summer and fall of 1931, amidst his accounts of Soviet politics, economics, and foreign policy, Barnes pursued his interest in the everyday life of the Russian people, writing about the willingness of Russian women to pay $7.50 for a ten cent pair of silk stockings from New York, and about their struggles to find fashionable clothing and cosmetics. He wrote of the uncomfortable need to share housing with one's former spouse after a divorce, and of the problems of the ostracized nuns he found living in a cubbyhole in the entryway of an old church.[50]

Thanks to a tip from Maurice Hindus, Barnes learned that Stalin's wife, Nadia Alliluieva, was a student in a school in Moscow. Throughout the fall, he searched, finally locating her at the All-Union Industrial Academy pursuing a three-year course to become a specialist in the artificial production of silk. Stalin's second wife and twenty-three years his junior, Alliluieva was the daughter of an old Georgian revolutionary who had long been Stalin's friend. Barnes found her engaged with her classmates in a chemistry experiment. They did not converse. His article pictured her as "setting an example in line with the Soviet policy of getting the housewife away from housework and into industry." He commented on the impact her studies might have on her two young children, and the headline writer in the *Herald Tribune* went even further: "First Lady of Soviet Land Completing 3-Year Technical Course in Moscow with only one day out of six to see how children are getting on."[51]

The Soviet leaders were traditionally quite secretive about their families. Barnes's finding Alliluieva was a real coup that won him recognition in *Time* magazine and elsewhere. He was pleased with himself and wrote his parents that he had "had a clean sweep with the story." He had shared it with Stan Richardson of the Associated Press for publication thirty-six hours later when "all his piece could do would be to lend prestige to mine." Of particular satisfaction was the fact that the *New York Times* was completely without coverage. Not until he was writing from Paris during his Christmas visit there did Barnes let his parents know that Hindus was his source, suggesting an awareness that his correspondence might not be secure.[52]

5

The problem of supplying the industrial workers with
more goods is a sufficiently urgent one, but that of
rushing goods into the villages to restore the shattered
morale of the peasant is still more urgent. The peasant,
be he individualist or collective farmer, is either
apathetic or hostile because in many cases too much of
his grain was taken by the government last year to
fulfill the arbitrary collection program, and because he
has not been supplied with clothing, shoes, sugar, tea
and other necessaries in exchange for his grain.

Ralph Barnes, *Herald Tribune*,
September 18, 1932, from Moscow

Such achievements as the Alliluieva story helped ease the sense of
isolation from the home office that made Barnes feel insecure,
especially in the first years in Moscow. He complained of the lack of
feedback and faithfully reported to his parents any indication of
approval from New York, or from the head of the European service,
Harold Scarborough in London: "I had a letter from the European
manager, saying he thought my first cables were 'excellently
handled.' " A. R. Holcombe, the managing editor, wrote that the
New York office felt Barnes was "taking hold of the situation in
good shape." He also assured Barnes that the *Herald Tribune*
management was "anxious that everything shall go well with your
family in Paris," and offered to "lend assistance at any time."[1]

Changes at the *Herald Tribune* brought comment in his letters: "I
was puzzled shortly after Suzanne's birth to receive from New York
a wire signed 'Wilcox' and including congratulations from him and
from Mr. Draper, the first assistant of Ogden Reid, the publisher. I

now learn from Esther and the Paris bureau that for some reason or other Mr. Holcombe resigned last week as managing editor, and that a Mr. Wilcox has replaced him. So I haven't the least idea who Wilcox is, or rather, what his background is. Esther says that Lee Stowe, head of the Paris bureau, thinks that the change is for the best." And so it proved. Grafton Stiles Wilcox was, according to Richard Kluger, "the first truly competent journalist to direct the news operation of the paper since Whitelaw Reid in his prime half a century earlier." With only a high school education, he had been a newspaperman in Waukegan and Chicago before spending sixteen years in Washington as the top correspondent for the Associated Press, the *Chicago Tribune*, and the *New York Tribune*. As managing editor, Wilcox was hardworking and fair, "a working journalist, no mere company man." Later on during his stay in Moscow, when Barnes was frequently in disfavor with the Soviet authorities, the *Herald Tribune* under Wilcox gave him full support.[2]

Family concerns, in both Paris and Salem, preoccupied Ralph during the fall of 1931. The separation from Esther and Joan had been difficult from the start. He took consolation from the fact that they had a number of old friends in Paris on whom Esther could rely. Ralph missed Joan's first birthday and felt his absence as she progressed: "She will be all grown up when I see her again." He took pride in her mischievousness and was against "too much taming." Her childhood illnesses caused him anxiety although they were usually over before he received the letters reporting them. Esther's pregnancy proceeded without complication. Her mother came from Portland for the new baby's birth. Ralph rejoiced at the safe delivery of his daughter Suzanne. "All the news from Paris is good news. The French doctor, according to Esther, described Suzanne as 'superbe.' "[3]

In Salem, the stock market crash had an impact on the previously comfortable living standards of the Barnes family. When he sold his business in the early twenties, Edward Barnes had invested the proceeds in Columbia Paper Company. With the onset of the depression, the company stopped paying dividends to its stockholders. As time went on, it was more and more necessary for Ralph and Esther to provide financial support for the folks in Salem. These problems and Ralph's frequent reassurances to his parents became a recurring theme of his correspondence.

The prospect of a Christmas reunion with his wife and daughters loomed large: "Within two or three days, Mother Parounagian will be in Paris with Joannie and Esther. They will have a great time together. What a jolly time the five of us will have in Paris together at Christmas!" He was adjusting to the Russian winter and reassuring about his health: "Of course it is easier here than elsewhere to pick up contagious diseases, simply because the population knows so little about sanitation." He was anxious to get away, "Eight or nine months is quite enough at one stretch in this country."[4]

The trip was long; he left Moscow the evening of December 15 and arrived in Paris early December 18, Esther's birthday. He found her "stunning. She doesn't seem to be affected by years. It is most difficult to believe that she is thirty now." As for the children, "Joannie is glorious; I'm enjoying her immensely. Suzanne is a fat, healthy appearing little devil; but she doesn't play such a conspicuous role in the household as does Joannie." There was a fireplace, a Christmas tree, a cozy apartment. They dined out, browsed bookstores, made an expedition to Chartres for the benefit of Esther's mother, but mostly they talked. For Ralph, being in Paris was a treat: "You can't imagine how attached I am to this city. Every time I go out into the streets, I bubble over with enthusiasm. Churches, cafes, narrow winding streets, broad boulevards, the bridges and embankments of the Seine, and a hundred other things."[5] The time passed all too quickly. Esther and Ralph made their plans for the immediate future. He would "come out" to Paris in May for a short visit; then Esther, her mother and the children would sail for the United States to return to Oregon for a time.

After a stop in Berlin, Barnes arrived in Moscow on January 14, bringing books, most importantly for his purposes the *Encyclopedia Britannica*, new clothes, blankets, and other necessities unavailable there. He settled into his old room in the Metropole Hotel. He was pleased to find that the *Herald Tribune* had used his photograph of the dynamited Cathedral of the Redeemer in the gravure section on January 10: "Guess I'll have to go in for photography."[6]

Upon his return, the Seventeenth Congress of the Communist Party met amid rumors that the Japanese were assisting remnants of the old Czarist Army in a planned attack on the Soviet Union. Indeed, one Soviet paper charged that the United States was behind the Japanese threat, encouraging an attack on the Soviet Union to distract the Japanese from China. Less than a month later, Moscow papers reported speculation that United States recognition of the Soviet government was near, precisely because of the Japanese threat in the Far East.[7]

The goals of the Second Five-year Plan were modified in light of the shortfalls of the First Plan. Greater emphasis was to be placed on consumer goods including food supplies. In fact, the summary of the plan forecast "abolition of the rationing system through reorganization of distribution and augmentation of the supplies of consumers' goods." Production in heavy industry would continue to expand, but at arithmetical rather than geometrical ratios. To secure the technical expertise they needed, the Soviet government struggled to convince its American advisors to continue working even though the government could no longer pay them in hard currency. But when Americans, out of work in the west, came for the jobs they knew must be available in the Soviet paradise, they created a problem leading to a requirement that those coming have roundtrip tickets. Barnes did not foresee wholesale expulsion, but warned that "only those foreigners who have some definite assurance should come for other than sightseeing purposes. There is no question that the situation of some American jobseekers has been decidedly difficult."[8]

Lyons credited Barnes with bringing the plight of the Americans to the attention of other reporters. In writing about the issue, Walter Duranty took a decidedly different view: "To this writer the most important features of the year just ended are the success in operating modern industrial plants on a mass-production scale and the first distinct evidence of an inflow of skilled foreign workers, with their wives and families, prepared to settle in the Soviet Union and work on a ruble basis. ... Unless conditions abroad improve and unless the Soviet Union fails to maintain her previous rate of progress, which seems improbable—indeed, everything seems to point to a great improvement in living standards in the coming twelve months—next December may well witness a real flood of immigration."[9]

Barnes's awareness of conditions in the Soviet Union did not prevent him from continuing his argument with his father: "Dad, I find Moscow much more invigorating than 'debasing'—the last word is yours." He regretted his six-year absence from the United States but

I think that you will agree that for Esther and me these six years have been crowded pretty full of interesting experiences. I think that for both of us life is more interesting than it was a decade ago. For my part, I find living most absorbing, more so, perhaps, with each year that passes. I cannot think of very many important things that Esther and I have sacrificed by following the paths that we have followed. We postponed having our youngsters somewhat longer than would otherwise have been the case; but we have two of them now, and they are about as healthy and attractive as one could wish. This separation is not satisfactory, but we both feel that it will work out all right eventually."[10]

Ralph reminded his father: "Your letters are most interesting always—don't put any more than necessary of paternal reproofs in them, though. Even though I am used to them, sometimes they go against the grain. After all, I'm an adult, thirty-two years old, and so far I haven't done so badly with life." His father's response must have been conciliatory because Ralph wrote: "Dad, I liked your reaction to my comments about your ideas. You wrote not as father to son, but as friend to friend, which was mighty satisfying. I'm glad that you didn't take offense at what I said. Your remarks in the letter indicate that your ideas have undergone something of a transformation in the past few years. I do not hold a brief for the Soviet regime, but I think that the experiment should be studied dispassionately." He continued to rely on his father's feedback: "I'm always grateful for your comments on my pieces. Your judgment as to which among them are the more interesting is much better than mine could possibly be."[11]

Building on his story of Madame Stalin, Barnes wrote about the lives of the wives of high Soviet officials who, he said, had to commit themselves to "hard work, with mighty little compensation in bettered living conditions, pleasant publicity, pretty clothes, increased prestige, or agreeable social duties." In fact, the choice of wives less devoted to Soviet ideals had ruined the careers of several government officials. Generally the wives of successful men shunned publicity while working in some capacity within the Soviet economy. The wife of the Soviet president, Mikhail Kalinin, managed a state farm in Siberia, while the wife of the Commissar for Education, A. S. Bubnov, clerked in one of Moscow's principal shops for foreigners. The contrast with the role played by the wives of their own political leaders proved interesting to American readers. The *Literary Digest* reprinted the entire article.[12]

Barnes used the coincidence of the Russian Easter falling on May Day, the international proletarian holiday, in 1932 to revisit embattled religion in the Soviet Union. It was clear, he wrote, that "preparations were being made to smother the religious observances in monster counter-demonstrations and in a barrage of propaganda." The official press announced that special stress should be placed "on the difference between Easter and the proletarian May Day and on the necessity of offering a firm resistance to attempts of the

Orthodox and sectarian clergy to make use of Easter in the struggle against completion of the spring sowing and the Five-year Plan." In anticipation of the holiday, the government released a series of pamphlets for children that included such scenarios as a priest conspiring with capitalists from unnamed western countries to lure the workers from their duties. The plight of religion in the Soviet Union was clearly an issue of concern to American readers. Barnes's story, with accompanying photographs of Russians churches destroyed or converted to secular purposes, took nearly a full page of the *Herald Tribune*.[13]

With other correspondents, Barnes journeyed in May to Dnieprostroy in southern Ukraine, site of the great hydroelectric development that was the centerpiece of the first Five-year Plan. He shared with his readers the "almost childlike ... continued repetition in this country of the claim that the Dnieprostroy turbines and generators are the biggest ever built, that the power to be generated when all nine of the projected turbines are in operation will be greater than that of any other single hydroelectric plant in the world, and finally that the Dnieprostroy is one of the key economic units which when taken together are to permit the Soviet Union 'to catch up with and surpass' the United States and other capitalist countries."

While he found this ironic since the designers and construction supervisors of the project, as well as its generators, turbines, and construction equipment, were American, Barnes sought to have his readers understand. From their viewpoint, the Soviet leadership was waging a virtual war to modernize and industrialize their backward country. To stimulate the interest of their "primitive" people in the achievements of the Five-year Plans, they resorted to the kind of propaganda familiar in wartime. Besides, Dnieprostroy was their vision, the twenty-five thousand workers constructing it, and occasionally losing their lives in the process, were Russian. The achievement was "truly Russian."[14]

With his family's departure for the United States pending, Barnes returned to Paris at the end of May. "It will be hard to have them leave, but there is nothing else to be done." He enjoyed the visit, delighting as always in Joan's mischievous qualities, and warning his parents not to try to "take the deviltry out of her. She will have plenty of time later to become serious." After their voyage, a brief stay in New York, and a long, hot train trip, Esther, her mother, and the children arrived in Oregon on June 26. Their immediate plan was to rent a house on the Oregon coast for the summer. Since Ralph's parents would be joining them, Ralph wrote: "Hope you have lots of drift-wood fires, and the like. You can imagine how much I wish that I could be there. Do have the best times ever. Write as often as you can, and tell me all about my little girls."[15]

During his absence in Paris, the *Herald Tribune* ran several mail articles he had sent. One was about a Soviet production of "Uncle Tom's Cabin," altered for Russian audiences by removing its religious overtones. It afforded "ample material to illustrate the way in which the Negro race was treated not so many years ago in America. Mrs. Stowe has always been charged in the South with exaggeration, but she is mild when compared with the producers of the Moscow version of the stage play." However, no attempt was made "to give the impression that the play illustrates the contemporary scene in America."[16]

A plan to film a motion picture depicting "the exploitation of the Negro in America from the days of slavery to the present" fell apart when the government withdrew its support. According to Barnes, "the Soviet authorities suppressed the film for fear that its appearance would prejudice American opinion against the Soviet Union." He observed that "since the occupation of Manchuria by Japan, the Soviet authorities more than ever have been eager for a rapprochement with the United States as a means, among other things, of strengthening the position of the U.S.S.R. in the Far East." The collapse of the project stranded twenty-two African Americans in Moscow, including the poet and novelist Langston Hughes. Four members of the group, McNary Lewis, Theodore Poston, Henry Lee Moon, and Lawrence Alberta, protested the Soviet move to the Communist International as compromising "12,000,000 Negroes of the United States and all the darker colonial peoples, while sacrificing furtherance of the Communist world revolution to the advantages to be gained from American recognition of the Soviet Union." It was, they said, "an ignoble concession to race prejudice, of a type for which the Communist party is continually berating the Christian Church, the Second Socialist International and other social-fascist organizations."[17]

Problems with the Five-year Plans were a recurrent theme through the summer and fall of 1932. Barnes interviewed American engineers who maintained that the entire industrial structure was "infested with a deadening bureaucracy which is rapidly bringing chaos." Inefficiencies were rampant: "the number of labor hours consumed in Soviet plants is five to ten times as great as in American plants and in some cases 100 times as great." They saw the urgent need for internal reorganization "supplemented by immediate steps to increase the quantity and variety of food provided to the workers and their families and to improve living conditions."[18]

A government decree favored the crafts cooperatives in the hope of expanding their production to supply the peasants in the countryside. Barnes explained: "The government is doing what it can to encourage collective farmers and individual peasants to bring their surplus produce into the newly established *kolkhoz* bazaars, but as in the past it meets a stumbling block in the shortage of goods of the type peasants want to exchange for their grain, vegetables, meats and fruits. The peasants are reluctant to part with their produce when they can have in return nothing more than paper rubles."[19]

The government acknowledged problems in the countryside but saw them as a temporary setback, as did Walter Duranty who attributed them to sabotage by the *kulaks* and resistance to change by older peasants: "Hence the present difficulties, which are widespread and frankly admitted, but will not prove more than a temporary setback, for the Kremlin is strong and resolute and has the youth of the country on its side." Barnes reported that American students doing a survey in the western Ukraine found the population "suffering severely from an acute shortage of food, confusion on collective farms and inefficient government agencies." They saw abandoned children in the streets. The peasants were leaving the villages, having "lost faith in the government's promises." Barnes foresaw a need to import large quantities: "The problem of supplying the industrial workers with more goods is a sufficiently urgent one, but that of rushing goods into the villages to restore the shattered morale of the peasant is still more urgent."[20]

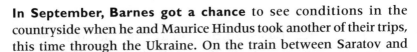

In September, Barnes got a chance to see conditions in the countryside when he and Maurice Hindus took another of their trips, this time through the Ukraine. On the train between Saratov and Kharkov, he wrote his parents:

Along the route, we have purchased excellent cooked chickens, tomatoes and watermelons. We found good butter in the market in Saratov before leaving. We had some bread with us, and have purchased more at intervals as we have progressed. We also have some jam for sweets, as well as tea and sugar, which are not to be had in this district, some German sausage and German cheese. With tea and sugar, one could live off the country quite well; this, despite the seriousness of the general food situation. The peasants seem to bring their best to the railway station.

We are travelling in a "hard" coach that is to say, one in which the bunks have no padding. My hip bones are sore as a result of the two nights on my bunk; but otherwise, I'm tiptop. I have slept well both nights. The peasants, and the other passengers, have been extremely interesting. In many of the villages through which we passed last evening, there were accordions to be heard in the distance. The land has been almost flat, with few trees except in the towns. Late yesterday, we passed quite close to the country which Hindus and I visited last summer, south of Voronezh. In the Volga region we found the peasant huts largely of logs with thatched roofs. Here in the Ukraine the huts are nearly all plastered with mud on the exterior, and then whitewashed. The whitewashing takes place a couple of times a year, so the huts always have a neat appearance—from the outside.[21]

On his return, Barnes wrote his parents that he had become ill and had faced obstacles in reporting on his trip:

Immediately upon my return (October 2) I attempted to send an extensive cable summing up the situation in the Ukraine. The censor took exception to about two-thirds of what I had written, so I decided to send the material by mail. After taking to bed with the fever, I reconsidered, and re-wrote—dictated—the cable, softening it and adding some pleasant things about cultural developments. This revised cable, which the censor passed, is under a Kharkov dateline, and bears the date of October 6th. Since then, I have sent off a piece of about 2,000 words describing our experiences in travel. Bill Stoneman filed the cable which has to do with the opening of Dnieprostroy, and bears an October 10 dateline. I missed that trip, as you know, because I was in bed. Incidentally, I am feeling quite myself again, and have the satisfaction of knowing that I am immune to several possible diseases from now on.[22]

In his "softened" cabled article, Barnes concluded that, despite the ample food available to westerners offering hard currency, "the Soviet government is facing a highly difficult situation in wide areas of the Ukraine, where the peasants are disheartened in consequence of hardships suffered last winter and spring, and where unfavorable crops this year promise further privation during the coming winter." During the past year, to meet the requirements of the cities, the government had taken grain needed by the peasants. Their deprivation had combined with the deaths of large numbers of horses and pigs who could not be adequately fed. Despite the adverse conditions, Barnes did not foresee revolution: "[E]ven in the Ukraine, the Soviet regime continues strong, and there is no sign of turbulence."[23]

In a mail article that appeared on the front page of the second section of the Sunday, September 25, *Herald Tribune*, after having been advertised in the paper beforehand, Barnes used a question-and-answer format to discuss everyday life in the Soviet Union. His sources, both official and unofficial, led him to a surprising conclusion: "[T]he intelligent, ambitious and industrious Soviet citizen is held back from completely outstripping his less well endowed neighbor more by the general economic backwardness of the country than by the laws of the state." Unless things changed, Barnes foresaw a greater differentiation of economic classes, in short a moving away from the Communist state. On the other hand, he saw the possibility that successful technicians and managers would go the way of the private trader of the NEP period: "When he seemed no longer necessary, he was destroyed."[24]

Bill Stoneman's help during Barnes's illness renewed an old alliance from Rome, where he and Barnes were accustomed to working together. Since Stoneman reported for the *Chicago Daily News*, the two were not in direct competition. Their collaboration during the Moscow period proved fruitful and helped Barnes to overcome the isolation he felt there. With other reporters such as Eugene Lyons, Linton Wells of the International News Service, and Harold Denny who succeeded Duranty for the *New York Times* in 1934, Barnes appears to have had a less close but friendly relationship. His letters were rarely critical of any correspondent, although he remarked to his father that while he thought Louis Fischer's articles in the *New York Nation* worth following, "I do not by any means agree with Fischer in general." Barnes was not alone in his assessment. Many of his colleagues viewed Louis Fischer as the American reporter who was the greatest apologist for the Soviet regime.[25]

In later memoirs, some of these colleagues left a picture of Barnes at this juncture of his career. Lyons mentioned "Ralph Barnes of the New York *Herald Tribune*, whose journalistic courage was always a notch or two higher than the Moscovite average (a fact that did not make him too popular in certain official areas)." His diaries show that the acerbic Malcolm Muggeridge was initially unimpressed with Barnes, but his memoirs offer the following:

The most notable activist among the press corps was Ralph Barnes, an earnest eager American reporter who kept us all on our toes. He used to pad about the streets of Moscow in rubber shoes hoping to come upon some newsworthy person or event, and endlessly apply for interviews with Stalin, which were rarely accorded, mostly to eminent visitors like H.G. Wells, and even then settled, if not drafted in advance. When as happened from time to time, Barnes disappeared from Moscow, there was great apprehension among the other correspondents. Where had he gone? What was he up to?"[26]

Economic problems combined with the Japanese threat to give urgency to Soviet hopes for American diplomatic recognition and provided Barnes with the material for several articles in the late summer and fall of 1932.[27] Because the American presidential election and the question of recognition were intertwined, the Soviets were watching the election closely, as was Ralph Barnes. He had kept up a running commentary in his letters to his father, despite their political differences: "I suppose that you are planning to be a good Republican. I must confess that I find but little to admire in Roosevelt; but I very much dislike the idea of Hoover sitting in the White House for another four years. I might vote for Norman Thomas, if I were in the States; merely as a matter of protest. I doubt, however, whether he would be of presidential calibre. Perhaps sincere and honest. At least, I have the impression that he is. Perhaps Hoover has both of those qualities, but his conservatism irritates me. Perhaps it is the party, and what it stands for, rather than the man, that I dislike."[28]

Closer to the November election, he had altered his outlook somewhat:

If I were in the States, I would probably vote for Roosevelt; though I have the impression that he is not strong personally. You know my feelings about the Republican Party. Nothing has happened in recent years to change that impression. However, I am not so foolish as to credit the depression to the G.O.P. [Former New York governor Alfred E.] Smith is undoubtedly a much stronger man than Roosevelt, and I am sorry that he did not have his chance this time, rather than four years ago. I had a letter from Phil Elliott earlier in the summer in which he—though he is a dry—expressed the view that Smith was the outstanding figure in American politics today. I think that the West has never begun to realize the calibre of the man. Some of his crude ways, plus his religion, have told mightily against him. But I suppose you will consider Moscow a curious post from which to pass out judgments on the American political scene. I concede that I should visit my country for a few weeks before becoming too categorical in my statements about it.[29]

After Franklin Roosevelt's overwhelming defeat of incumbent Herbert Hoover in the 1932 elections, Barnes found that the Soviets were cautious in light of the rebuffs they had encountered from previous administrations. The American State Department had prescribed three conditions for recognition: "First, acknowledgment by Moscow of liability for debts contracted by previous governments of Russia; second, agreement to make restitution to Americans whose properties were confiscated; third, disavowal of revolutionary activity in the United States." The last issue, Barnes noted, was the primary stumbling block.[30]

The fall saw Ralph Barnes's inclusion in the new edition of *Who's Who*. Edward Barnes sent along the clippings from the *Oregon Statesman*. Ralph was pleased but cautioned his proud father, "Please don't talk too much about it in Salem."[31] He wrote Esther of a reception to celebrate the October Revolution where he had a chance to talk with the playwright Afinogenov and the writer Leonid Leonov and of an evening at the Bolshoi: "God, I wish you were here, Esther. I am sure you would have enjoyed this evening immensely. How narrow Dad's view that there is little or no culture to be found here! But I fear that I am becoming more and more attached to this place— not that I am accepting Communism. It's simply that I find living here tremendously interesting. The place has been growing on me."[32]

A constant round of social gatherings among their small circle was a fixture of the Moscow correspondents' life. Occasionally included were American and British advisors to various Soviet enterprises and members of their families. Zara Witkin, an American engineer on an ill-fated odyssey of ideology and romance, was a regular for a time. The daughters of the American mining engineer J. H. Gillis, Faye and Beth, were popular additions. After recognition in 1933, members of the American diplomatic community, such as George Kennan and Charles Bohlen, joined the group.[33] The social life was itself a symbol of the isolation of the correspondents. Muggeridge compared it to the social life of the British in India: "Such parties took place at one embassy or another almost every evening, and reminded me very much of the British Raj; more or less the same guests turned up at all of them—and one had the same feeling, as in India, of being a little privileged isolated community having practically no contact with the surrounding country and its people. Ideological sahibs."[34]

In fact, reporters in Moscow could not escape the sense that their movement and their correspondence were under scrutiny. Barnes's letters alluded to the surveillance obliquely as when he assured his father, "the restraint evident in your letters is quite unnecessary. I do wish that you would say what you think; there is no danger whatever of my getting 'in bad' as a result of what you say. The Biblical quotation comes in handy: 'It is what goes out of me, and not what comes in which will damn or save me.' " Somewhat disingenuously, Barnes wrote at another point, "There is a good deal of speculation in rubles, but with a view of avoiding embarrassment for my newspaper, I change all my dollars at par. Speculation is illegal, as you probably know."[35] In another letter, he told his parents not to worry, that he was far from becoming a Communist, and remarked, "Might as well let the censor have a mouthful."

6

The battle between Joseph Stalin and the peasants, now being fought out in the rich granary of the North Caucasus, may determine whether or not collective agriculture in its present form is to endure in Soviet Russia. Nowhere else in the Soviet Union has the opposition to collectivization been so stubborn as in this area, especially the Kuban River Valley, south from Rostov, where the Kuban Cossacks with their independent traditions dwell. Stalin has met the opposition with an offensive in which night raids in search of hidden grain and mass exile have been the principal weapons.

Ralph Barnes, *Herald Tribune,*
March 5, 1933, from Rostov-on-Don

With the onset of winter 1932-1933, Barnes planned a number of trips around the country in his continuing effort to report on events and conditions outside Moscow, an effort other correspondents seldom made. Duranty, for example, wrote a series on the food shortage and the rural situation in November without ever leaving Moscow. He attributed the problems to the world depression and to sabotage by peasants resistant to collectivization.[1] Barnes found the trips, if arduous, immensely interesting:

I am sitting on a lower berth of a four-berth compartment. A Russian is sleeping on the berth immediately opposite, and two Russian engineers are playing cards on a two-step affair close by. The electric generator has been out of working order since this train left Vladivostok, so there is nothing but candle-light to be had, even in the international sleeping car. There is a candle burning on the stand at the window near which I am writing. I had dinner in the dining car a few minutes ago with the two engineers. The dining car is out of both sugar and bread, but they served a few meat-filled rolls as dessert, "extra." The engineers supplied me with both bread and sugar—the latter for the coffee, such as it was.

We had a discussion as to the relative merits of their system and ours. One of the engineers, a Communist party member, talked much in the manner of an old-time Baptist minister who had "got" religion. Not the least doubt in the world that theirs is the right system. Both the engineers conceded, however, that living conditions are bad here. They contend, only, that they will be better.[2]

Barnes toured several of the great Soviet industrial complexes, the iron and steel plants at Magnetogorsk, the tractor plant at Cheliabinsk, and the metallurgical works at Sverdlovsk, to prepare a series of articles marking the end of the First Five-year Plan. For several months, he had noted indications of trouble with both industrialization and collectivization. An unskilled work force, a high level of labor turnover, and the ongoing problems with a lack of machine tools, poor transportation, and a lack of coordination continued to plague Soviet industry. As an example of the last, he wrote of 1,200 partly completed trucks resting idle at the Nizhni Novgorod vehicle manufacturing plant because of the failure of a Moscow factory to provide needed electrical parts. To address the problem, the Soviet government threatened shirkers with the loss of their food cards, abolished thousands of bureaucratic positions, and finally introduced a new system of internal passports to control movement from the countryside to the cities. This last decree revived one of the most detested constraints of the Czarist regime, one whose abolition at the time of the Revolution had been seen as a major victory for individual freedom.[3]

A major challenge was in the countryside. In a *Pravda* pronouncement that Barnes reported, the Communist Party found the traitors within its own ranks: "Recently rural party units have become cluttered up with members having nothing in common with communism, and in some cases with kulaks who have changed their faces. Those members unable to carry out the party policy in the villages, those attempting treacherously to prevent realization of the rural economic program, must be eliminated. In a number of regions persons with party membership cards are the real organizers of kulak sabotage of grain collections. It is clear that enemies provided with party cards are more dangerous than plain counterrevolutionaries, and must be punished with all strictness by revolutionary law."

In his article, Barnes commented on the Soviet Communist party's practice of purging its membership, correctly anticipating a third major "cleansing" comparable with those in 1921 to crush the Menshevik element in the party and in 1929 to eliminate the Trotskyites. The procedure was well-established: "Every party member, whether or not charges have been preferred against him, must appear before representatives of the control commission and satisfy them of his orthodoxy." Sometimes such cleansing took place on a case-by-case basis, as recently when the two Old Bolsheviks Gregory Zinoviev, Leo Kamenev and their followers were expelled.[4] Long excused by Soviet apologists in the West, the purging occasioned Duranty's famous remark: "Why wail over broken eggs when you try to make an omelette?"[5] The process involved informers, often with a personal rather than a political ax to grind. The usual penalty was expulsion from the party, a serious threat to any Communist, but this time the government went further in sentencing two high party officials and an agricultural expert in the Dniepropetrovsk region of the Ukraine to be shot and eight others to be imprisoned, for their participation in a conspiracy cited as an example of "the fierce class resistance of the kulaks which is now present in the villages." Along with these harsh measures, Stalin offered a carrot, the restoration of Lenin's policy of fixed taxation of the peasant rather than requisitioning his grain. The peasant would thus know in advance what was required and, it was hoped, produce a surplus because it would be to his own benefit.[6]

Sensing that the rural crisis was creating turmoil within the leadership, Barnes wrote of the Politburo: "Joseph Stalin, the general secretary of the party's central committee, is, of course, the dominating figure in the 'Big Ten.' The other nine members are men on whom Stalin can depend, selected by means of a weeding-out process extending over a period of years. ... What Molotov and his colleagues may lack in other respects, they make up for in loyalty to Stalin." Public evidence of discord emerged before long. Several high officials, leaders of the Russian Socialist Republic, were ousted from the Central Committee. Others officially reprimanded included Alexei Rykov and M. P. Tomsky, who had been forced in 1930 to issue statements recanting their errors. Once again there followed what Barnes referred to as "the sorry spectacle of reiterated recantations and confessions of faith on the part of two highly placed Soviet officials."[7]

On successive Sundays in January 1933, the *Herald Tribune* featured Barnes's series of five analytical articles on the Soviet scene at the end of the Five-year Plan. Pieces mailed rather than cabled, they were thus quite frank. During the same period, the Soviet press was full of criticism of various shortcomings in the fulfillment of the plan, usually blaming "wreckers" or disguised *kulaks*. Each of Barnes's articles included what he hoped would be "interesting eyewitness material." His introduction was not sanguine: "The first Five-Year Plan is ended. Soviet Russia is under martial law, with death as the penalty for large-scale thefts. The food shortage is more severe than at any time since 1923. The standard of living for the bulk of the population has dropped steadily during the last two years. The peasants in large areas, notably the Ukraine and North Caucasus, are demoralized, and the prevailing agricultural system is revealing what may prove serious defects." Acknowledging that outside forces contributed to the failure of the plan, Barnes nevertheless maintained that the Kremlin had "bitten off more than it could chew."[8]

The next day, the paper ran an editorial that assigned considerable importance to Barnes's reports. Noting that the progress of the Five-year Plan "has put a heavy strain on Marxian doctrine" and that "the food shortage is now forcing a further retreat from orthodox communism," the *Herald Tribune* continued: "We have been inclined to agree with the many dispassionate students of the Russian experiment who believe that, from the point of view of those who do the heavy thinking in the Kremlin, the Marxian game is up. Against this assumption many persons in this country still vigorously protest, but the only test of conflicting opinions on the Soviet Union's future that can now be applied is a comprehensive survey of actual conditions there."[9]

Barnes's "comprehensive survey" continued with two articles on conditions in rural Russia. Again he included several interviews along with his own observations and background material. A number of peasants had spoken freely to him during his visits to the countryside. They recounted a life of shortage and deprivation, of losing their land and their livestock, of sons being sent away as "*kulaks*." The chairman of a commune Barnes visited frankly discussed the problems: "We have 350 souls here but during the last two years we have been able to secure only 1,000 meters of textiles, or less than three meters a person. And during that period we have had in all just ten pairs of boots and shoes. ... We had plenty of sugar in 1928-30—now we have none—and in those years there was much more tobacco and soap than there is now. During the last twelve months we have had but two small boxes of tobacco for the whole community and but 200 cakes of soap, and we were able to obtain those small amounts only by purchases at the high-priced commercial stores." They were however comparatively fortunate "in that, in contrast to the situation in some other regions, the government did not take too much grain from our section last winter. In fact, here in this Commune we are considered relatively well off. Last winter and spring several hundred persons, who had migrated from the Saratov region, came to us and to the near-by state farms, stating their willingness to work for their board alone. Our Commune took in ten families; we were unable to handle more."[10]

In the next piece, Barnes focused on the much more straitened conditions he had found in the Ukraine: "Grain, needed by the Ukrainian peasants as provisions, was stripped from the land a year ago by grain collectors desirous of making a good showing. The temporary or permanent migration of great masses of peasants, which followed, alone prevented real famine conditions. Horses and pigs, in fact, died off in large numbers. Last spring the ground was poorly prepared and badly sown by peasants disheartened by the hardships of winter. The recent harvest was in proportion."

Among the farms he visited in the Ukraine was a model commune in the Poltava region which had been founded in 1923 by a group of Bulgarian-Americans who were members of the Communist party. Despite its longevity, and the funds and equipment its supporters had sent from the United States, it too had seen shortages of bread and an abrupt decline in the standard of living because of government grain requisitions. Many of the Bulgarian-American founders had left, disillusioned by their experiences. Still the collective survived, better off than most of its neighbors.[11]

Barnes's December trip to Magnetogorsk provided the material for the fourth article of the series. To him, the iron and steel complex there, "the biggest single project of the Five-Year Plan" and one to which enormous economic and human resources had been dedicated, epitomized the Soviet Union's experience with industrialization. It was, he wrote, "one of the best laboratories in which to study the Five-Year Plan, and thus in which to glean facts calculated to throw some light on the future of industrialization in the U.S.S.R." He dismissed American reports that Magnetogorsk was a total failure as "far too hasty and too categorical." At the same time, he also dismissed many Soviet claims about the superiority of their planning. After all, no steel had been produced at the complex so far. Its construction and presumably its operation were compromised by the lack of adequate transport. Already problems had arisen with the blast furnaces. The local labor force was inadequate and poorly prepared. Bureaucratic disputes threatened to cripple the plant's productivity.

Barnes managed to convey to his readers the magnitude of the undertaking as well as the contrasts he found: a bustling boom town of two hundred thousand people where only grazing land and tumbledown peasants' huts had existed just three years before; sleighs rather than automobiles provided at the railway station; the array of nationalities gathered in the work force: "A slant-eyed Mongol and a Khirgis herdsman work side by side with a bearded Russian peasant and a Cossack horseman. In this new industrial metropolis the four men are equally out of their respective elements." The two photographs that ran with the article were themselves illustrative of the contrasts; one featured the towering, billowing smokestacks, the other a group of peasant women "resorting to a primitive method of mixing plaster," that is, stomping the wet plaster with their feet.

Both the location of Magnetogorsk and the feverish pace of its construction were determined by concerns other than the strictly economic: "Napoleon, on his famous invasion of Russia, advanced only as far as Moscow, but his army lacked the mechanized equipment which increases the mobility of military forces today. The armies of the capitalist countries, which appear in Soviet eyes as so many dangerous specters on the horizon, enjoy a thousand advantages in movement that Napoleon lacked. Joseph Stalin and his aides fear that the forces of the ever-expected capitalist 'intervention' may prove capable of penetrating further inland than did the French emperor. Most of all, perhaps, they fear an attack from the air. Thus they have hidden their biggest steel plant in this isolated region."[12]

Barnes continued the industrial theme in the final article of his survey, telling of his visits to Sverdlovsk and Cheliabinsk where heavy machinery and tractors were to be manufactured. Again he found serious construction delays as well as difficulties with product design. Elaborate buildings housed the bureaucracy and the secret police but the streets were so muddy that ordinary traffic could not pass. Sverdlovsk was also the former Ykaterinburg, site of the July 1918, execution of Czar Nicholas II and his family. At the revolutionary museum, Barnes heard the standard story of the execution, that it was the decision of the local Soviet to kill the royal family out of fear that the advancing Czechoslovak troops would free them. Modern scholars have determined that the decision was Lenin's and was communicated from Petrograd.[13]

While the series was running in the *Herald Tribune*, Barnes took another trip, this one with Bill Stoneman. In the North Caucasus, they found an agrarian crisis more extreme than anything Barnes had witnessed elsewhere. There the government had resorted to forced exile of recalcitrant peasants to the industrial labor camps of the far north. Barnes and Stoneman saw at least two groups of peasants being herded aboard trains by armed guards. They were told of a number of other such cases by people they met in the villages.

To meet the government's demands for grain, armed squads of party loyalists made night raids searching for the grain the peasants were rumored to have hidden:

> *Much as in the Ukraine a year ago, yet in a more merciless manner, villages have been stripped of their minimum bread provisions, so that thousands of peasants have been almost completely without bread— the mainstay of their diet—for two or more months. They are existing largely on limited and rapidly diminishing quantities of two or three vegetables. The bread shortage in the Kuban is becoming increasingly serious as the zero hunger months of March and April approach, the period before relief from spring vegetables can be expected. While to date there probably have been only a limited number of cases of death due directly to starvation, there have been many deaths resulting from disease attacking constitutions seriously undermined by lack of sufficient food.*[14]

The *Herald Tribune* editorialized the following day:

> *The picture which our Moscow correspondent sketches of famine throughout Soviet Russia and of terror in the Kuban area is ample confirmation of accounts of this tragic situation that have been published in France and Germany. It makes sad reading for the American people, who were always warmly sympathetic with the aspirations of the Russian masses under the harsh discipline of the Czar's Cossacks and secret police. This present situation means that the lot of the mujik under the Red dictatorship's soldiery and OGPU agents is so much harsher a tyranny that passive revolt against it has brought this great agricultural nation to the point of starvation.*

The famine, the editorial writer pointed out, was not the result of natural calamity or climatic conditions, but was man-made. Further

> *[t]he mass exile of disaffected folk into Russia's sub-arctic wilderness is a disastrous confession of weakness. So is the renovation of the Communist party, which has put scores of highly publicized 'heroes of the revolution' on the Kremlin's blacklist. Every one knows from the past that Russia's capacity for absorbing indignity and horror is enormous. But the history of Czarism proves that there is a limit to it.*

It has seemed probable that present conditions could prevail for a long time without serious reaction; but there is now at least room for the beginnings of doubt."[15]

In a second, longer article from his trip that appears to have been mailed out of the Soviet Union,[16] Barnes observed: "Stalin apparently is determined to accept nothing less than unconditional surrender from the peasant." He wrote anecdotally of his experiences in the North Caucasus, of the hungry begging from anyone with food, such as a privileged railroad worker, of scraps fought over by children and adults alike, of a nearly inedible bread substitute made of cornmeal. He and Stoneman prevailed on a peasant with a horse and wagon to take them across an iced-over river to the village of Poltaskaya. There they found many houses boarded up and were told by the remaining residents that as many as seven thousand persons had been sent away. Already fifteen hundred former Red soldiers and their families had settled in the town to replace them. The article combined incidents Barnes witnessed and those he only heard about with careful distinctions between the two.[17] It contained no hint of what several authors have asserted as fact, that Barnes and Stoneman were arrested in the Kuban and sent back to Moscow.[18] Neither did Barnes mention his being arrested in his letters home; however, he did include the following in a March letter to his parents: "You must not worry too much about my situation here. I am not going out of my way to get myself into a mess. I am in close touch with our London bureau, which is in charge of the HT foreign service, and know what the office there thinks about the situation. If I were to be under the necessity of leaving Moscow, I would not be without a job. Don't worry about that. I have assurances to the contrary. By the way, my relations with the powers-that-be here remain friendly."[19]

Barnes was pleased to report to his parents that as a result of his February famine story, "Duranty received two cables" from his home office. However, Duranty told the *New York Times* that "to the best of my knowledge there is no famine anywhere although partial crop failures [occurred in] some regions." Through that summer of 1933, against all the evidence, Duranty continued to deny the horrors that were occurring in the countryside.[20] The immediate impact of the February and March reports was the issuance of new regulations by the Soviet government banning foreign correspondents from travel in the Ukraine and North Caucasus.[21] This ban remained in effect through the summer and into the fall.

~

Barnes's attention was diverted from the famine story by several developments in the late winter and spring of 1933. Adolf Hitler came to power in Germany. In the United States, the depression became even more severe. One of Franklin Roosevelt's first acts as President was the temporary closing of American banks until their solvency could be assured. Ralph was determined not to allow the situation to interfere with the plan for Esther to join him in Moscow, leaving the two children with their grandparents in Oregon. "Dearest Girl," he wrote, "there are rumors of war and bank crashes and Fascism in Germany, and what not. God knows where we will all be a month from now. But under the circumstances it appears best to keep one's head. I hope you are doing that. From this end, it seems as if it were best to continue our plans for getting together."

He reassured her that the management of the *Herald Tribune* was supportive of the move. "Your letters these days sound pretty blue. I suppose that is largely because you have a lot of persons around you who are also blue. I know it is difficult to decide things under the present circumstances. As for coming over here, I am convinced it is the thing to do. We can't go on living like this."

As for Joan and Suzanne, "they should be able to get along for a time with care other than yours. I'm convinced it will not be best for them, but it will not be bad. We just ought to get together, Esther. And I am hoping that you are not letting any of Dad's mournful outbursts about 'leaving your babies' interfere with the plans … it will be great to be with you again, Esther. Wish you wouldn't worry so much about things. The whole world's in a mess. Why take it all so seriously? I've been thinking a lot lately of a cottage on a hill and a garden, with a lot of books."[22] Ralph prevailed. Esther would sail from New York on April 29 after settling Joan in Salem with the Barneses and Suzanne in Portland with her mother and sister Mary. To his mother, Ralph wrote more words of reassurance: "When you think about it, we are pretty lucky. Just think how much worse everything might be. The world seems to be hurrying toward some kind of catastrophe; but, on the whole, it will probably affect us much less than it does a great many other people."[23]

~

In Moscow, the attention of all the correspondents turned to the arrest of eight British technicians employed by the British firm Metropolitan-Vickers which had for years sold, installed, and serviced electrical machinery and turbines in the Soviet Union. Twenty-five Russian engineers were also arrested. Charges of conspiracy, sabotage and wrecking, later to become all-too-familiar during the Moscow show trials of 1936 and 1937, were brought by the O.G.P.U.[24] The outraged reaction of the British government and the foreign community in Moscow failed to dissuade the Soviet government from the public trial it planned.

Barnes conceived the idea of writing directly to Stalin for assurances as to the security of Americans working in the Soviet Union. Because of the absence of diplomatic relations between the two countries, their status seemed particularly uncertain: "In view of these circumstances," he wrote, "would it not be well for you personally to give some word of assurance to the Americans now in the U.S.S.R. and to those planning to come here for reasons of trade?"

To Barnes's intense satisfaction, Stalin responded in a letter delivered to the *Herald Tribune* bureau by a uniformed courier. The paper ran it in its entirety in both Russian and English:

March 20, 1933

Dear Mr. Barnes:

There is not the slightest ground for your fears about the security of American citizens here.

The U.S.S.R. is one of the few countries in the world in which display of hate or unfriendliness toward foreigners as foreigners is prohibited by law. There has been no case, nor can there be one, of any one becoming an object of persecution because of his nationality. This is especially true in the case of the foreign specialists in the U.S.S.R., including the Americans, whose work, in my opinion, is worthy of appreciation.

As for the few Englishmen, employees of Metro-Vickers, they are being prosecuted not as Englishmen but as persons who, according to the affirmation of the investigating authorities, have violated the law of the U.S.S.R. Is it not true that Russians are also being prosecuted? I cannot see what connection this case could have with American citizens.

At your service,

J. Stalin[25]

Barnes attributed his coup to "very good luck" and wrote his parents of the reaction of the rest of the journalistic community: "All conceded it was a first-class idea. Had a wire from Wilcox, the managing editor in New York, in which he said they were 'delighted' to have the letter and that they were playing the story in a prominent position on page one."[26] Some months later, Barnes sent his father a quote from a book published in London by a British reporter A. J. Cummings in which he described the letter to Stalin as "inspired less by the grave reflection that he and his compatriots might have anything to fear, than by the journalist's quick-witted recognition of a priceless opportunity to 'draw' Stalin, and tease him into a first-class 'scoop.' Stalin rose to the bait like a fat trout."[27] Despite his run of success, Barnes demurred at a suggestion by his father: "I am not ready yet to think seriously of a book; but of course I have that in mind for the future. I want to learn more about what is going on before I tackle anything so pretentious. There are plenty of half-baked volumes on the subject already."[28]

The Metro-Vickers trial ran through much of April with six of the eight originally charged being tried. One of the British defendants, William Lionel McDonald, confessed to the charges against him and implicated his fellows. Another, William Henry Thornton, signed a damning written deposition, only to recant, attributing his confession to O.G.P.U. pressure, then confess again. Although the prosecution had originally asked for the execution of the accused, the judge finally ordered McDonald and Thornton imprisoned for two and three years respectively, acquitted one of their fellows and expelled the other three from the Soviet Union.[29] The significance of the trial proved twofold: it was a foreshadowing of the later show trials with their staged confessions, while it distracted journalists, editors and readers alike from the much more important story of the famine.

In March, Barnes had also managed a long-sought interview with the Soviet Foreign Minister, Maxim Litvinov. The interview was granted with the proviso that he could not quote Litvinov directly; instead he had to attribute his stories to "official circles." He wrote to Salem: "Litvinov is very easy to talk with, and quite frank. He is pretty much worried about the Japs, as would be expected. Says he thinks that they want to get away with large sections of Asia." The two articles, one stressing Soviet willingness to disavow interference in American domestic affairs in return for diplomatic recognition and the other expressing fears of Japan, ran on March 29 and 30.[30] The necessary prerequisites for American recognition were falling into place.

~

In May, Ralph "went out" to meet Esther. After taking the train to
Berlin, he flew from there to Paris, a seven-hour flight with stops in
Leipzig, Frankfurt and Saarbrucken. The trip made him a convert to
air travel. From the plane, he wrote his parents a long descriptive
letter later printed in the Salem *Oregon Statesman*. Passing over the
areas that had seen the worst of the fighting during World War I,
Ralph noted the beauty of the villages but had a premonition of the
future: "It is awful to contemplate the prospect of another war which
would disrupt the peaceful pursuits of their inhabitants."[31] He met
Esther in Paris, and they vacationed in the French Pyrenees before
returning to Paris, where Ralph had a tonsillectomy. They arrived
in Moscow on June 10 after a train trip that Esther described to her
family:

> The sleepers dated from about 1913, and I don't think that anything
> had been done to them since, but they were very clean. The style and
> decorations were so different from the International "WagonLits" in
> western Europe. For one thing, the line is wide gauge, so the cars are
> very wide, and the ceilings are so high that it is more like a moving
> house than a railway car.
>   The interiors are in colored glass and mahogany panelling. The
> compartments are quite roomy, with one berth made up the length of
> the compartment and the other across. When not made up, there is a
> long bench, as in any compartment in Europe, with a small table and
> a chair. The berth lengthwise of the car is somewhat higher than the
> one across. That way, the one sleeping in the lower berth doesn't have
> someone over his head all the time. The diner was the first Russian one
> that I have been in. It dated back quite a few years also. The walls
> paneled with mahogany and a lighter wood, with rather faded painted
> wreaths of roses on the light wood. There were potted flowers,
> hydrangeas, on the tables, with a great abundance of colored paper
> bows and trimmings on the plants and pots. The road bed not being of
> the best, the meal was accompanied by a continual tinkle of glassware
> and bottles. We had very good roast chicken, with fried potatoes, black
> bread, and a sort of rye bread, and mineral water. Had a chocolate bar
> in our compartment for dessert.[32]

Esther found Moscow considerably improved since her 1927 visit.
She enjoyed meeting the American community and a visit to the
Chamberlins' dacha in the countryside, but most of all Ralph:
"Everyone here likes Ralph so much, and has said so many nice

things about him. I am sure you can realize what it means to us to be together again." Life in Moscow had its drawbacks: "When I think of those markets out in Oregon with such a variety of clean fresh vegetables it makes me almost weep." The routines of a homemaker, which Esther ordinarily enjoyed, were strenuous: "Trying to shop here sort of wears one out. It is quite a task to find something in the windows of the regular stores, selling new stuff, to get peppered up about. ... No one here gives a whoop whether you buy or not."[33]

They moved from the hotel into an apartment only to find the new Moscow subway being constructed right outside their door. Esther found a maid and gamely set up housekeeping, soon earning a reputation for her hospitality. Her letters record her constant loneliness for the children:

> How I wish Ralph could see the youngsters. I am beginning to realize what it has meant to him to be so far away from them. How I do miss them. I almost disgraced the family today by weeping on the street. We were coming along from the Metropole hotel, where Ralph gets his mail, when I saw a mother sitting on the curb of the busy street. She was trying to arrange her food kit of a few dry bread crusts, over which the flies were swarming, into a box which she had evidently found in the street. Beside her was a baby about Zannie's age, and of about the same coloring too. The baby was eagerly leaning over the edge of the box. Seemed well and happy, but you can imagine how it all struck me.[34]

But being together was so important that Esther agreed to stay longer than originally planned. Ralph wrote his parents and Esther's mother to ask if they were willing to take the children for a longer period. Mrs. Parounagian forwarded her letter to the Barneses in Salem, adding: "I think I have already expressed our willingness to care for Suzanne if Esther wants to stay longer, and I do not wonder that she does, especially as Ralph hopes to get home in the spring. If you wire them you may include our cordial approval. We had a laugh about their renting another apartment then writing to see if it's all right. I think they used to do those things years ago."[35]

~

Foreign correspondents were confined to Moscow through the summer and into the fall. The Soviets were determined to bring in a record harvest and in the meantime to suppress the story of mass starvation in the countryside. More and more, the reporters chafed at the restriction. A number of accounts exist about what followed.

The most disinterested is that of Zara Witkin, the American engineer whose journals of this period lay untouched in the Hoover Archives at Stanford University until they were edited and published by Michael Gelb in 1991. Witkin wrote of a meeting at the Barneses' apartment in August 1933. Present when Witkin was there were Walter Duranty, Eugene Lyons, Maurice Hindus, and William Stoneman. Earlier William S. Chamberlin, Louis Fischer, Stanley Richardson, and Linton Wells had been there as well.

Witkin wrote:

> *Barnes put the question. What should be done? Their duty was to "get the news," to which access was denied by the Soviet Government. Lyons responded that he was blocked because his agency, United Press International, had asked him not to antagonize the government. Duranty, confronted, answered that he would write nothing, "What are a few million dead Russians in a situation like this? Quite unimportant. This is just an incident in the sweeping historical changes here. I think the entire matter is exaggerated. Anyhow, we cannot write authoritatively because we are not permitted to go and see. I'm not going to write anything about it."*

Lyons and Stoneman protested, Duranty turned away to converse with Esther. Hindus, because he had only been allowed into the Soviet Union on this particular trip with the understanding that he would not visit the countryside, said he would not write of what he had not seen. Barnes then proposed that the group together demand permission to visit the rural areas. Stoneman and Lyons agreed but Duranty and Hindus demurred. They noted that Fischer would oppose such a move as well. Then,

> *A queer light played in Barnes's eyes and his football chin stuck out. He left the room abruptly. The other correspondents continued to converse. Under the friendly spell of Mrs. Barnes's hospitality the ugly question was temporarily relegated to the background.*
>
> *Suddenly Barnes re-entered the room. His face was flushed with excitement.*
>
> *"I shot the story!" he announced.*
>
> *Consternation reigned in the room. Barnes had telephoned a sizzling dispatch about the famine despite the restrictions of the censorship.*
>
> *"What did you send?" the men chorused.*
>
> *"I estimated the deaths by starvation to be at least a million."*

Barnes's article ran on August 21 under the headline "Millions Feared Dead of Hunger in South Russia." It appeared on page 7 of the paper and elicited no editorial comment. Witkin wrote that the *Times* in a strong message demanded of Duranty "where he was when these terrible conditions were developing and why he had remained silent." Dismissing "any report of a famine in Russia" as "an exaggeration or malignant propaganda," he estimated that three million had died "not so much from actual starvation as from manifold diseases due to lowered resistance and to general disease." Other correspondents, under pressure from their papers, confirmed the Barnes story. Rather than take on the entire American press corps just as negotiations for recognition were reaching fruition, the Soviets allowed Barnes to stay in Russia. But long after other reporters were allowed to leave Moscow for the countryside, he was restricted. Chamberlin later wrote: "The last to be allowed to leave Moscow was Ralph Barnes, of the *New York Herald Tribune*, whose courageous, honest reporting in the face of the harassments and disabilities of censorship should have won him a Pulitzer Prize, or some other mark of distinction." Chamberlin noted that Duranty was the first to be allowed to travel.[36]

A week later, Barnes reported that the grain crop currently being harvested was one of the biggest in Soviet history and "undoubtedly had the effect of raising the morale of the whole countryside which had been lowered seriously last winter and spring." He also wrote that new information showed that his estimate of one million dead was conservative. Duranty, on the other hand, in a series of articles on the "famine scare" in September wrote that he thought the "distressing facts had been exaggerated" and that in fact his own estimate was too high.[37] The true magnitude of the tragedy was obscured for many years, although Stalin himself told Churchill "ten millions" had lost their lives. He attributed most of the deaths to incidents in which *kulaks* were wiped out by their laborers. In fact, the accepted figures today indicate that eleven million died directly as a result of collectivization, with another three and a half million arrested and dying in the camps later.[38]

How little attention those in the West paid to the "famine" was suggested by a radio interview Barnes had with Dale Carnegie during his 1934 visit to the United States. Asked whether everyone in the Soviet Union had enough to eat, Barnes responded: "There is very little real hunger in the towns. But it is different in the villages. A year and a half ago, there was a real famine, due in part to the crop shortage. During that period, between three and seven million persons, most of them peasants, died from undernourishment and starvation." The apparently astonished Carnegie then said: "What, do you mean to say that millions of people have died of starvation in Russia during the last two years?" Barnes answered: "Yes, but it is difficult to determine precisely how many because the Soviets have published no figures. Today the situation is much improved and it is unlikely that such a tragedy will occur again." Carnegie then asked whether the Soviet government could have prevented the starvation and Barnes said: "Well, it wanted to collect large stores of grain because of fear of a war with Japan. In addition, the peasants disliked the idea of collective or cooperative farming; so they were refusing to work and the government determined to starve them into submission." Carnegie went on to a question about unemployment in the Soviet Union.[39]

The immediate crisis in the countryside came to an end with the fall harvest, bountiful thanks to a combination of coercion and good weather. The Soviet papers saluted Lazarus M. Kaganovitch, appointed by Stalin to accomplish the task, as the man of the hour who mobilized townsmen and the Red Army to harvest the grain. His achievement led Barnes to observe: "It is no reflection on Stalin to point out that dictators die, like other men, and that if dictatorships are to be perpetuated the dictators must have successors. Today no other Soviet leader appears so likely to be in a position to fill the boots of Joseph Djugashvelli (Stalin) as does Comrade Kaganovitch." Not that Kaganovitch was a potential Trotsky, a rival to Stalin's power. In fact, Barnes noted the care with which Kaganovitch attributed his success to Stalin's guidance and inspiration.[40]

7

The "aggressive designs" of Japan and Germany
against the Soviet Union were condemned by Josef V.
Stalin, Soviet dictator, in his keynote speech last night
at the opening session in the Kremlin of the
seventeenth Russian Communist party congress, the
first to convene since 1930. The speech was not made
public until today.

"Whoever wants peace and desires economic
relations with us will always have our full support,"
Stalin said, "but whoever attempts to attack our
country will meet with such powerful resistance that he
will never again *desire to shove his pig's snout into our
cabbage patch.*"

Ralph Barnes, *Herald Tribune*, January 28, 1934, from Moscow

With the harvest in, news in the fall of 1933 turned to the visit of
Colonel Charles Lindbergh and his wife Anne to the Soviet Union
and to the Soviet "stratospheric balloon" which reached record-
breaking altitudes with its crew of three men.[1] Also on the light
news note, an exchange between a grammar school in New Haven,
Connecticut, and a Moscow school led Barnes to the classroom of
Stalin's son Vasily. *Time* again noted Barnes's "keen nose" for a story
and his report that the children in the Soviet classroom paid particular
attention to the picture of the Pilgrims and the Indians that they
found "bourgeois" and "capitalistic," asking "Where are the Indians
today?"[2] The lighter stories provided occupation for Barnes who,
although he was allowed to visit Leningrad for Lindbergh's arrival
there, was otherwise still restricted to Moscow: "I have been barred
from traveling in the rural provinces, or districts, despite the fact
that other correspondents have been permitted to make such trips.

Failing to receive any satisfaction through the unofficial representative in Washington, the *Herald Tribune* management has written a letter of protest to Litvinov. They have backed me up in fine shape."[3]

Esther was distressed by reports in the Moscow papers of conditions in the United States: "Of course, the Russian papers print only strikes and atrocities for the working men. So we get a distorted picture. America will have to put in a Board of Censors like the newspaper men here have to contend with. I do hope that things will straighten out very soon. Something is wrong with our 'system,' but I am yet to see a better one."[4]

Her reports of life in Moscow emphasized practical considerations. She described the construction of the Moscow subway:

The digging is all being done by hand, and carried away in stretcher-like boxes by two men. They manage to move about six shovelfuls at a time. In spite of that, the work is progressing much faster than I expected. There are eleven Americans in charge of this section in front of the house. What a coincidence that they should be right here in our yard. They are mostly New York Jews. They drop in once in a while to look at a New York paper, and admire our house. It is most interesting to watch the workmen who are doing the digging. They are real peasant types, and come from all sections of the Soviet Union. Mongols, Tartars, Ukrainians, etc. They wear a funny conglomeration of clothes—fur hats, medium length patched coats with full skirts, and their feet and legs are wrapped up to the knees with the woven basket sandals over the wrappings for shoes.[5]

Hitler's consolidation of power in Germany and continued Japanese action in the Far East gave momentum to Soviet efforts to secure U. S. recognition. The trial of the Dutch Communist Marinus Van der Lubbe, accused of setting fire to the Reichstag building in Berlin, heightened Soviet awareness of Nazi hostility. Documents purporting to demonstrate a Japanese plot to seize the Soviet railway in Manchuria were released by the Soviet government while Japanese overflights of Soviet territory brought stern warnings.[6] Barnes wrote that the Soviets had abandoned their call for world revolution, adding that in fact, "It is no secret that a proletarian upheaval in any of the principal European states today would cause serious embarrassment in the Soviet capital." For the foreseeable future, Barnes saw the emphasis on cooperative relations with other countries continuing, but observed that when the Soviet Union had "a developed and well balanced industrial system backed by an efficiently functioning agriculture," other policies might prevail.[7]

Exchanges between Presidents Mikhail Kalinin and Franklin Roosevelt reached the point that Roosevelt invited the Soviet Foreign Minister, Litvinov, to Washington for face-to-face talks. Obstacles remained but Barnes viewed them as "neither sufficiently serious nor sufficiently difficult of solution" to delay recognition. Strong feelings in the United States muddied the question, but a *Herald Tribune* editorial writer observed, "It would be in no better keeping with the international proprieties or with American practice in the past to recognize a Russian regime that was making open or secret war upon our institutions, because it would facilitate the sale of a little more cotton, copper or machinery, than it would be to hold diplomatically aloof because Americans generally did not like the Bolshevik attitude toward religion or their nationalization of manpower."[8] Even the Republican *Herald Tribune* was prepared to forget unpaid debts and seized property so long as the Soviet government would afford the appropriate assurances that it would refrain from attempting to subvert the American system.

Unlike Duranty for the *Times*, Barnes did not accompany Litvinov to Washington, to the relief of Esther, who feared such a trip would compromise his chances of visiting the United States in the spring. Fortunately, the *Herald Tribune* "thought that the reaction from here was more important than having him there in Washington."[9] Litvinov's trip resulted in the anticipated diplomatic recognition in November, 1933. President Roosevelt nominated as ambassador William C. Bullitt, who had visited the new Soviet Union as a special representative of President Woodrow Wilson in 1919 and was a longtime advocate of diplomatic relations between the two countries.

Barnes summed up the reaction of the Soviet people to American recognition with two quotes from people on the street. One, a woman shoveling snow, was optimistic about the benefits to the Soviet standard of living: "As you see, we have neither good mittens nor good boots and our stomachs are nearly empty. If what you tell us is true, we should soon have plenty of everything." A policeman saw the advantage as greater security: "Now that the United States is with us, no one will try to attack us in the East."[10] Barnes assumed that recognition would bring more work for him because of "increased interest in everything having to do with the Soviet Union." Esther predicted another result: "It is interesting to think that there will soon be an American Embassy here, and Consulate. I certainly pity the first group that comes in. There will no doubt be another line-up in Russia—former American citizens trying to get back to America."[11]

~

Perhaps as a reflection of warming relationships, the ban on Barnes's travel was finally lifted. On November 28, he set out for an extended trip into Siberia and Central Asia, willingly missing the arrival of the American ambassador in order to gather material from afar. He felt secure because Eugene Lyons of the United Press, a "good correspondent," would cover for him in his absence. Because of "the cold weather and consequent travel difficulties," Esther would not accompany him. Bill Stoneman had already left for Siberia and his wife Majlys would stay with Esther in Moscow while the two men were gone. Friends within the American colony saw that the two women were entertained. Esther even felt a bit guilty, knowing of Ralph's hardships. Still she wrote home of dinners and concerts, and a banquet given by the correspondents for Ambassador Bullitt: "I sat between Louis Fischer and Karl Radek. They both kept me hopping, but I did enjoy them." A visitor to Moscow, Harpo Marx, joined the group, shopping with Esther and Majlys and taking them to the theater.[12]

Barnes's trip was by far the most ambitious he had undertaken. He and his secretary, Oscar Emma, chose to ride the "immigrant train" from Moscow to Novosibirsk rather than the more luxurious Trans-Siberian Express. It was, he wrote for the *Herald Tribune*, "a slower train along the Trans-Siberian Railroad, carrying peasants to the new agricultural districts in various parts of the Soviet hinterland and workmen and engineers to new industrial projects and mines in the Ural Mountain region and Siberia. They are pioneers going East, as Americans went West, to participate in the building of an empire." His article explored the parallels and contrasts between the two great migrations and demonstrated an acquaintance with Frederick Jackson Turner's theory about the role of the frontier in American history.[13]

> *Did the frontier play a role in pre-revolutionary Russian history similar to that which it played in the United States? It appears that here the role was appreciably more modest. Though in the peak years before the war—1907—more than 650,000 persons moved from European to Asiatic Russia, there was a steady counterflow due to disappointment with the new conditions. Dr. Gerold T. Robinson, associate professor of history at Columbia University, reaches the conclusion that the prerevolutionary migration eastward had no appreciable effect on the agricultural situation in European Russia in*

*part because the Jewish townsmen rather than the Russian peasants
were principally involved.*

Certainly the people Barnes met on the train were seeking a new
chance, as the American pioneers had done. He pointed to the
fecundity of the Russian peasant, and to Kremlin policy, as the two
factors "calculated to assure a substantial migration toward Asiatic
Russia." Not lost on Barnes was the irony of the Soviet government
utilizing capitalist incentives to accomplish its goals. Pay scales were
higher in the east, and peasants moving there to farm enjoyed a
five-year exemption from government requisition of grain and other
agricultural products. Perhaps the government's determination
would make up for the lack of "independent initiative" Barnes saw
in the peasants. The Trans-Siberian Railway took on a role similar
to that of the Union Pacific in the settlement of the American West,
with the important difference that it remained the only rail line,
while the Union Pacific was soon joined by other lines throughout
the west. Barnes found Russian officials quick to cite the parallels
with the American experience: "Today Siberia is America in its
youth."[14]

The four-day, two-thousand-mile rail trip between Moscow and
Novosibirsk was followed by tours of the capital of Western Siberia,
a conglomeration of log buildings and new concrete and brick
structures. Before being allowed to register in the hotel, Barnes had
to go to the disinfection house. Typhus from lice had been epidemic
in the area the previous winter and measures were being taken to
prevent its recurrence. Disinfected and relieved of fifty kopeks, he
explored the factories and mines in the area. He went on to Kuznetz,
a new city within 250 miles of the Mongolian border, where he and
Emma encountered a twenty-two year-old woman, Evgenie
Trophimovna Sack, in charge of the night shift for construction of
the blast furnace at a steel plant. Their exchange shed light on
women's attitudes toward their lives and work. She never wore
trousers to work, she told Barnes, "for I believe that when a woman
does so she loses her authority among men. If you are a woman, I
think you should be a woman, and let everybody know it." She
found that she had to work more carefully than if she were a man,
because when things went wrong, people would say: "What can
you expect of a woman?" Nevertheless, she enjoyed her work. She
expected one day to marry and have children but saw no reason that
would take her away from her career for more than a year with each
child.[15]

From Kuznetz, Barnes embarked on a 140-mile trip by sleigh and Siberian ponies to Altaiskiya in western Siberia. The sleigh trip took four and a half days. Each night he and Oscar Emma slept in peasant cottages and subsisted on black bread and tea. Barnes survived the sleigh trip better than Emma, who became ill and was sent back to Moscow from Altaiskiya. Barnes went on via the Turk-Siberian Railway through Semipalatinsk, along the eastern shores of Lake Balkash, through Alma Ata to Tashkent. Intended to replace the great camel caravans, the relatively new Turk-Siberian Railway was even more primitive than the "immigrant train" in its accommodations, and typically ran ten to twelve hours behind schedule. Since there was no dining car, Barnes joined his traveling companions at each station to fill his teakettle and buy butter, milk, bread, and "decidedly unappetizing" meat cakes. He carried his own bedding and shared his four-bunk compartment with other travelers, mostly young Russian men. "One never thinks of undressing—have not had my trousers off—except for a Russian vapor bath at Altaiskiya—since I left Kuznetz nine days ago."[16]

Barnes found Tashkent "something resembling a dream" and enjoyed his three days exploring there. Marco Polo's account of his own journey was Ralph's reading material as he traveled, but to return to Moscow in time to spend Christmas with Esther he had to forego trips to Samarkand and Bokhara. He arrived back in Moscow late on Christmas Eve. He and Esther pored over the letters and photographs of the children that had accumulated during his absence. He did not mention to his parents, but Esther did, his chagrin at learning that Walter Duranty had obtained an interview with Stalin. Given Duranty's long tenure in Moscow and his sympathetic attitude toward the regime, it was not surprising that he had secured such a coup. Esther loyally noted that there was "absolutely no reason for Ralph to feel down-hearted about it, but naturally he does."[17]

Duranty repaid Stalin's confidence fully. His article on the interview contained repeated references to likenesses between Stalin and Lenin and commented that Stalin "showed the same complete assurance and confidence in the future that characterizes every Soviet executive—and the rank and file for that matter—in the Soviet Union today. From high to low they feel they have 'crossed the divide' and that, although the road ahead may not be easy, it will be easier than the road behind them was."[18]

Barnes was perhaps consoled by the recognition he received in an article on foreign correspondence in New Outlook:

Known among his Moscow colleagues as "Scoop Barnes," Mr. Barnes is actually no longer a boy, but has retained all his cub reporter enthusiasm despite his ten years in Paris, Rome and Moscow. Barnes, on behalf of the New York Herald Tribune, *and Stoneman for the* Chicago Daily News, *were shipped back to Moscow by the Gay Pay Oo [O.G.P.U.] from the South of Russia for being the first of the resident Moscow correspondents to get an eyeful of the famine of 1932-33. Famine and disaster stories in the hinterland of Russia are* supposed to be covered, *if at all, from Moscow, and preferably by getting the details from reading the accounts in the Soviet official press. Barnes is still cub enough to think that spot news stories should be covered on the spot. What with Italy, Germany and Russia offering foreign correspondents the dubious collaboration of censorship bureaus, Barnes's field on the Continent is getting narrowed down.* [19]

Barnes took a good deal of kidding from his fellows when *Time*, in picking up his story about Vassily Stalin's report card, referred to him as "handsome Ralph Barnes." He wrote home that his colleagues were "quite convinced that the staff of *Time* must have got their ideas from a very much touched-up picture."[20]

In the early months of 1934, turnover among the reporters stationed in Moscow left Barnes as the "dean" of Moscow correspondents. Eugene Lyons, Stanley Richardson, Linton Wells, and Walter Duranty all left for other posts. Even Chamberlin moved to Berlin, before proceeding to Tokyo for the *Christian Science Monitor.* Joseph Baird replaced Lyons, Harold Denny followed Duranty, and Demery Bess came in Chamberlin's place. Barnes had reports from both John Elliott, the *Herald Tribune*'s Berlin correspondent, and Scarborough in London that the paper was happy with his work. He thought it foolish to change posts at that juncture. Instead he and Esther purchased an automobile, while assuring his parents that it would in the long run be an economy and would not interfere with their chances of going home to Oregon for a visit in late spring.

The establishment of the American Embassy affected their social life: "The American Colony is going, or has gone, socially mad. It is rather difficult to stay home." Moreover, "our apartment has become a sort of gathering place for the correspondents. They always know Ralph will be working, so they drop in at all hours of the evening. When they get started talking, they forget to go home." Joe and

Kathleen Barnes came briefly to Moscow. Ralph and Esther enjoyed their visit as well as their growing friendship with the third secretary at the American Embassy, George F. Kennan, and his wife Annelise.[21]

In March, Esther traveled to Vienna on a ten-day trip to buy supplies unavailable in Moscow. The trip occasioned a more open than usual letter to Salem:

> *I could come here quite inexpensively because a friend got a ticket for me in paper rubles. Now the gold ruble is 1 ruble 14 kopeks to the dollar. We buy with gold rubles, or dollars, in the Government store, Torgsin. Illegally, we buy from certain people the paper ruble at 45 to the dollar. Every foreigner who lives in Moscow does that, and the Russians know it, but realize that there is nothing to do until they can stabilize the gold and paper ruble. That is why we can send long cables to you. We pay in paper rubles. I am telling you something that I couldn't write from Moscow, but don't get excited about it. If we were to be arrested, the whole foreign colony would also. They all buy paper rubles from the "Black Bourse." Don't write anything about this in any letters to Moscow, for goodness sakes. ... Remember—**don't say anything about rubles or tickets in your letters**.*

The hoped-for Spring trip to Oregon was delayed but both Ralph and Esther agonized over their separation from their children. They advised their parents, particularly Mrs. Barnes, not to "cloister" them so much, but to see that they had chances to be with other children.[22]

The construction of the Moscow subway carried on outside their door. In a rush to finish a seven-mile stretch by the November anniversary of the Revolution, the government recruited "volunteers" to work on Saturdays. Joining them were a few American women resident in Moscow, fodder for two articles, as they were educated members of the Social Register. Esther wrote home that Ralph could not resist trying it himself: "Ralph found a shovel yesterday morning and spent two hours shoveling on the subway work in front of our house. As a result, he is feeling rather stiff this morning and has some blistered hands. The workmen and the girls got a lot of fun out of watching him. I think that he disrupted the work more than he helped. He has taken today off to recover."[23]

~

1934 saw renewed resolution in the Soviet drive toward an advanced economy. The revised Second Five-year Plan, the Kremlin announced, would by its completion make the Soviet Union "more advanced technically than any country in Europe" although its measurable goals were more modest than previously announced. The plan highlighted development in the East, trade with the United States, the promised end of rationing, and a pay scale based on merit. It included yet another effort to limit the bureaucracy through a reorganization of the party. Requirements for membership were made more exacting and competence rather than party membership would determine appointments and retention in high industrial posts. Stalin decreed an end to the chaos that disrupted rail transportation, threatening "the punishing hand of the party" to those who did not cooperate.[24]

A careful study by the Barneses' friend, the American engineer Zara Witkin, demonstrated that the much-vaunted First Five-year Plan actually called for less construction than that done in the United States each year from 1923 to 1932. Since the Soviet Union accomplished less than 60% of what had been planned, actual construction was about half that of the United States. Overhead costs were four or five times as great as in America. Foreign trade, especially with the United States, had been expected to spur the Soviet economy but despite the lifting of some barriers, trade with the United States proved to be no panacea. The anticipated credits were not forthcoming.[25]

The Soviets had launched an automobile industry based at Gorky, the old Nizhni Novgorod, and contracted with Henry Ford for access to his patents. In spite of tremendous effort and resources devoted to the project, production broke down almost completely in 1932. In May 1934, when Barnes was given permission to visit Gorky, he found evidence of improvement, although 1933 production had been 27,000 cars instead of the projected 140,000. A combination of management reorganization and a not very socialist piece-work system of payment made a difference. Barnes reported on plans to build an attractive, powerful car for the private consumer. In a country where the private ownership of automobiles was still virtually unknown, an "own your own car" movement arose, as an incentive to the best industrial workers and engineers. But the Soviet Union had a long way to go before it could hope to produce enough cars to meet demand, or to meet international engineering standards.[26]

Indeed, the manager of the Soviet Automobile and Tractor Trust visited Detroit and returned to chide his fellows. In *Izvestia* he wrote that those who claimed the Soviet Union had surpassed the United States in the automotive field "simply make themselves ridiculous." He cited the organization and high standards of the plants he visited and the discipline, training, and even the personal hygiene of the American worker. It was difficult, he observed, "to train a man who does not shave and seldom takes a bath to make automobile parts with exactness down to one-thousandth of a millimeter."[27] Despite such self-criticism, the familiar explanations for failures resurfaced: sabotage and "wrecking" encouraged by foreigners. The Kremlin ordered the arrest of several foreign engineers allegedly involved but then had them deported rather than risk the bad publicity and diplomatic embarrassment that resulted from the Metro-Vickers trial. In another case, a military tribunal sentenced seven Soviet citizens and a "Corean spy" to death and fifteen others to prison for an alleged conspiracy to share military information and sabotage railroads, presumably for the Japanese.[28]

But other moves seemed to signal a more open society. Restrictions on the practice of religion in Moslem regions were relaxed. School curricula and even children's toys were rescued from Marxist strictures. The O.G.P.U. was abolished and replaced by a Commissariat of Internal Affairs whose responsibilities were similar to those of Ministries of the Interior in western Europe. Barnes noted that the new organization was led by the same people who had run the O.G.P.U. When the new Soviet ambassador to the United States, Alexander Troyanovsky, said that the Soviet Union was a "full democracy," Barnes disputed the claim. Even if the Communist Party itself was democratic in its organization, a questionable premise in his eyes, it was a small ruling minority of perhaps three million in a nation of 160 million. The *Herald Tribune* editorialized in support of Barnes's position and the contrast with the American system he cited, noting that "it is notorious that Americans abroad look back on us and our ways with a tender and lenient affection."[29]

As before, relaxation of the pressures on the Soviet people was followed by renewed repression. A new law made treason punishable by death and by the exile to Siberia of the traitor's family, regardless of their involvement in his offense. The government imprisoned seventy-five clerics whose vocations as well as their German ancestral backgrounds made them liable to charges of conspiring against the state. Two incidents in which children became heroes for reporting their parents' crimes inspired Barnes to do an article on Soviet success in indoctrinating young people, recounting his conversations with school children.[30]

Through the early months of 1934, Moscow newspapers reflected continued concern about the menace of Japan, and increasing uneasiness about Nazi Germany. Stalin noted Nazi assertions of German racial superiority, reminding them that the Romans had thought themselves superior to the Franks and Teutons: "Ancient Rome had a certain justification for its belief in its superiority;

Germany today has no such justification. In any case, Germany should not forget that in the end all the other nations combined against Rome and overthrew her." The Soviet Union sought a pact with Germany in which each nation would guarantee the territorial integrity of the three Baltic republics, but negotiations led nowhere. The German-inspired abortive attempt by Austrian Nazis to take over their country, resulting in the assassination of Austrian Chancellor Engelbert Dollfuss, heightened Russian fears.[31]

Periodically the Soviets made gestures calculated to draw together nations fearful of Nazi Germany, but progress was tentative at best. Barnes recorded the Soviet reaction to the "Night of the Long Knives," Hitler's June 30 massacre of Ernst Röhm and other leaders of the Storm Troopers. Karl Radek, writing in *Izvestia*, foresaw a class war in Germany and the Nazis' ultimate overthrow because in destroying the Storm Troopers, they had alienated the lower middle class, "cutting off the branch on which they had perched themselves." Despite such optimism, the Soviet Communist leadership took the threat of Hitler seriously enough to make peace with old rivals. The French Socialist Party cemented an alliance with the French Communist party, with the full encouragement and probably at the instigation of Moscow. After years of bitter dispute and recrimination, the European Left seemed at last prepared to close ranks against a dangerous foe. Barnes's article recognized the Soviet role in the inception of the Popular Front, an anti-fascist alliance extending from the Center to the far Left, that later came to power in France, in Spain, and even in far away Chile.[32]

Just before his departure for the United States in August, Barnes wrote a piece recounting the observations of the American crusader for contraception, Margaret Sanger, on her visit to the Soviet Union. While applauding the availability of contraceptive devices, she decried the number of abortions there and foresaw dire results:

> It is common knowledge that the practice of abortion, if it becomes a habit, can do considerable harm to woman's sex life. Neuroses may develop and those in turn may result in frigidity. In this country woman is no longer economically dependent on man. If she becomes frigid she will not be dependent on him in any other way and, in fact, will no longer be interested in him. Likewise, she will have no further desire to bring children into the world. But she will develop a surplus energy which she must expend in some direction. In such cases, it is not inconceivable that she would push man out of the political sphere and promote the development of a matriarchy, or gynecocracy.

This remarkable analysis stands out among those of visitors to the Soviet Union but seems to have attracted little notice.[33]

The chance for Ralph to take some leave at last presented itself. Through the spring, Esther had pressed for the long-planned trip to Oregon. Initially, the plan was to go via the Trans-Siberian Railway and then by ship from Yokohama across the Pacific Ocean to Seattle. But they finally settled on a trip via New York to allow Ralph some time at the *Herald Tribune*'s home office.[34]

8

The heresy hunt which is always under way in this country is now being conducted with greatly increased vigor as a result of the Kremlin's decision, following the assassination of Sergei Kirov, to stamp out all opposition ruthlessly. For every person executed, imprisoned or exiled, from twenty to fifty persons are being called in for questioning, dismissed from their positions or expelled from the Communist party or the Young Communist League. The terror now in progress strikes not only at acts or intention to act but also at ideas expressed only in private conversation. Officials and others are being disciplined in a rigorous manner even for relating counter-revolutionary anecdotes.

Ralph Barnes, *Herald Tribune*, January 7, 1935, from Moscow

When they arrived in the United States for Ralph's first visit since 1926, Esther went immediately by train to Salem. Ralph remained in New York briefly, then spent a few days in Washington, where he reported on the current status of United States-Soviet negotiations on settlement of the debts of previous Russian regimes. The Soviets had so far refused to honor these debts, which included $86 million in Tsarist government bonds held by Americans, loans of $187 million from the United States to the government of Kerensky during World War I, and a $400 million claim for damages incurred during and after the Russian Revolution by American private and corporate property-holders. The United States government rejected the direct cash loan the Soviets were demanding to finance American exports in exchange for an agreement on debt settlement. Barnes's article pointed out that the Soviets were particularly constrained, because any agreement with the United States would cause demands from France and Great Britain for settlement of their debts, far larger than those owed the Americans.[1]

Sheldon Sackett, writing in Salem's *Oregon Statesman* in September, said Barnes also visited President Roosevelt's home in Hyde Park, New York, where Roosevelt "quizzed him minutely about Russian affairs." Esther's sister Mary mentioned such a visit in a letter that survives, but the asserted visit failed to become part of family lore. Barnes did not write for the *Herald Tribune* about the interview, and never mentioned it in his correspondence.[2]

Barnes crossed the continent for a month in Oregon, getting to know his children again and seeing family and old friends. He even managed a few days of relaxation at the Oregon coast. Despite his intention to have a private time, he agreed to the interview with an old schoolmate, Sackett, as well as another with a reporter from the *Oregonian*, David Hazen. He spoke at the Marion Hotel in Salem to a combined session of the Kiwanis, Rotary, Lions, and Business and Professional Women's clubs. Willamette University prevailed upon him to speak at a chapel convocation. He also did a radio interview on KEX in Portland. In each instance, he emphasized the stability and relative conservatism of the Soviet regime, and the counter-revolution in education and culture. He asserted that very little communism was practiced there: "It is a certainty that no serious threat exists to the long continuance of Soviet power. It is an equal certainty that the industrial development of Russia has been far more slow than the plans its leaders laid out called for." Barnes rejected the notion of a Communist threat in the United States: "Americans who talk about communism as though it were imminent in this country do not appreciate the vast differences in the temperament and background of American people from those in Russia. The Russian experiment could not be superimposed upon the United States." He correctly emphasized the Soviet government's interest in peace, and forecast, incorrectly as it turned out, greater liberalization and the lifting of the internal repression.[3]

Ralph and Esther went to California with Sackett and his wife, Beatrice. In Los Angeles, Ralph submitted to another interview in which he commented on the stature of writer Upton Sinclair, then a candidate for governor of California, in the Soviet Union. Sinclair's books were so popular that Russian readers saw the United States "through Sinclair spectacles." However, "most of the Communists are almost entirely against Sinclair. They place him in their classification as a 'Socialist,' which in their political scheme makes him much harder to get along with than a Democrat or Republican or a capitalist."[4]

Sinclair interested Barnes, and the trip to California turned into a bit of a busman's holiday as he gathered material for a three-part series for the *Herald Tribune* on the candidate and the California gubernatorial race. Earlier Sinclair, with his socialist "EPIC plan to End Poverty in California," had been seen as the front runner, but as the election approached he was given only an even chance. Barnes noted the gathering opposition and predicted that he would lose. He braved the hostility of Sinclair's protective wife to interview him in his garden in Palos Verdes and found the author-candidate more inclined to contemplation than political activity. Barnes recalled the experience of others:

> *When American radicals, such as Big Bill Haywood, arrived in Moscow in the early days after the October Revolution, they found that building a new order was quite a different thing from making soapbox speeches, leading strikes and in general railing against capitalism. Many of them were a total loss when it came to constructive labor. Now without by any means intending to class Sinclair with these others, it is fair to recall that he has passed a good deal of his life writing books and digging in his garden; he has had very little experience with practical affairs. Perhaps his real place is in his garden writing books and digging.[5]*

The vacation passed all too quickly. Soon Ralph boarded a plane for New York. The trip involved stops at Pendleton, Salt Lake City, Omaha, Chicago, Toledo, and Cleveland. On the plane, he wrote a farewell letter to his parents: "It was a glorious six weeks and I hope that in the near future we shall be able to have a longer period together. I am resolved not to remain away so long again. It was difficult before to return. From now on it will be much less difficult. I am much more independent than I was before. In any case, I will not want to remain in Moscow much longer, not more than two years, I think. And after that, quite seriously, I would like to have a breathing spell." He added, "Let us be happy in the knowledge that each of us loves the other. It is great for me to know, as I know, that I have fine people; and that Esther's people are of the same caliber."[6]

Esther remained in Oregon, their plans for reunion indefinite. In New York, Barnes lunched in the executive dining room of the *Herald Tribune* with owners Ogden and Helen Reid. They discussed Russia and communism in the United States, Cuba and elsewhere. He found the Reids complimentary of his work and encouraging about his future. Changes in staffing in Europe meant that Barnes would inherit the Berlin bureau which would, he assured his parents, "make it possible for us to come to the States more often." He found the plans to be rather far along: "I was glad to find, too, that Lee Stowe is not in disfavor in Paris. Probably he will be recalled to New York, but he will be given a good position there—one with a good deal of prestige. Scarborough, in London, appears to be on the road to demotion; and Elliott, of Berlin, will take his place as head of the European service. John Elliott and I are on the best of terms, so the change will be quite satisfactory with me. I like Elliott's type much better than Scarborough's."[7]

~

While in New York, Barnes combined visits to relatives and old friends with writing a long article, "Living under a Dictatorship." He observed that the Communist revolution in Russia had so far meant much greater change for ordinary citizens than had the fascist revolutions in Italy, Austria and Germany, where revolutions had consisted of "substitution of dictatorial control for democratic control of the old 'capitalistic institutions.' " He found the changes in the Soviet Union most striking in rural areas. About the nature of the regime, he had no doubts:

> As for political rights, the Soviet citizen has something of the form with virtually none of the substance. There are general elections for the hierarchy of Soviets, which is supposed to provide a democratic governmental system, after a fashion. Yet anyone at all acquainted with the Soviet Union knows that the real power is vested in the All-Union Communist party and its various organs. The party is composed of about 2,000,000 members and 1,000,000 candidates. The party, like an army, is commanded by a general staff in the form of the so-called "Politbureau" of the party's Central Committee. The "Politbureau" is composed of Joseph Stalin, secretary general of the party, and nine men who have proved their loyalty to him in past battles with deviationists. This "Big Ten" is like an interlocking directorate, for its members hold the bulk of the key executive and administrative positions in both government and party. Such elementary rights as free speech, free press and free assembly have no place whatever under the Soviet dictatorship. The individual is completely at the mercy of the state.[8]

This series, like the one he wrote on Mussolini's Italy when he left Rome, was another manifestation of an idea that continued to germinate in Barnes's mind. He had experienced Fascist Italy and

Communist Russia; soon he would have the opportunity to acquaint himself with Nazi Germany. Perhaps one day a book would be in order.

For readers of the journal *Editor and Publisher*, Barnes provided a description of a journalist's working conditions in the Soviet Union. American diplomatic recognition had improved the situation, and he had found the Embassy to be a great resource. Ambassador Bullitt's press conferences, open only to accredited correspondents of American news organizations and "off the record," were remarkably frank and helpful. Censorship was a problem, but the greatest challenge was getting accurate statements of fact. He said that he found the average Russian official "the most secretive person in the world."[9]

Barnes returned to Europe on the *S.S. Manhattan*, passing the time reading James Joyce's *Ulysses*. He traveled through London, Paris, and Berlin, meeting there with John Elliott whose place he would shortly take, with Ambassador William E. Dodd and his daughter Martha, and with William and Sonya Chamberlin. He arrived back in Moscow on November 25 after an absence of nearly four months. Rested and with renewed energy for his work, he found himself plunged into the holiday social activities of the American colony: "All of my old friends seem quite glad to have me back, but they rather resent the fact that Esther isn't along. Since returning, I have come to the conclusion that Esther is about the best-liked person in the colony. Everyone has asked about her. Everyone, without exception, likes her. That's a good deal in this place, where every one knows everyone else's affairs; and where it is not easy to keep an even temper. It's pretty lonesome in the apartment without Esther, but I am managing to keep busy most of the time."

The parties had their value for both the journalists and the diplomats. Although Barnes wrote home complaining of the late nights, he allowed that "the parties develop news, for they make for informal conversation with people who know things." Whitman Bassow, in his study of Moscow correspondents, said the diplomats included the correspondents in their social gatherings because they considered them the best-informed foreigners in Moscow. Clearly the correspondents considered themselves so. In a 1934 letter written after the United States had established diplomatic relations, Barnes observed: "I am seeing quite a good deal of some of the boys at the Embassy; they are a good bunch. Yet I am still convinced—and I have been in other capitals—that, on the whole, correspondents know more about what is happening than the diplomats. I presume that I flatter myself and my profession."[10]

~

During Barnes's leave, Samuel Rodman, the Moscow correspondent for the London *Observer* and for the Reuters News Agency, filed for the *Herald Tribune* from Moscow. To Barnes's relief, "decidedly little news of first importance" had happened during his absence. He had only a few days of filing routine stories before the lull ended with the December 1 assassination of Sergei Kirov, the starting point for the great terror that swept the Soviet Union from 1935 until 1938. The magnitude of the horror has been slow to penetrate western consciousness. But millions lost their lives and millions more their freedom, accused of, and in many cases forced to confess to, crimes that were the invention of their accusers.[11]

A member of the Politbureau and leader of the Communist Party in Leningrad, Kirov was a popular and able party figure with impeccable revolutionary credentials. His assassin was quickly identified as Leonid Nicolaev. Despite calls for revenge against the "capitalistic beasts" responsible for the assassination, Barnes initially wrote: "The Soviet regime, in the opinion of this correspondent, is stronger today than ever before, and thus will not feel a necessity to resort to terror on a wide scale" in response to the crime. Still he foresaw "repressive measures of one sort or another" and a setback to the movement to substitute judicial processes for "summary treatment of political cases." Barnes underestimated Stalin. Within hours, arrests, trials and executions were carried out.[12]

On December 3, the trial of 71 former "White Guards" was announced. These supposed members of units that fought against the Bolsheviks during the civil war were charged with plotting a revolt and hurried to a summary trial and execution. Barnes dismissed foreign reports of an impending counter-revolutionary uprising. However, he noted that even if the assassination had resulted from Nicolaev's personal grudge against Kirov, its effects would be felt widely. When events confirmed his prediction, Barnes struggled for an explanation: "Only yesterday a Russian of wide experience voiced to this correspondent the view that the seventy-one persons handed over to the military tribunal on Sunday would not be put to death, but would be sentenced to varying terms of imprisonment. Apparently there is no way to explain the Kremlin's response to the assassination of Kirov unless one falls back upon the thesis that Oriental and, if one will, barbarous traditions are still deeply rooted in this country."[13]

The tenor of the official response can be seen in a resolution passed by the Moscow section of the Communist Party in mid-December: "The abominable cunning agents of the class enemies, the coward scum of the former Zinoviev anti- party group, have torn Comrade Kirov from our ranks. We will stamp out every one of the vile counter-revolutionary followers of the Zinoviev anti-party." An *Izvestia* editorial warned against regarding the assassination as an isolated case: "Class enemies within the U.S.S.R. are scouts and sappers for the army of the world counterrevolution, which is still powerful. Their terroristic acts against representatives of Soviet power are, in reality, a continuation of the mass terror against the struggling workers and peasants."[14]

The evidence now available implicates Stalin in Kirov's murder, but that was not clear to the journalists in Moscow in 1934. Kirov had opposed Stalin in several important matters during the early thirties and was dangerously popular among party members. Stalin apparently saw his assassination as a chance to remove a potential rival and to impose a far more repressive regime on the country. Allegations of conspiracy soon implicated others who had disagreed with Stalin in the past, most notably Gregory Zinoviev and Leo Kamenev. The assassination was depicted as the first move in their effort to take over the leadership, not only in Leningrad, but also in the rest of the country. Barnes noted the irony of Karl Radek's denunciation of the conspiracy: "It is interesting to recall that Radek himself was once a prominent member of the Zinoviev-Trotsky opposition. When the opposition collapsed in 1927, Radek was one of the first to hurry to do penance."[15]

To Barnes, Stalin's intentions and methods became clearer: "The heresy hunt which is always under way in this country is now being conducted with greatly increased vigor as a result of the Kremlin's decision, following the assassination of Sergei Kirov, to stamp out all opposition ruthlessly. For every person executed, imprisoned or exiled, from twenty to fifty persons are being called in for questioning, dismissed from their positions or expelled from the Communist party or the Young Communist League. The terror now in progress strikes not only at acts or intention to act but also at ideas expressed only in private conversation." Stalin and his aides appeared to be "more concerned about their control of the party machine than about further resistance of opposition elements outside the ranks." But perhaps that was merely preparatory. The Politburo had made a decision "to leave no stone unturned to assure the absolute obedience and loyalty on the part of every party member as the first means of meeting resistance elsewhere whenever it may occur." Barnes, however, rejected the idea that any effective opposition existed within the party: "Whatever the number of dissenters, they have no means of expressing themselves and thus are no immediate menace to the present leadership."[16]

The increasingly tense situation heightened Barnes's frustrations with the censorship. He was also bothered by the return to Moscow of his old competitor Walter Duranty: "He will begin to write long essays on everything that has happened since he left and of course the *Times* will play them up. I'm preparing a counter-attack but it's tough going. In any other country, one would have a general idea of what was happening but here, it's a mass of conflicting rumors." Duranty's visit resulted in two feature articles in the *New York Times Magazine*. One lauded Soviet progress and Stalin's leadership without mentioning the terror in progress; the other justified the conditions of the workers and peasants in light of the greater goals of the regime. The *Herald Tribune* buried Barnes's work on inside pages: "I said to someone last night that I presumed that the gods were all lined up on the edge of Olympus laughing at me—but then, they probably take too little notice to laugh."[17]

Preoccupations with his work did not keep Ralph from missing Esther: "Still awaiting some word from Esther as to when she is leaving. Certainly hope that she doesn't postpone her departure much longer, for it is lonesome here without her." Nor was there further word on the reorganization of the *Herald Tribune*'s European service discussed while he was in New York. In the longer run, Ralph looked forward to a return to the United States: "I should like to come back to the United States after a couple of years, or more, and write about America. By that time I should have a background which should permit me to speak with some authority."[18]

At the meeting of the All-Union Congress of Soviets in late January and early February, Stalin and his principal henchman Viacheslav Molotov decried western criticism of their summary methods of dealing with the Kirov assassination.[19]

Speakers warned of the German and Japanese threats and boasted of Russia's readiness to respond to any danger. They were defiant in their attitude toward the United States. As Barnes wrote, Litvinov, with his diplomatic skill, "obtained American recognition for his government without definitely obliging it, even in the long run, to pay to the United States any part of the canceled Russian debt and claims." Trade with the United States had actually declined since recognition; with no American loans forthcoming, there was no reason to expect the situation to improve.[20] The Soviets also again proclaimed the support for world revolution they had downplayed during the negotiations with the United States. They welcomed a report by an American Communist, Moissaye J. Olgin, editor of the Yiddish language New York Communist daily *Freiheit* and a correspondent for *Pravda*, of growth in the ranks of American Communists. The Depression, the sweatshops, and strikes offered opportunities for the party to extend its influence, he argued. Particular progress, he said, was being made in Harlem, a place inhabited by "a backward, ignorant mass of 250,000 Negroes who live in hunger, poverty and disease."[21]

Olgin's claims inspired an editorial response from the *Herald Tribune*. It reminded its readers that predictions of the impending revolution had been made regularly since 1917, but doubted that Americans would ever accept the regimentation such a revolution would involve. Roy Wilkins, the head of the National Association for the Advancement of Colored People, responded to Olgin's remarks in a letter to the editor. He said that claims of advances in Harlem were "just one more example of the tactical stupidity of the American wing of the Communist Party." Not that American Negroes were content. "There is growing among them greater and greater distrust of the old order of things—political parties, courts of justice, profits and wages—indeed, the whole capitalist system. They long since have seen through the New Deal. They are ready for a change. Generations of practice at analyzing white folk in order to survive have made it certain, however, that the Negro will not aid a change from silk-hat stupidity to gnarled-hand stupidity."[22]

Through the early months of 1935, Barnes's stories chronicling the ongoing repression were juxtaposed with those about theater, film, juvenile crime in Moscow, and the opening of the Moscow subway, which despite Esther's misgivings ran quite well. Ordinary life went on while thousands were tried and sentenced to imprisonment or exile in Siberia. The sale abroad of the great art works in the Hermitage was halted. Soviet wives, like their husbands, could be jailed for failure to pay alimony. A hundred American vaudeville performers came to Russia only to find their contracts were fraudulent. The formerly reclusive Stalin became something of a man-about-town.

In Barnes's judgment, Stalin's "consummate dexterity" could be seen in events since the Kirov assassination. Barnes questioned the guilt of many who had been sentenced, but saw the ruthless response as very much in keeping with the nature of the regime, citing Lenin's remark that the 1871 Paris Commune had failed because of "insufficient severity." Those who remained in the party were in Barnes's estimation "better prepared than hitherto to carry out Stalin's bidding." He also pointed to some "carrots," particularly in Stalin's efforts to win back the peasantry "antagonized by forcible collectivization and its consequences, including the famine of 1933." He concluded that the changes had profound significance "not only for this country but for the whole world."[23]

In their renewed calls for world revolution, the Soviets had allowed themselves an indulgence they could not afford. On March 17, Adolf Hitler denounced the restrictions of the Versailles Treaty and announced the introduction of conscription. Reviewing the antagonism toward the Soviet Union reflected in Hitler's speeches and in his book *Mein Kampf*, the Soviet press chided the British for their "wavering policy" and "indecision" in the face of the Nazi threat: "Will this new act of militant National Socialism serve to sober those British and other foreign circles which nurse the illusion that, by directing German expansion eastward, they will succeed in preserving peace in the west and will render their homes safe amid the threatening flames?" The Soviets took comfort in dreams of revolutionary solidarity: "German Fascism will not succeed in bringing back to life the stinking corpse of bourgeois patriotism. The German workers, placed behind guns by Hitler for imperialistic adventures, will consider the great lessons of the class struggle, and will know how to use the guns properly."

Despite Soviet bravado, Barnes knew that the government was profoundly fearful of war. Even with all its efforts to modernize, it remained vulnerable on several counts: the "deplorable" state of its transportation system, the sullen bitterness of its peasantry, and its still fragile industrialization. Moreover, he noted, "There is a fixed idea here that, if the U.S.S.R. were to become involved in armed conflict with any capitalist power, other capitalist powers would not be adverse to seizing an opportunity of crippling the state which continues to proclaim world revolution as its ultimate goal."[24]

In Soviet eyes, the British in particular were seeking a compromise with Germany. The London correspondent of *Pravda* accused the British of a tendency "to support German aggressive designs at the expense of other countries." The Soviet Union, Barnes noted, "is thoroughly convinced of Adolf Hitler's 'aggressive designs' and thus stands for urgent and effective measures to meet the Nazi 'menace.' " Into this atmosphere of recrimination came Anthony Eden, Lord

Privy Seal in the British Cabinet, who arrived in Moscow on March 28 for talks with Soviet leaders, the first official visit by a British cabinet member since the Revolution. The Soviets sought assurances for the countries in eastern Europe similar to the security guaranteed to those in the west by the Locarno agreement, signed in October 1925 by delegates from Belgium, Czechoslovakia, France, Germany, Great Britain, Italy and Poland. They maintained that such an agreement would have meaning only "if each signatory nation was to be sure that, were it to be attacked by land, sea or air, the other signatory nations would be bound to hasten to its assistance." The talks, between Eden, Litvinov, and Stalin, were more cordial and productive than Barnes had anticipated. He reported that Eden had been impressed by Stalin's grasp of European affairs. The British apparently agreed not to put obstacles in the way of continental countries' unity in opposition to Hitler, thus opening the way for negotiation of a pact between the Soviet Union and France.[25]

Barnes's coverage of the Eden visit occasioned one of his recurrent bouts of insecurity. He rebounded in a few days, but his accumulated experience had not lessened his tendency to worry about the quality of the job he was doing.[26] His spirits were helped by Esther's presence. She had sailed from New York on the *Manhattan* on February 27, 1935. Ralph came out to meet her at the Soviet border. Both enjoyed the luxury of being together again. In one of her first social outings, Esther acted as hostess for a party the foreign correspondents gave for one of the censors who was being sent to the Consulate in Vienna: "Had a wild time struggling along in French, German, some words of Russian and English. I sat between two censors at the head of the table, which was a funny circumstance, as Ralph had been called down as being a 'bad boy' by the censors again, just a few days previous. We got along fine."[27]

The ramifications of German rearmament intruded on their reunion. Barnes's article on Soviet readiness began: "With the European situation giving cause for more alarm than at any time since 1914, the Soviets are going forward steadily with their defense preparations." Morale was high in the standing army that numbered 940 thousand and could call up two million trained reserves. Recent developments in the munitions, steel and chemical industries left the Soviets in a far better situation than the Russian Empire in 1914. On the other hand, Soviet efforts to improve transport ironically depended on importing rail equipment from the expected enemy, Germany.[28] The Soviets combined boastful claims of invincibility with efforts to enhance the country's international stature. Their diplomats impressed on British, French and Italian representatives,

Esther Barnes and Karl Radek in Moscow, 1935.

meeting at the Italian resort town of Stresa, the principle of the "indivisibility of peace." Even before the Stresa meetings, French Foreign Minister Pierre Laval and Soviet Ambassador Vladimir Potemkin had reached an agreement that ultimately led to the signing of the Franco-Soviet Pact on May 2. Barnes described the pact as essentially defensive, in contrast to the agreement between Russia and France before World War I, noting that at that time both France and Russia had territorial designs but "perhaps no other states in Europe are more interested today in preserving the territorial status quo than France and Soviet Russia."[29]

While accepting the Soviet stance for international peace, Barnes was more skeptical about Stalin's new crusade calling for the Soviet bureaucracy to overcome its "heartless and simply outrageous attitude toward the workers." Stalin decried the "famine" of men able to operate the machines of industrialization: "If we wish to provide our country with a sufficient number of men to 'saddle' technique and move it forward, we must first of all learn to know men, to appraise their capabilities." Barnes wrote that few considered Stalin "a man who gives much thought to what happens to individuals." "Perhaps," he added, "those persons who recall the aftermath of the assassination of Sergei Kirov will be prepared to take Stalin's words with a grain of salt." Still he noted that Stalin seemed to be emerging from his usual seclusion, even to the point of making radio addresses.[30] Barnes saw a trend, a "Soviet stampede back to what in some circles at least, will be called common sense." He ticked off Stalin's speech, editorials about motherhood and the duty of Soviet youth to honor their parents, even the presentation of Shakespeare's "Romeo and Juliet" to introduce Soviet children to "true love." These changes followed upon others that had occurred since 1931: differentiated wages, a return to fundamental education and standard textbooks, renewed use of traditional children's stories and toys, more style in women's clothes, jazz bands. The authorities seemed intent on "rehabilitating the Soviet family and restoring it to the place from which it had been dislodged as the bulwark of society." They decried divorce and called for mobilization of public opinion against men who abandoned their wives and children.[31]

Through the spring, the *Herald Tribune* management occasionally indicated that plans for the reassignments discussed in New York were proceeding. The illness of the managing editor, Wilcox, slowed things down. Ralph and Esther were both anxious for the change because it would give them an opportunity to reunite their family. They were especially concerned about Joan, whom they felt to be too isolated; they were relieved when Ralph's parents enrolled her in kindergarten. When the Oregon State House burned to the ground in May, Ralph and Esther worried about the effect on Joan. The Capitol was just a block from the elder Barneses' home and its steps had been one of Joan's favorite play areas.[32] Finally on June 10, Barnes received a telegram from John Elliott in the Berlin bureau confirming that the change of assignments was coming. Typically, he fretted about his limited knowledge of German and the fact that, in his preoccupation with the Soviet Union, he had not devoted much time to studying the German situation. But he again welcomed Elliott's assignment as head of the European service: "He is a good level-headed chap, and he and I get along very well together."[33]

With their departure from the Soviet Union now certain, Ralph and Esther traveled through the southern part of the country, accompanied by Ralph's assistant. They visited the Kuban, where Ralph had traveled with Bill Stoneman during the famine. Ralph surveyed peasants at the railway stations along the way and sent a dispatch from Kavkazkaya in the North Caucasus reporting an improvement in conditions: "After difficult years, Kuban obviously is returning to its place as one of the richest grain-growing regions in the country. By almost unanimous report, a majority of the collectives are working better than formerly. There is appreciably less grumbling among the collective farmers than there was a year or two ago, and they are much better prepared to cope with the problems of harvesting."[34]

Esther wrote a more detailed account of their trip through the Kuban:

We rode around in farm carts, visiting collective farms and eating with the peasants. That was where we made our first and only attempt to sleep under the stars. Walked all over in the dark, looking for a spot, and finally arranged ourselves on a hay stack. Even with mosquito netting, we were driven from there by mosquitos, and finally spent the rest of the night in the middle of the road. Luckily there was no traffic, or we would have been stepped on. Washed and bathed next morning in the local river, and got breakfast from a Cossack peasant woman. Sat on her dirt floor porch, surrounded by cats, chickens and pigs, while she started a fire in her outdoor stove and fried some eggs, made tea with our tea and our sugar, served homemade black bread, no butter, and fresh cherries off the trees. The cats and chickens cleaned my plate off when I finished, but at that stage, one doesn't mind. Had lots of fun with the peasants later, and had a glorious drive across the Russian countryside just at dusk, on a flat buggy, or cart, with two galloping horses, beautiful moon too.

The trio traveled by train and slept on the "hard" coach, which turned out to be cooler than the first class cars. "The only real excitement," Esther wrote, "was when two pigs were discovered in sacks under the seats of the coach. They had been quiet, and no one but the owner knew they were there until the conductor came through, and one of the pigs, by chance, squealed. At first, no one admitted ownership, and finally they confessed that they would have had to be late for work if they had waited for the train on which they could transport the pigs. They paid a small fine, and went their way badly scared."[35]

The travelers changed to automobile for the trip from Vladikavkaz to Tiflis over the Georgia Military Highway, stopping at a small, "primitive" hotel, eating their fill of *shashlik* and trout, and talking with Georgian mountaineers whom the government had gathered into collective farms. The old Georgian castles scattered in the valleys reminded them of those along the Rhine or in the Pyrenees. Because of Esther's Armenian background, a major objective of the trip was a visit to Soviet Armenia. Their stay in Erivan, the capital, was short, but Esther was happy just being there "because I know Father would have wanted me to come." They attended services, "very much like Catholic services," at the monastery of Etchiadzin, the seat of the head of the Armenian Church, the *katholikos*. Noting the small number of elderly men resident there, Ralph and Esther concluded that the church in Armenia was gradually fading away, if not so rapidly as the Russian Orthodox Church. Told that Esther's father was of Armenian descent, one archbishop quoted an old proverb: "A stone only has its real value in its proper place," meaning, Esther wrote, "that if I were an Armenian I should be in Armenia. He made no other comments."[36]

Despite Esther's misgivings, they chose the hour airplane trip from Erivan back to Tiflis rather than a fourteen-hour train trip. They went on by rail to Batum on the Black Sea and boarded a freighter for a "not very comfortable" trip to Poti, where Ralph wrote about local claims that the Greeks had plagiarized their legend of Jason and the Golden Fleece. Another dispatch from Poti told of the effort to create on the Black Sea coast a "Soviet Florida" to supply the country with citrus fruits through a land reclamation project. The travelers took a passenger steamer to Sotchi where they enjoyed three days of beach and sun before going on to Yalta, Balaklava and Sebastopol. From Kharkov, Esther returned by train to Moscow while Ralph and Shumack visited collective farms near Poltava and the tractor factory in Kharkov. They flew back to Moscow on a six-passenger, single-engine monoplane, flying low enough and slow enough for a good view of the countryside.[37]

Back in Moscow, reality quickly exerted itself. In the view of Soviet commentator Karl Radek, Mussolini's attempt to take over Ethiopia threatened to upset the unstable balance of power because it distracted Italy from the much more important issue of German "aggressive designs." The Seventh Comintern brought Communists from all over the world to be instructed on the new course they were to follow in light of the Fascist threat to the Soviet homeland. Barnes summarized the new policy: "In those countries which still have 'bourgeois democratic' regimes, Communists are to ally themselves, so far as possible, with those regimes. Thus they are to cooperate not only with Socialists, but also apparently with bourgeois liberals and the like—with all those who are prepared to combat Fascism." It was such a reversal of course that Barnes wondered if Communists around the world would follow it: "Some one has suggested that the Communist appeal for a united front of

Communists and Socialists is reminiscent of the words of Racine, 'I embrace my rival, but it is the better to choke him.' If the quotation is apt, it remains so when the Comintern goes further, as it is doing, and calls for the support of 'bourgeois democracy' against Fascism. The question arises when it will cease embracing and begin choking."[38]

Although calls to make common cause against the Fascist enemy predominated, the Soviets were not entirely consistent during the Comintern gathering. Barnes wrote that Ambassador Bullitt was under orders to "follow closely the seventh congress of the Communist International with a view to detecting possible violation of the Soviet government's undertaking, given when it was recognized by the United States, to refrain from propaganda in American territory." Speakers encouraged American Communists in their efforts to eliminate "right-wing opportunists," that is, followers of Leon Trotsky. The delegates welcomed plans for a Communist-led longshoremen's strike on the American Pacific Coast in the hope that, in the course of the struggle, "close collaboration can be established among the seamen and dock workers of all countries in a decisive battle against the bourgeoisie." Members of the Young Communist League around the world were instructed to join youth organizations of all kinds, including church groups, and then to "fight for influence" in those groups.[39] No attempt was made to maintain the fiction that the Comintern was independent of the Soviet government. Stalin was recognized as "the leader in the struggle to overthrow not only Fascism but also capitalism."[40]

The final sessions of the Comintern meeting coincided with the Barneses' preparations for the move to Berlin. Joseph Phillips, who had held the *Herald Tribune*'s Rome post, arrived to succeed Barnes in Moscow. The round of welcoming and farewell parties ("We didn't realize that we were so popular") as well as the usual run of visitors to Moscow with letters of introduction led Esther to write that she would "shoot the next visiting fireman who puts his head through the door." Even the censors whom Barnes had battled so often gave them a party.[41]

The last articles Barnes filed from Moscow reflected both the recent trip and familiar issues. He wrote of the results of the Soviet government's compromise that allowed each collectivized farmer an acre of land and a limited number of livestock of his own. The new policy served as "a stimulus to individual initiative" and, because it had helped to bring Soviet agriculture out of its 1932-33 slump, "had an important effect in improving the general Soviet picture."[42] A second piece reviewed the status of organized religion in the country, noting the decline of the Russian Orthodox Church, the Armenian Church and the Orthodox Church of Georgia, and the end to the period immediately after the Revolution when Protestant Churches enjoyed a brief freedom. Islam, he observed, was "holding on somewhat more tenaciously," in part because its "religious practices are obligatory on the Moslem believer and enter into his daily life to a greater degree than like practices prescribed by Christian creeds." Another factor was undoubtedly the government policy of greater tolerance for religion in the "Oriental" portions of the U.S.S.R. Still Barnes foresaw that religion was "doomed to something approaching extinction" because of the hostility toward it from young people of all backgrounds. He quoted a peasant woman on a collective farm near Poltava: "We have five children and they insist on taking down the icons. Since we came here, five years ago, I have become used to getting along without God."[43]

Before leaving Moscow, Barnes managed to score one last coup, his August 13 letter to Stalin. Recounting the assertions of the Comintern conference, he asked if they did not in fact violate the Soviet government's pledge to President Roosevelt to refrain from subversive activity in the United States. The letter, which went unanswered, was printed in the *Herald Tribune* on Sunday, August 25. That very day, in Moscow, Ambassador Bullitt delivered a formal diplomatic note protesting "the 'flagrant violation' of Soviet pledges of non-interference in the internal affairs of the United States." Other countries, including Great Britain and Italy, joined in objecting to Communist propaganda within their borders. The Soviet government vigorously rejected the protest, on the familiar grounds of the Comintern's independence. Barnes correctly perceived that the American State Department was not prepared to take drastic action, such as the expulsion of consular representatives, despite the Soviets' inadequate response to the note.[44]

Once again, Barnes's initiative brought congratulations from New York. Although he looked forward to the new challenges in Germany, he and Esther both left Moscow with regret. Ralph was concerned that Esther would find her Moscow friends hard to replace. Neither expected to find Berlin as congenial.[45]

Part III. Berlin:
September 1935—March 1939

With the violently anti-Jewish wing of the Nazi party now apparently in the saddle, further anti-Semitic measures, supplementing those decreed by the Reichstag here last night withdrawing citizenship from Jews and forbidding Jewish-"Aryan" (gentile) marriages, are expected to be enacted soon. Re-establishment of the ghetto is now under way, as is manifest in the recent decision to establish separate schools for Jews. Two months ago Julius Streicher, anti-Semitic Nazi leader of Franconia, urged on the government the ghetto policy with all its implications. Streicher had his way in the matter of the schools, and again last night in the enactment of the anti-Jewish laws. There are definite indications that Chancellor Adolf Hitler is prepared to go much further along the lines which Streicher and others of his crew are pointing out, with elimination of all the Jews in Germany as their ultimate aim.

Ralph Barnes, *Herald Tribune*,
September 17, 1935, from Nuremberg, Germany

Ralph and Esther Barnes arrived in Berlin on Sunday, September 1, 1935. Exactly four years later, German forces invaded Poland to initiate the terrible destruction of World War II. The seventeen years since the end of World War I had only heightened the insecurity and resentment of the German people. In fact, Germany had been defeated; the German Emperor, Wilhelm II, had abdicated and the German Army had agreed to the armistice to avoid fighting on German soil. But the circumstances of the defeat allowed the legend of the "stab in the back" to fester in the democratic republic that grew out of the debacle. For many Germans, the new government had forever compromised itself by accepting the harsh terms of peace from the French commander, Marshal Ferdinand Foch, in the railcar at Compiègne. Although there had been no alternative, the German people believed they had been robbed of victory, "stabbed in the back" by politicians of the newly declared republic who had betrayed the glorious German army.

The victorious allies actually intensified the blockade of Germany that winter. People already malnourished as a result of wartime shortages suffered further, a bitter memory easily revived in later adversity. Meanwhile, an elected assembly dominated by the Social Democrats, the Catholic Center Party, and the Progressive party met at Weimar, the home of Goethe, to create a constitution for the new polity, consciously removing itself from the Prussian tradition of the German Empire. At its inception, the Weimar Republic was threatened from the Left that sought a revolution on the Russian model, but the German social system even in defeat did not collapse as Russia's had. The conservative forces in Germany were too strong, and the working classes were not especially radical. After the first few months, there was no real danger of a Communist revolution, although the Right used that specter for its own purposes throughout the Weimar Republic. In fact, the Right was a far greater threat. It did not recognize the legitimacy of the republic, yet most of the Weimar bureaucracy and judiciary were rightist leftovers from the empire who were unsympathetic with the republic.

Another disturbing element was the Free Corps. When the war ended, many of the troops refused to disband and formed mercenary units that were hired by the political parties, generally those on the extreme Right or Left. Those still in the army sympathized with these groups and created ties with them. Attracted to this murky realm was a thirty-year-old soldier who had fought in the trenches for four years, had been wounded, and had won the Iron Cross. Despite his fervor for the German cause, Adolf Hitler had never risen above the rank of corporal and was regarded by his captain as an hysteric. The war over, he returned to Munich and went to work for the army as an education officer, assigned to promote the army's concept of nationalism.

Hitler joined the German Workers' Party, a nationalist, anti-Semitic group whose tract *Bolshevism from Moses to Lenin* indicated its ideas.

Within a short time he emerged as its leader and transformed it into the National Socialist Party. In cooperation with General Erich Ludendorff, a celebrated military commander, the party attempted to overthrow the Weimar government in the 1923 Beer Hall Putsch. When it failed, Hitler was tried and found guilty of high treason. But the courts were sympathetic and gave him the minimum sentence, five years. He served only eight and a half months, enough time to write his testament *Mein Kampf*. The legendary Ludendorff was acquitted of any responsibility for the attempted coup.

Germany suffered during this period, its economy ravaged by hyperinflation that had its greatest impact on the middle classes, many of whom developed an intense hatred of those they considered responsible: the French, the Socialists, German liberals, the Jews. But in 1924, under the leadership of the chancellor Gustav Stresemann of the conservative People's Party, the economy and the political life of Germany began to stabilize. Foreign, particularly American, investment built German industry. Germany was admitted to the League of Nations and gained substantial reductions in the huge reparations imposed on it at Versailles. In 1925 Field Marshal Paul von Hindenburg was persuaded to run for president and was elected. Although a monarchist, he supported the republic.

As long as prosperity lasted, the Weimar Republic was able to withstand the pressures assailing it from Right and Left. But the stock market crash on Wall Street caused American investors to withdraw from Germany. Factories closed; unemployment skyrocketed. Heinrich Brüning, the leader of the Catholic Center Party, became chancellor at the head of a coalition government. When the coalition broke down in July 1930, Chancellor Brüning convinced President Hindenburg to dissolve the Reichstag. From that point on, those who had the president's ear controlled the government. Reichstag elections in September confirmed the decline of the moderate forces and the rise of parties on both ends of the political spectrum.[1] In the streets, the Communists and the Nazis fought continuously, creating the perception, if not the reality, of a breakdown in the public order. By 1932, the Nazi militia, the *Sturmabteilung* or S.A., had four hundred thousand members, its ranks swelled by the unemployed. The army, only a quarter the size of the S.A., was helpless to control it, especially since the army leadership viewed the S.A. as a useful counterpoint to the Communists. More and more, the Right came to see Hitler and the National Socialists as distasteful but convenient tools for their own ends.

In the 1932 presidential elections, Hitler ran against Hindenburg. Hitler lost but the campaign gave him national prominence. In physical and mental decline, Hindenburg was a pawn of those closest to him. His advisor General Kurt von Schleicher envisioned a National Front of all moderate and right parties, including the Nazis. He forced Brüning out of the government and arranged for his protégé, Franz von Papen, a member of the extreme right of the Center Party, to become chancellor. Hindenburg developed a great affection for Papen, who conceived a strategy of calling repeated elections in the hope that the Nazis would run out of funds to campaign. The plan seemed to be working. Nazi representation in the Reichstag dropped from 230 seats after the July 1932 elections to 196 seats in the November balloting. Finding Papen too independent, and perhaps jealous of his relationship with Hindenburg, Schleicher brought down his government. Hindenburg insisted that Schleicher assume the role of chancellor. Papen then turned to Hitler, offering to serve as vice-chancellor to Hitler's chancellor and also to convince Hindenburg to make the appointment. The President disdained Hitler, but trusted Papen's promise to control him. On January 30, 1933, Hitler became chancellor legally. In the end Germany rejected democracy, voting in the majority for the two parties that promised to abandon it, the Communists and the Nazis.

As chancellor, Hitler first cultivated the image of a moderate who needed extra-constitutional powers to deal with extremists. The Reichstag Fire on February 27, 1933, provided an excellent opportunity for the Nazis, who portrayed the fire as the beginning of a bloody communist insurrection.[2] A presidential decree suspended all civil guarantees and allowed the national government to take over the state governments. After the March elections, the Nationalists joined the Nazis, still not in the majority, to push through a two-thirds vote giving the government plenary powers to deal with the emergency. The Center Party supported the government. By the end of March, Hitler was a dictator. Through the course of the summer, the other parties and the trade unions were outlawed; the S.A. took over police functions; the first concentration camp, at Dachau, opened.

The Army remained an obstacle to Hitler's consolidation of power. The generals and the wealthy conservative elements who had supported the Nazi movement distrusted the S.A., viewed by the Army as a rival and by the conservatives as the "left-wing" of the Nazi party. To secure their own power, Hermann Göring and Heinrich Himmler encouraged Hitler to move against the S.A. Anticipating Hindenburg's imminent demise, Hitler approached the Army commander Werner von Blomberg with an offer to destroy the S.A. if the Army would support him for president when Hindenburg died. In June 1934 the S.A. was purged; its leaders, including Ernst Röhm, long Hitler's close comrade, were killed. Hitler also took the opportunity to order the deaths of Gregor Strasser, a former lieutenant who had become too independent, Schleicher and others. In August, Hindenburg died. The offices of president and chancellor were merged in Hitler's person, and 88 percent of the electorate approved the move in a plebiscite. Hitler took the title of *Führer;* members of the armed forces took an oath of loyalty to him personally rather than to the constitution or the state.

In office, Hitler moved quickly to restore Germany to full status among nations, particularly regarding rearmament. At the World Disarmament Conference in 1933, German representatives maintained that according to the Versailles Treaty, German disarmament had been a prelude to universal disarmament; since no such disarmament had taken place, Germany should be permitted to rearm. In the fall of 1933, Hitler pulled Germany out of the League of Nations. In March 1935 he abrogated the military provisions of the Versailles Treaty and introduced universal conscription. The *Luftwaffe* came out from under wraps. In no case did other nations offer more than token protest.[3]

In September, 1935, Ralph Barnes arrived on the scene, his Berlin assignment a welcome sign of the *Herald Tribune*'s confidence in him. Despite his regrets at leaving Moscow, he embraced the new challenge. He was anxious to build his language skills and orient himself to his new setting: "So far, I am very much at sea here, but I presume that things will work out all right. I am fortunate in that the Italo-Abyssinian conflict is occupying the principal attention abroad. There is less space for news out of here than there would be otherwise. I need a breathing time." He settled into the *Herald Tribune* offices on Hermann Göring Strasse, while he and Esther moved into a pension until they could find more permanent accommodations. As they had feared, living costs were "fantastic, especially food prices. I believe that one could dine well in New York at hardly more than half the cost here. Several of the correspondents here say that over the past year they have gone into debt." On the other hand, Esther enjoyed the relief from Moscow's proletarian stringencies: "Of course, it has been fun coming to a real city again where you can see nice things, eat out, and window shop."[4]

Barnes began his Berlin tour by gaining access to army maneuvers, something no foreign correspondent had previously managed.

Unable to secure official permission, "I decided to take a chance as an ordinary layman. The maneuvers were announced as 'public.' ... I was the only foreign correspondent with the German news-papermen." Observing the maneuvers, Barnes identified the tactic that later became chillingly familiar, *Blitzkrieg*: "at least in the early stages of the next war, the new German Army, now being constructed with the old Reichswehr as a base, will go forth on wheels almost en masse and at a swift pace."[5]

Having plunged in, Barnes went on to his next challenge with his usual curiosity and earnestness. Esther rode the train as far as Nuremberg with Ralph on his way to cover the annual National Socialist Party Congress, then went on to Zurich. Her letters from there record their initial impressions. She was, she wrote, glad she was not staying in Nuremberg because the train and city were "swarming with Nazis." She was not sure how much she and Ralph would like Berlin: "One is quite conscious of the fact that we are foreigners, and not too welcome. Foreign journalists especially are not welcome." She was "anxious to get back to Ralph so we can start looking for a place to live. It's going to be hard, for rents are high. My idea was to get a place and fix it all up so that I could come home and get the youngsters."[6]

By 1935, the Nazi government had gained full control of the news sources in Germany, both formal and informal, and had limited its citizens' access to foreign news. For foreign correspondents, finding the truth became very complicated, particularly since Germans were afraid to be seen with them because they were often under surveillance. Barnes's experience in developing sources under similarly difficult circumstances in Moscow and Rome served him well. Eleanor Bancroft, who as a young woman worked for the *Herald Tribune* bureau in Berlin, recalled such contacts as "Fatty" and "Oleg's father." Great care had to be exercised. Correspondents were constantly aware that they could not depend on the confidentiality of their mail, telegrams, or telephone calls. They also knew that their homes and offices could be searched at any time.[7]

The Barnes papers include a letter addressed to Esther, dated January 13, 1947. Written in German on the stationery of the Christian Democratic Party, it came from a man named Ernst Lemmer. In it, he asked Esther Barnes to provide a statement defending him against charges of involvement with the Nazis. He reminded her of the "significant relationship" that developed in the late 1930s between Lemmer, Ralph Barnes and Prentice Gilbert, the American *chargé d'affaires* in Berlin, of their many meetings in the Barnes apartment and of their conversations that "served the purpose of

informing American diplomacy on the criminal policy of the Nazis."
One can sympathize with Lemmer, trying to clear his name during
the aggressive de-nazification of the Allied Occupation, even though
his two best witnesses, Barnes and Gilbert, were dead. There is no
record of Esther's response.

Officially, the process of gathering the news, verifying its
authenticity, and understanding what it meant, was freer in Germany
than in the Soviet Union. Direct censorship was not so rigorous
because the more difficult to monitor long distance telephone had
replaced the cable as the most used vehicle to transmit news. Usually
articles were dictated by phone to Paris or London and then sent
across the Atlantic by cable to New York. Nevertheless, correspondents who wanted to keep their jobs imposed a kind of self-
censorship, knowing they would be held responsible for what
appeared in their papers at home. Between 1933 and 1937, Germany
formally expelled nineteen foreign journalists, and five others left
after warnings and harassment. During the same period, thirteen
Jewish correspondents chose to leave. Shirer wrote that correspondents were anxious to avoid expulsion because they were
never sure their employers would understand. Louis Lochner, the
Associated Press correspondent, summarized the direction he and
his colleagues received from their superiors: "to tell no untruth, but
to report only as much of the truth without distorting the picture, as
would enable us to remain at our posts. Ejection was the one thing
our superiors did not want."[8] It was a difficult line to walk.

More than eight hundred thousand people crowded into the
medieval city of Nuremberg to celebrate Nazi triumphs. "The Party
Day of Freedom," Germany's escape from the military limitations of
Versailles, was the official theme of the week-long congress. But
another theme quickly emerged in a special edition of *Der Stürmer*,
the viciously anti-Semitic party newspaper edited by Julius Streicher.
Barnes reported its headline: "Murderers from the Beginning of
History—Jewish Bolshevism from Moses to the Comintern." Hitler's
proclamation, read to the opening session, warned of the enemies:
"Jewish Marxism and parliamentary democracy which is related to
it," "politically and morally pernicious Center parties,"and "certain
elements of stupid and reactionary bourgeoisie." While Hitler did
not propose "a campaign against Christianity as such," he promised
to "combat those clergymen who have mistaken their calling, who
should have been politicians and not pastors." The main thing was
to unite in the face of "the Jewish Bolshevist danger."[9]

Hitler called a special session of the Reichstag to meet in
Nuremberg during the Congress. The Reichstag's president, Hermann

Göring, proclaimed "laws for the protection of German blood and German honor" that forbade marriage and extra-marital relations between Jews and Germans, prohibited the employment of Germans in Jewish households, and deprived Jews of their German citizenship. Göring argued a need to preserve "the Germanic and Nordic purity of the race" and to protect "our women and girls with every means at our disposal." Barnes wrote that the violently anti-Jewish elements in the party were now clearly in the ascendancy, and he anticipated a series of moves "with the elimination of all the Jews in Germany as their ultimate aim." He noted the dissent of Hjalmar Schacht, Reichsbank president and Minister of Economics, who opposed action against the Jews that might endanger the German economy.[10]

Probably with the help of his *Encyclopedia Britannica,* Barnes compared for *Herald Tribune* readers the Nazi measures to those of the Third and Fourth Lateran Councils of the Catholic Church in the twelfth and thirteenth centuries, that "renewed the series of old restrictions including one forbidding gentiles to enter the service of Jews or be otherwise subordinated to them." He noted that the edicts of the Councils laid the foundations for the ghetto system that spread rapidly through Europe and disappeared finally only with the capitulation of Rome to Italian troops in 1870.

> The decisions of the Lateran Councils and the subsequent developments find striking parallels in the anti-Jewish laws passed by the Reichstag at Nuremberg this week, and in the additional points in the anti-Jewish program to be carried out. Apparently, the ultimate aim—to be realized over a period of years—is to make it impossible for a Jew to earn his living in Germany ... it is important to note that during the earlier periods of persecution the Jews had recourses which are not open to them in Germany today. Before, there were two avenues of escape: through flight and baptism. Now that the Nazis have made the issue purely racial rather than religious, baptism no longer is an effective solution. The 50,000 Jewish Christians in Germany today are hardly in a more favorable position than are 500,000 Israelites who have retained their faith.

Barnes also noted that "in the past Jews fleeing from persecution in one country often were welcomed in another because of the wealth which they took with them. This was the case with the Marranos, Jews who fled from Spain to the Netherlands at the end of the sixteenth century. Today Jews who emigrate from Germany are not permitted to take their wealth."[11]

From his coverage of the 1935 Nazi Party Congress until he left Germany in March of 1939, Barnes recorded the ever-intensifying campaign against the Jews. In her exhaustive study of American press coverage of the coming of the Holocaust, Deborah Lipstadt, a scholar at Emory University, included Ralph Barnes in her short list of nine reporters "who understood the true nature of Nazism and its fanatic hatred of Jews." Barnes worked hard to convey to his readers the virulence of Nazi anti-Semitism, not only reporting events but also quoting extensively from the speeches of Nazi leaders and from German newspapers and other internal propaganda. He painstakingly recorded the pre-conditioning that made the Holocaust possible.[12]

Back in Berlin, the German government appeared to welcome the intensification of the Ethiopian crisis, since it distracted international attention from Germany's expansionist policies. Long the object of Italian nationalist aims, Ethiopia, or Abyssinia, was an independent African nation bordering the Italian colony of Somaliland. In 1896, Italian troops had suffered a humiliating defeat at the hands of the Emperor of Abyssinia. Mussolini was determined to avenge that defeat and to enlarge Italy's colonial empire. Through border incidents and other pressures, he provoked Emperor Haile Selassie into an appeal to the League of Nations. Anxious negotiations through the spring and summer of 1935 yielded no settlement, and Italian forces invaded Ethiopia on October 3. Germany took advantage of the distraction of the powers to pursue its aims in Austria, where Italy acted as the only brake on German designs.[13]

The Reich's domestic policies suggested Nazi intentions. Barnes noted some restiveness because of a food shortage largely created by the government's determination to make Germany self-sufficient in foodstuffs. The German people were "paying for an ardent nationalism to which they may or may not have given active support." Although he warned against exaggerating the unrest, Barnes wrote of a good deal of grumbling. Special courts had been set up to handle those whose words or actions were considered "detrimental to the state and its institutions." According to Barnes's information, the police were watching closely the people in the butter lines for expressions of dissatisfaction.[14]

A French expert, Lelarge d'Ervau, concluded that Nazi policies had put the country in a much better position to withstand a blockade than during World War I. D'Ervau's study was printed in the journal of the French general staff and, Barnes conceded, was partly intended "to awaken the French public to the alleged German menace." Nevertheless Barnes found D'Ervau's conclusions compelling. Aside from foodstuffs, Germany was addressing its shortage of raw materials through the accumulation of strategic stores. It had a very advanced industrial base, a transportation system with excellent railways, and "a new network of superb motor highways of a military importance which cannot be underestimated."[15] The Nazi leaders maintained that their efforts were defensive in nature. Göring noted in a speech that "we are working night and day in three shifts." He continued: "We now have an example, comrades, of what it means to be defenseless and at the mercy of other nations armed to the teeth. Adolf Hitler has saved Germany from becoming another Ethiopia."[16]

D'Ervau's was not the only warning that Barnes recorded. An article by Winston Churchill, British Chancellor of the Exchequer and First Lord of the Admiralty during World War I, but now in political eclipse, attracted considerable attention. Barnes quoted extensively from the piece. Churchill wrote, "We cannot tell whether Hitler will be the man who will once again let loose upon the world a war in which civilization will irretrievably succumb, or whether he will go down in history as the man who restored honor and peace of mind to the great German nation and brought them back, serene, helpful and strong, to the European family circle." Still, he warned that "Hitler's triumphant career has been borne forward not only by a passionate love of Germany, but by currents of hatred so intense as to sear the souls of those who swim upon them." Churchill's examples were the purge of June 30, 1934, and the policy toward the Jews: "Every kind of persecution, grave or petty, on world-famous scientists, writers and composers, at the top, to wretched little Jewish children in the nation's schools, was practised, was glorified and still is being practised and glorified." Finally he asked, "Can we really believe that a hierarchy and society built upon such deeds can be entrusted with possession of the most prodigious military machine yet planned among men?" Churchill's query brought German protests to the British government and a ban on the *Strand* magazine in which it had appeared.[17]

Fall 1935 saw Hitler respond to internal opposition to Nazi measures against the Jews. Resistance came from the churches and from the financial community led by Minister of Economics Hjalmar Schacht. Hitler launched a campaign against the Christian churches, partly because of their stand against government anti-Semitism and partly because the Nazis were determined to eliminate any independent focus of strength or loyalty within Germany. So-called neutral committees were created to govern the Evangelical Protestant Church in an attempt to quiet church opposition. But the Confessional faction of the church rejected a committee-issued manifesto sanctioning the Nazi principles of "race, blood and soil." Barnes documented the emergence of Pastor Martin Niemöller as the leader of the Christian resistance. The former submarine commander defied Nazi orders, telling his congregation, "we must remember Martin Luther and the power of faith. We had hoped during these days for a relaxation of tension. Instead, a new and violent storm has burst over our heads. But, strong in faith, we are afraid of nothing."[18]

Government reaction was swift. The church's publications and pronouncements were censored, its right to train and ordain clergy was restricted, its financial underpinnings were stripped away. Barnes's articles educated his American readers, accustomed to the separation of church and state, about the German churches' dependence on the government for financial support. Niemöller was barred from speaking. He and his associates were threatened with prosecution for treason. Barnes found the situation for Catholics at least as tense: "Feeling has been running high among Catholic church folk for a long time because of the Nazi system of mocking their priests in public speeches, in newspaper articles and caricatures. These feelings were not smoothed by sentences of imprisonment for Catholics who removed Nazi anti-Catholic posters from the walls of their houses and cloisters." He wrote of the Nazis' early expectation that the Church would be one of the pillars of their power. Instead "it has become increasingly evident that these hopes have been shattered and that the Church, both Protestant and Roman Catholic, offers more tangible resistance against the 'new Germany' than any other body."[19]

In the meantime, German Jews, fearful of new confiscatory laws, rushed to sell their businesses and their assets in a vain effort to salvage some level of financial security. Their selling drove down prices on the Berlin Stock Exchange, while buyers paid only a third or a fourth, sometimes only 5 or 10 percent, of the value of their businesses. Schacht protested to Hitler, less out of concern for the

Jews than because of the effect on the German economy and on German standing abroad. Although Schacht was regularly attacked by hard-line Nazis such as Julius Streicher, Hitler appeared for the moment to waver. Barnes noted again the prevalent expectation that "the Nazi regime gradually would shift to a more moderate course."[20]

During November, Esther and Ralph left Berlin for a trip to Vienna because, as Esther explained in a letter, "Ralph thinks that Vienna may come into some prominence soon." Their visit gave Esther the chance to write more openly about their situation: "I guess we will have to ask the HT to help us out about bringing the youngsters over because I don't see any chance of our saving enough for me even to get home. Also please caution Father B about writing so plainly about our sending money to Oregon. We are not supposed to send one cent of our income or even to have any of our income outside of Germany. Not even for insurance or our children. We are expecting to be jumped on any minute but until they do we won't look for trouble. These dictators haven't the least bit of sense and in some ways the Germans are worse than the Russians. They are heaps more efficient and decidedly more pigheaded."[21]

Barnes reported his Vienna observations in mail articles that appeared in the *Herald Tribune* two weeks later. Austrian tensions had eased somewhat. Berlin had cautioned the Austrian Nazis that "the time was not ripe" for unification with Germany or *Anschluss*. Barnes wrote, "In the period of despair immediately following the war Austria would gladly have become incorporated in the German Reich, but the entente ruled otherwise. Now that Hitler has shown his hand, the majority of the Austrian people are opposed definitely to *anschluss*." He found the government of Austria in a dilemma. For a number of years, Austria had relied on Mussolini for support against threats, internal and external, to the country's sovereignty, specifically in July 1934 when Mussolini thwarted an attempted Nazi coup by moving Italian forces to the Brenner Pass. Now, Mussolini's Ethiopian adventure distracted him from Austria's concerns while Austria's closeness to Italy endangered her relations with Britain and France.[22]

While Austria too was under a dictatorship, that of Kurt von Schuschnigg, Barnes concluded that it was rather mild. Both the Nazis and the Socialists were open in their opposition to the regime; political cabarets indulged in satirical swipes at the government without police interference. Looming also was the possibility of a Hapsburg restoration, a prospect not unwelcome to many in the government but violently opposed by both the Nazis and the Left.[23]

Back in Berlin, Barnes returned to the Ethiopian crisis. The British
and French governments had been embarrassed by the Hoare-Laval
Pact granting concessions to Mussolini in Ethiopia. Named for their
two foreign ministers, Samuel Hoare and Pierre Laval, the pact was
interpreted as an agreement to look the other way on Ethiopia in
order to maintain good relations with Mussolini. Although Germany
was not an active party to the negotiations, she nevertheless had a
telling effect: "It might be argued that if the Nazi 'menace' were
non-existent, the ill-fated Anglo-French peace proposals never
would have been made. Sir Samuel Hoare would not have resigned
as British Foreign Secretary, Edouard Herriot would not have thrown
up the leadership of the Radical Socialist party in France, and the
British and French governments would not have been shaken to
their foundations."[24]

Domestically, Germans faced a Christmas troubled by food
shortages and by deeper concerns: "The expression commonly heard
in Berlin during these pre-festival days is 'Nothing will happen until
after Christmas.' " But Berliners feared further moves against the
opposition within both the Catholic and Evangelical Churches. Many
of the faithful were offended by the Nazi celebration of the Winter
Solstice with its overtones of the pagan past. For Jews, the
atmosphere was even more menacing. In a year-end article reviewing
1935, Barnes pointed to rearmament and the Nuremberg legislation
against the Jews as the key events.[25]

Through the holidays, the Barneses stayed in the apartment of
London *Times* correspondent Jimmy Holburn while his family was
away. They had dinner Christmas night with Bill Shirer, whom they
had known in Paris, and his Austrian wife Tess. Esther's reports of
their holiday round of parties suggest that they had found a
welcoming circle in Berlin. Esther had finally secured a suitable,
although expensive, apartment near the Tiergarten. They moved in
right after Christmas, recovering furniture and other belongings
stored since Esther's 1931-2 stay in Paris.

Particularly worried about Joan's situation in Salem, both Ralph
and Esther were anxious to reunite their family. Ralph's parents'
perilous finances complicated their plans. In a letter a friend carried
to New York for mailing, Esther was able to write to her mother and
sister and take them into her confidence about her in-laws'
circumstances:

You have probably been wondering just why we don't come to some decision about the youngsters. You don't know and I am not supposed to tell but you will have to know sometime. We are having to pay $100 a month on the interest and mortgage on the house or we will lose the house and all the mill stocks. ... If we can just hold on until next year and the mill moratorium is over, then we will have saved money. If Mr. Barnes should lose everything then you can imagine what he would do and even if he didn't we would still have them to support all their lives. ...I know the Barneses feel that we can't afford to take Joan and still help them. They must not have that idea. Goodness knows into what depths they will sink when we do take her away. She does need to be with children and not with Nonna B. [Mrs. Barnes] all the time. Can you write your advice—cover up the financial side some way so the censor won't learn too much. All letters are opened to see whether money is enclosed. I don't know how much they read or remember.[26]

Pressed as they were by the financial situation and by their concerns for their children, Ralph and Esther were acutely aware that their problems paled in comparison to those of the people around them. Through January and February 1936, Barnes's stories largely focused on the Nazi government's further moves against the Jews and the churches, and the domestic reaction they engendered. The Confessional Church called for "a return to the Catacombs" rather than submitting to the government-sponsored program that would mean "the Nazification of the Protestant Church in Germany."[27] Barnes wrote of an American Jewish writer, Elias Tobenkin, who interviewed Germans in many walks of life and reported their expressions of sympathy for their Jewish neighbors. Tobenkin also met Jews who felt "they must not do anything to bring disgrace on themselves or their country—Germany."[28]

The Catholic bishops of Germany issued a pastoral letter defying government edicts and cautioning the faithful against efforts "to shatter the faith of old and young and to pave the way for a new hedonism." Barnes interpreted the letter as implying strongly that Catholics should not read Nazi propaganda literature or attend Nazi meetings and training camps. At St. Matthew's church in Berlin, he heard the priest follow the reading of the pastoral letter with a strong statement that the Church would continue to accept true converts, Jew or Gentile: "When Christ brought His message to this world, He did so for all mankind, and not for especial races." Despite its 1933 Concordat with the Vatican, the Nazi government responded by an attack on the Catholic Youth Movement, first arresting its leader, Monsignor Ludwig Wolker, then a hundred others associated with the organization. Barnes's sources suggested that those arrested would be charged with fomenting a Communist conspiracy, information soon confirmed by "inspired" editorials accusing the youth groups of high treason against the Nazi state involving "cooperation with the Comintern and with Soviet diplomats." He thought the real motive simpler: "The leaders of the Reich have already announced their plans for mobilizing the children of the land in compulsory Nazi youth organizations, and they are not prepared to permit a body such as the Catholic Church, which is not within the totalitarian structure, to conduct a strong competing youth movement." Barnes was reminded of the *Kulturkampf,* the great nineteenth-century battle between Chancellor Otto von Bismarck and the Catholic Church, one of the few contests that Bismarck lost. In this case, he concluded, Hitler had the advantage of greater control over German society.[29]

The Confessional Church too faced a new onslaught. By now nine thousand of the sixteen thousand evangelical churches adhered to Martin Niemöller's movement in opposition to the government that continued to suppress its publications and threaten its leaders. Barnes noted: "It is commonly said in Germany today that the rise of the Nazi regime has resulted in a closer co-operation between the Catholics and the Protestants of the Reich than at any time since the Reformation."[30]

With the 1936 Olympic Games coming to Germany, the government issued a new book calling for the political education of German athletes, since "non-political, so-called 'neutral' sportsmen" were "unthinkable." The book referred to Jews as "surpassed even by the lowest Negro tribes," while maintaining that the Catholic Church was "inimical to the people." German athletes were to be educated in Nazi principles: "Those who do not yet understand the task which faces our efforts in German history must become adjusted to the fact that National Socialism declines to grant the honors of victory to those athletes and sportsmen who, through their behavior or attitude, show they fail to comprehend or decline to comprehend the fateful questions which they face." Victors must be "pioneers in political influence."[31]

German athletes were not the only focus of Nazi efforts to "educate." As Barnes had anticipated, the previously voluntary membership in Nazi youth organizations was now made compulsory for all children ten and over. In the *Herald Tribune,* Barnes observed that "no feature of contemporary European dictatorships is more impressive than the way in which they have brought every possible agency to bear to win their youth." He pointed to Italian and Soviet successes in propagandizing their youth and predicted: "If, despite economic woes and the like, the Nazi regime succeeds in holding together for the coming five years, it will be in a position to tap new sources of strength which—other things remaining equal—will have an increasingly stimulating effect. By the end of that period those Germans who are in their impressionable early 'teens today will have been successfully propagandized, and will begin to make their weight felt in the Nazi state."[32] Barnes's estimate of the timing coincides almost exactly with the onset of the Holocaust.

10

The movement of the troops at noon was timed to
coincide with the extraordinary session of the
Reichstag in the Kroll Opera House in Berlin, before
which Chancellor Adolf Hitler, amid deafening cheers,
announced the unilateral scrapping of those clauses of
the Versailles "diktat" which provided for a permanent
demilitarized region on the German side of the Franco-
German frontier.

The Locarno pact, based in part on the provision for
the demilitarized zone, collapsed as German soldiers set
foot on the soil of the area from which they had been
barred. Hitler completed the liquidation of the Locarno
treaty by declaring that from today Germany does not
consider herself bound by its provisions.

Ralph Barnes, *Herald Tribune,* March 8, 1936, from Berlin

Although European attention continued to focus on the Ethiopian
crisis, Barnes cautioned his readers on Sunday, February 2, 1936,
that "the real problem is Germany." His article showed how the
lessons of 1918 were driving Hitler's rearmament and his
mobilization of the German economy. Kaiser Wilhelm had a
formidable army at the beginning of World War I but failed to prepare
for a long war. Hitler would not make the same mistake. Barnes
restated the elements of Hitler's program to equip the country for
war: "the provision of domestic substitutes for products such as
petroleum which Germany is lacking; the construction of a superb
network of motor highways; the stimulation of the motor vehicle
industry; the relocation of essential industries away from the
frontiers; the control of foreign trade ... to make the Reich relatively

self-sufficient in foodstuffs; the mobilization of children from ten to eighteen years old in compulsory youth organizations and the provision of a period of disciplined labor for youth in the semi-military *Arbeitdienst*." These efforts were not without cost. Barnes estimated that German workers had seen a 20 percent reduction in real wages over three years. Over the same period, the gold reserves of the Reichsbank had dropped from nine hundred million marks to less than eighty million. Taxes and government debt had increased substantially. Nevertheless, Barnes reminded his readers of the advantage a dictatorship like Germany had over the democracies, at least temporarily, in the control it could exert over its economy.[1]

On February 22, Barnes wrote an article downplaying rumors that Germany's next move would be the military occupation of the Rhineland, the German territory adjacent to France, Luxembourg, Belgium, and Holland that had been demilitarized in the Versailles Treaty. While recognizing its importance to the Reich government, he found general consensus that action had been postponed, partly because of "warnings from Paris and London" and partly because the army was not ready. While subsequent scholarship has proven him right about the military, his conclusion was wrong. Although Army leaders opposed a move into the Rhineland, Hitler soon overrode their objections.[2] Barnes's first clue to his mistake came in an article he found in an influential German economic weekly, *Der Deutsche Volkswirt*. The editor, who was close to the government, hinted that Hitler would demand remilitarization, particularly in light of the recent Franco-Soviet mutual assistance treaty. The move would abrogate the Locarno Pact of 1925 in which Germany, France, Belgium, Italy and Great Britain had guaranteed the current border arrangements in western Europe. Late on March 6, Hitler called for a special session of the Reichstag for the next day to be preceded by a meeting with the ambassadors of the other four Locarno signatories. Still, Barnes wrote: "The immediate occupation of the Rhineland by German troops is thought unlikely."[3]

Barnes's March 7 article set the scene:

> The delicate European peace structure was shaken today as German troops marched into the demilitarized Rhine zone in violation of the Versailles Treaty, occupying the principal cities of the area for the first time since the World War. The movement of the troops at noon was timed to coincide with the extraordinary session of the Reichstag in the Kroll Opera House in Berlin, before which Chancellor Adolf Hitler, amid deafening cheers, announced the unilateral scrapping of those clauses of the Versailles "diktat" which provided for a permanent demilitarized region on the German side of the Franco-German border.

Hitler explained his action as the necessary German response to the Franco-Soviet Pact and included "two firm resolutions:" "First, we resolve not to give way before any force or any power in connection with the re-establishment of our honor, and to submit honorably to the most severe privations rather than capitulate. Second, we resolve now, more firmly than before, to work toward understanding between the peoples of Europe and especially for understanding with our western peoples and neighbors. Now, at the end of three years, and with today, I believe I may consider concluded the struggle to obtain equal rights for Germany." While offering new and more comprehensive peace treaties, he finished his speech with a warning: "I will not permit the terror of the Communist International dictatorship of hatred to be spread over the German people. I tremble for Europe at the thought of what would happen to our old, overcrowded continent if the chaos of the bolshevik revolution were to prove successful through the penetration westward of that destructive Asiatic way of looking at the world."[4]

Hitler then dissolved the Reichstag and called for elections on March 29 as a plebiscite on his actions. The move into the Rhineland was followed by a flurry of diplomatic activity, but by no military response. The Germans maintained publicly that the army had been prepared to meet resistance. Postwar access to the archives and to some of the military leadership has led scholars to conclude that the German army planned to withdraw if it encountered military opposition. Hitler himself later admitted that the time following the army's march into the Rhineland was "the most nerve-racking in my life. If the French had then marched into the Rhineland, we would have had to withdraw with our tails between our legs, for the military resources at our disposal would have been wholly inadequate even for moderate resistance."[5] But no one called his bluff. While the western powers conferred in London, Hitler proclaimed his peaceful intentions: "I do not desire military glory. I am looking for an entirely different kind of glory. In fact, the only monument I should care to have is one as a peacemaker."[6]

French protests did cause the German government to take certain precautionary measures, but Barnes concluded that a French and Belgian military response in the absence of British support would have little effect. While he maintained that the Reich was "not yet ready for war," Barnes recognized the potential of the panzer units and the air force. Ordinary German people had little grasp of the seriousness of the crisis and accepted Hitler's explanation of the move. Diplomatic activity continued with the censure of Germany by the League of Nations and a variety of proposals to calm French fears. Hitler at first rejected an invitation for German diplomats to join the London meetings but shortly acquiesced, apparently as a result of internal pressures, brought particularly by Schacht.[7]

Esther's letters reflect the uncertainties of the period: "We haven't any idea how this will all turn out. We don't expect war, but there have been some rather heated remarks made. Ralph says that I am to start home the minute that things should break. It won't be a matter of days, but of hours, until things would be rather warm. We can only hope for the best."[8]

While the diplomatic maneuvering proceeded to its inconclusive end, the election campaign was being waged in Germany. Hitler and his lieutenants toured the country, with special attention to the Rhineland, making the case for support of the Reich government. Not that there was much question in Barnes's mind as to how the election would turn out: "Tomorrow the German people will go to the polls—spontaneously or otherwise—and cast their ballots so *Reichsführer* Adolf Hitler can convince the world that 'like one man' they stand back of him and his policies of 'peace on earth and freedom.' " Still, as he later wrote his parents, "the balloting was pretty much of a farce, yet the great majority of the German people approve Hitler's action in occupying the Rhine Zone."[9]

Covering both the crisis and the electoral campaign was a challenge. Barnes's by-line appeared in the *Herald Tribune* no less than thirty times between March 6 and April 5, for the most part over articles of considerable substance. The exhausting period put a strain on his family life. Esther wrote: "The amount of time I see Ralph now would almost make one think he was doing military service. Like he's coming home weekends or something. He hasn't had dinner at home in the evening since the Reichstag meeting on March 7th. I get him out of bed, see that his clothes are ready, feed him and he is off to work. He is usually so tired and sleepy, engrossed in thought about his work that we hardly have a chance to converse. He was feeling partly all in until the sun started shining a few days ago and now he looks much better. Work is not so pressing since the storm has moved somewhat to London."[10]

It was also a time of self-doubt for Ralph. In a March 22 letter to his parents, Esther wrote: "He always feels that his stories are not what they should be, so naturally his mind is never off his work. Some of the New York papers came in today, and he was feeling a little cheered up. Thought that they weren't quite so bad as he had expected. I don't think that Ralph will ever get over worrying that way, so I don't try to pull him out of the depths he gets into at times."

By April, he was in better humor and wrote home: "Things went badly for a time just before the Rhineland invasion, I hope that now I am in the swing, and that there will not be another slump ... I'm packing in background, so that soon I should be functioning more intelligently."[11]

Despite the pressures of covering the Rhineland crisis, Barnes continued through the winter and spring of 1936 to share everyday German life with *Herald Tribune* readers. He wrote of the new government initiative to increase the birth rate through a monthly stipend to families with more than four children and of another directive which said the failure of candidates for party leadership to marry by age twenty-six would be construed "as a reflection on the candidate's power of decision, his personal courage and his attitude toward life," ironic in light of the fact that Hitler had never married. Barnes provided a sampling of the realities of life under a totalitarian regime: the banning of Charlie Chaplin's film "Modern Times;" the elimination of Goethe's poetry from the schools; the arming of boys from ten to fourteen with javelins to help convince them of "the invincibility of the German race;" the expanded use of the *"Heil* Hitler" salute in the military; and the development of a "Germanized" form of the Sermon on the Mount.[12]

The rigors and uncertainties of life in Berlin and, even more, international tensions made Ralph and Esther hesitate to bring their daughters from Oregon to Berlin: "If there is any chance of sanctions, or anything like that, this is no place for Joan and Suzanne."[13] But ultimately the decision was made. Esther's sister Mary would bring six-year-old Joan and four-year-old Suzanne to Germany in June. Before his daughters' arrival, however, Ralph had his own opportunity to travel. The new German airship, the *Hindenburg*, would be making its maiden voyage to the United States, and he wanted to be on it. The zeppelins themselves were a cause of controversy, since their designer and builder, Hugo Eckener, had refused to allow the *Hindenburg* and its sister ship the *Graf Zeppelin* to be used for propaganda purposes during the recent electoral campaign.[14] Ralph left home for the airship's base at Fredrichshafen not at all sure he would manage to secure passage. He learned just a half hour before takeoff that he would be among the fifty-one passengers and fifty-six crew members aboard. A photograph shows Barnes at his typewriter in one of the luxurious airship's lounges. From the passenger list, it appears he was the only correspondent from an American newspaper on board, although the three U. S. wire services were represented. Barnes radioed his stories of the *Hindenburg* and the sixty-one-hour flight, describing the airship's amenities and the view of icebergs, whales and fishing boats as it flew 450 feet above the Atlantic.[15]

After landing at Lakehurst, New Jersey, Barnes spent several days in New York and Washington. He wrote his parents to describe the visit and explain why he could not come home: "You can imagine how much I should like to come to Oregon to see all of you, but you will readily understand why I think it better not to come. The trip on the Zeppelin proved a great personal experience, and I am indebted to the paper for it. I don't want to carry things too far." He was encouraged by his welcome in New York: "The talks here have been more helpful than those a year and a half ago. I'm getting many ideas. No one seems to have any serious complaints with the Berlin bureau—only helpful suggestions."[16]

His trip to Washington provided worthwhile contacts:

I returned last night from two delightful and profitable days in Washington. I saw a good deal of Al Warner, the Washington correspondent for the Herald Tribune, *and of other men in the bureau, two of whom I had known quite well before. Also, I saw Joe Baird and Stan Richardson, of Moscow days—both are now stationed there. I attended two of Secretary of State Hull's press conferences; and had a talk with Under-Secretary of State Phillips at his office. The Chief of the Press Bureau of the State Department arranged a long talk with an expert in the trade section of the Department. … Thursday night, I attended the party at the White House which the President and Mrs. Roosevelt gave for the Press.[17]*

His visit to New York also gave Barnes the chance to lay the groundwork for a project which had been taking shape in his mind: "Lee Stowe took me up to see Knopf, the publisher, about my 'book' on *Under Three Dictatorships* and Maurice Hindus took me to see Harrison-Smith, publishers, regarding the same matter. The 'book' is still in the back of my head but it was well to see the publishers anyway.[18]

Barnes sailed from New York with his old colleague from Paris *Herald* days, Al Laney, now a sportswriter for the *Herald Tribune* on his way to the Berlin Olympics. Another shipmate was Thomas W. Lamont, the J. P. Morgan partner who had been a delegate to the Young Conference on reparations that Barnes covered with Lee Stowe in 1929. They discussed the German financial outlook over lunch on board. Otherwise Barnes passed his time with deck tennis, ping pong, and swimming, "plus a small amount of dancing," and read Walter Duranty's account of his Moscow years, *I Write As I Please.* After the ship landed at Southampton, Ralph went on to London and Paris before arriving in Berlin on May 29.[19] He found Esther immersed in preparations for the children's arrival. Ralph went to Hamburg to meet the girls and their Aunt Mary Parounagian. After such a long time apart, Suzanne asked her aunt, "Is that my Papa Ralph?" Soon they were comfortable together, with the children climbing all over Ralph during the three and a half hour train trip to Berlin. Even Esther seemed a bit strange to the girls when she met them at the station. Joan told her she did not look "like Mamma." With her usual knack, Esther had readied the apartment. Mary found it "lovely, in a very nice district, the diplomatic district, to be exact, with a very chic entrance. Each room is very spacious, with the exception of the central bedroom, which Esther and I have. Ralph is sleeping in the sun-room, which is very attractive, with a red-tiled floor, day-bed, unpainted wood furniture, and red accessories. ... The children's room is very cute. The huge windows, which open out, are curtained with a pretty blue."[20]

Becoming a family required some adjustments, particularly in light of the demands that kept Ralph at work late into the night. "Mornings

Joan and Suzanne Barnes with Hermann Göring's lion cub at the Berlin Zoo.

are quite impossible around here as we devote all of our efforts to keeping the girls toned down so Ralph can sleep." When he was available, he enjoyed his daughters, who remember the games and funny rituals of their life with him. He was occasionally a disciplinarian; Joan remembers him as the only person who ever spanked her, "And I needed it." Having each been an "only child" in their respective grandmothers' houses, they had to learn to share the attention of their parents. Ralph too had to make an adjustment, according to his daughters. Although they had endured long separations during their twelve-year marriage, he was accustomed to Esther's total attention and availability when they were together.[21]

Mary found her sister's life in Berlin interesting if very expensive. She toured the Berlin area extensively and reported her impressions in her letters home, enjoying the historical and cultural aspects of the region, but disturbed by the pervasive Nazi presence. She also provided insights into Ralph's work routine: "all of Ralph's stories are telephoned out. He has two regular calls each night to Paris, 7:45 and 11:45. The stories are picked up there by a machine and then cabled to N.Y. Quite a wonderful system. The Bourse and weather reports always go at 7:45, a financial expert writes them."[22]

~

While his family settled in, Barnes was preoccupied with the economic and international policies of the Reich government. In a cautionary piece, he quoted Dr. Goebbels: "Our whole strength and courage are required in the struggle for the attainment of complete equality of rights for the German people." "Equality of rights" had become, Barnes wrote, a codeword for the "right of all Germans to live under the Reich government. Hitler still hopes to include within the borders of the Reich at least part of those territories in eastern and southeastern Europe which are predominantly German in population or for a long period under German sovereignty, and to accomplish much along that line without overt aggression." It would, he wrote, "seem fair to ask whether other great powers should attempt, through the League, to negotiate agreements which Hitler— even though he were to agree to them—would be sure to violate. Unless Geneva were fully prepared to punish the violation, the only result would be to lower further its prestige, which already is at a very low ebb."[23]

In the domestic realm, Barnes had predicted that the government would undertake no new moves because of the coming Olympics. That restraint was severely taxed by a four-thousand-word memorial issued by the leaders of the Confessional movement, including Pastor Niemöller. First sent directly to the government and later circulated, it denounced the escalating deification of Hitler and added: "It is a heavy burden for the Evangelical conscience to realize that in Germany, which purports to be a state in which the law is supreme, there are still concentration camps, and that the activities of the Gestapo are not subject to legal control." Explicit in its charges, the memorial cited Nazi spokesmen like Göring, Rosenberg, and Goebbels, as well as listing specific offenses.[24]

The Reich government made no immediate reply. In fact, it was preparing for the Olympics by carefully cleansing Berlin of all evidence of the anti-Jewish campaign and of persecution of the Catholic and Confessional Churches. So successful was this effort that when Barnes and Bill Shirer lunched with a group of American businessmen visiting for the Olympics, they were chided for being "unfair" to the Nazis. The group, which included Norman Chandler, the publisher of the *Los Angeles Times*, had met with Dr. Goebbels and was impressed with what seemed to be a pleasant, well-run country. Another summer visitor was Charles Lindbergh. His impression of the destructive potential of aviation led to a toast in which he said, "To bombers, may they fly slower; to pursuit planes, may they fly swifter." To curb the bombers, he called for a security system that "rests in intelligence not in force." Barnes talked to Lindbergh briefly, off the record. He reported that the aviator remembered him from Leningrad and Moscow, "without my suggesting it." Lindbergh was "jovial" although, as Barnes reminded his parents, "Lindbergh is highly unpopular with American newspapermen, on the whole, because he is so touchy about publicity. One can understand that, in part, because of the kidnapping episode."[25]

To Barnes's relief, his paper sent sportswriters to cover the actual athletic competition at the Olympic Games. He provided material on the extensive construction and other preparations for the Games, their opening in late June and closing in mid-August, and "color" pieces. When an American woman managed to get close enough to kiss Hitler, he reported her elation and the consternation of the Führer's guards. He, Esther and Mary attended a number of events and sent their impressions in letters to their families. When Germany finished first, the United States second and Italy third in the Games, Avery Brundage, the president of the United States Olympic Committee, called for American organizers to address the challenge of countries like Germany and Italy where athletics were organized on a national basis.[26]

The Olympic Games had hardly ended when the Confessional Church resumed its defiance of the government with a two-thousand-word letter read in all its churches. Barnes was able to obtain the text in advance for the *Herald Tribune*. He was present at the Jesus Christ Church in Dahlem when Pastor Niemöller read the message to his congregation, ending with a charge to action: "We call upon the servants of the church to bear witness to the Gospel of Jesus Christ without compromise and without fear of men. Many have been sent to prison and concentration camp, have had to suffer expulsion and other trials. We do not know what may still be in store for us. But whatever this may be we are bound to be obedient to our Heavenly Father!" Again, there was no immediate response from the German authorities.[27]

The Roman Catholic Church, on the other hand, seemed to be moving to a rapprochement with the government, as Hitler ordered the re-examination of all pending court cases against Catholic priests and religious. Driving this compromise was the church's reaction to the Spanish Civil War and its appeal to Hitler for a "church-state truce as a means of forming a united front against 'world bolshevism.' "[28] The Spanish Civil War began in July, when a group of generals rebelled against the government, only to find that the two sides were relatively even in strength. Instead of a quick "surgical" coup, the country was confronted with a civil war between the Loyalists, who supported the government, and the Nationalists, who favored the insurgency. The intrinsically Spanish issues involved in the Civil War were soon lost as it became internationalized. Depending on one's outlook, the Loyalists were viewed as communists or as parliamentary democrats, and the Nationalists as fascists or as the saviors of Christian civilization. As the legitimate government, the Loyalists sought support from France and Great Britain, but were largely disappointed. They then turned to the Soviet Union which directly and indirectly through the Communist parties around the world provided weapons and manpower. The Nationalists received increasing support from Italy and Germany, who defied efforts to cut off arms supplies to both sides and who soon put troops and aircraft into the war.[29]

In an article the *Herald Tribune* featured prominently in its Sunday, August 30, edition, Barnes compared the European situation with that of 1913, finding parallels in "a vicious circle of accusations and counter-accusations, accompanied by an equally vicious circle of armaments" along with the preoccupation with the "Russian peril." The article also pointed to trends in journalism, citing a book by Theodore Wolf, the former editor of the *Berliner Tageblatt* , in which

Wolf described pre-war press campaigns "in terms he might well employ today." Wolf had written:

> *Everywhere all too unrestrained, the press shattered the air with its cries, and every time a pause seemed to be coming, it howled still louder and brought a scolding echo from the other side. Journalists were artificially working themselves up and presenting cool calculations in the form of passion, or yielding to the intoxification of their own chimeras. They brought to the market triumphantly every poor little dispute that could be swollen into an "affair." They were constantly searching for new materials for the drama of hatred, constantly declaring that the nation had been insulted; always defending their threatened country as they sat well fixed in their editorial chairs.*

Barnes did not note, as he might have, that the comparison was most apt with the controlled press of Germany and Italy in 1936. Scholars such as Franklin R. Gannon, R. Cockett, and Eugen Weber have noted that the British press was already markedly pacifist, while the French press, much of it controlled by right-wing financial interests, was most obsessed with internal "enemies," that is, the Popular Front.[30]

The annual Nazi Party Congress at Nuremberg occasioned an embarrassment for Barnes. With advance word on Hitler's main speech to the congress, he submitted an article saying that Hitler would the next day call for the "diplomatic isolation" of the Soviet Union, declaring that Germany would no longer sit at an international conference in which the Soviet Union was included, nor would it be party to a pact which the Soviet Union signed. But when Hitler actually gave his speech, it was considerably toned down. Barnes explained in his follow-up article that Hitler's advisers feared the British reaction and persuaded Hitler to moderate his tone. Ralph's chagrin was evident in a letter to Salem: "I am not very proud of my coverage at Nuremberg. Perhaps you will have noticed that on the next to the last day—Sunday—I predicted that Hitler would say certain things in his speech Monday night. Well, he failed to say them. I should have known better than to be so categorical."[31] Oratorical attacks on the Soviet Union continued in part as a rationale for the sacrifices Hitler was demanding from the German people. At Nuremberg he had announced a Four-Year Plan to assure German self-sufficiency. As the outlines of the plan emerged, Barnes wrote that the government was exploring the use of ration cards to control demand and escalating efforts to find substitutes that would enable Germany to stop importing oil, certain metals, and textiles.[32]

Hitler's extension of compulsory military service from one to two years and army maneuvers at Bad Nauheim gave Barnes the occasion for two long articles on the German Army, which he depicted as a "powerful instrument of diplomacy." As impressed as he and other observers had been with the level of training of the army, they were equally impressed by the high morale and camaraderie between officers and men: "The unanimous testimony of foreign military experts who have had contact with the new army supports the view that a new relationship between officers and men exists. The war, they say, started the process of change, for it was found that rudeness on the part of the officers in dealing with their men, degenerating in many cases into brutality, served to undermine the morale. During the Nazi era humane treatment of the men has been encouraged, especially as a means of counteracting subversive Communist elements in the ranks."[33]

The violence of the Nazi campaign against Soviet Russia
and "Jewish Bolshevism" was further increased at the
fourth congress of the Nazi party here today as Dr.
Paul Joseph Goebbels, Reich Minister of Propaganda
and Public Enlightenment, and Dr. Alfred Rosenberg,
the Nazi party's cultural director, exhausted invectives
in their attacks on these traditional enemies of the
Third Reich.

The two leaders appealed for a world crusade against
Bolshevism and Judaism. It is fair to say that in
unrestrained verbal attacks by a responsible member
of the government on the political system of a foreign
state's government, Goebbels's speech of today was
almost unequaled in modern times.

Issuing his warning to the world, Goebbels asserted
that "events in Spain illustrate that Moscow has not
diminished, and has even increased, its determination
to foment world revolution."

Ralph Barnes, *Herald Tribune,*
September 11, 1936, from Nuremberg

International tensions heightened during the fall of 1936 because
of the Spanish Civil War. Rampant violations of the Non-intervention
Pact by the Italians and Germans in favor of the Nationalists, and
the Soviet Union in favor of the Loyalists, brought charges and
counter-charges, while Britain and France clung to the diplomatic
facade of neutrality. One important effect of the polarization was a
new closeness between Germany and Italy. Meeting in Munich,
Hitler and Galeazzo Ciano, the Italian foreign minister and son-in-
law of Mussolini, issued a communiqué announcing German/Italian

cooperation on European issues, particularly in the face of the Communist peril. Germany recognized Mussolini's conquest of Ethiopia. Barnes compared the agreement to the "Holy Alliance" of 1815 when the rulers of Russia, Prussia and Austria banded together to preserve European civilization as they defined it.[1]

From Munich, Ralph joined Esther and the children for a few days rest in Berchtesgaden. He wrote his parents a probably unwelcome reaction to the re-election of Franklin Roosevelt:

> *The country is changing, and it had better change. The New Deal is only a beginning. We shall have to reconstruct the country, or have it done in a violent manner. The worst enemy today, in my mind, is not the Communist, but rather the die-hard Republican, who fails to see that things must change. Through his obstinacy and ignorance, he sows the seeds of Communism. Today, the Republican of the die-hard mold has a certain power, while the Communist has almost none. Of course, many of those who voted for Landon are not die-hards. Yet I feel that Roosevelt is on the right track, and that the Republican party in full power would not meet the situation as effectively. I do not mean that Roosevelt has been right, in my mind, in every detail, but I mean that he is right in principle.[2]*

A few days later, Germany made another move designed to contain the "Bolshevik menace" when Joachim von Ribbentrop signed the Anti-Comintern Pact with Japan. While the text of the agreement did not mention the Soviet Union, Ribbentrop made its intent clear: "Japan will not suffer expansion of communism in eastern Asia. Germany is a bulwark against this pestilence in the heart of Europe. Finally, Italy, as *Il Duce* has stated, will carry the anti-Bolshevist banner in the south." Barnes's reading of London papers suggested that while the Anti-Comintern Pact might bring closer cooperation between Britain and France, it could just as easily drive Britain into greater isolation, even though several commentators hinted broadly "that the new German-Japanese treaty may serve as a serious menace not only to the Soviet Union but to the British Empire."

The German government's international moves were accompanied by further repressive measures at home. Goebbels limited art and literary criticism in the Third Reich to those who "approach their work with purity of heart and from the National Socialist viewpoint." Barnes suggested that since Goebbels was a writer, perhaps he had felt "the sting of the critics' lash." Other measures made Hitler Youth pre-military training compulsory for all children aged ten through eighteen, and prescribed severe penalties for evasion of the economic laws regarding the holding of property or resources abroad. The

Nobel laureate, Thomas Mann, who had left Germany when Hitler came to power, and thirty-eight others, all resident abroad, were deprived of their German citizenship.[3]

Even in matters unrelated to the regime, the Nazi leaders controlled information. When the attention of the world focused on the love affair between the King of England, Edward VIII, and the American divorcée Wallis Warfield Simpson, Barnes found the German people kept in the dark. An official statement was issued: "It is reported that there are differences at present between the King of England and the British government. Since the causes seem to be of a private character, the German press does not choose to take any note of them, either through news items or comment." The story occupied the New York papers for weeks. But only when Edward formally abdicated did the story appear in German papers, and then with what Barnes described as a "holier than thou" attitude. He cited one Berlin paper's assertion that only in the Third Reich "where the personal honor, not only of every German subject but also of foreign sovereigns, is protected," had the press behaved with proper decorum.[4]

As 1936 drew to a close, the German economy once more came to the forefront. Shortages in foodstuffs and raw materials took their toll on the standard of living. The Reich government blamed the shortages on the loss of German colonies after World War I. Hjalmar Schacht explicitly stated the case: "Germany has living space too small for her population. She has made every effort—certainly more than any other people—to get everything possible out of her small territory. Despite all these efforts, the space is insufficient. The difficulty in the case of raw materials is even greater than that in the case of foodstuffs. The existence of the German people cannot be supported by commercial agreements of whatever character. The allotment of colonial territory is the obvious solution of the existing difficulties." With its colonies restored, Germany would "produce there infinitely more food and raw material than are now produced under the present arrangement." Schacht reiterated his view in an article published in the American quarterly *Foreign Affairs*, maintaining that "the German colonial problem is not a problem of imperialism. It is not a mere problem of prestige. It is simply and solely a problem of economic existence." The text of the article was widely reprinted in German newspapers with much favorable editorial comment.[5]

In a closed meeting of government leaders, Hitler named Hermann Göring to head his four-year plan for economic self-sufficiency. No attempt was made to hide the fact that the plan was the result of lessons learned during the World War. Noting British forecasts of a breakdown of the German economy, Barnes cautioned against such comforting assumptions, reminding his readers that "economics is far from being an exact science, and that to come to Berlin, Rome or Moscow steeped in the tenets of the English classical school, from Adam Smith through Alfred Marshall, and in little else, is to be lost." He reminded his readers that, despite the economic difficulties, the Nazi government had in the last year strengthened its political control over the country: "Police power and propaganda can be effective instruments when handled skillfully, under contemporary conditions."[6]

The Christmas season of 1936 brought an expansion of Nazi attempts to replace the Christian holiday with the older celebrations of the winter solstice. The efforts were unsuccessful, both among observant Christians and more secular Germans, who nevertheless clung to the traditional combination of the pagan Christmas tree and the celebration of the birth of Christ. In a Christmas radio broadcast, Rudolf Hess "thanked God for having blessed the German people by sending Adolf Hitler to lead them."[7] Despite the atmosphere surrounding them, the Barnes family enjoyed their first Christmas together since 1931. Ralph confessed to being "just an overgrown boy," so great was his delight in the festivities. They were joined by Bill and Tess Shirer for Christmas dinner.[8]

The Barnes celebration of the Christmas holidays was interrupted by a new international crisis over foreign involvement in the Spanish Civil War. The French government protested Germany's policy of providing arms and "volunteers" to the Spanish rebels, while the Spanish Loyalist navy seized a German freighter in the Mediterranean. The German navy responded by stopping two Spanish merchant ships. The war scare raged both in Europe and in the United States, leading Barnes to write that the Soviet Union, Italy, and Germany all bore some responsibility although Germany and Italy appeared "to have intervened in force on the side of the insurgents before the Soviets acted to send substantial aid to the loyalists." Recognizing the Spanish situation as a symptom rather than a cause, Barnes assessed the international situation:

> *If no great power will fight when* Der Führer *moves to obtain 'limited objectives,' then a general European war is much less likely than otherwise it would be. If Britain is not going to fight to keep*

*Germany out of eastern and central Europe, then there is some reason
to doubt whether France will invade the Rhineland in an effort to halt
Der Führer in the east. Soviet Russia might move, but however strong
the Soviets would prove to be when defending their own soil, they are
likely to be outclassed by German troops in a match of strength on
territory lying between the German and Soviet borders.*[9]

In a wide-ranging speech early in 1937 celebrating his fourth
anniversary in power, Hitler assured his listeners that the "era of so-
called surprises" was over. Germany had achieved a position of
equality with other states and would seek cooperative solutions to
international problems. At the same time, he formally withdrew
Germany's signature from Article 231 of the Versailles Treaty, the
war guilt clause that read: "The Allied and Associated Governments
affirm and Germany accepts the responsibility of Germany and her
allies for causing all the loss and damage to which the Allied and
Associated Governments and their nationals have been subjected as
a consequence of the war imposed upon them by the aggression of
Germany and her allies." The clause had been the portion of the
treaty most offensive to Germans of all political persuasions. Scholars
of the period had in general rejected its validity. In fact, some months
before, Barnes had written his parents that as a result of his own
reading on the issue, "I am now convinced that the war was not
such a one-sided matter as the propaganda of the time caused us to
believe. There was blame on the side of the Allies, too."[10]

Barnes began his anniversary analysis of Hitler's four years as
chancellor by reminding his readers of the conditions under which
Hitler had come to power, how Hindenburg, who had reportedly
once said that he would not trust Hitler with the ministry of posts,
had reluctantly appointed him. Many intelligent Germans, he wrote,
referred to Hitler at the time as "that cheap Austrian demagogue" or
"that incompetent charlatan." Shortly after coming to power, Hitler
issued a manifesto asking for dictatorial powers for four years and
promising to restore "national discipline," to reorganize the German
economy, and to achieve for Germany equal standing in the family
of nations. Barnes found "an astonishing correlation between his
promise and—on the surface at least—his accomplishment, of course
at a cost which the Nazis avoid counting in public." It was, he
thought, "one of the most remarkable examples in modern history
of vision, tactical ability and will power utilized by a single man to
gain a specific end." The article reflected Barnes's deeply held
conviction that Hitler should not be underestimated.[11]

In a companion piece examining the prospects for the coming four years, Barnes emphasized the economic goals of the Nazi regime. He drew parallels with the state control that Stalin had established in the Soviet Union, while noting that Hitler had shown no intention to abolish private property. Whatever the accomplishments, Barnes wrote, "It is still fair to ask whether the goal justifies the cost, and even whether the goal itself is good regardless of the cost."[12] His service in Moscow continued to inform his reporting from Germany. From a distance, Barnes was watching the events in his former post where the famous show trials were underway. Grigori Zinoviev and Lev Kamenev had led off with many other prominent Communist leaders publicly confessing to a variety of crimes against the Soviet Union, Stalin, and humanity in general. Barnes wrote his father: "Perhaps you will have read reports of the Moscow trial. In some ways it is more fantastic than those which went before. Everyone confesses to everything—all kinds of skullduggery. I do not believe that these men are guilty of all the things that they confess to. But I am mystified, like most others."[13]

Tensions between the Reich government and the churches resurfaced in 1937. Despite the alliance forged by their mutual support for the Franco forces in Spain, Germany and the Roman Catholic Church were on a collision course over the education of young people. In two pastoral letters, the Catholic bishops of Germany called upon the faithful to fight anticipated efforts of the government to eliminate Catholic schools. A few days later, Barnes reported that the government would require all children to attend non-denominational state schools. The curriculum in the state schools was avidly Nazi. As an example, Barnes cited the state of Anhalt, where it was decreed that children be taught that "Jesus waged an unrelenting fight against the Jewish spirit and that in fact from a racial viewpoint He did not belong to Jewry." Baron Paul von Eltz-Ruebenbach, the minister of posts and transport since before Hitler came to power, resigned from the cabinet because he could not as a Catholic support the government policy. The Cardinal Archbishop of Munich, Michael Faulhaber, strongly criticized the government before a supportive audience of five thousand. He reminded the government that the Concordat was not a "*diktat*," and its repudiation put into question any agreement that Germany might sign.[14]

In spurious elections, parents were pressured to withdraw support from the religious schools. The controversy simmered with no solution until Pope Pius XI took the unusual step of circulating a pastoral letter to all parishes in Germany. In it, he condemned the violations of the Concordat and decried Nazi policies: "Whoever attaches more than a mundane meaning or worldly value to the ideas of race, nation, state or form of government, and turns them into a heathen idol, falsifies the divinely created order." The government responded with charges that the Catholic Church had violated the Concordat. Attacks on the church and particularly on the clergy accelerated, with a number of trials for treason and other offenses. Meanwhile Catholic schools were closed.[15]

For the Protestant opposition, too, 1937 proved to be decisive. The government used a variety of means to control the Confessional movement, including the withdrawal of financial support, travel restrictions, organized boycotts and finally arrest and imprisonment. Pastor Niemöller, persisting in his defiance, was jailed by the Gestapo in July. Still the resistance continued. While recognizing that motivations were both religious and political, Barnes wrote "In Germany today Protestant and Catholic churches are the only institutions which have not been effectively whipped into line with the totalitarian system."[16]

For Jewish Germans, life became ever more difficult. Reminding his readers that Jews had been eliminated from the political and social life of the capital and were gradually being forced out of its economic life, Barnes wrote a February article asserting that Nazi policies in some of the provinces were enough to convince observers that "relatively speaking, cosmopolitan Berlin is tolerant." He questioned the recurring proposition that a reaction to current policies could ameliorate some of the more stringent restrictions, by pointing out the intensive anti-Jewish propaganda to which young people were exposed in schools and elsewhere. A few weeks later he wrote of a textbook adopted for use in elementary schools which included, along with attacks on Catholics, Britain, France and the United States, the subheadings: "Jews—enemies of the nation," "Jews destroy German nature," "The Jew—the great swindler," and "The Jewish lust for power—a danger to Germany."[17]

When New York Mayor Fiorello La Guardia in a speech before the women's division of the American Jewish Congress criticized Hitler as a fanatic who endangered the peace of the world, the German reaction was swift and violent. Although Secretary of State Cordell Hull promptly expressed official regret for La Guardia's statement, the invective continued. Barnes catalogued some of the references to La Guardia in German newspapers who referred to him as "a dirty Talmud Jew, a Jewish boob, a procurer, a master New York gangster, an underworld character, a blackmailer, a man with cheap-joint brains, an impertinent Jewish lout, a filthy character, a well poisoner, a war profiteer, and a Jewish inciter and apostle." The writers threatened revenge and expanded their protests to include indictments of American civilization, government, institutions, and people. So virulent were the attacks that Ambassador William Dodd protested. When the attacks promptly ceased, Barnes noted that the Foreign Office had apparently won out over Goebbels at the Propaganda Ministry.

The restraint was short-lived. A few days later one paper, the *Nachausgabe*, suggested an amendment to the United States Constitution that would allow the federal government "to protect Germany and her *Führer* against such mean attacks and thus do its share to safeguard the peace of the world." An editorial in *Der Angriff*, Goebbels' paper, indicted the United States as a land of strikes and gangsters where millions lived in misery amidst the greatest wealth in the world, and asked: "What is the explanation of the fact that those who dwell in the midst of plenty and who consider themselves entitled to instruct us cannot get rid of their misery as we do?"[18]

$\sim$

Ralph and Esther found a small house to rent for the summer outside Kladow, a little town in the lake region west of Berlin near the Havel See. The house was only a short walk through woods to a beach, and had a yard with fruit trees and room to garden. They bought a secondhand car, a 1934 Adler cabriolet, and sublet their Berlin apartment. Esther welcomed the chance for the children to have play space and for herself to have some privacy "where I don't have to be an animal in the zoo for the Germans sitting around watching." When Ralph bought the girls a toy farm set, Esther wrote that "luckily the girls are 'Aryan' or the Government would probably confiscate it." They were in Kladow when the telephone call came from Paris informing them of the crash of the airship *Hindenburg* in New Jersey. Because of Ralph's trip the previous year, the disaster struck close to home. He had in fact declined an invitation for this voyage.[19]

While Esther had looked forward to the summer away from Berlin to provide some respite from the constant social demands of the city, her usual hospitality prevailed and the Kladow house became a retreat for other correspondents and their families. But Ralph's work schedule did not lighten. A Saturday off was a rare event. The prospect of his thirty-eighth birthday seemed to increase the pressure: "I feel I must get a lot done before I reach the forty mark." As to the future, "most elderly newspapermen advise young newspapermen to get out of it early. After one is 45 there is little future in the profession itself, unless one has made the reputation of a 'Duranty' and of course I haven't. Joe Barnes has insisted from time to time that I must begin to write for periodicals and the like—and he's right—but I find it sufficiently difficult keeping up with the work as correspondent of one newspaper. In part, of course, that is because the NYT has a big bureau here. In Rome and Moscow, it was easier." The *New York Times* Berlin bureau was staffed at the time by Otto D. Tolischus, Guido Enderis, and C. Brooks Peters. Frederick T. Birchall, formerly the managing editor of the *Times*, became a special writer for the paper in 1932, based in Berlin but traveling about Europe.[20]

Esther felt the competition was taking its toll: "He won't give up trying to compete with four men in the New York Times bureau. He will have to stop soon, as he can't continue at this rate. Don't say anything about this or he will be angry at me. There is nothing to worry about, but he just puts too much effort into his work; and I sometimes wonder if it is all appreciated." Some of Ralph's work habits were described a few years later by Martha Dodd, the daughter of the American ambassador: "Once or twice my father and mother were amused and slightly annoyed at [Ralph's] midnight appearance at the Embassy. He is supposed to have gotten William Bullitt out of bed on various occasions in Moscow. My father simply invited him, and on one occasion Bill Shirer who accompanied him, upstairs to his bedroom, to discuss the matter they were so eagerly pursuing."[21]

Summer 1937 saw the continuation of the Spanish Civil War, a meeting of the World Chamber of Commerce in Berlin, and the end to the last of the territorial restrictions of the Versailles Treaty, when Germany resumed full sovereignty over the provinces of Upper Silesia, a section of the German Empire under Polish sovereignty since the war. The first change the Nazi government imposed was the extension of the anti-Semitic regulations in German law to the restored provinces. The priority was consistent with other aspects of German policy, as Barnes noted in a July 18 article: "Notwithstanding Germany's other domestic and foreign political concerns, the anti-Jewish drive in the Third Reich is being carried on systematically and relentlessly with the twofold aim apparently of forcing as many Jews as possible out of the country and reducing those remaining to the status of inhabitants of the ghettos in the Middle Ages."[22]

Anti-Semitism was fundamental to the German drive against modern art that climaxed during the summer of 1937. In a speech at the opening of the new House of German Art, Hitler blamed the Jews for the degeneracy of German art before the Nazis took power. "Jews," he said, *put art on the same level as fashion designing—something new every season. Jewish art critics were really playing the game of the Jewish art dealers. They have undermined German taste and have even succeeded in persuading the German people that there is no such thing as national art. We had futurism, expressionism, realism and even cubism and Dadaism. Could insanity in art go to any greater limits? How deeply this corruption of taste had eaten into the German mind was shown in the material submitted by artists in the House of German Art. There were pictures with green skies and purple seas. There were paintings which could be explained only by abnormal eyesight or willful fraud on the part of the painter.*

In Hitler's eyes, Impressionist painters and sculptors were "dangerous lunatics" who should be sterilized to keep them from passing on their madness. "The National Socialists have cleansed the political and economic life of Germany. We will also clean up artistic life."[23]

Despite the government's best efforts, crowds flocked to the exhibit of "degenerate" art and largely ignored the approved German art. Barnes wrote two long mail pieces exploring the plight of art and artists under dictatorship, and comparing Hitler's moves to those of Mussolini and Stalin that he had witnessed during his time in Italy and the Soviet Union. He concluded that the contemporary dictatorships did not benefit the arts: "No one of the three dictatorships has produced an outstanding school in any field of art or literature." For many, the explanation of Hitler's actions could be found in his own failure to become a recognized artist: "Does the *Führer's* frustrated ambition, it is being asked here, explain the new campaign in the Third Reich to regiment the arts, especially painting and sculpture? Is it not possible that Hitler is dictating ruthlessly in this field to compensate for his own failure as an artist, sort of a vicarious act of creation? He cannot create good art, so he will dictate what is 'good' and what is 'bad.' He will be the supreme critic; he will mold the art life of Germany." Hitler was, Barnes noted, "a man of limited culture," inclined to condemn what he did not understand.[24]

As the summer passed, Esther's concerns about Ralph took on concrete form: "He had lost weight, his whole facial expression had changed, and he was so nervous and irritable." Physicians diagnosed Graves disease with exophthalmus, a thyroid disorder, and Ralph entered a Berlin hospital in August for treatment and surgery to remove the diseased thyroid gland. He was lonely in the hospital, since he was restricted to one visitor a day and very limited activity.

His frustration was intensified when he was unable to cover the Nazi expulsion of Norman Ebbutt, the longtime correspondent of *The Times* of London.[25]

Barnes's stay in the hospital provided an opportunity to tackle Erich Maria Remarque's *All Quiet on the Western Front* in the original German. The book was banned in Germany, and brought him to serious speculation about the next war. After three weeks he was able to leave the hospital for the Kladow retreat and a brief vacation with the family. Still his doctors were not pleased with the pace of his recovery and concluded that he should go to Italy for the sun, the time-honored cure-all of German medicine. John Elliott, the European manager for the *Herald Tribune*, made arrangements for temporary coverage in Berlin. Ralph spent three weeks on the island of Ischia near Naples, returning to Berlin on October 20 and resuming work a week later. But his recovery was slow and incomplete. During his absence, the Barneses' good friends Bill and Tess Shirer had departed from Berlin. Unhappy with the merger of the Universal Service and the International News Service that made him second man in Berlin, Shirer resigned. He joined the Columbia Broadcasting System's European service, under Edward R. Murrow, and moved to Vienna. Both Ralph and Esther felt the loss, but the couples maintained their friendship despite the separation.

After the summer at Kladow, Esther's immediate concern was enrolling the children in school but not, as she wrote to Salem, a public school: "Wish you could see the school books, then you would understand." Ralph was in agreement. When they settled on the Anglo-American school, he wrote to explain: "We decided on that expensive and distant institution because German schools, with their intensive Nazi propaganda, were what seemed to us an impossible alternative."[26]

∽

Although no new measures against the Jews had been enacted for some time, Barnes reminded his readers once again of their plight in a December 1937 article. He noted that revenues from the tax levied on those wishing to emigrate had jumped from 17,500,000 marks in fiscal year 1933-34, Hitler's first year in power, to 70,000,000 marks in 1936-37. Jewish retailers and manufacturers had been forced to sell their businesses at bargain rates, because they had lost both suppliers and customers from Nazi pressure not to deal with Jewish companies. Many had already left the country, but Barnes pointed to the problem of middle-aged people with small financial resources whose experience was limited to the retail business and who spoke no language other than German. Even more tragic was the situation of the twenty thousand Jews originally from Poland, Austria or Russia, who had become naturalized German citizens at the time of World War I. Now they had been deprived of their citizenship and of their livelihood and ordered to leave the country. Their options were stark: "With no European country nowadays admitting a stateless individual without a passport, these unfortunates have the alternative of being jailed or deported from the neighbor country for entering it illegally—or go to prison or concentration camp in Germany for failure to obey the deportation order."[27]

~

December brought changes at the *Herald Tribune* that Ralph and Esther greeted with some dismay. Esther wrote home to express their feelings:

> *The poor H.T., they seem to be starting an economy campaign or something. It all hit us yesterday. Ralph began getting wires from Paris. The poor Foreign Service finds itself to be Cinderella after midnight. They have turned over the editorial and financial management of the foreign service to Larry Hills, the editor and manager of the Paris Herald Tribune. Ralph used to be under him on the Herald and learned to know him as the "so and so" that he is. John Elliott has been reduced to Paris correspondent. The Munich and Warsaw stringmen have been fired. So far they haven't made any drastic changes affecting Ralph or his office. Only informed the bureaus to leave more stuff to the agencies and cover only the high spots. That may make Ralph's work lighter but it takes some of the kick out of his job. We are being very philosophical about it all. We feel now like retrenching for a while until we get our debts all paid and then start looking around. I am anxious for Ralph to get out of the foreign service. It is alright for a time but one can't grow old in such a job. Make a name and then get into something else is my idea. This job may become impossible under Hills and the H.T. has been treating the foreign service as an unnecessary luxury lately. The owner seems to be "falling in his soup" more often and this change may have come at one of these moments. Hills must have been a very good drinking companion on this trip to N.Y. He is due back to Europe after Christmas then things may happen. We aren't worried about Ralph's standing in New York but one has to feel a certain amount of*

appreciation and backing to get the right results from one's job. If Hills
begins dictating what angles to write from it might be unpleasant.[28]

Esther's analysis proved correct. Hills, still in charge of the Paris
Herald, had been contacted by Wilbur Forrest and asked to lead an
effort to reduce expenditure. He welcomed the opportunity, writing
New York that he had intended to raise the issue of the expenses of
the foreign correspondents for "I think a great deal of money is being
spent unnecessarily, if the results were to be appraised." The
announcement that Hills would replace Elliott as European manager
was greeted with dismay by the correspondents all over Europe.
John Whitaker, who had left the *Herald Tribune* to join the *Chicago
Daily News*, wrote Elliott of Hills: "He represents everything which
is bad in American journalism. He boasted during the Versailles
Conference era that he got his publisher [Frank Munsey] to come
out against the League because it would make the paper different
from the rest and build circulation. He has accepted humiliating
terms for advertising from certain governments. He proudly claims
that his chief accomplishment is in chiseling down salaries and
cheating reporters into writing for by-lines and promises. He has
the integrity of a cockroach."

Walter B. Kerr, who was Elliott's assistant in Paris, recalled that
"everyone understood it to mean that the *Herald Tribune* was dropping
out of the fight with the *Times*, that we were no longer to compete
with the *Times*, at a crucial time in the history of the world. And this
mattered to us. We were not working for money; we were working
for the paper. ... We felt we could adjust to almost any financial
requirements of the paper, that if they were stringent we could think
of a way to minimize their effect. But no one asked."

The memo Hills issued to the bureaus made their plight clear: "It
is no longer the desire even to attempt to run parallel with the New
York Times in special dispatches from Europe. Relying more than
ever on the agencies [Associated Press and United Press] for routine
[stories] what the paper wants from our service are dispatches that
in a sense seem exclusive in news, as well as presentation. This
means short stories, as well as long. Crisp cables of human interest
or humorous type cables are greatly appreciated. Big beats in Europe
in these days are not very likely."[29]

Barnes, along with a number of the other correspondents,
including Joseph Barnes from Moscow and Don Minifee from Rome,
met with Hills in Paris at the first of the year. All were receptive to
the need for economy. The *New York Times* correspondents too were
under orders to cut costs, in part because of a steep increase in the

cost of newsprint. Esther wryly observed that it might all be worth it if there were "some recompense at the paper mill end," a reference to the largely worthless stock Edward Barnes held in the Salem paper mill. Still, the prospect of Larry Hills in charge was depressing. Barnes later wrote that during these conversations, Hills "failed to ask a single question about the German situation."[30]

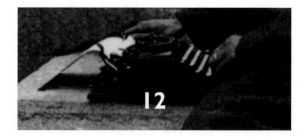

12

Moving swiftly to crush the "revolt" by the
conservative clique of the German officers' corps,
Chancellor Adolf Hitler has carried out one of the most
sensational purges in contemporary history. Official
announcement was made last night of the summary
dismissal from their posts of thirteen army and air
force generals. Implied were similar dismissals of an
undisclosed number of officers of lower rank.

A separate communiqué revealed the resignations,
"for reasons of health," of Field Marshal Werner von
Blomberg and Colonel General Werner von Fritsch, who
have been respectively, War Minister and chief of the
army command.

Ralph Barnes, *Herald Tribune*, February 5, 1938, from Berlin

Larry Hills had maintained that "big beats" were unlikely in Europe
in 1938. Barnes—and Hitler—soon proved him wrong. Through
January, the stories Barnes filed dealt with familiar topics. The
exigencies of the Four-year Plan with its shortages of butter, eggs
and milk, had made the German housewife's usual Christmas baking
a failure. Fully one-third of the national income was being absorbed
by the government while short-term debt continued to mount. A
labor shortage was forcing German women out of the home and
into the factories, despite Nazi views on a woman's proper role. In
the face of new, even harsher government measures, Jewish leaders
appealed to foreign governments to accept Jewish immigrants, and
begged the Nazi regime not to deprive Jews of their ability to earn a
living. Instead they found other countries such as Yugoslavia and
Rumania adopting anti-Semitic measures. While the usual tensions

continued within the Nazi government, Göring seemed more and more to be emerging as Hitler's partner and anointed successor.[1]

On January 30, Barnes warily reported the first evidence of a crisis that profoundly affected the course of European affairs. Since the days of Frederick the Great, the position of the army within German society had been unassailable, as evidenced by the old joke referring to Prussia not as a country with an army but an army with a country.[2] Many in Germany viewed the army as the one force capable of counterbalancing the power of Hitler and the Nazis. True, the army had been brought within the Nazi orbit after the 1934 Purge of the S.A. when all soldiers began to be required to swear an oath of loyalty to Adolf Hitler. Equally true, the current minister of war, Field Marshal Werner von Blomberg, was clearly "Hitler's man," to the growing dismay of his fellow officers. In fact, Blomberg was under pressure on several fronts for his position was resented by two powerful figures in the Nazi establishment, Hermann Göring and Heinrich Himmler.

Blomberg, a fifty-nine year old widower, played into the hands of his opponents by marrying Eva Gruhn, the twenty-five year-old daughter of a Berlin masseuse. He had advised Hitler that his intended bride was "a child of the people,"and Hitler and Göring had agreed to serve as witnesses at their wedding. The marriage was considered an affront by the aristocratic officers' caste of the German Army, particularly when it developed that Fraulein Gruhn's background was rather more shady than Blomberg had revealed, perhaps because he was not fully aware of it. For several days a crisis had been brewing, but it was not until Saturday night, January 29, that Barnes got wind of a meeting between a group of high officers and Hitler: "I knew definitely that something serious was up, and that it had to do with Blomberg's marriage. Of course, I didn't know all the details, and I was under the definite necessity of writing cautiously at first."[3]

The article was indeed cautious, although Barnes later maintained he had "told a lot to anyone prepared to read between the lines." A scheduled appearance by Blomberg on January 28 had been canceled because of "urgent duties." Rumors circulated that he might resign and that other issues beyond the marriage were involved. In addition, Barnes cited strains between the Nazi government and Germany's major industrialists as well as the ongoing question of the loyalty of the monarchists to the regime. Festivities the next day celebrating the anniversary of Hitler's accession to power did not include a previously planned meeting of the Reichstag. Hitler made no public statement. Neither Blomberg, Göring, nor *Wehrmacht* commander-in-chief Werner von Fritsch joined Hitler on the balcony of the chancellory for the traditional torchlight parade. Barnes compared the "charged" atmosphere to that at the time of the Röhm Purge. He wrote of having learned of conferences held throughout the previous week at the War Ministry, meetings in which Göring, and perhaps Hitler himself, had participated. In diplomatic circles, he found speculation that the controversy over the Blomberg marriage was only "a manifestation of something which goes deeper," "a restlessness within the army as a result of certain phases of the Nazi set-up."[4]

In an article printed on February 2, Barnes wrote that Blomberg's resignation was a "foregone conclusion" although its announcement might be delayed. He anticipated some reorganization of the command structure due to Nazi opposition to "an influential bloc of generals, imbued with the conservative traditions of the old army." The crisis had clearly moved beyond the relatively petty issue of Blomberg's marriage. By the next day, Barnes was aware that Hitler was considering assuming the role of minister of war. General von Fritsch, a soldier known for his integrity and, unlike Blomberg, for his independence from the Nazis, was rumored to have resigned or threatened resignation. Barnes speculated that other generals might follow his lead, but concluded that "some sort of patchwork compromise appears the most likely outcome." Hitler, he thought, wanted to avoid the kind of "extreme disciplinary measures" that Stalin was currently visiting on the Soviet High Command. A day later, Barnes reported that the tension continued in the inner circles, although the German people knew nothing of the crisis because no mention of it was made in the German press.[5]

In fact, *Herald Tribune* editors were becoming somewhat nervous about the story because, as Barnes later wrote, "for a long time, the agencies and other newspapers failed to come in with confirmation of the stories I was sending." Their uneasy queries turned to congratulatory messages when the German government officially announced what Barnes called "one of the most sensational purges in contemporary history." Blomberg and Fritsch were out, Hitler assumed the Ministry of War, a number of other generals were removed, and some officers were rumored to be under detention. Hitler had also used the occasion to make other changes; the conservative aristocrat Konstantin von Neurath was replaced by Joachim von Ribbentrop as foreign minister and three key ambassadors, those representing Germany in Japan, Austria, and Italy, were recalled. While Barnes cautioned that it was as yet unclear "how far the purge of the fighting forces would extend or what in sum would be its ultimate consequences," still he presented the possibility that Hitler had "precipitated a series of developments which will change the whole course of the German state."[6]

Later historians agreed with his conclusion, seeing the Blomberg-Fritsch affair as signaling a shift of power in Germany. Certainly it ended the chance that the army would moderate Hitler's aggressive actions. It also caused many conservatives to become increasingly disillusioned with the regime. A particularly sordid aspect of the entire affair did not at the time come to light. The effectiveness of General von Fritsch's opposition had been compromised by accusations of homosexuality concocted by Himmler and accepted by Hitler and Göring. Fritsch seems to have been so stunned by the charges, which were accompanied by an "identification" by a known blackmailer, that he withdrew from the fight at a key juncture. He was the most highly regarded member of the General Staff, and its resistance to Hitler collapsed without his leadership.[7]

The immediate question was whether the purge meant "an increase in influence for the adventurous elements of the Nazi party, and thus an increased danger to the peace of the world?" Barnes noted that "reports from Vienna say that the Austrian Nazis have been stirred up and are restless again, seeing in the recent dramatic events in Germany signs that *Der Führer* is taking steps preparatory to the long awaited *Anschluss*." A February 20 meeting of the Reichstag had been announced. Already speculation about its agenda was rampant.[8]

Hitler seldom disappointed those looking for news. On February 12, he met with Kurt von Schuschnigg, the Austrian chancellor, at Hitler's retreat in the Obersalzburg. The meeting had not been announced by either side, and its proceedings were kept secret, the official communiqué saying merely that the two men had discussed "all questions outstanding" between their countries. Barnes wrote of German "irritation" at a Vienna statement that the meeting "was being held with the 1936 amity accord as a basis and with the proviso that there would be no steps to put Austrian Nazis in the Schuschnigg cabinet." In fact, precisely that outcome shortly followed with the appointment of Nazi Arthur Seyss-Inquart as minister of the interior, responsible for the internal security of the country. In other moves, the Austrian government announced an end to the prohibition against National Socialist Party activity and propaganda in Austria, and an amnesty for those previously convicted of such activity. "Austria is ours!" boasted jubilant Nazis in Berlin.[9]

Not quite. In a desperate attempt to preserve his country's independence, on March 9, after some days of preparation, Schuschnigg announced a plebiscite. To be held on Sunday, March 13, it would give Austrians the opportunity to vote yes or no "for a free and German Austria, an independent and social Austria, a Christian and united Austria; for peace and employment and for the equality of all who stand for their people and their nation." Somehow news of the plan had leaked and the Germans were aware of it the day before Schuschnigg's announcement. Hitler was outraged; the atmosphere in Berlin was tense with anticipation of his next move. Late on March 10, "trying to find what was up," Barnes tracked down a source who "at first said that the situation was so delicate that it would be better not to talk about it. Under persuasion, however, the person in question loosened up somewhat and said, among other things, that events were moving so swiftly that already even the press comments in the Berlin early morning editions were out of date. When asked outright if Hitler would march in, he shrugged his shoulders. He spoke of 'anger and grim determination.' "[10]

Shortly after midnight on March 12, Barnes filed his story: "The most formidable army mobilized by Germany since the World War was being concentrated yesterday in Bavaria for the invasion of Austria. More than 50,000 troops, both regular army men and members of Nazi uniformed organizations, were assembling as an expeditionary force, together with 200 bombing planes and pursuit craft." Already the Germans had closed their border with Austria, allowing neither trains nor motor vehicles to cross. Faced with the prospect of invasion, Schuschnigg agreed to the German demand that the plebiscite be canceled. Having secured Mussolini's assent, Hitler raised the ante. The German ultimatum now included the resignation of Schuschnigg and his government and the appointment of Seyss-Inquart as Chancellor, with the understanding that Seyss-Inquart would then request German troops to help "restore order."[11]

In fact, several hours passed while the elderly Austrian president, Wilhelm Miklas, resisted German pressure, but the ultimate result was determined. No help was forthcoming from the other European states; Austria's army was no match for Germany's; the country's leaders bowed to superior force. In Berlin, the implication was clear to Barnes: "Yesterday German soldiers carrying swastika flags marched or rumbled into the territory of a foreign state. That this step was taken in response to an urgent request from the *Führer's* new puppet in Vienna is of little consequence. There is no end to the possibilities of this kind. It takes little stretch of the imagination to see Konrad Henlein [the Nazi leader in Czechoslovakia] as the next in line of puppets, heading a one-man provisional government in Prague and begging the *Führer* to dispatch German soldiers to Austria's northern neighbor 'to restore order and prevent bloodshed.' "[12]

In one of his informal man-on-the-street surveys in Berlin, Barnes found great expectations: "If views expressed here today by more than twenty Berliners of the lower and middle classes are typical, the masses of this city are wholly convinced that the conquest of Austria is only the first step in a grandiose program under which Chancellor Hitler will build a greatly enlarged central European state and force the return of the former German African colonies in the bargain." One worker, snapping his fingers, told Barnes *"Der Führer* will take the Polish Corridor like this."[13]

To his parents, Barnes wrote, "Once again we have had excitement here, and I have been working like the dickens. Austria has gone Nazi, and is controlled by German bayonets. One of the finest cities in Europe promises to lose in very short order some of its lovely features. I can be thankful only that Esther and I, on two occasions, saw Vienna as it was. Undoubtedly, it will never be quite the same again." He knew Austria was only the beginning: "It will be interesting to note the future moves of Paris and London. Of course, the great French Democracy would be governmentless at this time, and thus almost completely impotent. There doesn't seem to be much danger of war, simply because none wants to fight. German troops may march almost at will, since there is no resistance."[14]

Almost lost among the headlines of February and March of 1938 was the effective *denouement* of the struggle between the Christian churches and the National Socialist government. On February 7, the trial of Pastor Niemöller, who had been imprisoned since July, finally began. On the grounds that "the testimony was of a nature involving danger to the state and people," the court ignored Niemöller's vigorous protests and closed the trial to the public. Barnes noted: "The trial is closely linked with other dramatic events in progress in the Reich. If, as has been widely asserted, the radical elements in the Nazi party are being exalted to a position of new power and prestige in the reorganization and purge which Chancellor Adolf Hitler is carrying out, then the fate of Niemöller and the Church may have been sealed in advance. Long before the political crisis reached a critical stage a few days ago the view was held in some circles that the Church was fighting a losing battle."[15]

The special court freed Niemöller after a month-long trial, but the secret police arrested him again within a few hours. The news quickly spread through Berlin and among Niemöller's parishioners in Dahlem, a Berlin suburb, that he had been sent to the Sachsenhausen-Oranianburg concentration camp. Barnes reported what he knew about the camp: that it had opened about a year before and was filled to its capacity of 3,500 prisoners, who were employed at field labor and guarded by units of the *Schutz Staffel* or S.S., Hitler's elite bodyguard. The sense of foreboding among Niemöller's supporters was heightened by the remark of a high Nazi official: "There will no longer be a Pastor Niemöller."[16]

The changes in the *Herald Tribune*'s European management continued to rankle Barnes. He complained to his parents of having to respond to the "deluge" of letters from Larry Hills in his new role as director of the European service. The paper's management had been concerned about Barnes's stories on the Blomberg-Fritsch crisis, but "New York soon had to change its tune; and before the week was out, I had a message of congratulations from our managing editor in New York, Wilcox, forwarded from Paris. Hills seemed to think it necessary to add his own word to that of Wilcox—but in a most grudging manner." He was glad to receive reassuring letters from his colleague Sonia Tomara: "The second letter was intended to inform me of the impression my dispatches on the internal crisis in Germany had made in New York. She summed it up by writing: 'I repeat, your stock here is very high.' She had discussed the dispatches with Wilcox, managing editor; Walter Millis, who took in the military maneuvers with me a year and a half ago, of the editorial staff; with Wilbur Forrest, representing Ogden Reid, the owner of the Herald Tribune; and with Geoffrey Parsons, who dominates the editorial page." Not wanting to seem to be bragging, Barnes cautioned his parents: "This information is for you folks only, and is not for broadcasting, but I know that you will be interested and understand."[17]

Barnes was sufficiently restless to respond favorably when his father sent him an article about the new Nieman Fellowships that provided journalists an opportunity for study and reflection at Harvard University. Barnes reasoned: "I have had a good deal of practical experience with 'totalitarian' states—the dictatorships—perhaps it would be a good thing to read the theory, and think a bit some distance from the battle. A year in the States wouldn't do us any harm." But maybe he would be too old to qualify, or would not be eligible because he already had his master's degree. Perhaps his colleague Walter Lippmann could help. The possibility of the fellowship had great attractions:

> *If we were to take a scholarship, do the things we have in mind, then afterwards, we could look around a bit. I feel almost certain that with the added prestige of a year of special work at Harvard on the "Dictatorships," and related service—the background—I would be somewhat more in demand than at present. That is to say, I would have somewhat more prestige than at present. If in the interval, Hills were to have taken the* Herald Tribune *service on down hill, I could offer my services to the* New York Times. *I think, from what I have heard, that I am not entirely without prestige in that organization. Then, perhaps, at Harvard, I could get the long-awaited "book" under way.*[18]

As it turned out, the application deadline for 1938-39 had passed. The idea of a Nieman Fellowship and a year in the United States was put off for consideration later. Anyway, he assured his parents, "I'm still working with all the enthusiasm of a cub reporter." His work on the Blomberg-Fritsch affair had had its benefits: "Here in Berlin, the word has got about that I knew a lot about what was happening at the beginning of the crisis, and it has got about both in German and foreign circles. That kind of thing is cumulative. During the crisis I kept in touch with the sort of person—I mean, passed on to that type of person the information—who will be more inclined than in the past to favor me when there is a story to be divulged." His sources were all-important. When the *Herald Tribune* office moved to Wilhelmstrasse 80-A, between the Reich Chancellery and the Air Ministry, he welcomed the "good company."[19]

Both Ralph and Esther were bemused by happenings in their distant home country:

> *Ralph and I were laughing last night while reading* Time *when we noticed that the best seller this last year was Dale Carnegie's book on "How to make (sic) friends etc." What is happening to the States anyway? Did you remember that this person was on the same boat when Ralph and I came home in '34. That was evidently before he made his great discovery and wrote his book because everyone on the boat considered him Public Pest No. 1. He used to bore me to tears. He*

wrote to me after I got home wanting me to stop in New York on the way back to Russia and have lunch with him (adding that his aunt was with him so it would be quite proper) as he wanted me to buy some old Russian china for him. Do you also remember that he was the one who made arrangements for Ralph to speak over the radio in New York and interviewed him on that occasion. I never answered his letter.[20]

After the *Anschluss*, Barnes had written his parents: "Perhaps, though, we will have some relative quiet, now that the 'Big Man' has chewed off another big bite, which he will have to digest." But only three days later, he filed a story in which he wrote: "With Germany and Austria now united in a new empire of 75,000,000 population, there were signs tonight that additional dramatic developments might not be as distant as was first believed." Citing Hitler's famous telegram to Mussolini when the latter acquiesced in Germany's takeover of Austria, "Mussolini, I shall never forget this," Barnes pointed out that the *Anschluss*, rather than causing a strain between Hitler and Mussolini, had in fact strengthened the alliance, leaving Great Britain, France and the Soviet Union as the only possible brakes on Hitler's ambitions in central and eastern Europe. The article also predicted not only where Germany would look next, but that Hungary and Poland might also participate in a "first partition of Czechoslovakia," a demand that later surprised Neville Chamberlain at the Munich Conference.[21]

As Barnes expected, the issue of the three million Sudeten Germans soon came to the fore. Before World War I, they had been a part of the dominant German population of the Austrian Empire. As the boundary-lines were drawn at Versailles, they found themselves a minority in the new Czechoslovakia. Indeed, despite the best efforts of the peacemakers at Versailles, most of the countries of central and eastern Europe had to contend with substantial minority populations.[22] The Sudetens were distinguished from the other groups by Hitler's immediate interest in them, an interest neither the Weimar nor the Imperial German government had earlier shown. Throughout the crisis, no free election was held to determine if all or even a majority of Sudeten Germans were any more eager to join Nazi Germany than the Austrians as a whole had been. Still they had their grievances against the Czech government. In their sense of injury, they coalesced around the political leadership of the former *gymnasium* instructor, Konrad Henlein, whose tactics and goals were at first ambiguous, but who later was clearly a pawn of the Nazis. Since 1935, the Sudeten German party had had the second largest representation in the Czechoslovak national parliament. Both in parliament and in the streets, Henlein's followers disrupted political and civic life. Their actions were supported by diplomatic pressure and by the controlled press in Germany, who repeatedly attacked the Czech government for a variety of offenses including "the expropriation of German-owned properties in connection with defense construction in the border regions, suppression of German Nazi Party activities in the Sudetenland, prohibition of the sale of *Mein Kampf*, and failure to suppress anti-Nazi publications of the German Social Democrats and other emigrés who had fled to Czechoslovakia after Hitler seized power."[23]

On March 18, Hitler met with another special session of the Reichstag to defend his moves in Austria. Pleading Germany's commitment to peace, he did not mention Czechoslovakia specifically in his triumphant speech but warned: "Let it be understood, above all, that a great people with a feeling of honor cannot in the long run look on passively while masses numbering millions of racial kinsmen are being suppressed." Germany's newspapers chimed in, warning of the Bolshevik penetration of Czechoslovakia and decrying the treatment of Germans there. Through March and early April, as Nazi Germany prepared for the nationwide plebiscite planned to endorse the *Anschluss*, the attacks on Czechoslovakia heightened. On April 24, in a speech at Karlsbad, the Sudeten Nazi Henlein made a series of demands that took the form of an ultimatum and, if met, would have seriously undermined the integrity of the Czechoslovak state. German support for his actions was immediately forthcoming.[24]

In May, a crisis ensued when the Czechs, as well as the British and French military attachés in Berlin, received word of the massing of German forces along the Czech border. Theoretically, Czechoslovakia was protected by its 1925 Alliance for Mutual Defense with France and its 1935 Alliance with the Soviet Union, although the latter required that France take up arms in defense of Czechoslovakia before the alliance came into effect. The Czechs mobilized their army along the German frontier. The British and French ambassadors immediately sought an explanation from the German foreign ministry, which denied any unusual troop movements. The tension heightened when Czech border guards killed two Sudeten German motorcyclists. Barnes wrote that the Germans seemed to be playing a dangerous game because "events might force Hitler to go beyond the limits of his original plan in order to preserve his prestige."[25]

Writing on May 25, Barnes returned to this theme: "One of the most dangerous features of the situation is the circulation of the idea that Chancellor Adolf Hitler has suffered a diplomatic defeat. The folly of such tactics is apparent to any one who understands the sensitivity of high Nazi quarters." By that time, it was "clear that the reports of German troop concentrations last week end were seriously exaggerated." Barnes observed, "*Der Führer* is likely to continue to be successful on the European chessboard as long as he can dictate the moment of his moves. It is probable now that he is hunting a way out of the present impasse, since there is danger that circumstances, and not he himself, might be dictator."[26]

Weeks later, Hitler's deputy Rudolf Hess decried the Czech mobilization as "a game which for irresponsibility hardly was equaled in the history of civilized nations." He declared, "It is clear to every one: first that this state [Czechoslovakia] is no longer in a position to maintain law and order within its own frontiers and no longer can protect the lives of its own citizens; second, that this state has become the danger center of all Europe. ... It is our most earnest wish that finally the days of sacrifice will be over for the Sudeten German people, that days will dawn which will show that their sacrifices have been worth while."[27]

The crisis caused the British Embassy to charter a railroad car for the possible evacuation of women and children from Berlin. Ralph himself was not immune from concern, as shown in a letter Esther wrote from Belgium late in May: "Won't you be surprised to get a letter from me from here. No more so than I am to be here altho we were talking of having a vacation out of Germany this year. This is the first time I have had a breath of free air since we went to Vienna in December '35. I can hardly get used to a free country." With the crisis, "the newspaper men got all excited and Ralph and Jimmy Holburn especially. Ralph made me pack and be ready to go any moment. Then Sunday the 22nd he and Jimmy decided to ship Margaret and me with the four children to Belgium. So off we went at 11:30 Sunday night arriving in Brussels Monday noon. We stayed there until Wednesday when we moved up here to the coast."[28] Belgium fulfilled her expectations: "It is nice to be able to buy all the butter and fresh eggs and fresh vegetables. The shopkeepers are so helpful. A little capitalist competition is a good thing once in a while." She wondered if she could get the children back to Berlin, "The girls both dislike it so much. They are so happy to be away from there."[29]

From Germany, Barnes reported a new campaign against the Jews. Raids on Jewish-owned cafés resulted in the detention of non-Jewish patrons, including foreigners. A Nazi magazine for young women asserted:

Fashionable padded shoulders and small waists, short skirts and bare necks are such a menace to our women's spiritual poise that our racial and population experts have good reason to rebel. Jewish influence in these particulars can become a danger to our birthrate. Jewish taste will always be influenced by racial feelings and can never conform to Nordic taste. International fashions provide a means for the Jew both to do business and rule in a racial sense. He has used best the French fashion world as a means to power, and has spread his taste throughout the entire world. Jewish fashions lead to spiritual decadence, profane the relationship between the sexes and cripple our racial substance.[30]

More serious was a government move that forbade Jews leaving the country to take any funds whatsoever. Previously they had to surrender 85 percent of their fortune to take out the remainder; now not even that was allowed. Since few foreign countries would accept immigrants without funds, Jewish Germans were more than ever prisoners. Another decree, requiring the registration of all non-corporate Jewish-owned property in Germany, including that owned by Jews who were foreign nationals, was widely seen as a precursor to confiscation. In what Barnes characterized as "the biggest anti-Semitic drive in the Third Reich since 1935," Jews were arrested by the secret police, menaced by Nazi mobs, and saw their livelihood threatened by a new boycott movement. In Austria, too, the situation of the Jews was reported "becoming more critical daily." Barnes's articles referred to Jewish "desperation" and the "harrowing times" they were experiencing while the authorities were announcing that the new campaign "had just begun." Its goal, in Barnes's judgment, was "to drive the Jews in Germany deeper into a modern ghetto, and then from the territory of the Third Reich."[31]

In another article, Barnes compared the campaign, and its motivation, to the recent purges in the Soviet Union, as "part of a general purge of so-called 'undesirable elements' which may prove a burden or cause trouble in case of war. The two clean-ups are alike in that in part they are motivated by national defense considerations. They are unlike in that, while under the Soviet the drive has been directed primarily against 'non-Stalinite' elements within the Communist party extending high into the ranks of the leadership, in Germany efforts are being concentrated for rounding up and liquidating 'foreign elements' within the Reich frontiers," including, he noted, non-Aryan Russian emigrés. Ralph joined Esther and the children at Le Coq sur Mer on July 6. He found the family well: "Esther is stunning, with her good coat of tan; and both of the girls are all browned up." Finances were as always a concern, but Ralph tried to be reassuring to his parents: "You, Mother and Dad, must not overwork. Try to keep cheerful always, because we shall all stick together, even if things get a little worse. Esther and I are not worrying about the situation even though everything is not as perfect as it might be. The principal thing is to keep well and happy. We love you very much, and we don't want you worrying about financial trifles. Life's too short."[32]

13

Field Marshal General Hermann Wilhelm Goering,
Chancellor Adolf Hitler's closest adviser and virtual
War Minister of Nazi Germany, dropped a verbal
bombshell here today which reverberated throughout a
Europe made nervous by the Czech-German dispute
over the Sudeten German territory.

What was left of the delicately balanced peace
structure was shaken severely by the belligerent
remarks which Der Fuehrer's "faithful Paladin"
literally shouted into the ears of 20,000 members of
the Labor Front and other guests assembled in Leopold
Hall. His half-hour speech, a scheduled event of the
tenth Nazi party rally, was broadcast, so that it was
heard throughout Germany and beyond.

This tirade combined a devastating attack on the
Czechs as a miserable fragment of a race devoid of
culture, proud boasts of Germany's bristling
armaments, war chests and invincibility, and finally an
appeal for the unswerving loyalty of the nation to its
leader in the present crisis, whatever he might
command.

Ralph Barnes, *Herald Tribune*,
September 11, 1938, from Nuremberg

When he returned from his Belgian holiday on July 23, Barnes was
caught up immediately in a new Czech crisis. His first articles
documented German moves to enhance military preparedness and
ongoing attacks on Czechoslovakia in the German press. Under the
circumstances, leaving Belgium was difficult for Esther: "We will
soon be back to 'Heiling.' Heavens, what a relief it has been to be

away from Germans for awhile." She and the girls arrived in Berlin August 3. A week later, she wrote: "I sort of feel like keeping my suitcases packed. The tension hasn't let up any. It was only felt in the colony before; now even natives sense it here. Terrible feeling. I just go on from day to day making no plans."[1]

German actions seemed carefully calculated to increase the tension. While a British mediator, Lord Walter Runciman, worked to reach a peaceful solution to the Sudeten issue, the German government decreed a "test mobilization" which brought more than 1,200,000 men under arms for war games in various parts of the country. Stocks fell sharply on the German stock market. Barnes observed that the Nazi leaders had succeeded not only in scaring the other powers, but their own people as well: "Never before since Hitler assumed power have Germans generally manifested so much anxiety as to the possibility of war." The German press heightened its vituperative attacks on Czechoslovakia, manufacturing accounts of a "terror" against the Sudeten Germans: "From all Sudeten German districts come alarming reports of the bloody and violent methods of the Czechs, the shameful action of the unleashed mobs like a cloud of horror over the tortured land." This particular article, published August 30 in *Der Angriff*, Goebbels' paper, continued: "In this last hour the tortured Sudeten Germans direct an appeal to the conscience of the world to halt the raging and storming of the Czechs and put a final end to the life which the Germans of this state must endure."[2]

Beyond the threats and bluster, however, Barnes questioned whether Germany was ready for war. In a long and rather prescient analysis which ran in the *Herald Tribune* on Sunday, September 4, and in the *Washington Post* on the same day, he wrote: "Germany's economic unpreparedness for a prolonged armed conflict may still cast the die in favor of peace in a critical hour, especially if in the end the Reich's leaders realize that their hopes for localization of the conflict and a short surprise blow at an unprepared enemy are futile." The stresses placed on the country's material and capital resources and on its labor force by rearmament and the drive for economic self-sufficiency would in fact handicap Germany in the case of a long war. Already its credit structure was strained "almost to the breaking point," and the option of financing a war through inflation was untenable. While Germany might look to Hungary and Yugoslavia for food and raw materials in an effort to overcome a blockade, in Barnes's view, the Italian alliance would be a liability "since Italy's economic war preparedness and financial power are still inferior to Germany's."[3]

On September 5, the French at last responded to the German "test mobilization" by calling up some of their reserves and canceling Army leaves. The gesture was largely ignored by the Germans, who used the annual Nazi Party meeting at Nuremberg as another opportunity for Hitler to warn Europe that Germany was "determined not to capitulate before anyone." In a speech many observers feared was the announcement of an invasion, Hermann Göring attacked the Czechs: "A miserable chip of a race without *Kultur*—nobody knows where they came from—is oppressing a civilized minority, but behind all this is Moscow—the grimace of the eternal Jewish devils." In his closing address, Hitler demanded that the Czech President Eduard Beneš come to terms with the Sudetens: "I am no longer willing to countenance the oppression of the German population in Czechoslovakia." He declared: "No European state has made more sacrifices for peace than has Germany, but there are limits."[4]

Esther's September 13 letter to her family in Portland gave a sense of the helplessness:

Nothing special to write today. No one seems to know any more about what is going to happen than we did last night before Hitler's speech. I wonder how much longer Europe can stand the tension which seems terrific. Thank heavens Ralph will be home from Nuremberg this afternoon. I feel better when he is around. One doesn't feel quite so cut off from the rest of the world as the correspondents do hear things. We are scheduled to have a blackout and mock air raids in the next few days. That doesn't add anything to one's peace of mind. I have no definite plans about where to go if things blow up. Naturally I will head for home if things really start but there will certainly be a rush and there are certainly enough Americans that will be of the same mind. The neutral boats are already booked until the middle of October with the tourist traffic and Jewish emigrants. Am sorry to say we haven't much faith in the arrangements that could be made by our diplomatic corps but we may have to depend on them.

We are expecting a pretty miserable lot of newspapermen back from Nuremberg. They all admit that this year has been the worst they have ever gone through, complete disorganization as far as they were concerned and no cooperation. I haven't talked with Ralph since he went. Had one short note after his arrival. He was able to wrangle a room in town so didn't have to stay on the train that was arranged for correspondents. They say the train was terrible, beds weren't made all week, most of the time no drinking water on the train, and so far away from the center of things.[5]

British Prime Minister Neville Chamberlain's decision to fly to Berchtesgaden for a meeting with Hitler was widely welcomed as the last chance for peace. From Berchtesgaden, Barnes wrote that "Chamberlain's courageous pilgrimage to Hitler's mountain retreat seems to have decreased immensely the dangers of war." The joint communiqué issued after the meeting included the familiar euphemism of a "full and frank exchange of views" to describe the encounter. Barnes's understanding was that the prime minister had asked Hitler what he wanted, and that Hitler had made his wishes clear: "inclusion of the Sudetens within the Reich, with a plebiscite either now to establish their desire to come in, or later to confirm a *fait accompli*."[6]

Agreeing to return to Germany within a few days, Chamberlain flew to London and, with the French, pressured Czechoslovakia into accepting Hitler's demands while at the same time agreeing to protect the remainder of the country's territory. In the Berlin press, however, the talk was of a wholesale partition of Czechoslovakia, a "cancer in the heart of Europe." As the *Berliner Borsenzeitung* explained to its readers: "Czechoslovakia is nothing but a colony of Bolshevism in central Europe. This fact must not be ignored when the future of Czechoslovakia is decided." The problem Barnes had anticipated in March came to the fore in September: Poland and Hungary, supported by Mussolini, demanded their pieces of Czech territory.[7]

The attention of the world shifted to Bad Godesburg on the Rhine, where Hitler and Chamberlain were to have their second meeting. Hitler came to receive the " 'gift' of a good slice of Czechoslovakia," Barnes wrote. "The gift was forced almost at the point of the bayonet for the new Supreme War Lord's prolonged game of sabre-rattling and his implied threat to invade the Sudeten territory had pushed Europe to the verge of general war. To prevent such a conflict Britain and France succumbed and 'sold out' Czechoslovakia, the state which was the handiwork and once the pride of the democracies." Barnes made the significance of the German triumph clear for his readers: "It was Bismarck, Hitler's great predecessor as German empire-builder, who once said, 'He who controls Bohemia (the western portion of Czechoslovakia) holds the key to Europe.' " Barnes's colleague, Ed Beattie of the Associated Press, left a picture of him at work in Godesburg:

> There was only one touch of calm in the scene. Ralph Barnes of the
> New York Herald Tribune, one of the finest newspapermen in Europe,
> sat at a small table, waiting for a direct call to New York and busy
> writing his piece. Ralph had a marvelous power of concentration—

only he or a boss riveter could have concentrated there that night. He interrupted his work only to rise every so often and shout: "Listen you guys. Was it Bismarck or Napoleon who said, 'Who rules Bohemia, rules Europe'?"[8]

Now, however, new demands appeared to imperil the settlement. While Hitler and Chamberlain held their series of meetings, rumor was rampant in Godesberg: the two had disagreed; they were friendly; German troops were poised to invade Czechoslovakia; detachments of the Sudeten Free Corps, organized in the Reich, were filtering across the border. Barnes gave credence to reports that Hitler was "insisting on a full settlement of the Sudeten issue—in line with his views—within eight days." Midway through the talks, Chamberlain issued a statement citing the sensitive nature of the negotiations and the danger inherent in their disruption: "There should be a determination on the part of all parties and on the part of all concerned to insure that local conditions in Czechoslovakia are such as not in any way to interfere with the progress of the conversations." He appealed "most earnestly, therefore, to everybody to assist in maintaining a state of orderliness and to refrain from action of any kind that would be likely to lead to incidents."[9]

September 23 was a trying day of messages back and forth and meetings at lower levels. Finally Hitler and Chamberlain met about ten o'clock at night. When their meeting broke up in the early hours of Saturday, September 24, the British prime minister responded to reporters' questions with the statement: "I do not consider the situation hopeless. I am going home this morning to present new proposals to the Czechs. It is up to them." As far as Barnes could determine, the talks had ended in "virtual deadlock," with Hitler issuing an October 1 deadline for meeting his demands. He refused Chamberlain's requests for a pledge not to undertake military action while the talks with the Czech government proceeded. Instead he demanded the immediate withdrawal of the Czech army from the disputed areas. Barnes also noted reports that Hitler had refused to guarantee the future borders of Czechoslovakia unless the claims of Hungary and Poland were settled.[10]

In an article forwarded from Berlin later on September 24, Barnes listed the apparent preparations for war: anti-aircraft precautions, further call-up of men for service, the requisition of motor vehicles, military flights from Tempelhof Airport. His conclusion about the Godesburg meeting was tentative: "[W]hatever else may be said about the British Prime Minister, he has succeeded at least in retarding once again the supreme war lord's invasion of Czechoslovakia, and thus possibly once again preserving the peace in Europe." In fact, the German government was orchestrating a series of moves designed to heighten the already unbearable tension. In a September 26 speech before Nazi party loyalists in the Sportspalast, Hitler repeatedly attacked the Czech president, Eduard Beneš. Although his speech did not entirely close the door on the efforts of Chamberlain, it was widely rumored that Hitler had moved up the date for a response from Czechoslovakia from October 1 to September 28. On September 27, masses of troops with their mechanized equipment moved through the most important streets of Berlin in a calculated show of force. Barnes reported its effect on the people of Berlin:

> Berliners enjoy the colorful goose-stepping demonstrations of German festival days, but most of them are watching Hitler's current big parade in grim silence, except in the case of the most ardent Nazi supporters, including youngsters who know nothing first-hand of the World War. There is little enthusiasm at this stage for the Czechoslovakia adventure, not because of a lack of sympathy for the Sudeten Germans, but because of a growing fear that Hitler's tactics may involve the Reich in a real war, with Great Britain, France and the Soviet Union among its enemies. The expressionless or sad faces watching the detachments roll by in the streets tell the story.[11]

In his September 27 dispatch, Barnes mentioned that the British newspapers had ordered their correspondents and their families to leave Germany and that many Americans resident in Berlin were sending their families out of the country. Once again, Esther and the children left, this time for Norway. Before their departure Esther wrote her family:

> Well, perhaps by the time this reaches you I will be back in Berlin or on the boat for home. I won't even attempt to give you an idea of what my feelings are at this point. Will try to get another letter off to you as soon as I get out of this place. Never before have I realized what pawns 'the people' are in this game of life. I don't know whether or not you understand what I mean. Will make myself clearer later. The girls are fine and in good shape for their trip. Of course we would love to see you all but hate so to leave our Ralph. The price is much too great for Europe to pay that we would have the trip home. We love you so but please don't worry. Surely things will come out alright.[12]

They were accompanied by a young American woman, Eleanor Trampler. Married to a German musician, she worked in the *Herald Tribune* bureau for Barnes and had become a close friend of the family. Norway had been chosen for their exile because if war actually came, they could find passage to the United States more easily from Scandinavia than from the Channel ports. In Oslo, the little party joined Mary Deuel, the wife of the *Chicago Daily News* correspondent, and her two children.

∼

Meanwhile, tensions eased palpably in Berlin with the announcement of a four-power conference to be held in Munich. Chamberlain had appealed to Mussolini who telephoned Hitler and persuaded him to agree to the conference just an hour before the mobilization of German troops was planned for 2 P. M. September 28. Reports on British and French radio spread the news around Berlin as Hitler prepared to leave for Munich. Again Barnes's dispatch recorded the public's apparent lack of enthusiasm for war: "It was interesting to note the difference in the spontaneous 'Heils' which greeted Hitler when he left this German capital and the comparatively thin applause given to Dr. Paul Joseph Goebbels when—ignoring tomorrow's meeting and the international diplomatic steps preceding it—the Minister of Propaganda expounded national enthusiasm at this critical hour at a mass meeting summoned in the Lustgarten."[13]

The Munich Conference was a day-long affair. Mussolini met Hitler's train at Kufstein in Austria and the two continued on to Munich. Chamberlain and the French representative, Premier Edouard Daladier, flew from London and Paris respectively. Held in the *Führerhaus*, an ornate structure commemorating the early days of the Nazi movement, talks began at 12:45 P. M. Thursday, September 29, and ended at 1:00 the next morning with an agreement whereby the German army would begin occupying the German areas of Czechoslovakia at midnight. The occupation was phased over ten days, with final borders to be determined by an international commission that in fact was never convened. Britain and France offered to guarantee the new Czech borders, while Germany and Italy would do so only after the demands of the Poles and Hungarians had been met. As they left the meeting, Barnes noted that Hitler and Mussolini were "literally beaming" while Chamberlain and Daladier appeared "wan and dejected."[14]

In a dispatch the next day, Barnes summed up the conference and the hopes it engendered:

It now seems clear that the last seventy-two hours have seen the beginning of a turning point in European history. During that period war clouds have cleared; that is the most important single fact. Had not Mussolini intervened, in response to Chamberlain's appeal, Hitler might have marched precipitately into Czechoslovakia without an agreement as to procedure. Europe was mobilizing, apparently to halt him. In view of the combined resources of Germany's potential enemies there was a good chance, at least, of Hitler and National Socialism (Nazism) disappearing in a war. If on the eve of an invasion he had backed down, the blow to his prestige would have been severe. If Hitler was in a hole he is now out of it, and more. At the cost, perhaps, of "a few Sudeten villages" he has soared to new heights of power and prestige.[15]

Barnes's skepticism surfaced in an article he wrote for the Sunday, October 9, edition of the *Herald Tribune*:

It was only human that there should have been widespread rejoicing abroad over the fact that through the Munich conference peace was preserved for the present—throughout the world the masses fervently desire peace. Yet, after this is said, there remains something of a paradox in the picture of France and Great Britain going into frenzied jubilation at a moment when Chancellor Adolf Hitler, an Austro-German, once considered an upstart and demagogue, had succeeded in reversing some of the major decisions of 1918-19, and thus had opened avenues of new power and prestige for the renascent German empire.

Barnes dismissed Hitler's pledge to Chamberlain that he had no further aspirations in Europe and merely sought redress of Germany's colonial claims. He also predicted another result of Munich, the Soviet Union's "turning her broad back in disgust and dis-illusionment with everything European" and looking to other means to preserve its security. Subsequent scholarship has confirmed the relationship between Munich and the Nazi-Soviet Pact of August, 1939.[16]

~

After Munich Barnes, exhausted and plagued by a chest cold, sought and received a two-week vacation. Rather than joining Esther and the girls in Norway, he headed for the south of France in search of sunshine. On his way, he stopped in Paris where he conferred with John Elliott who was about to leave for New York. Barnes also visited with Bill Shirer and his boss, Edward R. Murrow, the head correspondent for the Columbia Broadcasting System in Europe. Barnes had participated in one of Shirer's broadcasts from Berlin.

From the Riviera, he wrote his parents his private assessment of Munich: "the situation is better than if there had been war. When it comes, the war may be more terrible than it would have been if it had come earlier; but no one can be sure of the future." His coverage of Munich had earned him praise from New York and a "merit" raise, one that did not make up for the salary cut he and other correspondents had taken earlier in the year when the European service was reorganized. Still, he encouraged his father to keep things, such as efforts by the State of Oregon to take over the family house for construction of a government building, in perspective: "Do take good care of yourself, and if eventually the State wants the old house, don't take it too much to heart. Over here in this part of the world so much unhappiness is caused by forced emigration— the forced separation of families for political reasons. We see so much human misfortune from such causes that the simple loss of an old home seems like a small matter. On the whole we are pretty fortunate."[17]

In Norway, Esther was enjoying a countryside that reminded her of her Oregon home and reveling in "heaps of vegetables, good milk, real cream and pleasant company." She dreaded the return to Berlin:

> Our feelings of the last few weeks in Berlin have been such that it is now impossible to describe them. We were all so fed up and disgusted with the Nazis. To sit there and read German papers with their lies and propaganda knowing that the "so & so" Hitler was leading Europe into war and there seemed to be nothing one could do about it worked me up into an awful state. If it hadn't been for the girls I would have sat on but I didn't want them to live through the experience. The greater part of the Germans themselves were terribly jittery but so many of the dumb ones with faith thought Hitler had some divine power of getting what he wanted without endangering them. So far he has and that is why it is going to be so darned hard to go back there and see the fools crow about their "wonderful leader."

Esther also wrote of "another matter" she could not mention in her letters from Berlin: "Julie, Ralph's assistant, has at last decided to get out as are so many of the Jews. New York has promised to pay her way to N.Y. and will give her a job so I guess she is going. It is hard for her to go as she will have to leave her 82 year old mother and sister. Her mother probably can't live much longer and doesn't want to leave Germany. Julie feels that she must think of herself and her sister so she plans to go ahead and prepare to bring over her sister. This war scare has made them realize that they have no future in Germany. It's their only chance to get out."[18] Reluctantly, Esther and the children returned to Berlin on October 20. Ralph joined them there on October 25.

His return was delayed by meetings in Paris where he pressed Larry Hills for an expansion of the Berlin bureau. The volume of news had become overwhelming and he wanted to add Walter B. Kerr as his assistant. Kerr had been assistant to John Elliott in Paris, but that bureau was to be downgraded. Kerr had reported from Prague during the Czech crisis and had come to Munich for the conference, where he and Barnes had conceived a plan for him to move to Berlin. Somewhat to his surprise, Barnes found Hills willing to pursue the issue with New York.[19]

No change was effected before Berlin was again the center of the world's attention. In his November 9 dispatch, Barnes anticipated the horror to come and assigned responsibility: "A half-million Jews of greater Germany were faced tonight with a police-controlled regime of ruthless persecution, as plans were laid by Nazi authorities following the news from Paris of the death of Ernst vom Rath, secretary of the German Embassy, who was shot on Monday by a seventeen-year-old Polish Jew."[20] During the night the storm broke: "An anti-Semitic terror, unprecedented in civilized countries since the Middle Ages, was sweeping the Greater Reich today as Nazi authorities, ably supported by mobs, dealt blow upon blow against the panic-stricken 500,000 persons who now compose German Jewry. Man hunts, shootings, suicides, invasion of Jewish homes, mass arrests, orders for deportation, wholesale destruction of Jewish property, looting and defiling and burning of synagogues featured this most serious blot on the record of the regime of Chancellor Adolf Hitler in its dealings with Jews of the Reich."

Goebbels explained *Kristallnacht*, as the rampage came to be called because of all the broken glass, as the expression of "the rightful and comprehensible indignation of the German people over the cowardly Jewish murder of a German diplomat." Barnes dismissed this explanation from the beginning: "Obviously the word that the 'lid was off' for mob violence came from high Nazi quarters. In fact, the Nazi hoodlums were told to go to it." He added, "The spontaneous factor appeared to have played relatively a small role in today's terror. There were plenty of Nazi strong-arm squads ready to act, but it may be assumed that they would not have gone *en masse* to their work of destruction unless they had instructions to do so. All of this violence occurred among a people—the German people—which in the past enjoyed a tradition for discipline under adequate police protection."

As to the reaction of the ordinary German citizen, Barnes wrote: "In Berlin, at least, many thousands of Germans were disgusted and even angered by what was done. The thousands of persons in custody were known to include some non-Jews who were too frank in expressing in the streets their disapproval." Still, he noted, "many German citizens who failed to take active part in the orgy approved of it in principle. Perhaps the population was about equally divided on the issue. One of the most revolting features was the manner in which many parents took their small children to see the show. Whether they approved or not, thousands of the curious roamed the principal thoroughfares in which Jewish enterprises are concentrated to watch the wreckers at their systematic operations."[21]

A day later, Barnes wrote: "In answer to the assertion today by Propaganda Minister Paul Joseph Goebbels that yesterday's terror was 'wholly spontaneous,' it can only be repeated that there is every possible circumstantial evidence that it was organized and directed from above. The big scale wreckings started almost simultaneously in the small hours of Thursday morning in scores of centers throughout the Reich." Nor did he accept the premise that the violence could not be controlled:

> As for the question of police protection, if the regular police forces had been unable in fact to cope with what Goebbels termed the 'manifestation of the popular will,' Elite Guard and Storm Troop detachments could have been mobilized at a moment's notice. The fact is that, when questioned, police agents on duty in Berlin streets admitted they were not interfering with the hoodlums in their work. Moreover, scores of riot calls to the police stations were ignored. Curiously enough, when one foreign correspondent telephoned to the Berlin police headquarters in the Alexanderplatz and asked why police protection was not being provided, the official on duty said that his officers were not dealing with the matter because it was in the hands of the Propaganda Ministry—the department headed by Goebbels.[22]

By Friday, Barnes continued, the terror had "passed from its gangster-orgy stage, marked by man hunts, pillage and destruction of Jewish property—including the burning, bombing and defiling of synagogues—to what might be termed a 'legal stage.' " The new round of harsh decrees that he anticipated was announced the next day. Barnes summarized the measures for his readers:

Following five and half years in which the Jew was forced gradually to his knees in an economic sense, he now is struck to the ground, so to speak, as a response to the assassination of a German in Paris. First he was forced to submit to the destruction of a considerable share of his commercial property through Nazi mob violence. Now he must pay the bill for all the damage so that his enterprises will be in good order when they are presented for a song to an "Aryan." Simultaneously, the Jew is barred from doing business in the Reich except on the smallest scale. Stripped of the bulk of what means he has and prevented from obtaining more, he nevertheless must pay a huge collective fine for the crime committed in Paris.[23]

The fine of 1,000,000,000 marks ($400,000,000) was estimated by Goebbels to constitute about one-eighth of the total value of Jewish property; Barnes's sources set the figure at one-third to one-half. But the combination of the earlier economic restrictions and the arrest of some 35,000 adult male Jews during *Kristallnacht* meant that "actual hunger and perhaps worse will be the lot of large numbers unless relief is provided immediately." Because Jewish relief organizations were banned, help could only come from the German government or from abroad, although Barnes noted that "many German families throughout the nation secretly are providing relief to Jews in individual cases."[24]

The international reaction to *Kristallnacht* only excited a wave of abuse in German newspapers that condemned the criticism as originating from Britain and the United States and accused them of being hypocritical considering, respectively, their treatment of the Palestinians and Negroes. The Berlin press tried to downplay the significance of President Roosevelt's recall of the American ambassador, Hugh R. Wilson, to Washington. In a dispatch from New York to *Der Angriff*, a German reporter maintained that "the majority of 'Jewish newspapers' carrying 'outrageous lies about Germany' were not finding a sale because 'the reader in the United States has had his fill of Jewish agitation.' " But the international reaction, long on protest, was short on concrete proposals. Barnes wrote of a Dutch effort to enlist Britain, France, Belgium, Switzerland, and Denmark in setting up border camps to provide a safe haven for Jews until permanent homes could be secured.[25]

While the rioting and mob action had ended, German Jews were subjected to the ongoing threat of arrest. Barnes wrote that in Frankfurt, members of the S.S. "halted passing pedestrians and demanded proof of 'Aryan' descent, and when this was not forthcoming herded them off to prison." The Nazi government announced that eight thousand apartments would soon be available in Berlin when their Jewish occupants were evicted. Barnes reported indications that wealthy Jews in prison were being "held for ransom" until they paid what the authorities considered to be their share of the fine levied on the Jewish community. Meanwhile, the Nazis' worst Jew-baiter, Julius Streicher, announced in a speech that he would soon demonstrate that the Pope, Pius XI, had Jewish ancestors, the only possible explanation for his efforts to assist the Jews.[26]

The German government responded to the recall of the American ambassador by ordering Hans H. Dieckhoff, its ambassador in Washington, back to Berlin. He would report, the communiqué read, on the "mood in the United States and on the peculiar attitude apparent there regarding German domestic affairs."

"Nowhere else," the *Völkischer Beobachter* said,

> is there so little understanding of the Jewish problem as in the United States, where not only elderly ladies with a complex, such as Dorothy Thompson, but also ambitious presidents, are helpless in the net of propaganda spread by Jewish finance. To recognize the full extent of Jewish influence in America, one should glance at the list of the President's advisers, the owners of the big banks, the proprietors and editors of the newspapers and the powerful men in the sphere of motion picture films.[27]

Such attacks continued, but Barnes also reported word of a German effort to move Jews to Latin America linked with a drive to improve its export market there. It was, Barnes remarked, "the first occasion on which the Nazi regime had manifested willingness to play an active role in solving the problem for which it is responsible—that of finding suitable areas for the settlement of German Jews driven to despair by persecution within the Reich." The shocked reaction of many nations to *Kristallnacht* and its aftermath had an effect on Germany's world trade. It was therefore perfectly possible that Berlin's motive was "to secure foreign trade advantages."[28]

In a November 22 dispatch, Barnes explored the linkage between the Munich Conference and the current drive against the Jews. He quoted at length from an article in *Das Schwarze Korps*, the organ of the S.S., in which he said the Nazis revealed for the first time their true feelings about the Munich Conference: "The implication was that the ruthlessness of the present anti-Jewish policy in the Reich was a consequence of the apparent weakness displayed by Britain and France during the September international crisis." The writer for *Das Schwarze Korps* noted that in 1933, there were those in Nazi circles who wished to solve the Jewish problem immediately "by the most brutal means." He continued:

In principle this view was correct, but at that time it had to remain a theory because we did not have the military power we possess today. In 1933 the Jews might have succeeded in provoking other nations to start a war of revenge against us. Today the worst of the democratic powers will think twice before they try that. We shall now complete the solution of the Jewish problem because it is necessary, because we do not any longer take notice of the world's shouting, and finally, because no one in the world can prevent us from doing so.

The problem is clear. It means the complete elimination and absolute segregation of the Jews. It is not merely the elimination of the Jews from German economic life, but much more than this. It cannot be expected of any German that he should live under the same roof with Jews recognized as race murderers and criminal enemies of the German people. The Jews must therefore be hunted out of our houses and residential districts, and housed in streets and blocks where they will keep to themselves. They must be branded, and the right must be taken from them of disposing in Germany of their real property or mortgages.

German policy would soon render all Jews destitute, the newspaper explained: "In line with their intrinsic nature, they would all sink to criminality ... Were we to permit this, it would result in a conspiracy of the underworld such as may perhaps be possible in the United States but certainly not in Germany. In the face of such a development, we should be confronted with the hard necessity of exterminating this Jewish underworld exactly as we in our orderly state exterminate criminals—with fire and sword. This would be the end of Jewry, indeed, its annihilation."[29]

This chilling specter was reinforced by ongoing efforts to confine Jews to specific areas that Barnes compared to the "pale of settlement" in Czarist Russia. Plans were afoot to require all Jews to wear a yellow badge. The property and financial holdings of Jews were confiscated. Meanwhile, more than 160,000 Jews applied for visas at the American embassy. A British committee sponsored a program in which Jewish children, allowed to leave Germany with one *deutschmark* and what little they could carry, were brought to Britain. Nevertheless, Barnes doubted that all of this horror would have "a profound and permanent effect in alienating any of the great mass of the inhabitants of this country from the regime of Chancellor Adolf Hitler and his aides."

In reaching this conclusion, Barnes drew on the experience of an English reporter following the 1934 "Night of Long Knives" in Germany and his own experience with the government-sponsored famine in the Soviet Union. In a recent book, *Insanity Fair*, the London *Times* reporter, Donald Reed, had written of his expectation that the Nazi killings on June 30, 1934, would be a lasting shock for the German people. Instead they were "quickly forgotten. ... How small a thing is the killing of even several hundred people in the life of so great a country." Barnes had expected the horror of the famine to weaken the Soviet regime but found that it did not.

Now, he asserted, "the plain fact is that the German people today have, so to speak, peace, bread and circuses, and much hard work to do, to boot. As long as they have all these things they—the great bulk of them—are not going to be very long or very seriously concerned over the fate of the half million which makes up the Jewish population of greater Germany." Barnes attributed this to the widely held perception that the Jews were somehow responsible for the postwar hardships in Germany, to the success of Nazi anti-Semitic propaganda, and to "emotional apathy—or a sort of resignation to fate, or perhaps even callousness" that he found widespread among Germans, although on some the events of November had made "an indelible impression—on humanitarian grounds."[30]

In fact, the German government seemed to have turned its attention once more to the international situation. Barnes saw the declaration of peace and amity signed by Germany and France on December 6 as a step in Hitler's plan to restore to Germany the gains made in the Treaty of Brest-Litovsk. That March 1918 treaty, negotiated by Erich von Ludendorff and Leon Trotsky between the German Empire and Soviet Russian, left Germany in control of Russian Poland and the Baltic states of Estonia, Latvia, and Lithuania, and created an "independent" Ukraine obliged to supply the grain needs of the German Empire. With Germany's defeat on the western front in November 1918, the Brest-Litovsk Treaty was abrogated and Germany lost those lands. In Barnes's view, "Almost from the birth of his regime Hitler has been engaged in a carefully calculated campaign to neutralize France along with Great Britain, so that, without being troubled by the back-door menace which defeated Ludendorff, he may be able to return to Ludendorff's design, building on more solid foundations." To further its aims, the German government was actively encouraging the creation of a satellite Ukrainian state, described by Barnes as including "all of the Ukrainian Soviet Socialist Republic, a constituent republic of the Soviet Union, as well as the Soviet Crimea, a good slice of Poland, an ample corner of Rumania and, finally, Ruthenia." This strategy was combined with new efforts to speed up Germany's economic mobilization for war.[31]

Christmas 1938 provided one example of the Nazi lack of restraint Barnes had noted. Far more than in previous years, Nazis were willing to risk offense to Christians by promoting their Winter Solstice celebration. To give his readers a sense of the atmosphere, Barnes quoted from the S.S. paper, *Das Schwarze Korps* :

Who at the season really believes he is commemorating the birth of Christ rather than the truly meaningful victory of life over the powers of death—as manifest to the Nordic man on this consecrated night of the solstice? No nation on earth has as good a right as have we to the solemn commemoration of this consecrated night. This night belongs to us. We observed it while the learned scribes of Rome and Byzantium were still arguing over whether the birthday of the founder of their religion should be observed on the first or the sixth of January. And the holiness of our sacred night [Weinachten] was of such powerful force that a hundred years after the advent of Christ, the Christian Church was forced to change the day of the birth of Christ to enjoy the benefits of the uninterrupted life force of unconquerable sources and strength. ...

The night belongs to us. We celebrated it with flaring bonfires and with burning wheels rolling from the mountains into the valleys amidst a garb of sparks when no alien missionary yet had entered Germania's forest bringing an alien gospel.

Christ was "nothing other than the old Germanic mother of Heaven, Fricka." Another new version of "Silent Night" was presented as a hymn to the race.[32]

For the Barnes family, the holidays took on a special significance. Esther wrote home that they included the American Jewish correspondent of the Jewish Telegraph Agency and his wife, Vic and Selma Bernstein, in their Thanksgiving celebration, and bade goodbye to Julie Rothschild just before the New Year. Christmas greetings from friends were more than usually meaningful: "Isn't it funny how much enjoyment one can get from knowing that your friends are interested in you. Have you noticed how much closer people hang together in time of stress like this last year?" Prospects for the New Year were not encouraging: "I can't say that I am looking forward to 1939 with great enthusiasm. I have usually been quite optimistic about starting a new year; but 1938 sort of took it out of me." Ralph urged his parents to keep their problems in perspective: "Keep smiling and for goodness sakes don't let stupid financial affairs get you down. If you, or we, were in the position of some of the families we know in this God-forsaken part of the world, you and we would have something to worry about."[33]

⁓

A German dispute with the American government carried over into the new year. Speaking in Cleveland on December 18, Harold Ickes, a close associate of President Roosevelt and the secretary of the interior in his administration, condemned the Nazis for their anti-Semitic outrages. Incensed, the German government demanded a repudiation of his remarks. When the State Department refused, the Nazis orchestrated a new wave of attacks on the United States in the German press. A "humorous" article in *Das Schwarze Korps* made a New Year's prediction that "the Negroes in the United States will increase in number mysteriously during the summer. However, it will be discovered that these people are not Negroes but white American citizens who have turned black in the face after hearing the lies sent out over the air by the broadcasting companies of the United States."[34]

In three early January dispatches, Barnes reviewed 1938, summarized current conditions in Germany, and looked toward international affairs in 1939. Recognizing the "enormous increase in German military strength," he asked who would resist Hitler: "Perhaps, as in 1938, the supreme war lord will get what he wants in 1939 simply through threatening to employ force." Barnes anticipated a coordinated effort on the part of Germany, Italy and Japan to keep the pressure on the other powers through crises in different parts of the world. Drawing from the annual economic survey produced by the state-owned *Reichkreditgesellschaft*, he pictured an economy strained by rearmament, the building of fortifications, and the absorption of new territories into the Reich. Germany had attempted to deal with its labor shortage by putting women to work in factories and fields and by importing labor, mostly from Italy. Attempts to move toward more conservative financing of the public debt had failed, while the amount of currency in circulation had increased by 38 percent.[35]

Radicals within the Nazi Party were pleased by Hitler's decree restoring the *Sturm Abteilung*, the Storm Troopers, to the position they had enjoyed before the 1934 Purge. He assigned the exultant S.A. the responsibility for pre- and post-military training, raising its prestige, as Barnes noted, and undermining "the conservative clique within the officers' corps." Clearly this move, which risked offending the military, was another manifestation of Hitler's sense of his personal power after his triumph at Munich. Three days later, Hitler had an unprecedented meeting with several hundred of the highest officers in all three branches of the German armed services. Barnes learned that they had been "harangued" and then entertained at dinner but he was unable to break through security to learn what topics had been discussed.[36]

Esther's letters reflected the tension:

Yes, we are sitting again on top of a boiling teakettle. I must say that I can't get excited. We can do nothing but wait until after the Nazi anniversary celebration on January 30th, Monday. It would be nice if we were to know then just what was going to happen. The Deuels have just had their home leave postponed until conditions at home and abroad are improved. They are terribly upset and disappointed. Mary Deuel and I are now searching the map to find a place where we haven't been to evacuate to, if the need arises. We still think Norway was an excellent idea; at least we know the ropes.[37]

In his anniversary speech, Hitler attributed U.S. press attacks on Germany to "a gigantic Jewish capitalistic propaganda" and "literally prophesied that, in the case of a war fomented 'by international Jewish financiers,' the result would not be Bolshevization of the world, and thus 'the victory of Jewry,' but rather 'annihilation of the Jewish race in Europe.' " With a demand for the return of Germany's former colonies and veiled threats against the Church and its clergy, the speech was, Barnes concluded, "one of the most confusing and oracular" of Hitler's career.[38]

When two days later the United States agreed to sell American military planes to France, a new storm of indignation and denunciation burst from the German press. President Roosevelt came in for particular abuse because, it was reported, he had told the Senate Armed Services Committee that "America's frontier lies in France." Clearly Washington had become "the center of war-mongering agitation against the totalitarian states." Britain and France were warned to keep their hands off Spain, as Franco's victory seemed imminent. No negotiations were possible: "For a complete settlement of the Spanish question, it is clear that there must be a total military victory carried to the point where the last Red hireling has left Spanish soil, or an armistice followed by unconditional surrender of the remainder of the Red Army."[39]

Early in the year Esther had written of rumors about the plans of the *Herald Tribune* management: "Some definite changes are coming in the next few weeks in our service, but we don't know how it will affect us. We should know something before the end of the month." After sending off his report on Hitler's January 31 speech to the Reichstag, Barnes wrote home: "I find the work fascinating still, though it is hard going sometimes. I seem to be able to get a good deal of material in the papers. There are rumors of a new shake-up in the foreign service; which I am told is not to be to my disadvantage. I'll let you know the details when I hear them."[40]

Two weeks later, he sent off a cable to his parents: "OFFERED ACCEPTED HEADSHIP LONDON BUREAU MOVING MARCH." He followed with a long letter:

> *I just finished dispatching a wire to you, announcing that we have been offered the London post, and that we have accepted. Something has been in the air for weeks, but we couldn't get anything very definite on the matter. We decided not to say too much to you until there was something concrete to write about. Yesterday a telephone call from Moscow routed me out of bed. Half asleep, I heard Joe Barnes say over the wire that he had been offered Berlin, so that I could go on to London. The "brilliant" Mr. Hills, our European manager, had wired Joe Barnes in Moscow, but had sent me a letter by ordinary mail which reached me at about 6:00 this afternoon.*

Ralph explained his decision to accept the transfer:

> *As you know, I have considered Berlin in recent years about the most fascinating post possible. It still is fascinating; but have been here three and one-half years, and have covered the rise of Germany, up to a point, and in my opinion we are wise now in going to London while the opportunity is offered to us. We have had nearly nine years under dictatorships, so it will be strange, at first, harder in some ways, perhaps, but easier in many others. One important point is that a person who wants to become, to a small degree, at least, an expert on European affairs, must know something about the British Isles.*

The new assignment lifted his spirits: "A little more than a year ago it looked rather black for us when 'Brother Hills' took over the European service management to reduce costs; but a good news-year seems to have counteracted anything that he could do. At least, New York seems to have sufficient confidence in me to offer me what they consider the best position on this side of the water, that is, the best correspondent's post. Everything will come out all right in the wash."[41]

A theme through several of Barnes's last articles from Germany was the dominant influence of the "radicals" in Nazi inner circles. He pictured Hermann Göring, Hitler's designated heir, as a voice of relative moderation, pitted against Goebbels, Himmler and von Ribbentrop. Barnes thought Himmler in particular "may bear watching" with his control of the police and the S.S. While Göring occasionally got his way, the radicals more frequently won out because they reflected Hitler: "No longer can there be any doubt that the *Führer* is engaged in what for him is a holy war, a crusade in which there are two principles and related tenets: First, the unification of the German nation in a single-minded, regimented, militarized eternal state. Second, the destruction of Bolshevism. A corollary, of course, is the liquidation of 'Jewish power.' In the prosecution of his 'holy war' Hitler is as fervent as Torquemada; to understand his methods it is necessary to go back to the religious wars."[42]

While Barnes anticipated a new attack on the church, he did not as late as March 6 expect moves that might lead to war, reiterating points he had made before: "Germany is in no condition to wage war on a large scale, and especially not a war which would last for more than a few months. The raw materials stored in the Reich are pitiably low, the four-year plan to provide domestic raw materials with substitutes has not progressed sufficiently to be an effective aid, and the once superb rail transportation system of the Reich has deteriorated appreciably through neglect. Moreover, the shortage of skilled industrial workers and farm laborers would develop into an acute problem in case of general mobilization." Despite his years of experience with Hitler and his regime, Barnes still assumed that practical considerations would forestall catastrophe.[43]

Leaving Germany was complicated by Joan's bronchitis, then Suzanne's appendectomy. Ralph and Esther decided that he would go ahead to London, in order to spend some time with Joseph Driscoll whom he was replacing. Ralph shared his plans with his parents: "I hope to get a couple weeks off, soon after my arrival in England, to spend in the English countryside alone, resting, reading, riding my German bicycle, and getting the feel of the land, talking with all sorts of people."[44]

Part IV. The Coming of War:
March 1939—November 1940

This morning, nearly forty-eight hours after the fighting forces of Fuehrer Adolf Hitler began their invasion of Poland, the question as to whether this attack without warning was to plunge Europe, and perhaps the world, into another disastrous war was still undecided.

Just before 8 o'clock last night Prime Minister Neville Chamberlain told an impatient and angry House of Commons that thus far Berlin had not replied to the identical ultimatums dispatched there by London and Paris on Friday night, and that the British and French governments were consulting as to how much further time should be given to Hitler in which to answer.

Apparently a fleeting hope that Premier Benito Mussolini of Italy might forestall war was having a good deal to do with the signal to the British and French commanders to begin marching. Yet Chamberlain told the Commons that, however much his government appreciated the efforts of Rome, it could not participate in the five-power conference which Il Duce proposes while "Poland is being subjected to invasion, her towns under bombardment and while Danzig is being made subject to unilateral settlements by force."

Ralph Barnes, *Herald Tribune,*
September 3, 1939, from London

Barnes arrived in London on March 12, settling for the time being in a small boarding house near Hyde Park. A day later, in defiance of the agreements signed at Munich, the Germans entered Prague to take over the remainder of Czechoslovakia. The family took the news calmly: "I talked with Esther by phone a few nights ago; and at that time all was well with the family in Berlin. Up to that time Esther was not seriously concerned about the new international crisis; but there have been developments since which put a much graver stamp on the situation. Britain seems to be stiffening her stand. I think that the chances are against a real conflict within the next couple of weeks. Nevertheless, we want to be on the safe side, so I may suggest to Esther that she hasten her preparations for departure."[1]

Esther was initially cool: "Well, here we are still sitting. Can't seem to get out of this place. It would be a joke on us if we got caught, after running out of here twice before—once to Belgium, and once to Norway. ... Do you suppose that there is really one peaceful place left in the world?"[2]

Another week passed before her next letter, still from Berlin:

Poor Ralph was so mad when he learned what I have had to do to get our things out of here. He thought that he had everything in order when he left. Maybe some day I will settle down and write you some of my experiences this past week. A woman alone is just so much dirt under a man's feet in this country, and it is almost impossible to get anything official done.

People in the offices haven't the slightest idea of what they are there for, and no one knows just what one has to do to get out of here. They completely disregard the fact that we are American citizens, and tried to make us go out as emigrants, and prove that we were not Jewish. ... I shall not say any more about that until I cool down a little.

I am not paying any attention to the political situation in Europe, but am going about the things that have to be done. I am glad that I don't have to sit here in Berlin during the next few months, not knowing from one day to the next whether I should be getting out or not. I shall at least be on the other side for a change.[3]

Finally on April 3, Esther, Joan and Suzanne were able to leave Berlin: "All of our American friends were so lovely to us. We had twenty or more down to see us off. We got on to the boat about 10:30 Monday night. Did I give three cheers when the train crossed the border from Germany into Holland!"[4]

Meanwhile, Ralph was orienting himself to his new assignment but a bit chagrined that he had not anticipated the new crisis: "Curiously enough, the situation began to reach a head on the night that I arrived in London. Apparently there was no advance notice in Berlin of what was to happen; or if there was, I was asleep."[5] He made his planned trip through the countryside, visiting Cambridge, Lincoln, Doncaster and Leeds. The first article to appear under his byline from Britain was datelined Leeds, and reported that ordinary people in England were still hoping that war could be avoided but were sure that Hitler represented a threat and must be stopped. Support for Chamberlain was greater than one would guess reading British newspapers, Barnes wrote: "Though he condemns Hitler and sees the potential menace in the authoritarian regimes, the man in the street is by no means convinced that war is the only way out. He may think Chamberlain should be a little more firm, but he is prepared to give him the benefit of the doubt, provisionally. The feeling that 'he kept us out of war' is still strong."[6]

The initial response of the Chamberlain government to the German takeover of Czechoslovakia was hesitant. The Prime Minister seemed stunned by Hitler's total betrayal of the Munich agreements. As the pressures Barnes perceived in the countryside were combined with those in the House of Commons, the government signaled its resolve through joint military staff talks with the French and by encouraging volunteers to join the Territorial Army, a force corresponding roughly to the National Guard in the United States. The government was still unwilling to introduce conscription, although Barnes noted that "French and other European leaders, as well as many influential Britons, think conscription in some form is the only answer, if Britain's apparent determination to stand up to Hitler is to command support."[7]

Clearly, considerable diplomatic maneuvering was taking place behind the scenes. Rumors of a pending guarantee to Poland and Rumania surfaced but Barnes reported the problems of a common front against German aggression:

> In diplomatic quarters the view was current today that once again the Soviet Union might be "left out in the cold," as the British government continued its efforts to establish a system of mutual assistance. Apart from the fact that some influential British leaders desire to avoid covenants with the Bolsheviks, Poland and Rumania, it is understood, are reluctant to make commitments under an agreement to which the Soviet Union would be a party. A Polish spokesman in London was emphatic in stating that Poland could not accept a scheme which

would involve "even a peaceful invasion of Polish territory by Soviet troops." The Poles, of course, fear that, once in the country, the Russians might remain. As for the Rumanians, they fear that "a peaceful Russian invasion" might mean to them the loss of Bessarabia, which was Russian territory before the World War.[8]

In Germany, the Nazis were waging against Poland the same kind of vigorous press campaign as they had against Czechoslovakia before Munich. The Polish foreign minister, Colonel Josef Beck, made an emergency trip to London to seek aid. The *Herald Tribune* reported "on good authority, but without official confirmation, that the British government had decided to offer Poland a unilateral guaranty against aggression by Germany, thus reversing Great Britain's traditional policy of avoiding formal commitments on the Continent." Excluded from the guaranty were the former German territories of Danzig and the Polish Corridor, now under Polish control. The British indicated that they were still open to a negotiated settlement on the two areas lost to Germany at the end of World War I but still largely German in population. On March 31, Chamberlain announced the new policy in a formal statement before the House of Commons.[9]

On April 3, again addressing the House, Chamberlain indicated that he would extend Britain's support to the nations from the Baltic to the Black Sea. He emphasized that his plans contained "no threat to Germany so long as Germany will be a good neighbor." He concluded: "I trust that our action will prove to be the turning point— not towards war, which wins nothing, cures nothing, ends nothing— but toward a more wholesome peace era in which reason will take the place of force and threats will make way for cool and well marshaled argument." His statement won the support of Anthony Eden, Alfred Duff Cooper, and Winston Churchill, all Conservatives who had parted with their government over its appeasement policy.[10]

The Italian invasion of Albania on Good Friday, April 7, disturbed British calculations. Away in Scotland when the crisis hit, Chamberlain returned for meetings with his cabinet and with American Ambassador Joseph P. Kennedy. Mussolini's action, combined with the adherence of Franco's Spain to the Anti-Comintern Pact, threatened France and the British position in the Mediterranean. Nevertheless, the *Herald Tribune* reported: "Britain, like France, has not the slightest intention of going to war over Albania, any more than it did over Czecho-Slovakia. Having written King Zog's kingdom off the map, London and Paris will concentrate on saving Greece, Turkey, Rumania and Poland—and possibly Yugoslavia and Bulgaria, as well—from the acquisitive powers of the Rome-Berlin axis."[11]

Barnes wrote that, in fact, the invasion of Albania hardly deterred Chamberlain from his efforts to reach an understanding with Mussolini: "Persons close to him say that Chamberlain still thinks that, because of *Il Duce*'s own long-time interest, there is a chance of detaching him from his partner, Adolf Hitler, in the Rome-Berlin axis." Chamberlain's policy was opposed by many in the Foreign Office. Barnes quoted one anonymous observer: "Distinct whiffs of appeasement are floating across from Downing Street." The venerable Liberal David Lloyd George warned: "We have been fooled, and fooled repeatedly. Now we are to be fooled again by infinitely cleverer men. I beg the British people not to allow this great country to be made the laughing stock."[12]

Chamberlain extended British pledges of "full military support" to Rumania and Greece. President Roosevelt entered the fray with dramatic telegrams to Hitler and Mussolini requesting assurances that they would not attack a list of thirty-one countries in Europe and the Middle East. Well-received in Britain, the telegrams set the German Foreign Office to work. Through diplomatic pressure, Germany secured statements from the majority of the countries Roosevelt had listed to the effect that they had no fear of German aggression. In a Reichstag speech full of heavy-handed sarcasm, Hitler read out the responses and attacked Roosevelt. Barnes quoted a provincial Yorkshire paper that compared the countries to "an intended victim of gangsters who feels a revolver in the small of his back and is bidden to assure the passing policeman that he needs no assistance and is only having a pleasant chat with his good friend."[13]

~

Barnes covered these events while still getting his bearings in Britain and beginning to establish the contacts he needed. He found his assistant, Frank Kelley, to be an able journalist. He sent his parents a picture of how the bureau worked:

The work for tonight is pretty well cleaned up, so I shall get off a short letter to you. I have done about 1,000 words on the general situation—diplomatic activity—since there were few "spot-news" developments of outstanding importance to report. Whether there is news or not, we have a [minimum] five minute call to New York, telephone, so it is well to send something when possible; otherwise the time would be wasted. The Cockney clerk—Williams—who transmits the stuff, gets it over at the rate of almost 200 words per minute, which is fast. He filed *my 1,100 words tonight in just six minutes. The recording machines in New York are excellent, much better, very much better, than those at present in the Paris office. At the rate Williams gets the material over, the telephone transmission is but little more than half as costly as the cable, press rate, about two and one half cents per word. Telephonic transmission is 15 shillings ($3.60) per minute. The transmission errors are fewer than one might expect.[14]*

Ralph and Esther encountered many old friends in London. Aside from the Stonemans, they saw Paul Cremona and his wife. Cremona had been a correspondent for the *Christian Science Monitor* in Rome during Ralph's time there. Recently expelled from Italy by the Fascist government, he now worked for the British Broadcasting Company. Bill Shirer, too, was briefly in England. Ralph dined with him and Ed Murrow at Simpson's-in-the-Strand, just a short walk from the *Herald Tribune* offices. Their Berlin acquaintance Martha Dodd, daughter of the then American ambassador to Berlin, had published a book about her experiences in Germany. In her chapter on the press corps, she had written:

Another young and animated couple, who were in Berlin during the last two years of my stay, were the Ralph Barneses who had spent five years in Moscow as Herald Tribune *correspondent. Ralph was the most painstaking, nervous, and maddening newspaper hound I have ever met. He had a naivete about news-gathering that was extraordinary in one of his years and experience. Every bit of information, no matter how trivial or unconnected it was, he would track down to its last source, sacrificing no one and no thing in his attempt to lay its ghost. Sometimes he would have something when he finally got there but as often as not he would find himself holding the bag. He was extremely excitable and definitely didn't like the Nazis. But he had neither the cynicism nor the incisive keenness, the "nose for news," that many of his colleagues had. He went about the whole business of news-hunting in an earnest, passionate, stammering way. Sometimes he got scoops through this procedure, sometimes he was left out on a limb. He was erratic and had most endearing traits of character and wore a continual expression of intense worry on his face. He was extremely argumentative and tenacious and many a night Bill Shirer, my brother, the two wives, Ralph, and I stayed up late at night heatedly discussing various theoretical approaches to Fascism. He was sensitive and had a child-like innocence of personality, cherishing a hurt or a grudge a long time. But I was devoted to him and his strangely beautiful, passive and understanding wife, Esther.[15]*

Barnes wrote his father:

Dad, you have mentioned Martha Dodd's book in three letters, including that in which you typed her comment of this branch of the Barnes family. What she said about me was amusing and, I think, not very consistent. But I suppose that I have some of the characteristics she mentioned. Walter Duranty was accustomed to say in Moscow that it is better to be damned than not to be quoted. Martha was extremely anti-Nazi and pro-Soviet, a fact which resulted in disagreements between us on political topics. Though, of course, I held no brief for the Nazi set-up, I tried to maintain a somewhat more balanced view. I liked her personally, and she almost invariably invited Esther and me to her small parties at the Embassy. She and Bill Shirer almost always agreed on political topics, so they got along famously.[16]

Despite Barnes's ambition and competitiveness, he was gracious when his colleagues were recognized: "I have just learned that Louis Lochner, head of the Associated Press bureau in Berlin, received the Pulitzer Prize for 1938. He is a first class reporter; I am glad for him. Seldom before, I think, has an agency man, in contrast to a special correspondent, been given the award. Lochner has worked long and hard. I met him first at Baden Baden in 1929."[17]

The uncertainties of the international situation made the Barnes family reluctant to sign the three-year lease customarily required to rent apartments or houses in London. Esther wrote to Salem: "Who wants to sign up for anything these days, with Hitler and Mussolini still loose in Europe." She continued, "What fun it is to write anything we feel about things over here in England, where there is no postal censorship as there was in Germany. Joan and Suzanne are planning a special celebration of Hitler's birthday. They have a little booklet of pictures of Hitler which they plan to burn and dance around while it is burning. Do we sound like barbarians? We can't feel otherwise after our stay in that country." Another letter told of the efforts of a German friend to get out of Germany but cautioned: "Don't say too much about that. One never knows how news gets back to the Fatherland these days."[18]

In the end, they took a cottage at the beach for the summer. Esther and the girls settled at Lancing on the Sussex coast, a little more than an hour by train from London, so that Ralph could join them on weekends, arriving late Saturday night and returning Monday afternoon. As Esther explained: "We really can live down here cheaper than in London, and as we have nothing to hold us there it is grand to be here. Next year we may not be able to do it. When we take on a place in London we don't expect to be able to afford to leave it again." As at Kladow and despite intentions to the contrary, the house at Lancing became that summer a haven for friends, both those stationed in London and those passing through.

⁓

The international situation and its effect on British life dominated Barnes's reporting. The government finally mounted a credible deterrent to Hitler's ambitions with serious measures for military preparedness. Sir John Simon, the chancellor of the Exchequer, went to the House of Commons to introduce the largest peace-time budget in British history, with a 57 percent increase in military spending. Revenue would be raised through an increase in the surtax affecting Britons with higher incomes and through taxes on automobile and motorbike owners.[19]

Limited conscription soon followed over the objection of the Labour and Liberal minorities, who castigated the Chamberlain government for abandoning its vow against a peacetime draft. Barnes reminded his readers that in the Great War, Britain had only turned to conscription in early 1916, after its volunteer army had been decimated. Looking back still further, he pointed out that only twenty-four thousand of Wellington's force at Waterloo were British, the rest being the soldiers of Britain's allies or hired troops: "To put it bluntly, Britain opened her purse liberally, but husbanded the blood of her manhood." This new policy, dismissed by the German press as "compulsory gymnastics," would provide a trained reserve of one million men in five years.[20]

Diplomatic maneuvering continued as Britain tried to find a way to bring the Soviet Union into the front against Hitler without offending other allies. In an article without a byline, the *Herald Tribune* reported Chamberlain's double dilemma: "Britain's decision not to enter any military alliance with Russia at present was believed to have been dictated by fear of its effect on Japan, Spain, Portugal, Poland, Rumania and other nations, including most of those in Latin America, which are fervently 'anti-Red.' Britain does not wish to damage her 'friendship' with such states, or to give the Berlin-Rome-Tokio triangle any excuse for aggressive action against 'Bolshevism.' " Furthermore, "In informed opinion Britain's rejection of the triple alliance project may also be put down to Prime Minister Chamberlain's fear of offending a small but influential section of his own Conservative party, the so-called 'church crowd' of elderly clergymen and retired army colonels, who 'would rather die on a bed of honor than have anything to do with those godless Reds.' "[21]

But, as German pressure on Poland over the question of Danzig rose, so too did pressure on the British government to reach an understanding with the Soviet Union. David Lloyd George stated the case: "Without Russia, the three guarantees to Poland, Rumania and Greece are the most reckless commitments any country has entered into. I say more: They are demented pledges. To meet the great deficiency in our forces it is proposed to have 200,000 conscripts in leisurely installments of 50,000. That is madness. The government needs Russia, but it does not want Russia. Without Russia there would be two alternatives if the government were called on to redeem its pledges: It might be that within a few days or weeks they would face certain disaster, or skulk out on their pledges, as they have done before." The tortuous process of building a front against German aggression continued with the adhesion of Turkey to the Anglo-French understanding. But when the Chamberlain government finally offered an alliance to the Soviet Union, it was rebuffed because Estonia, Latvia and Lithuania, more afraid of the Soviets than the Germans, refused to be included as the Soviets demanded.[22]

Chamberlain maintained his position, as in a speech to a Conservative women's gathering that Frank Kelley reported: "In many minds, the danger spot in Europe today is Danzig, where our assurances to Poland are clear and concise. Although we would be glad to see the differences between Poland and Germany amicably settled by discussion, although we think that they could and should be so settled, if any attempt were made to change the situation by force in such a way as to threaten Polish independence, why, then, that would inevitably start a general conflagration in which this country would be involved." In the same speech, the prime minister rather plaintively defended his past policies, noting that he was the "target of a lot of rotten eggs, but that does not keep me awake, because I believe I have the support of the women of this country. They have a clearer vision than some of those whose sight is obscured by party or personal prejudice. You have watched the old umbrella going 'round, and you have, I believe, approved our efforts, strenuous and up to now successful, to keep Europe out of war. ... It has never been part of our policy to be meddlesome busybodies, interfering in other people's concerns."[23]

When Hitler abandoned the 1935 Anglo-German naval accord in which Germany had agreed to limit the size of its navy, Barnes undertook a three-part series on "Seapower." His major theme was the continued confidence Britain put in its navy, the "vital lifeline." He included a recapitulation of his visit to Kiel for the German naval review the previous summer, a review closed to foreign naval attachés because of their greater knowledge, but open to journalists. After studying recent technical works on naval power, Barnes speculated on the impact of increased use of submarines and air power on war at sea.[24]

~

The press of events had given Barnes little opportunity for the broader coverage that had characterized his filing from Moscow and Berlin. Through the spring and summer of 1939, however, he and Kelley did attempt to give their readers a sense that issues other than the threat of war touched the lives of ordinary Britons. They wrote about the royal family, a submarine tragedy that took ninety-nine lives, and a manuscript find that suggested that Shakespeare had not only "written Shakespeare" but perhaps parts of works attributed to other authors as well. Barnes attempted to accompany King George VI and Queen Elizabeth on their state trip to the United States in May and June, but found that no American correspondents were to be included.[25]

Both he and Esther confessed to homesickness: "Often Esther and I long for a sight of Oregon. Though our experiences in Europe have been fascinating, living has just not been as comfortable as it would have been some place, or almost any place, west of the Cascade mountains." The Sussex coast, they assured their families, did not compare with that of Oregon. Ralph even revived an old scheme for some time in the United States:

> Yesterday afternoon I had tea with Walter Lippmann and his new
> wife, and had a most interesting conversation on the political situation.
> Though he has been associated with the Herald Tribune for a long
> time, I had not met him before—he is quite charming.
>
> I also discussed with Lippmann the Nieman Fellowships at
> Harvard. I still have in mind to try for one of them next year, if things
> look up financially. I do want to make a break soon, to provide time
> for thinking things over—some solid reading. As much as anything
> else, I think that it would be good for us to have a breath of American
> air. Lippmann was enthusiastic about the idea; said that he would
> push the project, both with the Tribune and with Harvard, and
> expressed the view that there would be no question about an award,
> were I to apply. He plays a considerable role in Harvard affairs, and a
> year ago was a member of the committee which decided how the
> Nieman money should be used. I shall take advantage of the

opportunity only if things open up financially, of course. Applications do not have to be in until early next year.[26]

In light of the international situation, Esther was anxious for Ralph to take his three-week vacation:

I am afraid that Hitler may be starting something the end of July. If he is going to start something I hope he does it then and doesn't wait until the end of August, or September, just when we plan to go back to London. Goebbels has been spouting this week-end, and the press has quite a bit to say about Danzig. I suppose that it will come; but here's hoping it comes while we are still out of London. Air-raids there give me the creeps. We brought our gas-masks down with us. There is a civil and military aviation field not far from here. Planes are flying around most of the time, but not quite as bad as at Kladow."[27]

~

"Ominous reports" of German plans for Danzig led again to a strong British statement, this time by the foreign minister, Lord Halifax, warning that any use of force to alter Danzig's status would mean war. Barnes wrote that this stand found widespread support with all parties "reflecting a national unity on foreign policy such as this country perhaps has not attained at any other time since the World War." Several leading British newspapers took editorial stances demanding that Winston Churchill be included in the cabinet. Barnes explained to his readers that such an appointment would be a symbol of British determination and a signal of the definitive end of the policy of appeasement, because Churchill had for years "warned the government of the danger which *Der Führer's* regime involved and demanded both resistance to his demands and British rearmament to the teeth. Looked at askance for years as a 'dangerous firebrand,' he now has had the satisfaction of seeing the government adopt, in succession, almost all the policies he advocated. His prestige in the House of Commons and throughout the country now is great. He is considered one of the ablest administrators in the country, and also enjoys a reputation as a military strategist."[28]

While not yet ready to bring his greatest critic into the government, Chamberlain continued his hard line, promising British support if the Polish government resisted an attempt "to settle the status of Danzig by unilateral action organized by surreptitious methods." He sent 120 British bombers over France for a war exercise and asked Parliament for new increases in the arms budget. Perhaps most telling, the prime minister announced plans for a test mobilization of the fleet in August, in conjunction with Royal Air Force and army maneuvers. Barnes saw in the naval concentration a clear message to Hitler and Mussolini. But he noted that, in the war of nerves being played out that summer, two developments concerned British and French leaders: "First the slow progress of the negotiations to bring Soviet Russia into full collaboration in the 'peace front' and, second, the failure of the Congress of the United States to respond to the efforts of President Roosevelt to relax the embargo on American war supplies to belligerents." The view from London was that "a certainty of full Anglo-French-Soviet collaboration from the outset in case of a new aggression and of unlimited American supplies to former Allies in case of war" might deter Hitler.[29]

Not until the end of July had the negotiations with the Soviet Union progressed to the point that the British government was able to announce high level military staff talks to coordinate strategy. High-ranking officers were dispatched to Moscow to reach an understanding, without which the Soviets were unwilling to proceed. Over the objections of the Labor opposition and of Winston Churchill, Chamberlain sought an adjournment of Parliament for its regular summer break. The two Houses were not expected to reconvene until October 3.[30]

Before going to Lancing for his own vacation, Barnes wrote an article evoking the summer twenty-five years before, when Europe had descended into war. Reminding his readers of the long-held belief that Germany had gone to war in 1914 in part because England had not clearly indicated its intention to join the opposition, Barnes wrote: "If today it comes to a fight in which Britain is involved, neither Chancellor Adolf Hitler nor anyone else can plead that London has failed to make its position clear in advance."[31]

In a long mail article, Barnes provided his readers with an analysis of German strategy, a *blitzkrieg* to bring the war to a swift, successful conclusion. He detailed British plans to safeguard their cities from bombing attacks. Nor would Britain remain on the defensive in the air: "Britain would not be the first to bomb large urban areas, but if Germany were to resort to this sort of massacre of civilians, the country undoubtedly would retaliate."[32]

In her letters, Esther reflected the opinion that war was likely: "Just a month until I will have to think of going back to London. As you say, it would be nice to know whether or not we are returning to London, or really coming home to the States. I am positive something will start just when we get back to London. I don't see how in the world the international situation can be worked out otherwise, unless Hitler can slip out of it with a very clever diplomatic move. He has gone too far to just let it pass off without making some move." Still they found an apartment in Hempstead so that they could move to London in the fall. Although Barnes interrupted his vacation to cover the king's review of the assembled fleet, Esther wrote that the family had a "jolly time while Ralph has been here. I haven't seen Ralph so well and so much himself for years. Can be thankful for some things, I guess. We have had a wonderful time together."[33]

The storm clouds were sufficiently threatening that Chamberlain called his cabinet back to London for a meeting August 22, but before the ministers could gather the thunderbolt came: Germany and the Soviet Union had agreed to sign a non-aggression pact, destroying the British effort to form a common front against Hitler. In London, Frank Kelley wrote the story of the British reaction while Barnes hastened up from Lancing, all thought of vacation abandoned.[34] He reported the government's communiqué maintaining that the Nazi-Soviet Pact would not change its obligations to Poland and that there was nothing in the Polish-German difficulties to justify the 'use of force involving a European war, with all its tragic consequences." . He found the British people undaunted, with "little excitement manifest in the streets."[35]

When, on August 23, the actual signing of the Nazi-Soviet Pact was announced, Barnes wrote that the British were asking the obvious question: "Has Josef V. Stalin in effect opened the path to the German subjugation of Poland and unrestricted German hegemony over the bulk of Eastern Europe to the Soviet frontiers?" The government sought the approval of a war powers bill. Speaking in its support, Chamberlain reminded his listeners of their cause: "If, in spite of all our efforts to find a way of peace—and God knows I have done my best—if, in spite of all that, we find ourselves forced to embark upon a struggle which is bound to be fraught with suffering and misery for all mankind and the end of which no man can foresee; if that should happen, we shall not be fighting for the political future of a far-away city in a foreign land. We shall be fighting for the preservation of those principles of which I have spoken, and the destruction of which would involve the destruction of all possibilities of peace and security." The bill passed the House of Commons with only four dissenters.[36]

In an off-the-record interview recounted by James Reston in his memoirs, the American correspondents found the American ambassador Joseph P. Kennedy still opposed to war: "I don't care if Germany carves up Poland with British support. I'm for appeasement

100 percent, and if 1000 percent is more than 100 percent, I'm for it 1000 percent." Reston continued that Ralph Barnes, among the reporters present, asked Kennedy: "Have you been telling this to Mr. Chamberlain?" The ambassador responded: "I've been telling him every chance I had every day for more than a year."[37]

Hitler soon made the price of "peace" clear. He summoned the British ambassador, Nevile Henderson, to the Chancellery and scheduled later meetings with the French, Italian and Japanese ambassadors. Immediately after the interview, Henderson flew to London bringing reports that Barnes understood to indicate a 'take it or leave it' offer, with Hitler threatening to go to war unless his demands were met. From what Barnes could learn, Hitler's terms were the immediate return of Danzig to the Reich and direct negotiations with Poland for the return of the other Polish territories which had been a part of the German Empire. While the British signed a new five-year treaty of alliance with Poland, rumors of a renewed Chamberlain effort toward appeasement were denied. Still, in two meetings to consider Hitler's demand, the Cabinet was split. Barnes wrote: "Although apparently there is accord among Prime Minister Neville Chamberlain and his aides that the full demands of *Der Führer* are unacceptable, one portion of the government, it is understood, desires to go further than the other in leaving the door open in the hope of conciliating Hitler."[38]

On August 27, Barnes was interviewed on NBC radio for broadcast in the United States. Asked whether Britain would "live up to her pledged word" or abandon Poland to avoid war, Barnes responded:

Officials at Whitehall are tight-lipped, but it was figured in some way officially that Britain will stand irrevocably by the letter and spirit of the Anglo-Polish pact signed here two days ago. Now, if these words are to be taken at their face value, obviously there can be no capitulation. However, it is said that the British reply will not be the last word. The belief is current in official and some unofficial quarters here that this respite resulting from Hitler's interview with Henderson is a very good thing in the present war of nerves.

The question arises as to just what the message which Hitler dispatched contained. Persons close to British governmental quarters say that of the hour and fifteen minutes which Sir Nevile Henderson spent with Hitler, one hour and ten minutes was taken up by a sermon delivered by Hitler. He is noted for delivering such sermons to diplomats when they call upon him. Also the question arises as to why three cabinet sessions are necessary to prepare a reply to this message of the Führer. The official explanation is that Britain does not intend to

*be rushed into irrevocable action. Again, it is clear that London intends
to give Hitler time to think things over. There is also the idea that by
the time the Cabinet convenes tomorrow at noon something may turn
up. There is no definite indication as to what this might be, but the
British Government is grasping at the straw that there might be some
development which would put a different face on the picture.*[39]

In an article he filed the same evening, Barnes catalogued the
rumors and denials swirling about London: that Britain's delay in
responding was due to its efforts to secure American support, that
Mussolini would again bring the parties to the conference table,
that a mysterious visitor had arrived from Berlin with new proposals.
As to the outcome, he reported: "One of the prevailing theories here
about the strategic situation, if it comes to a fight, involves the
supposition that at the outset the Germans will concentrate on a
steamroller push into Poland and remain almost entirely on the
defensive in the west. Thus, it is suggested, Hitler may refrain from
any serious bombing of France and Britain, trusting, apparently, that
the British and French will not desire to risk killing German civilians
from the air except in retaliation to German bombings." Once Hitler
had accomplished his objectives in Poland, he would seek an
armistice, and Barnes asked whether "London and Paris would not
be prepared to accept the *Führer's* armistice and peace proposals rather
than face the prospect of a long-drawn-out war."[40]

Clearly, the perception that Britain and France would or could in
fact do little to aid Poland was commonly held. Nevertheless, the
British Cabinet sent Nevile Henderson back to Berlin with a strong
message for Hitler and began the process of putting the country on a
war footing. Although the term had not begun, London's one million
school children assembled at their schools with their gas masks and
emergency rations as a test of evacuation plans. Chamberlain assured
a supportive House of Commons that Britain would honor its pledges
to Poland, as Poland rejected German demands for immediate cession
of the disputed territories.[41]

~

When finally, in the early hours of September 1, the invasion of
Poland came, it seemed almost anticlimactic. The British government,
despite its pledges, did not declare war but instead issued an
ultimatum to Hitler demanding an immediate suspension of the
invasion and a withdrawal of his forces from Poland. When the
twenty-four hour deadline on the ultimatum expired without a

response, Britain declared war but not before Chamberlain had faced what Barnes described as an "impatient and angry House of Commons" unconvinced of the government's resolve. During the session held the evening of September 2, Arthur Greenwood, acting head of the Labour Party, expressed the sentiments of the House: "I hope, therefore, that tomorrow the right honorable gentleman—and no one would care to be in his shoes tonight—will be able to tell us the mind of the British Government, that there shall be no more devices for dragging out what has been dragged out for the last two days. The moment we look like weakening, from that moment the dictatorship knows we are beaten. We are not beaten, we shall not be beaten, and we cannot be beaten, but delay is dangerous."[42]

The next day, when Chamberlain announced the state of war to the House, Barnes quoted from his remarks: "This is a sad day for all of us, and for none is it sadder than for me. Everything I worked for, everything I hoped for, everything I believed through my public life has crashed in ruins. There is but one thing left for me, and that is that I hope with what strength and power I have, to forward the cause for which we have all sacrificed so much. I cannot tell what part I may be allowed to play. I trust that I may live to see the day when Hitlerism has been destroyed, so as to restore Liberty in Europe." Chamberlain reshuffled his cabinet to address the reality of war, finally bringing in his old nemesis, Winston Churchill, as First Lord of the Admiralty. Barnes wrote: "The great majority of Britons, now girding themselves for what may be a long, grueling struggle, rejoiced when they learned that the man who is in many respects the outstanding figure in British public life today—Churchill—had been designated as civilian chief of Britain's great naval power."[43]

London was immediately beset with a number of air-raid warnings. During that busy September Sunday, the alarms forced Barnes to retire to shelters several times but the warnings turned out to be false. Days before, the American Embassy had urged Americans resident in Britain or traveling in the country to leave. Many had crowded to the available ships. Now came word that one of those ships, the *Athenia*, had been torpedoed. Forty-four lives were lost, and the survivors told harrowing stories of their rescue. Esther wrote her family from the new cottage, Meadway on Ald Salts Road in Lancing, where she and the children had settled: "We kept thinking that surely things wouldn't blow up, until they did; and then we thought that surely it couldn't last; and I did want to avoid the expense of the trip to the States. Now, so far, I am comfy and happy here, considering everything, and since the *Athenia* disaster I am really afraid to start out on the ocean. Maybe I am a coward, but I do feel safer with my feet on dry land. Reading about the experiences of people on that boat, I do hate to have the girls go through it. I feel I want to be near Ralph too."[44]

Willing to give up his London post to be at the scene of the action, Barnes applied to be one of the ten American correspondents who would accompany the British Expeditionary Force to France. He was accepted and scheduled to leave in mid-October. The *Herald Tribune* offered to pay passage for Esther and the children to the United States. From New York, their old friend Rida Stowe wired an invitation for them to stay with her as long as they wished. But Alice Rogers, the wife of Newell Rogers of the International News Service, came to Lancing to live with Esther, and Esther decided to stay. She assured her family: "I hope that you are not too worried about us all. It seems so calm and peaceful now that we can hardly realize that there is a war on." But the war had its anxieties: "I don't know where any of my Berlin friends are."[45]

In Poland, the German forces met gallant but futile resistance. On September 10, Barnes wrote that the British government would "prosecute the war at the side of France until the present German regime was broken or all Polish territory was evacuated by the Germans." The Cabinet planned for a war of three years duration and discouraged the comforting assumption that Hitler's regime was crumbling. Prime Minister Chamberlain went to France, where he and the French leaders agreed on a tentative strategy of "continuously worrying the Germans on the Western Front as a cat worries a mouse, but no dismal offensives against the strongly fortified German line" while searching out another point at which attack would be more effective, and enforcing a total economic blockade. The plans reflected the strong influence of the memory of the First World War on the highest councils of the British and French governments and general staffs.[46]

On September 17, Poland was attacked by the Soviet Union, as had been agreed in the still secret protocols of the Nazi-Soviet Pact. Despite their pledges to Poland, Barnes found the British unwilling to declare war on the Soviet Union, fearing to throw it "irrevocably into the enemy camp." In his dispatch, Barnes went on to suggest that while the door was open for German-Soviet cooperation to the detriment of other countries in eastern Europe, the feeling was strong that in the long run such a policy "would not only bring the German frontier to a sphere in which the Soviets—uncertain allies at the best—might take effective military action, action that is against the Germans. It would also enlarge appreciably the territory over which the Reich would be under the necessity of exerting effective military control." While recognizing that this speculation might be wishful thinking, Barnes again pointed to the lessons of World War I when the need for a large army in the East to enforce the Treaty of Brest-Litovsk kept the German Empire from wielding strength at a critical time on the western front.[47]

With Barnes among the war correspondents going to France would be Bill Stoneman for the *Chicago Daily News*, Webb Miller, and the author John Gunther who was now with the National Broadcasting Company. Unhappy with his situation at the *Herald Tribune*, Lee Stowe had joined the *Chicago Daily News* and come to London to replace Stoneman. Edward Angley, recruited to the *Herald Tribune* from the Associated Press, would come to London to replace Barnes. But Ralph's plans went badly awry. He explained in a letter to Salem: "Well, I didn't last long in this war. Undoubtedly you will have learned before this letter arrives that I'm in the hospital, again; this time with what seems to be stones in my gall bladder ... This mess, of course, has been a disappointment, but I'm trying to be philosophical. The New York office seems to be taking it all right. Joe Barnes, who is leaving Berlin, may come over here temporarily. Ed Angley arrived several days before my attack, so things were better than they would be otherwise."[48]

The *Herald Tribune* was understanding, even to an "unheard-of sympathetic letter" from Larry Hills. Esther felt she had had a premonition: "To say that I am happy to be here where I could be with Ralph through this is putting it mildly. I assure you that I will certainly be firm about the length of his convalescence. Ralph has had these attacks for about a year, and has carried on in spite of complete examinations in Berlin; and the professor there failed to spot this. Second time a German doctor has slipped up on a diagnosis." She shared Ralph's disappointment in not going with the British Expeditionary Force, but both were grateful that the attack had taken place in London and not at the front.[49] Their letters tell the tale of medical care in 1939. He was kept in bed for fourteen days after his surgery, then allowed up in a wheel chair. He did not go home to Lancing until three weeks after the operation. Esther said he was being "unusually brave and patient." She was impressed with the skill of the British surgeons: "You should see his scar— wonderful job. The Germans may be good at the operation stunt, but they certainly haven't made a study of cutting to avoid bad scars."[50]

Barnes settled at Lancing for his convalescence. He would return to his post as head of the London Bureau while Ed Angley went to France in his place. The *Herald Tribune* had also bolstered the London staff with the addition of Tania Long, Barnes's former assistant in Berlin. Barnes thought he might succeed Angley with the British forces later "if the war lasts long enough." In the meantime, he was "eager to get what news there is to be had in this country." As it turned out, this phase of the war came to be called the "Sitzkrieg" since there was virtually no action on the Western Front. With Esther's help Ralph filed a mail article that he had been working on before he became ill, but his byline did not begin to appear regularly in the *Herald Tribune* until he returned to work in November. His first article dealt with an alleged plan for a German invasion of the Netherlands. He wrote a long piece on the military and diplomatic implications of such a move, concluding: "If the invasion materializes, there will be an end once and for all to any thought that Britain might make peace before the eclipse of the Nazi regime or the thorough defeat of Nazi arms." He pointed out that since the sixteenth century, it had been consistent British policy to keep a strong continental power out of the Low Countries, a policy she had gone to war four times to defend.[51]

With Edward Angley filing for the *Herald Tribune* from France, Barnes took as his "beat" the sea war, recognizing the key role of the British Navy in the country's defense and in its offensive potential. Hitler too recognized that importance and had launched a number of initiatives against British ships with some success. Barnes reviewed the 1939 edition of the authoritative *Jane's Fighting Ships* for his readers and reported on what he learned during time spent aboard a British torpedo boat and a destroyer out of Portsmouth.[52]

Barnes's old friend, Leland Stowe, was a part of the party at Portsmouth and left an affectionate portrait of Ralph at that juncture of his career:

After the final toast to the King we had an opportunity to chat with some of the keenest, most impressive officers in the British armed services. They asked all sorts of pertinent questions about Germany, so someone said: "Ask Barnes. He worked a long time in Germany." Then they asked about Russia and somebody said the same thing. When they got around to Italy and France, Barnes was still having the ball passed to him. These officers were extremely well informed, but they were soon hammering Ralph with questions. He answered quietly and factually. "No, I wouldn't quite say that. You see, Stalin also has to take into consideration. ... " British naval captains and commanders listened avidly. They were obviously impressed, and the one person in the room who was not conscious of this fact was the big, bear-like Oregonian who, after fourteen years in Europe, was as unmistakably American as Will Rogers or a Texas longhorn.[53]

The naval war and the Soviet invasion of Finland dominated Barnes's dispatches through November and December. The British tightened their naval blockade, even seizing goods bound for Germany from neutral ships. With submarines and magnetic mines dropped from aircraft, the Germans tried to destroy Britain's shipping lifeline. Barnes wrote of the mobilization of the wooden vessels of the fishing fleet to sweep coastal waters for mines, and went along on minesweeping operations. The first real naval battle of the war ended with the sinking by the pocket battleship *Deutschland* of an armed merchant vessel, the *Rawalpindi*, off Iceland with the loss of all but a few of her crew, as the *Deutschland* attempted to swamp the lifeboats. Despite the losses, Winston Churchill assured the House of Commons that Britain was winning the sea war: "We are buffeted by the waves but the ancient tides flow steady and strong in our favor."[54]

By now, many of the correspondents who had gone to France were returning, Bill Stoneman among them. Esther hoped that Ralph would not go at all. Their wartime Christmas was not very elaborate but Ralph wrote of his pleasure in being with his daughters: "They are growing up very fast. I find them more interesting than when they were younger." Ralph assured his parents of his contentment: "I'm looking forward eagerly to the work ahead. Once again I must say that I can't imagine any other profession in which I would be half as happy as I am in this one. It's fun. Even if I had an ample independent income I would stay in it, I suppose, simply because I like it. Or perhaps I should say that I am quite sure I would." Esther was not optimistic in her New Year's wishes, "Here's hoping that this poor old world will have peace in 1940. But I suppose that is too much to ask."[55]

A management shuffle in New York encouraged Barnes greatly:

The best news out of New York is that my namesake, Joe Barnes, has been appointed Foreign News Editor of the Herald Tribune, *a position which has not existed before. He will put things in order in New York, where he will be stationed. The appointment is important because Joe is a good newspaper man; has high standards of journalism; is intelligent, knows Europe intimately, knows the problems inside a European bureau. It is good, too, that we know each other well personally, our acquaintance extending back to the Moscow bureau days. Joe was in the Moscow bureau, following Phillips, who followed me in that position. Then Joe followed me in the Berlin bureau, after spending several weeks with me in Berlin, after I had been assigned to the London post. Joe is the author of an authoritative work on the Near East and he was in Moscow writing while we were there, long before he came with the* Herald Tribune. *He is a distinguished linguist. I am pleased that he is to be Foreign News Editor in the* Herald Tribune *home office.*[56]

Beach Conger succeeded Joe Barnes in Berlin.

The war exacted its price, even when little seemed to be happening. Ralph did not notice the rationing because he usually ate in restaurants. Esther coped as first butter, then margarine, then meat were added to the list: "I find that imagination goes a long way in combatting rationing. One thing that makes it so much easier here is that we have eggs, which we didn't have in Berlin." Heating coal was in short supply. Ralph was fond of telling his friends that, in his experience, Siberia was better heated than London. In Lancing, Esther sustained bruises in a fall through the ceiling while trying to thaw frozen pipes in the attic. But she reassured her mother: "Please go on the old idea that 'No news is good news.' We are carrying on very well. We always thought that we couldn't live without central heating in the house. Well, we can and, although it isn't too comfortable, we seem to be thriving." In fact, as the censor finally allowed the newspapers to admit, it was the coldest winter in Britain in a hundred years.[57]

To Ralph's sister Ruth and her husband, Esther wrote affirming her decision to remain in England: "It would have been nice to have come home, but I don't regret so far my decision to stay here near Ralph. It is too nice having at least these twenty-four hours together each week. It is even worth whatever we have to face this spring from the Germans. I may regret keeping the girls over here—they are my only worry. We have at least had some grand times together this winter."[58] Esther was not alone in anticipating the next German move. While the western front in France remained quiet, rumors of a planned German attack on the Low Countries led in January to the cancellation of leaves for the British Expeditionary Force. The scare proved to be a false alarm, and leaves were restored a few days later.[59]

British spirits were raised when the British Admiralty dispatched a force of several ships to Norwegian waters to rescue 326 British seamen seized from merchant vessels and being held on the German ship *Altmark*. After the *Altmark* had run aground while trying to ram the British destroyer *Cossack*, a boarding party fought its way aboard and removed the seamen. Amid British exultation, Barnes noted: "The affair has served to bring to a head in an explosive situation the whole issue of belligerent and neutral rights in war time. Norway protests to Britain; Germany protests to Norway, and Britain seeks to explain, stating that the action was necessary because of Norway's failure to discover and remove the British prisoners when the *Altmark* was at Bergen; Berlin warns also that there may be 'the gravest consequences'; Oslo speaks of Britain's 'gross violation' of Norway's sovereignty, and in effect demands the return of the British seamen." Chamberlain defended the Navy's action and the *Herald Tribune* noted Winston Churchill's leadership role in the entire affair.[60]

From his new post in New York, Joe Barnes proposed that Barnes undertake an expedition to Russia, either through Germany or through Turkey. But the German army's April 8 invasion of Denmark and then Norway changed the *Herald Tribune*'s plans for his next assignment. New York immediately asked him to return to Berlin and reorganize the bureau there. He spent thirty-six hours with Esther and the girls before flying from the nearby Shoreham airport to Amsterdam to await a German visa. He and Esther both welcomed the chance for him to be on both sides of the war.[61]

15

Under the escort of gray-uniformed Nazi officers, a small group of American and other foreign newspaper men are witnessing, 1,300 yards from the German front line, the final phase of what may be recorded as one of the decisive battles of history.

Here in the shattered Flemish town of Bergues, afire at several points, the rattle and roar of battle on land and in the air is about us and above us.

Still held by the broken remnants of a great Anglo-French army, Dunkerque, seven miles to the west, is marked by a vast cloud of pale smoke, seemingly motionless. Parts of the port are in flames. The church towers and other landmarks in the suburbs of the city outside the area of fire are plainly visible. Besides Dunkerque, hard-pressed Allied forces still hold today a rapidly diminishing strip of coastline. From there they are now making their last stand.

... Roadside battlefields strewn with wrecked tanks, guns and other engines of war, as well as wrecked trucks and buses, demolished cities and towns, demolished bridges, provisional camps crowded with French and British prisoners, columns of German troops, columns of French and Belgian civilian refugees in great numbers, columns of Allied prisoners, newly made graves marked with steel helmets of the dead, very occasionally unburied corpses, cadavers of horses and cattle, smashed planes, and, above all, squadron upon squadron of German bombers—these passed before our eyes with the rapidity of the shifting pictures in a kaleidoscope.

Ralph Barnes, *Herald Tribune,*
June 5, 1940, from Bergues, Belgium

"Amsterdam," Barnes wrote to Salem,

is the center for news coming out of Germany. The British newspapers have their correspondents here to pick up what information they can about the enemy. I have found here many acquaintances and friends on both sides, many I had known in Berlin, others I have come to know in London, still others elsewhere. Almost all of them live at this hotel; though not the Germans. It has been good to come to know Beach Conger. He is a fine chap, and we get along very well together. Conger is stationed here temporarily, awaiting developments. You will have seen his by-line in the Herald Tribune. *He was at our Berlin Bureau, wrote some dispatches obnoxious to the German authorities, so was forced to leave Germany on very short notice.*

Barnes expected to be in Berlin from one to three months and looked forward to a "tremendously interesting experience."[1]

During the two weeks Barnes remained in Amsterdam waiting for his visa, he filed three stories. In two of them, he assessed Britain's situation as its participation in the war at last accelerated: "Great Britain goes into real action on the northern front possessing vast potential resources in materials, manpower and nervous energy which thus far have been tapped and mobilized to but a relatively small degree." That fact had two sides: "Those untapped reserves might mean that in a long drawn-out struggle Britain would be capable of taking severe punishment in defense and of inflicting severe punishment in offense. On the other hand, there are British critics of the present war program who assert that the scale of the effort which will be necessary has not yet been envisioned by the government and that the current rate of progress is dangerously slow."[2]

In his survey of Britain's readiness, Barnes alluded to shortages in machine tools and alloyed steel, as well as in skilled labor. He had found great numbers of young men not yet in uniform, "1,000,000 men still officially listed as unemployed," and little utilization of women in the labor force, particularly compared to Germany. He reported asking a union leader in Birmingham, just before the German invasion of Scandinavia, about the apparent emergence of a "peace now" sentiment among organized labor. The labor official responded: "I should judge that 80 per cent of the 14,000 members in this district are for a vigorous prosecution of the war. We look at it in this way: In case of defeat we would lose under Hitler the union through which we carry on our struggle. We must defeat Hitlerism, but make sure that in the process we don't get Nazism in this country."[3]

By April 25, Barnes was in Berlin, taking over the *Herald Tribune* bureau from Russell Hill, who remained to serve as his assistant. Barnes stayed at the Hotel Esplanade on Bellevuestrasse. The neighborhood was a familiar one, near the family's old apartment and the former location of the *Herald Tribune* bureau on Göringstrasse. He filed his first story, one about the German threat that if the British bombed German towns of no military importance, as the Germans maintained had happened, they could expect "a rude awakening and receive bomb for bomb." In a quick survey of opinion, he found: "In neutral quarters here the view is general that, in either case, the further spread of the conflict—either into new territory, or in the air, or both—is virtually inevitable. There is evidence that large masses of Germans at home as well as in the fighting forces expect both peace and victory by next winter."[4]

Barnes wrote the requisite series of "what it's like in Berlin" articles. Berliners in their cafes were drinking malt coffee or beer that was "slightly weaker than in peace time, but still better than that of most other countries," and automobiles were almost completely absent from the streets on the weekends, because gasoline was unavailable for recreational use. The German blackout was even stricter than the British one, and food rationing was much tighter except that sugar seemed more widely obtainable. He found the German people united and determined because they believed that defeat would mean "the liquidation of the German state and the splitting up of the German people." Even among people who opposed the Nazi regime, Barnes found a commitment. He quoted one young woman: "I don't like the Nazis and I detest the war, but if it's a question of England or Germany, well, I'm for Germany. My friends feel that way about it, too." A longtime acquaintance told him: "These English don't know what they are up against. They're still thinking in terms of the last war. They fail to realize what the airplane means to the German strength in this war. And another thing, these Nazis are organizers. You can't imagine how they have got this country organized."[5]

In the first days of May, Allied troops in Norway were forced to withdraw, leaving that country to Germany and precipitating a Cabinet crisis in Britain that ultimately elevated Winston Churchill to prime minister. Barnes wrote that the outcome in Norway was "a very real boost to German morale. Many Germans may think this war is a great catastrophe, but most of them are thrilled by military victory." The German government exulted in its triumph, and accused the British of an effort to expand the war into the Mediterranean, the Balkans and the Middle East. By May 7, the palpable tension in

Berlin indicated that a new move was pending. Barnes suggested to his readers that talk of areas to the south was a feint to cover "the long awaited march to the westward." On May 10, when the Germans attacked in Holland, Belgium, and Luxembourg with air power and artillery, Hitler as the Supreme War Lord issued a proclamation to his troops: "The struggle which begins today will decide the fate of the German nation for the next 1,000 years."[6]

Through the day and evening Barnes and Russell Hill monitored official bulletins and dispatches to report the drama on the western front, where Hitler was reported to have joined his troops. Given the sources, the news from the front was enthusiastically positive and, unfortunately for the Luxembourgers, Belgians and Dutch, largely correct: "German troops reached the River Ijssel in the early hours of Friday afternoon and have crossed the River Maas on to Dutch territory at several points. Maastricht and the bridges over the Albert Canal (west of that town) are in our hands. Malmedy is taken. Further to the south, German troops advancing through Luxembourg have crossed the Belgian frontier." The attacks were justified by the claim that the Dutch had declared a state of war with Germany and the Belgians had invited French and British troops into their countries. When the Dutch and Belgian ambassadors presented notes at the German Foreign Office declaring that a state of war existed and protesting the invasion, the German news agency dismissed the communications as filled with "impudence, insolence and dumbness."[7]

Waiting for the call so that he could send his dispatches, Ralph wrote Esther hoping that in light of the German action she had "decided to move a little westward, even though it may seem a nuisance." He complained of not having letters from her, although he was sure she had written. When his call finally came through, Ralph heard from New York that Esther and the children had left their home on the Channel to stay with English friends inland. A call from the *Herald Tribune* bureau had urged them to move quickly. They departed Lancing in an hour and a half.[8]

With alarming speed, the Germans advanced through the Low Countries. From Berlin, which was peaceful and untouched, Barnes and Russell Hill reported the war by sifting through the German press and official pronouncements. An eyewitness account of the first day of hostilities by a German aerial machine-gunner enabled Barnes to give his readers the flavor of German enthusiasm for the advance. The importance of the air arm proved to be a consistent theme as the Germans in thirty-six hours captured the great Belgian fortress at Liège, Eben Emael, that had held up the German advance through Belgium for twelve critical days during the First World War. The Germans insisted, too, that they controlled the air over northern France, claiming to have destroyed 681 French and British planes while losing only sixty-one of their own, with fifteen more missing. The Dutch flooded their land to no avail. Within only a few days, the Dutch royal family fled to London to establish a government-in-exile and the Dutch army surrendered.[9]

When stories of "secret weapons" appeared in the press, both Barnes and Russell Hill tried to separate the truth from the propaganda, noting for example the probability that the revolutionary means of assault that had captured Eben Emael in so short a time involved the landing of parachute troops. Clearly the air force was key to Germany's success, with massive bombardments of Rotterdam forcing that city's capitulation. Already France was being dismissed as an enemy, while Barnes noted "the press and official quarters alike placed the greatest emphasis also on the fact that Dutch air bases, as well as those 'soon to be secured' in Belgium place the German air arm within full striking distance of Great Britain."[10]

The German papers reported that English, French and Belgian troops were being thrown back across a wide front as the Germans simply bypassed the fortified Maginot Line on which the French had staked their security. In their elation, the Germans trumpeted the destiny of their race and their leader. Barnes quoted Robert Ley, the head of the German Labor Front, calling Hitler "the greatest of the great," born to conquer Europe while "We German men of the present must march as the standard-bearers of a new and better world, a world of reason and insight. For us there is no longer a road back. This is our sacred and invincible Idea: We believe we must annihilate false illusions and madness, and create instead of a recurrently warring and therefore doomed Europe, an orderly, reasonable and sensible Europe. This we believe! For this we are marching!"[11]

On May 18, eight days into the offensive, Barnes wrote that Brussels and Antwerp had fallen. Nearby airfields, only twenty minutes flying time from Dover, were in German hands, and Churchill warned his people Britain would be the next battlefield, even as he desperately tried to shore up French resistance. Barnes found "a distinct effort in high quarters here to convey the impression today that if France, not to speak of Belgium, should lay down her arms, she would be granted generous terms, and even concessions. If France were to follow such a course, much human life would be saved and great material destruction avoided, it was pointed out. This veiled appeal to France was put forward under the Nazi thesis that 'England is Germany's real enemy.' The implication was that Britain would not be treated so generously." On the 19th, Barnes presented the first accounts of a wedge being driven through the Allied lines with the immediate potential of leaving the forces to the north "faced with the alternative of capitulation or being driven into the sea." The next day, he noted, "Every effort was being made to damage the reputation of the British command and British troops. In an apparent attempt to give the impression that the British were leaving their allies in the lurch, the high command today wrote: 'English troops are engaged in forced marches toward Channel ports.' "[12]

Day to day, reports available in Berlin "painted a picture of an Allied debacle which suggested the first stages of the collapse of the armies of Napoleon III in the Franco-Prussian War." With German news as his only source, Barnes attempted to track the advance of the German forces. He wrote that "Once again the German high command claimed complete command of the air, and cited the devastating work carried out by German bombers and other aircraft in all sectors to prepare the way for the land forces." Mechanized divisions swept into northern France, going around the Maginot Line and encountering little resistance. In a move that Barnes compared to General William Sherman's March to the Sea in the American Civil War, another German force cut through to the Channel coast in France, reportedly covering forty-eight miles in one day. The Reich army pressed from east, west, and south on the shrinking territory, trapping more than a million men of the Allied armies. The Germans boasted of sinking or damaging many of the vessels sent from England to rescue Allied troops.

Barnes left no doubt as to the threat to Britain, again reminding his readers in one of his characteristic history lessons, "With a varying galaxy of allies, Britain has waged four previous wars to keep a strong continental power out of the Low Countries, but she is now faced with the menace of an immensely strong continental power which is on the eve, apparently, of completing its control over the whole coast line commanding Britain, from far to the north in Norway to the Somme, and perhaps farther to the southward in France. Moreover, this continental power, Germany, possesses an air force which is a threat to Britain infinitely more formidable than that presented by Napoleon."[13]

A day later, Barnes picked up evidence of a pause in the German advance but was cautious in drawing any conclusions. In fact, military historians have struggled to explain the German hesitation that ultimately allowed the rescue of many of the men trapped at

Dunkirk. The pause, for whatever reason, was accompanied by an attempt to dampen the expectations of the German people. Barnes quoted from a semi-official military commentary: "In connection with the fighting in Flanders and Artois, it can be said conclusively, first, that the enveloped enemy is extraordinarily strong in numbers; second, that he consists of select troops; and, third, that he possesses effective, first-class equipment. It can be added that, in any case, the enemy has not collapsed." And in an editorial in the *Lokal Anzeiger*, he found the following: "In view of the extent of the operations and the strength of the enemy,' this journal wrote, 'tremendous tasks remain before our troops. They will be faced by an enemy trying with desperate courage to break through the ring of iron which has been thrown about him. They must also be ready to repel relief attacks which Gen. Weygand may undertake from the west and the south. We do not know whether this will help them. Yet the official communique reported not only that the enveloped enemy is putting up a brave and stubborn resistance, but also is attempting to break out near Arras." Barnes speculated that this new tack might mean the Germans were encountering stiffer resistance than before or "that they are telling 'bear' stories in order to make the subsequent victory all the more imposing."[14]

By May 24, the French ports of Boulogne and Calais were reported captured, although Barnes found the high command "strangely silent" on the victories. From the intelligence he could gather, Barnes suggested tentatively that the French were either "incapable of carrying out or unwilling to carry out counter-thrusts" to relieve the trapped armies, and that the Germans were intent on finishing off those armies before turning south into France. He asserted once again that Britain was the ultimate goal. Indeed, he wrote a day later, in Nazi quarters there was talk of the occupation of London "within a few weeks."[15]

~

The threat to Britain increased Barnes's concerns for his family and he was relieved to get news of them, as he wrote Esther on May 25 in a letter sent by the Pan American Clipper to meet her in New York:

> *I received the news over the wire tonight that you and the girls were enroute to Dublin and would sail on the* **President Roosevelt.** *Under the circumstances it was the best possible news I could have. I knew earlier of course of your plans to go home via Ireland. Your*

messages from time to time by telephone have cheered me up. The best thing about the situation here is that I have had no time to think—in fact, have tried not to think. I do hope, Girl, that you are not taking it all too tragically. Don't worry; I've been sufficiently depressed, terribly depressed, but I'm thankful to be able to say that, though my lip has quivered sometimes, I've kept it stiff enough not to throw up the sponge. ... God, how I pray that everything will go all right with you and the girls on the way across.

In the same letter, writing over several days, Ralph confided: "Things have not gone very well with the job, Girl. I came in in a bad mood for it, as you know. I've made mistakes here, rather bad ones. Please tell Al Laney, when you see him, that it will be difficult for him to realize what his wire meant to me—I received it today. It was replete with terribly exaggerated praise of a poor job; the fact that he was interested enough to send it was what mattered." He finished his letter with encouragement and with an echo of his insecurities: "Esther, please do take things philosophically. We'll stick together, and that's what counts most with us. As you know, I am seriously concerned about my work, because I have been hitting on two cylinders and, as indicated above, have made serious mistakes in judgment. But I'll hold myself together, and perhaps be the better for the experience. ... So don't worry about me. I do love you so very much, Girl, and I miss you. Kiss Joannie and Zannie for me."[16]

Esther, Joan, and Suzanne crossed Ireland to Galway where the United States liner *President Roosevelt* was being sent to evacuate Americans from Europe. With them was Florence, the young daughter of Bill and Majlys Stoneman, who had been a regular visitor at the Lancing cottage. Tania Long, in Galway to cover the story of the evacuation for the *Herald Tribune*, wrote of the little town crowded with weary travelers, of the lack of organization and conflicting information, and of the protests of Irish-Americans unable to afford passage. When the liner arrived in Galway harbor, extraordinary measures were taken to protect her from sabotage. The tension of the evacuation was heightened by Nazi broadcasts charging that the British intended to torpedo the ship and blame it on Germany in an effort to bring the United States into the war. Esther later told a reporter: 'The Irish people I met, especially those in Dublin, insisted we should not go on the steamer, saying that the *Roosevelt* was doomed."

On June 2, 723 passengers, including 130 children, sailed on the *Roosevelt*, a ship built to accommodate fewer than 500. After a trip Esther characterized as "the roughest passage I ever made," the

Roosevelt docked safely in New York on June 10. Esther wrote her mother and sister: "How wonderful it is to be here out of the whole thing ... the girls and I feel now that we never want to see Europe again." Soon she would travel across the continent to Oregon, but not without regret: "I do hate to get too far from Ralph and my only source of news of him. Bless his heart he has been so worried about us. It was a grand thing for him as far as the job was concerned to go back to Berlin at the time he did. Tell Mother and Father Barnes not to worry about Ralph. He will come out alright and he wouldn't want them to worry."[17]

Meanwhile, from Berlin, Barnes continued to monitor Nazi accounts that assumed success in taking Dunkirk and boasted of the pending conquest of Britain. He anticipated extensive bombing designed "to silence the British air force, and thus obtain complete air supremacy over Britain, but also to cripple the whole land defense system in southeast England." Still unclear was whether the attempt to reduce Britain would begin immediately or await the crushing of French resistance. The German people had no hint of the tremendous rescue operation that between May 27 and June 4, under constant attack from the *Luftwaffe*, removed more than 330,000 British and Allied troops to relative safety in Britain. According to German sources, their aerial attacks were frustrating evacuation efforts. Barnes could not determine how the rescue was going. Instead the German press and official statements focused on the unconditional surrender of the Belgian king, Leopold III. The next day, Thursday, the Germans were boasting of the collapse of French and British resistance in the sector and "overwhelming losses" to the rescue operation, but on Friday they admitted that because of poor flying conditions, the British had probably been able "to transport large numbers of troops back to their island."[18]

Although the drama of Dunkirk had not come to a close, the Germans, inspired by their successes, planned an expedition for the foreign press to the conquered areas. The reporters traveled together under the watchful eyes of their German guides. On May 30, Ralph began a letter to Esther: "I'm off to the West tomorrow morning. It will be gruesome, but I want to see it—if I'm to be in this game I have to do it. We are supposed to be going clear to the coast opposite the chalk cliffs. How I thank God you are not on the other side. ... Tess [Shirer] has been having a hell of a time trying to decide what to do. She's still in Switzerland, has been interested in your plans.

We are to be gone nearly a week—Wally [Deuel], Fred [Oechsner] and some of the others you know are to be on the trip. I think I ought to hear at least one gun go off before I leave Europe."

The next morning, he added to his letter:

We have just stopped at Charlottenburg, enroute to Cologne. We are continuing from there to Aachen, then Brussels, I'm told. Later we are to see Calais, and perhaps Dunkirk, if it is taken by the time we reach that quarter. George Axelson, of the NY Times, a jovial Swedish-American is sitting across from me, the only other representative of an American outfit nearby. It has been warm recently but today it is overcast and cooler; at last I have an opportunity to wear on a campaign the shoes I purchased to march into Madrid. Do you remember, Girl? At Calais I will be close to Cap Gris Nez, where I went to cover the Channel swim of Gertrude Ederle. Times have changed since then.[19]

Barnes's first dispatch from the west is datelined "With the German Army in sight of Dunkirk, June 2." "For the most part," he told his readers, "we have taken the path of the right flank of the [German] army, from devastated Maubeuge, through Le Cateau, Cambrai, Arras and St. Omer and then on to Boulogne and Calais, before continuing here." Although they did not see the actual fighting, they felt its presence: "Here in Bergues we are far in advance of the German artillery positions, which we have not seen. But we know they are there. Occasionally there is the weird whistle of a shell passing overhead—one of the distinctive sounds of battle. An Allied dump of small-arms ammunition on a hill at the end of the town is afire. The exploding cartridges suggest an endless string of firecrackers set off by small boys in July."

The little party encountered soldiers and the remaining inhabitants: "Like frightened animals, uncertain whether to dive back into their holes or come out into the daylight, they peer from doorways and cellarways of houses and shops which are not completely demolished. Many women and children are among them." A tired priest told them of the first shell landing in the church garden, killing fifteen of his parishioners who had taken refuge there. Through the day, images crowded in: "Roadside battlefields strewn with wrecked tanks, guns and other engines of war, as well as wrecked trucks and buses, demolished cities and towns, demolished bridges, provisional camps crowded with French and British prisoners, columns of German troops, columns of French and Belgian civilian refugees in great numbers, columns of Allied prisoners, newly made graves marked with steel helmets of the dead, very occasionally unburied corpses, cadavers of horses and cattle, smashed planes, and, above all, squadron upon squadron of German bombers—these passed before our eyes with the rapidity of the shifting pictures in a kaleidoscope."

When the party stopped at Boulogne, Barnes told his readers, he stripped down and went for a swim in the Channel, perhaps in an attempt to erase another image: "The scene which stands out most vividly in my mind is that of a crossroads near the foot of Cassel Heights, which were stormed and taken by the Germans. In the grass close by the highway line, a handsome black-haired Briton in khaki battle dress, a youth of hardly more than twenty, lay with his face turned upward. At least he had died without suffering. The bullet which took his life hit the right side of his forehead squarely. For some reason, he was not wearing his steel helmet. It was strapped to his back."[20]

Approaching Dunkirk just as it fell, Barnes and his colleagues found the city in ruins, the debris still in flame from the bombing attacks, and the city's civilians just emerging from cellars and air raid shelters. The docks were strewn with the bodies of French soldiers. There was no way of knowing how many inhabitants had been killed; it would be weeks before all the bodies could be recovered. Those who lived could at first speak only of the loved ones they had lost and of the terror the airplanes had inflicted, particularly in the three days of bombardment that had preceded the armistice. As the day wore on, the survivors repeatedly complained that the British troops had not defended the town, had come through only to board their ships. In fact, Barnes saw signs of stubborn and costly British resistance and of the attempt to rescue the French wounded from the docks. Thousands of Allied military vehicles were abandoned in ditches to prevent their use by the enemy. In the harbor were the remnants of sunken and capsized vessels. The reporters could not doubt the evidence of "one of the greatest military debacles in history."[21]

Barnes filed the fourth of his "war front" dispatches from Cologne as his party of journalists completed their six-day trip through the battlefields. In it, he recounted the signs of preparations for the assault on Great Britain. "This drive," he reminded his readers, "has not only opened the way for an attempted subjugation of Britain, but also has made it impossible for Britain to render more than feeble support to France." Everywhere he had seen evidence of the British expeditionary force, "massed tanks, trucks and field guns of British make, half destroyed military stores, here a stray helmet of characteristic design, there a litter of British uniforms, by the wayside the uninterred corpse of a youngster from across the Channel not yet reached by the burial squad, freshly made graves marked as those of Britons, and then in columns along the road and in provisional camps the forlorn British prisoners."

Too, the correspondents had seen indications of the movement of German forces from the north to the southern front for the offensive against France: "Infantry afoot, infantry on bicycles, infantry in trucks, horse-drawn field artillery, motor howitzers, motorized anti-aircraft artillery, columns of tanks, horse-drawn supply trains, motorized supply columns—all these we've seen marching or rolling southward." Their progress was generally undeterred because the German bombers had carefully avoided damaging the roadways and the French, in their retreat, had largely failed to destroy the bridges. Barnes observed, "It would be hard to exaggerate the height of the physical condition and morale of the German Army, as it goes into the new offensive. The morale is that of victors who are being well cared for. Even the infantrymen whom we have seen marching along in the hot noonday sun appear in excellent spirits. Deeply bronzed, these youngsters—all of them seem young—give the impression of being on nothing more serious than a hiking expedition."[22]

Back in Berlin, Barnes found jubilation in official circles and among ordinary people. Victory seemingly assured, Mussolini had just announced that Italy would join the fight against France and Britain. Along a 217-mile front extending from near the coast to northeast of the city of Rheims in the province of Champagne, the German forces were reportedly everywhere successful, with some detachments within twenty-five miles of Paris. The *Hamburger Fremdenblatt* maintained that it was "now too late for the United States to rescue Great Britain and France as it did in 1917." Military sources were also quick to point out that this time the battle would not end in a German defeat as had happened on the Marne early in World War I, when the French army halted the German advance outside Paris. In fact, the German advance followed very closely the plans laid out by Field Marshal Alfred von Schlieffen, the Chief of the General Staff before World War I. He called for a strong right wing that would envelop Paris and encircle the French Army. Now the Germans were poised for just that outcome.[23]

The following day, the fate of Paris came to the fore. The Germans reminded the French of 1870-71, when the armies of Prussia besieged the city, and of what aerial bombing could do, warning, "If Paris continues to be defended as a fortified city the French must bear full responsibility for what may happen to it." Barnes wrote: "In suggesting the policy which would be followed toward Paris as a 'defended city,' the military spokesman suggested that the French should pursue, with respect to their capital, the course followed by the Belgians with respect to Brussels. He recalled that, having been evacuated by troops, Brussels capitulated 'peaceably.' "

The French made their decision quickly, declaring Paris an open city on June 13 in an effort to avoid the destruction wrought on Warsaw when the Germans captured the Polish capital in September, 1939. It was not immediately clear to Barnes in Berlin whether the Germans would be satisfied with the French action. Other bulletins that day claimed the capture of more than 100,000 military prisoners during the eight days of the "second offensive," and stressed German successes that threatened to trap a substantial portion of the French army against the Maginot Line. Nothing was mentioned of earlier troop movements to the west and south of Paris, but Barnes cautioned his readers against "assuming that the failure of the high command to provide full details every day of the progress of the offensive means that a serious setback or even a halt has been experienced."[24]

Indeed, the next day, Barnes noted, "The Nazi bulletins assert that, taking on the character of a rout, the French retreat has become disorderly, and that the French command no longer exercises full control over its forces. Thrusting forward like spearheads at various points along the line, swift-moving German mechanized detachments, it was said, are overtaking and breaking through retreating French units. Often on such occasions, according to the Nazi claim, the French abandon their equipment and scatter in all directions."

The capitulation of Paris was announced when the German army had entered the city. Barnes quoted the official military commentary at length, writing:

"The French," it said, "intended originally to defend Paris, but decided they did not have at their disposal the means, including troops, for the defense. Because of British pressure, the French command considered displaying a resistance which would have been short and entirely useless. In view of the possible destruction of the city, the plan was abandoned.

"In the eleventh hour reason has won, and thus Paris has been spared the fate of Warsaw. There is an impression that the changed plan was contrary to the wishes of the British, who probably would rather have seen Paris devastated because of the propaganda value of such a development. For the first time the French have actually

*opposed the wishes of the British with success, apparently because they
realized that in the end they alone would have to pay the piper."*

*As to the manner in which Paris is to be treated, this commentary
added: "Despite all the indignities which Paris has inflicted on the
German people during the last twenty-five years, the German soldiers
will avoid all unnecessary destruction and, through their discipline
and deportment, will provide the population with a picture of the
German Army which will stand out in sharp contrast with the rioting
of the undisciplined French troops in the occupied territories of the
Rhine and the Ruhr after the last war."*

To give his readers a sense of the Nazi attitude toward the capture
of Paris, Barnes translated an editorial from the party newspaper
Volkischer Beobachter,

*"The fortress of Paris," this journal wrote, "is one of the two great
symbols of that world which declared eternal enmity against us. From
Paris and London have come all the grief and misery, all the insults
and challenges, which the German people have been forced to endure
since those days in the autumn of 1918 when the generation of our
fathers died on the battlefield over which their revenging sons are now
marching as victors. Even more than London, Paris was for centuries
the breeding place and starting point of all French expeditions against
Germany. Paris is more than a capital. Paris is not only the idol of
France but also the birthplace and spiritual center of the democratic
century, to which the French Revolution gave its stamp. In Paris the
motto Liberty, Equality and Fraternity was born, a motto which swept
away all borders between ability and disability, value and
worthlessness. In Paris Jews were* persona grata *at court and Negroes*
persona grata *in salons."*[25]

On June 15, the fortress of Verdun, unconquered by the Germans
during the First World War despite a long and bloody siege, fell. As
the situation of the French Army deteriorated, talk of an armistice
circulated. The newly installed French cabinet headquartered at
Bordeaux and headed by the aged hero of Verdun, Marshal Philippe
Petain, asked the Reich government for its terms for peace. But Barnes
concluded that Hitler would accept only "unconditional capitulation,
without anything in the nature of a preliminary armistice or
negotiations." While the German leader flew to Munich to confer
with Mussolini about the peace settlement, the *Volkischer Beobachter*
rejected any accommodation with the French: "The plutocrats had
decades, years, months and weeks at their disposal in which to come
to a decent understanding with Germany. They neglected their

opportunity for decades, years, months and weeks. Now it is expected that the sins of twenty years, the misdeeds of twenty years, will be forgotten in twenty-four hours."[26]

Memories of 1918 lived on as the Germans contemplated the opportunity for revenge. Moreover, every effort was to be made to secure the resources of France for the fight against Britain. Although the German terms were not revealed, pending a French reply, Barnes speculated about their nature: "Persistent reports are current that *Der Führer*, with Mussolini, will demand, among other points, the handing over of the French fleet intact, the opening of the way for military occupation of Corsica and of the French territories and colonies in North Africa, and a definite undertaking for the delivery forthwith of huge quantities of military stores and possibly other materials. France is to be drained so that her ally, Britain, can be crushed."[27]

Circumstances prevented Barnes from reporting on the settlement reached between the German government and the so-called "Vichy" regime of Marshal Petain. Part of France, including Paris, was occupied by the German army; the other part was to be left in tenuous independence so long as its government was cooperative.[28]

16

As France waited for armistice terms and Great Britain faced possible invasion, a drama was being unrolled today in eastern Europe which, under other circumstances, would have attracted primary attention.

With half a million or more Soviet troops occupying the three Baltic states of Lithuania, Latvia and Estonia, the Soviet-German pact of non-aggression of last August, which at no time was based on anything more substantial than opportunism appeared to have been liquidated in fact, though not in theory.

To put it bluntly, the Wilhelmstrasse, and presumably Fuehrer Adolf Hitler himself, are angered by this abrupt occupation in force of the Baltic states by the Red Army.

In effect, the Soviet-German pact of August recognized this area as a sphere of Soviet influence, but this was the case only because at the time it suited the purposes of Der Fuehrer. He and his aides will not forget the act of Moscow in sending a powerful mechanized army into the Baltic area while the bulk of the German fighting forces is occupied in the west.

Ralph Barnes, *Herald Tribune,* June 20, 1940, from Berlin

Through the weeks of German conquest in the west, Barnes's output did not reflect the difficult time he was going through personally. Esther, in New York, had received two cables from him between her arrival on June 10 and a letter she wrote to her family on June 17. He was, she wrote, "well and busy—doing a grand job." In fact, he was just pulling out of what he later described to her as "a hell of a depression. I felt that I had done a rotten job for a good many days. Tried to walk it off nights in the garden near where we used to live."[1]

The two talked by telephone June 19 when Esther was at the *Herald Tribune* office as Ralph called in to file his story for the day. As Ralph wrote a week later, "It was so very good to talk with you. Your voice sounded so natural; what you told me cheered me up." He needed cheering up the next day when, as he put it, "things went smash." The story Barnes filed on June 19 appeared in the June 20 edition of the *Herald Tribune* and resulted in his expulsion from Germany. Barnes's dispatch told of the German reaction to the Soviet occupation of Lithuania, Latvia, and Estonia. The Soviet move, he said, meant that "the Soviet-German pact of non-aggression of last August, which at no time was based on anything more substantial than opportunism, appeared to have been liquidated in fact, though not in theory."

Barnes recounted reports of German troop movements in East Prussia near the border of the Baltic republics. He did not predict immediate hostilities but suggested, "Assuming a Hitler fully victorious in the west, it is not difficult to picture what could happen. The very acts of Moscow today, even though they are condoned for the present by the Nazi press, even though they were envisaged theoretically in the Soviet-German arrangement, might be used later by Berlin as a pretext for a settlement of accounts with the Soviet Union. Most observers have found it difficult to envisage Hitler, not preoccupied elsewhere, leaving undisturbed in Soviet hands a territory which was conquered centuries ago by Teutonic knights and which up to 1939 was dominated to some degree by their descendants in the form of the Baltic barons." Barnes reminded his readers of the famous passage in *Mein Kampf* where Hitler wrote: "When we speak nowadays about new territory in Europe we can think in the first place only of Russia and the border states under her shadow."[2]

The German reaction was immediate. On June 21, Donald R. Heath, the American Chargé d'Affaires in Berlin, sent a communiqué to the State Department:

At the press conference this morning, the official spokesman of the Foreign Office read a statement which he indicated was subscribed to by the Minister of Propaganda [Josef Goebbels], barring correspondents Ralph Barnes and R. L. Hill of the New York Herald Tribune staff from press conferences and press communications with their newspaper on the ground that they had:

1. Indulged in false, hateful, and sensational reporting.

2. Endangered German interests.

3. Abused privileges granted by the Reich to foreign correspondents.

It was later indicated that they would be expelled from Germany within twenty-four hours, possibly tonight. At request of the two correspondents, I called on the press spokesman of the Foreign Office, Dr. Schmidt, who said that he would refer the matter again to the Minister of Propaganda and inform me whether the decision could be annulled.

He telephoned this evening and said that the minister had consented only to extend for seven days the period which the correspondents might remain in Germany.[3]

To Wilcox and Barnes in New York, Ralph cabled his explanation of events:

I was expelled because of the story on Soviet-German relations. The occasion was employed to expel Russell because of irritation with him on other counts. The fact that the Herald Tribune *is in disfavor played a role. I have been told on excellent authority that there was discussion of barring all* Herald Tribune *correspondents from the country. The Embassy has been told that another correspondent may come in, but my information is that the authorities intend to be choosy about it.* Herald Tribune *editorials cause more irritation in the Wilhelmstrasse than those of any other American newspaper.[4]*

Esther knew from her conversations with Joe Barnes in New York that "everyone on the paper was behind Ralph."[5] His colleagues, the other correspondents, supported him. In his diary, Bill Shirer wrote that while the article on German-Soviet relations was the stated reason for Barnes's expulsion, he thought the real one was "Nazi hate of the *Herald Tribune*'s editorial policy and its insistence on maintaining fearlessly independent correspondents here—the only New York paper that does." He and Ralph walked in the Tiergarten, Ralph depressed and "not quite realizing that he had more integrity than any of us who are allowed to stay." Shirer wrote again of the incident in his later memoirs, mentioning that talk of a cooling of German-Soviet relations was current in Berlin in June of 1940: "But we were not allowed to say so. Two or three times I had tried to slip past the censors a story of the new crisis in Russian-German relations but they had cut it out." Shirer thought that Barnes's story came mostly from contacts in the Soviet Embassy in Berlin. Barnes "had more guts than the rest of us in trying to get a big story through. The threatened breakup of the collaboration between Hitler and Stalin, who we were sure hated each other's guts, was important news. It would affect the course of the war."[6]

Howard K. Smith, in the fall of 1941, after the Nazi invasion of the Soviet Union and after Berlin was no longer safe from British bombing raids, wrote of walking down the Wilhelmstrasse: "The last building on the Street before you turn is where the New York *Herald Tribune* office was until the *Tribune*'s correspondent Ralph Barnes was kicked out for saying German-Russian relations were not so cordial and might lead to an eventual conflict. Every time I pass the place, I remember that last night I spent with him in his office before he caught the train, drinking cognac because he was very sad about being thrown out; Berlin was a good spot then."[7]

In his later study of foreign correspondents, Robert W. Desmond wrote of Barnes's expulsion. He referred to Barnes's suggestion, made "with characteristic prescience," of the possibility of conflict between Germany and the Soviet Union within a year, noting: "He was correct, almost to the day." In a footnote, Desmond added: "It is not possible to say what the basis may have been or the source for Barnes's assessment of the situation. His integrity and professionalism as a correspondent were beyond question. As this writer can attest on the basis of personal friendship and familiarity with his work, there can be little doubt that he had good reason for writing as he did." One possible source, Desmond suggested, was Dr. Karl Bömer, the director of the foreign press section of the Ministry of Foreign Affairs and spokesman for the Ministry of Propaganda. At a party at the Bulgarian embassy, of uncertain date but sometime during this period, Bömer, apparently intoxicated, let slip a reference to an attack on the Soviet Union. Certainly such an attack was planned long before it took place in June of 1941. Whether for this indiscretion or for other offenses, Bömer was arrested by the Gestapo, was later released, and died fighting on the eastern front.[8]

His expulsion plunged Barnes deeper into depression as he worried about his future. Three weeks later, writing Esther from Bucharest, his mood had not lifted:

> *I'd give anything to be back there, as you probably have guessed, just sort of to retrieve my situation. You know of course that I feel I bungled things; that I was not clever, as I should have been. I suppose I had got the feeling after such a long experience under governments of this sort that I was immune; that I knew what I could write and what I couldn't. … I have the advantage of knowing I have done an honest job; but it is bad not to be clever. You know the sort of cleverness I mean. Knowing how to tell the story as it is, without being liquidated.*

Often I have felt that I should have gone out stronger in 1933 on the famine, but if I had, I would have been booted out in short order. In this case, the situation was complicated by the fact that the Herald Tribune *was without an available substitute, a fact which causes me to feel worse than I would have otherwise.*

Ralph added more about the period before he left Berlin: "You would be amused to learn how greetings were conveyed to me from various personalities on the Wilhelmstrasse. The prevailing view among those quarters—excluding the personalities definitely unfriendly—was that the story which caused my expulsion was right, but of course should not have been written."[9]

~

From Germany, Barnes went to Budapest, then on to Bucharest. His assignment was to review the situation in the Balkans, then move on around the eastern Mediterranean to Egypt. As he made his way to Egypt, he regularly filed stories designed to explain to his readers the complex situation in southeastern Europe and the Near East. A region of border disputes and sharp ethnic rivalries, the area had long been subject to the imperialist designs of the Russian, Austrian, and Ottoman Empires. Hungary, Rumania, Bulgaria, Greece, and Yugoslavia found themselves ill-equipped to face the new challenges from Germany, Italy, and the Soviet Union. Germany's military success was impressive to the relatively weak rulers in the area, and its trade patterns had created a certain dependency. That same success caused the Soviet Union to look to the region in an effort to protect its own flanks.

From Rumania, Barnes reported on the dilemma of a country trapped between two overwhelming neighbors. Meeting little resistance, the Soviet Army was completing its occupation of the Rumanian territories of Bessarabia and northern Bukovina. At the same time, Germany would allow Rumania little latitude and had found an ally there in the semi-fascist Iron Guard, still a powerful political force despite the government's efforts to crush it. Rumania's king, Carol II, renounced what Barnes characterized as "the defunct guaranties of assistance against aggression" given by London and Paris on April 13, 1939. Rumania had "cut loose from defeated France and beleaguered Britain and had tied her fortunes to a Germany which is now overwhelmingly dominant on the continent of Europe."

For one sector of Rumanian society, the effects of the new alliance were immediate. Barnes noted that Jews were henceforth "barred from all political activity and direction of business enterprises." While invoking Rumania's traditional tolerance of minorities, the new prime minister, Ion Gigurtu, issued an ominous warning: "I speak of the minorities which are prepared to collaborate with sincerity and loyalty in the life of the state. I omit those which have repaid our traditional hospitality by offenses and insults. We cannot forget those offenses and insults and will not permit them to be forgotten, since the members of such minorities cannot be fused into the framework of the new Rumanian state." While Barnes assured his readers that the reports of pogroms on a large scale were highly exaggerated, he pointed out that the new policies "provide an incentive to anti-Semitic action by mobs of hotheads." He continued, "Fearing the worst, great masses of Jews in the country are seeking desperately a means of escape."[10]

Aside from its location in the heart of the Balkans, Rumania's greatest value to Germany was its large oil reserves. King Carol and his new government immediately expelled the British engineers and technicians who had operated refineries and overseen drilling. Clearly, Germany was attempting to position itself in case of an effective British blockade of the Continent. Barnes wrote: "Leaving out of consideration the issue of supplies of industrial raw materials, including those needed for munitions, the food situation on the Continent is potentially serious. In this quarter, for example, crops are extremely bad. Faced with German demands for food, the Balkan granary will be in no position to export without decreasing amounts available for home consumption. A blockaded Continent would face something approaching famine next winter." In that case, he thought Germany's dilemma would push it toward a confrontation with the Soviet Union, returning to the theme that had gotten him expelled.[11]

Bulgaria too found itself caught between Germany and the Soviet Union and watched the relationship between the two uneasily. Bulgaria's traditional affinity for Russia, regardless of the regime in power there, would no doubt arouse German suspicions. The Bulgarians had little doubt that their country and the other Balkan states would be at best "little more than dependent units in an economic system dictated from Berlin, and possibly Rome." Nevertheless, the historic rivalries among the Balkan countries appeared to preclude any kind of common front against Soviet or German intrusion.[12]

Moving on to Istanbul, Barnes found the people and leaders of Turkey feeling a particular vulnerability, facing their ancient Russian enemy and the new German threat without being able to count on their traditional ally, Great Britain. The German ambassador to Turkey was the egregious Franz von Papen. He had just been called home, at the same time that the Rumanian and Bulgarian premiers and foreign ministers had been summoned to Berlin. Barnes reported much speculation about German intentions. Meanwhile, Turkey had moved to fortify its European frontiers in order to defend the Straits of the Bosporus, an opening to the west long coveted by Russia. Turkey was counting, Barnes wrote, on the continued success of its historic practice of "playing off one would-be vulture against another."[13]

From Turkey's capital, Ankara, Barnes filed a dispatch outlining the Turkish effort to bring about an understanding between the Soviet Union and Great Britain. "Besides providing a bulwark against the German menace," he explained, "such an entente, it is thought here, would liquidate the danger of an attack by Soviet Russia, since a rearrangement between Moscow and London would un-questionably imply the maintenance of an independent and unpartitioned Turkey, Britain's 'silent ally.' " The Turks, he noted, "tend to believe in the instability of German-Soviet relations and in an eventual rupture." Despite their long experience of the Russian threat, the Turkish government did not expect a Soviet attack: "Why, it is asked, should the Russians risk military action which would cripple them offensively in the face of the German threat?"

From Ankara, he wrote Esther reflecting on the year just past: "Girl, it is so hard for me to believe that a year ago at this time I was starting my holiday in Lancing. What a happy time that was. I shall not soon forget the morning I saw in the *Times* the news that the Soviet-German pact was about to be signed, the development which sent me packing back to London. I recall how I went down to the beach to tell the children goodbye. Well, some time in the not distant future we shall be on the beach together again."[14]

~

Barnes then turned his attention to the territories formerly part of the Turkish Empire but governed by the French and British through League of Nations mandates since World War I. Beirut, then a part of French-held Syria, was his next stop. He also visited Aleppo, Damascus and Baalbek, and managed to contract dysentery. His one dispatch dealt with the decision of the French military authorities to abide by a decree from the Vichy government that called for the detention of male subjects of Britain as well as of Holland, Belgium, Poland, Norway, the former Czechoslovakia and other areas under German domination, to prevent them from participating in the war against Germany. The Vichy decision was a response to Britain's attack on the French navy at Oran in North Africa, an effort to keep the French ships from falling into German hands.[15]

From Jerusalem, then under British rule, Barnes filed one story, summarizing his journey from Berlin and reiterating his conclusions about the trap in which Rumania, Yugoslavia, Bulgaria and Turkey found themselves, and their varying responses. He noted talk of an agreement with the Soviets to form a kind of pan-Slavic union as a means of resisting Hitler, but thought German power was "too formidable for either Sofia or Belgrade to risk falling in with a plan of that sort in the near future."[16] Otherwise unable to file anything of significance from Jerusalem because of the British censorship, Barnes moved on to Cairo. There he found a large British military and naval contingent, a reflection of the strategic importance of the Suez Canal for British communication with its Indian empire. British control of the area was threatened by the Italians in their neighboring colony of Libya, as well as by both German and Italian efforts to control the Mediterranean. On June 10, 1940, when German success in the West had been assured, Italy at last declared war, determined to share in the spoils of victory. The Italians began massing forces near the border of Egypt, anticipating an easy conquest of the Suez Canal while Britain was occupied with the defense of its island home.

Barnes's work in Jerusalem proved not to be a total loss, as the British authorities in Cairo allowed him to send his series of three articles that ran in the *Herald Tribune* on August 31 and September 1 and 2. Recalling the Arab revolt during the First World War, Barnes explored what their role might be in this war: "If the opportunity offers, will they indulge in widespread subversive activity against the British? Will the Arabs in Palestine revolt? If so, will they receive supplies or even active armed support from adjacent or near-by Arab states? What have the Germans and Italians been up to in the Arab world?"

For his readers' benefit, he explained precisely the territory he was writing about:

> *The area in question includes Iraq, an "independent" state in alliance with Great Britain and in which Britain still maintains military air bases; Syria and Lebanon, still under French mandate and occupied by military forces which have capitulated under the terms of the Franco-*

German armistice; Palestine, where the government of British officials and the British Army had its hands full in peace time suppressing the strife between Arabs and Jews, and, finally, Transjordan, which, although still included in the sphere of the British mandate, has been separated from Palestine and provided with an Arab government under British tutelage.[17]

Aside from their wish for independence, Arab discontent with their British governors had its base in the Balfour Declaration during World War I supporting the creation of a Jewish homeland in Palestine. The decades since had seen an increasing number of Jewish immigrants who bought up land, causing the Arabs to fear "that they would be deprived of their livelihood and would ultimately pass under Jewish domination." These fears had occasioned an Arab revolt in 1936 under the nominal command of the Mufti of Jerusalem, a religious leader whom the British forced to leave the country. Arab violence was met with Jewish retaliation, and guerrilla warfare spread through the territory, lasting well into 1939. Despite the war clouds then threatening in Europe, the British brought an army of 18,000 men to Palestine to control the rising.

Barnes noted, "Undoubtedly, the systematic and stringent measures which were carried out by the British military were the primary cause for the exhaustion of the revolt. Conflicting counsels within the Arab leadership, despite the dominant role of the Mufti in exile, contributed to restoring order. The feuds of great Arab families, as well as gangsterism, came into the picture later, and in many cases, in the closing stages of the uprising, Arab killed Arab." The direction of the Arab resistance was an ongoing issue: "By Western standards, both within and without Palestine, the general run of leaders of the Arab movement, if such it may be called, is pathetically weak, and Arab family feuds tend to prevent any considerable number of leaders from making any sustained effort in unison." This division enhanced the role of the Mufti who, although he had alienated many of the more moderate Arab leaders by his ruthless methods, still enjoyed considerable prestige among the people of Palestine. Certainly, the revolt had succeeded in making "the Palestine Arab problem an issue of primary interest throughout the Arab world." Barnes observed that the British themselves recognized this reality when they invited delegates from Iraq, Transjordan, Yemen, Saudi Arabia, and Egypt to a London conference on Palestine in 1939.[18]

In the third article of his series, Barnes explored the efforts of Germany and Italy to gain influence among the Arabs. The most obvious were the radio broadcasts from Berlin in Arabic, by an Iraqi journalist Yunis El-Bahri, whom Barnes characterized as the "Lord Haw Haw of the Levant," comparing him to William Joyce, the British fascist who broadcast from Berlin to Great Britain. El-Bahri's commentary was anti-Jewish and anti-British. In measuring El-Bahri's effect, Barnes wrote: "Though conceding that El-Bahri indulges in the grossest sort of exaggeration, Arab observers say he knows how to tune his message to the ear of his people, and that the message makes an impression. His sense of humor adds appreciably to his vogue."

More difficult to evaluate were persistent rumors of German and Italian intrigues with various Arab leaders including Ibn Saud of Saudi Arabia and the exiled Mufti of Jerusalem, Haj Amin Effendi Al Hussein. Despite German efforts, the British authorities and neutral observers were confident that Ibn Saud, "who has displayed signs of real statesmanship," would not ally himself with the Nazis. They were less sure of the Mufti, particularly since it was widely held that the Germans had helped to finance the 1936 rising.

How far the Axis would be able to go in the Middle East was a subject of controversy. Weighing in their favor was the "haunting fear among the large masses of Arabs in Palestine of eventual Jewish domination" as well as German military success in Europe. On the other hand, Barnes found those who believed that the Arabs would in the end reject the totalitarian states. All conceded that "the best British propaganda would be a British military victory, such as successfully resisting the German attempt to invade Great Britain or Italian aggression in Egypt."

~

Some of Ralph's letters from this period survive; Esther's, for the most part, do not. In the best of circumstances, letters took more than two weeks to travel between Egypt and Oregon, and one could never be sure that a letter would reach its intended reader. While getting settled at the Metropolitan Hotel in Cairo, Ralph wrote Esther: "I rather hoped you would wire to the Legation here. I also hoped to find a letter waiting there, but no luck. I inquired as recently as this morning. The mails are terribly slow, I know; hope you have some letters underway. Knowing you, I can imagine that the uncertainty has caused you to write little. My letters enroute here probably will reach you in a hodge-podge, since some of them were forwarded air mail and clipper, others straight. I take it N.Y. would inform me if there were any unusual developments at home." He worried about whether his pieces were making it into the paper:

> I can imagine, of course, that major interest in concentrated on the battle for England, and that this part of the world is considered in N.Y. a relatively small pie. Well, I'm doing my best anyhow to learn something about it. I've been doing more reading than usual, apart from running around to make contacts and the like. ... As for reading, I finished some time ago the book by George Antonius, an Arab, on the Arab movement—The Arab Awakening. It was both helpful and interesting. Meanwhile I delved into some good printed material on the Palestine question proper. Some of this provided background for the series. Since coming here I have read carefully a 400-page work on the history of the Suez Canal, a volume which has a good deal of the modern history of Egypt included within its covers. Now I am well into Lawrence's Seven Pillars of Wisdom, which is fascinating. I had had no idea that the man was able to write as he did. Wish you would read it or parts of it, Girl. I'm sure you would enjoy a good deal of it.

His expulsion from Germany still rankled:

> It will not be easy working in these parts, but I am resolved to dig in, with the hope of sort of retrieving my position. I am rather afraid that my prestige is not what it might be in N.Y. But I'm sticking, at least, and I intend to stick. ... Girl, I miss you a very great deal. Do wish so much that we could have a good long talk. Hope you are keeping your courage up. Some way or other everything will turn out all right in the end. You said something like that in one of the two letters; you must go on feeling about it that way. We are so much better off than Europeans in general. It's hell to think of England being shot up like it is.

Money worries continued to press: "Wish I could get a picture of the domestic financial situation. I presume this loan will make it considerably harder; on the other hand I am spending considerably less money—very much less—-than I would be spending if I were in London. It's expensive as hell here, but the office has to worry about that. I love you and miss you. Kiss Joannie and Zannie for me and give Mother and Dad my love. Girl, your Ralph."[19]

A cable from Wilcox in New York assuring Barnes that money was on the way and congratulating him for the Palestine series lessened a bit his sense of isolation, but the themes of loneliness and frustration at being away from the main events of the war recur in his letters. At the same time, the "making the best of it" facet of his character generally dominated. He filed spot news stories based on military communiqués. Despite the peril faced on the home island, the British were substantially strengthening their forces to protect the Suez Canal and their all-important communications with India. The danger of Italian encroachment was real, although for the moment they confined themselves to an aerial attack on Tel Aviv with its large Jewish population.[20]

For the first time, Barnes became an accredited war correspondent, meaning that he was assigned to a particular military force and wore "a boy scout uniform with shoulder emblems which say 'Foreign War Correspondent.' To date my costume consists of khaki drill shorts and short-sleeved shirt, light-weight golf socks, and the British equivalent for our overseas cap. I also affect a wide brown leather belt with all the necessary equipment for a holster, but with neither holster nor gun. The costume is quite comfortable, though I find the heat bearable without bare knees and arms. I've been hotter in N.Y. than at any time here."[21]

Ralph's next letter was from Cairo:

> I returned last night from my first desert trip. Hope you will have seen the initial result in tomorrow morning's Tribune. Though we failed to get very far forward it was a fascinating experience. The A.P. here says N.Y. is very much interested in the situation, so I suppose I got a fair play. Yet the piece lacked real eye-witness stuff, which it should have contained, simply because there was no possibility of getting it. I did get a fairly decent idea of the strategic situation and some sort of picture of the terrain; apparently the desert doesn't vary a great deal in its main features. Of course the chaps who have been far forward before the main action began had a considerable advantage over me. They knew exactly what things looked like. I arrived too late for that. Yet I was in a position to have the first story under a desert dateline; only one other correspondent was on this expedition: Clifford of the Daily Mail.

He described life with the British Army: "One night we slept in dug-outs and another on the open desert. We had part of our meals in the messes of the officers—almost always tent affairs—and part out of tins which we carried with us. I'd better say cans. At one place I was presented with a military servant who sirred me all over the place. Nice fellow; typical butler type. I found it rather embarrassing; kept saying I could take care of things for myself."

The concern about doing a good job was ongoing: "I hope N.Y. will realize that there must be a considerable interval without dispatches during trips. I missed dispatches during the first two days of the offensive, simply because I was in the field. As you can imagine communications for press messages are rather limited in the desert. I do hope that I can put up a good showing. I've got to, Girl."[22]

As he had warned Esther, Ralph's dispatches from Egypt appeared intermittently in the *Herald Tribune*. When he was away from Cairo, either with the army or for a brief period with the navy, he did not file until his return. His articles were generally short, reflecting in part the difficulty with transmission, but also the fact that the paper was crowded with the dramatic story of the Battle of Britain. In addition, his dispatches had to be passed by the British military censor which limited his scope.

Barnes chronicled the beginnings of the North African war: "Desert warfare of the modern mechanized sort—in which camels are absent—is in full swing today as Premier Benito Mussolini's colonial legions, both white and black, move cautiously eastward from Libya along the Mediterranean coastal region in the long-expected Fascist invasion of Egypt." British strategy, which Barnes characterized as a "come hither" defense, involved drawing the Italian forces into Egypt, exposing the flanks of the army to armored attack from the south and bombardment from ships in the Mediterranean. The British were stretched thin, but Barnes was sanguine: "What the British army in Egypt lacks in numbers it makes up in the quality of the troops. It is literally true to say that the desert combat forces of today are composed largely of crack detachments whose names are renowned throughout the world. These first-class British units are backed up by a contingent of New Zealanders and Australians on whose fighting qualities no slur has ever been cast."[23]

As he had done throughout his career, Barnes looked for interesting sidelights. He interviewed the three Italian journalists captured by the British army. Asked about Italian prospects, one responded: "Of course we think we are going to win and win quickly. It won't be a long war, at least we hope it won't. We've gone to war to make an empire —for better living space. We don't want to be cooped up in the Mediterranean." [24]

Back in the field, Barnes assessed the progress of the Desert War. The Italian forces had advanced with great speed but limited effect: "Yet the figures show that the Fascist land forces experienced difficulty in hitting anything. Since the Italians crossed the frontier two weeks ago, the British Army has lost in killed and wounded an almost ridiculously small number of men, and a good share of these were lost because of enemy aerial activity." He allowed a British mechanized cavalry officer to tell the story of desert warfare:

The Eyeties were shooting the sky full of red, white and green tracer bullets about the size of ping pong balls. I suppose they had decided to wave their national colors about in the desert night. Anyhow, we didn't suffer from that fire. They were searching the sky with searchlights too, and then there were lights from their lorries.

In the daytime it was a pretty picture. From my position on a bluff above the coastal belt, the enemy's left flank column close to the sea looked like some enormous worm crawling along, and the worm was raising an awful cloud of sand. Sand clouds far away, toward the coast, and much closer by as well, contributed toward the picture of chaos.

The Eyeties were coming along the bluff as well as along the coast. You'd see in the distance a group of curiously distorted objects—almost always fantastically elongated—and the objects would be moving forward in the sand and dust. The crazy distortions were tricks of the desert mirage, a factor we've got to contend with always out here.

As the objects came within range of 2,000 yards they would slowly take the shapes of motor vehicles, and always motor cycles would be in advance. Often tanks would come next, but hardly ever armored cars— we've seen but few enemy armored cars in this advance.

After the tanks would be first-class Italian lorries (trucks), six-wheeled affairs which are doing a good job in the desert. They carry almost everything, these lorries, including field guns and even tanks— until they think tanks may be needed. One of their prize tricks is to rush a gun-carrying lorry forward, swing it about, let the side down and begin firing away with the gun still resting on the lorry bottom. They are good at that. But our artillery has had several good shoots. We've administered a good deal more punishment to them than they have to us.[25]

In another dispatch, Barnes detailed the experience of a French detachment who had chosen to leave Syria and fight on after the capitulation of the Vichy government to Germany and Italy. Barnes encountered them when they had been withdrawn from the front after several days of fighting. He found relations between the two nationalities amicable: "Though the French commander was clearly proud of his outfit, he insisted on talking about what he described as the superior accuracy of the British artillery in recent engagements rather than about the exploits of his own men. News of the gallantry of these Frenchmen has spread rapidly in the desert, and at various points British officers have told me how the unit had conducted itself under fire." As Barnes was leaving, the French commander called him aside and said, "There's been a lot of propaganda to the effect that we are being badly treated by the British. There's not a word of truth in it, and we are very glad to be here with our allies."[26]

In early October, Barnes had his opportunity to go to sea with the British Mediterranean fleet. His report of the ships emerging unscathed from attacks by Italian bombers and then air-launched torpedoes earned him a citation in *Time* magazine. A few days later Barnes filed a story about an expedition to Malta to reinforce the beleaguered British forces there:

> *I was aboard one of the vessels which steamed into the island's harbor on a moon-lit night, landed their contingents, then steamed out again to rejoin the main body of the fleet and return to their base.*
>
> *A glance at the map will show that Malta is only a little more than a long-range gun shot from the southern tip of southern Sicily, about twenty minutes by fast bomber. The fact that in the face of the new aerial threat this island citadel is still being held and regularly supplied by the British provides evidence that the predominant sea power of Britain continues to play a major role in the Mediterranean, even though none could pretend that the British fleet exercises absolute control of these waters.*

He concluded his account of the reinforcement, "I have now been at Malta, but I have seen nothing of the island except shadows in the night. Many hours before dawn we were out of the harbor and steaming eastward at high speed. Disembarkation had been carried out without any sign of the Italian enemy."[27]

~

On October 10, the *Herald Tribune* printed Barnes's dispatch advocating a strong British stand in the Middle East and North Africa. His opinion was unequivocal: "Assuming that it is worth while for Great Britain to hold her present position in Egypt and the Near East, a British government which failed to make heroic efforts to rush to this quarter all possible reinforcements on land, in the air and on the sea would be guilty of the wildest folly." He cited indications that the Axis would make the Near East the next focus of their activity and warned against underestimating the efforts the enemy would make: "If Hitler's aerial offensive over Britain has failed, as is widely believed here, in such a way as to ruin his dreams of invasion, he must take extra precautions to make certain that his next ventures are not abortive."

The article went on to reject the easy alternatives:

In recent weeks there has been a tendency in certain official quarters to feed the British public exaggerated hopes of imminent assistance on a large scale by the French forces remaining in Syria, and of a "holy war" in which substantial portions of Islam would rise up to smite the Italian invaders, with their German friends, if they should come.

The most recent reliable information from Beirut indicates that the Italian-German armistice commission in Syria is leaning over backward to avoid offending either the Syrians or the French. The bulk of the French Army there is reported following a "wait-and-see" policy which is fundamentally neither anti-British nor pro-British, but pro-French. In the end, the British may secure much additional aid from these forces, but not before a lot of water runs over the dam.

The prospect of a "holy war" conjures up in some minds a dramatic picture of Arab tribesmen dashing or trotting across desert wastes on camels and horses. Some sheiks and petty rulers have talked, it is true, of a "holy war," but I have yet to find an observer with experience in the Near East who has discovered that this sort of talk has yet developed into anything of military significance.[28]

Another foray into the desert brought Barnes and other correspondents closer to actual warfare than they had been previously. For the most part, the British Army had thus far been involved in skirmishes intended to harass the invading Italian army. Barnes found the troops in good spirits and eager "have a go" at the Italians. They were still short of *matériel* but Barnes anticipated an offensive.[29]

Although he had been in Egypt only a short time, Barnes had already earned the nickname "Field Marshal" from his colleagues and enhanced his reputation for dogged persistence. Martin Agronsky, who reported for the National Broadcasting Company, later remembered Barnes during this period in a conversation with Lee Stowe. "You know, I'm just a beginner compared with him, but I never knew anyone who had so much enthusiasm. He always has to know everything about everything. Down in Libya he had to know just how they loaded the bombs and how the gunners operated. He asked more questions than the rest of us put together. Out in the desert he got interested in the stars, so he bought several books on astronomy as soon as we got back to Cairo." Agronsky added, "You know, he's done an awful lot to help us younger fellows."[30]

Barnes's "biggest" story while reporting from Egypt and Libya, both in terms of its import and its length, was his account of a British bombing raid over Italian lines in the western Egyptian desert. Asked how Barnes had managed to get aboard an RAF bomber, the British press liaison told Stowe that the RAF did not customarily allow correspondents to go on bombing runs,

> *But you know how it is with the Field Marshal when he gets his mind on something. We'd been out on the desert several days. One day Ralph comes up to me and says: "Listen, Tommy. Bish wants to take me on a raid with him." I tried to talk him out of it. Told him it wasn't supposed to be done. He had his heart set on it. How could you really tell what a bombing raid was like if you had never been on one? Finally I told him if Bish asked him to take a little ride and I didn't know anything about it—well, I couldn't give permission for a jaunt like that, but of course if it had already happened—I made one thing very clear. Even if he went, maybe the censorship wouldn't pass his story; so why go to all that trouble when the story might be spiked anyway? Well, you know Ralph. He was perfectly willing to take a chance on the censors' passing the story. So he slipped away with Bish on a daylight raid. He wrote a perfectly swell story—the best story anybody has yet written out of Libya. Sure they passed it. You can trust Ralph for that. I wish we had ten men like him, covering this war here right now. I mean ten reporters who were almost as good. Yes, there's only one Ralph Barnes. God, you should have seen him playing rugger with the boys of Seventy-seven Squadron out on the desert. He bloody well laid a couple of them out flat.[31]*

It was a good story. Barnes gave his readers a sense of the experience, from the bulky parachute slung round his waist, to the cold in the cabin at twenty thousand feet, to the drowsiness that only access to an oxygen tank could relieve, to the tension as the aircraft approached its target.

> *It was warmer in the plane, for we had descended steadily. The altimeter read 13,000, then 12,500 and finally, a couple of miles or so offshore, down to 12,000 feet. A jumble of evacuated native huts was visible a short distance east of the headland. … As we swept over the headlands I noted a series of small dust clouds a short distance southward. Then there were faint outlines of what I presumed to be a fortified camp, an area roughly circular, covered with tiny dots in an irregular pattern, something like fly specks on light brown wallpaper. I decided that these specks were trucks and other motor vehicles.*
>
> *Another minute or two went by. The observer remained busy with his bomb sights. The squadron leader at the controls was almost motionless. "Right steady." As he took aim the observer was directing*

the squadron leader: "Left, left, steady—steady, steady." The last two
"steadies" were long drawn out. In his right hand the observer held a
small button attached to a cord. He pressed the button.[32]

~

Both the anxieties and the small pleasures of his time in Egypt are
reflected in the letters Ralph wrote to Esther, still writing into a
vacuum because of the lack of communication from her.

I am sending this letter by air mail in the hope that it will reach you in
time for our wedding anniversary and Zannie's birthday. Since I
suppose it will get through to you much later, the expression of the
hope may cause you to smile. Of course I can have no idea how long it
does take a letter to reach Oregon; suppose it must be a very long time,
even with airmail stamps on it. As you can imagine I have had a good
deal of work to do recently. It's been rather maddening because of all
the obstacles placed in our way. This morning I began working on a
piece. It got through to the telegraph office about 4:30 this afternoon
after I had managed to get five stamps or sets of initials on it. That's
literally true. It was only a small part of the day's story at that. None
of us can go to the front at present; there's a bar on anything like that.
We've thought of changing our shoulder badges from "war
correspondent" to "peace correspondent." The more there is happening
the further we must stay behind. We may get up later, but God only
knows whether we will. You may have noted—it's no longer a secret
here—that the British have captured three Italian newspapermen. We
probably will have a chance to talk with them later. It's a dramatic
situation; all the glamour of the Middle East about the campaign. I
arrived here just about the right time. I haven't any idea of whether
any of my stuff is getting through. Transmission delays are simply
terrible.

He was lonely but encouraging: "I shall be thinking about you,
Esther, on our anniversary, and about Zannie and Joannie too on
Zannie's birthday. This letter should have been written several weeks
ago. Hope you will forgive me. Please, Girl, don't become too
depressed about this separation. We will have to change our habits
after the war is over. Sort of be together. Meanwhile keep a stiff
upper lip. Kiss Joannie and Zannie for me, and tell Mother that I am
going to write a birthday letter very soon now. I love you and miss
you very much, Girl. Let's stick together."[33]

Esther's letters reflected her efforts to cope with living with Ralph's parents and with the family's financial difficulties. She had paid the "S.O.B." in New York the money they owed and wrote, "I talked to Ruth about what we were doing for the family. She said she had a pretty good idea we were doing something but didn't know to what extent. ... I still don't think your mother realizes where the money is coming from. I have talked things all over with your Dad and we have worked things out very well." She tried to encourage Ralph, "Had such a nice letter from Joe Barnes the other day. He said to try to convince you to forget about getting thrown out. Reports from R.H. [probably Russell Hill and referring to the Berlin bureau] are that the H.T. could reopen and that you would be welcome. What do you think of that? We are so enjoying your articles and they are so well written. I am quite surprised. Looks like you will be getting your share of excitement before too long. I suppose it is useless to ask you to be careful."

Her life had its constraints but she was philosophical:

> *I find enough to do to keep me as happy as I could be anywhere without you, Ralph. Ruth said she didn't see how I could stand it but I do get along much better with your father than she ever did. I find Joan rebelling against them sometimes but I manage to get it to come out alright. It is the hardest nights when the whole family go off to bed at eight thirty or nine and I am left all alone. I do get a chance to read then—how nice it would be if you could just come down for the week end. I do miss you so. ... We are all busy now keeping the leaves raked up. I love getting out in the yard to work and I think I have at last convinced your mother that it is quite proper for me to work outside and that I don't care what anyone thinks. ... We plan Thanksgiving in Portland and Christmas. God—I wish you were going to be with us—miss you so—Take care of yourself and remember I love you.*[34]

It is not clear that this letter reached Ralph, but he was meanwhile writing of the difficulties of his professional life. "You can't imagine how much routine there is in getting dispatches through—stamp upon stamp, and initials after initials. In all our time on this side of the Atlantic, I have never experienced anything like it. But everyone is in the same boat, of course. That is some consolation." His remote location made for difficulties, "It's rather odd not knowing anything about what is happening to your dispatches. Did I tell you that I had a wire some time ago saying that two of them had been twenty-four hours or so in transmission? That's about all they have told me. Russia before the war was child's play compared to this. Here you have to spend about one-half your time going through the routine, or making complaints because the routine had gone wrong."

He missed his books, worried about his daughters' adjustment to U.S. schools, and complained that he could not even picture them since he did not know if they were living in Salem or Portland. He had still heard nothing since he left Bucharest. He wrote Suzanne for her birthday, wishing he could be there and providing great detail of his travels. On October 10, he sent a cable to Esther: "CABLE LEGATION DETAILING LENGTHILY HEALTH FINANCE SCHOOLING WHERE LIVING HUNGRY NEWS. SUGGEST INQUIRE PACIFIC AIRMAIL FEELING FINE ENJOYING WORK LOVE YOU."[35]

Barnes's time in Egypt was cut short when Italian forces invaded Greece on October 28. Fooled by the British strategy that allowed his forces to advance in Egypt, Mussolini was anxious to impress his German ally with further proof of his military prowess. To his embarrassment, the Greeks put up a stiff resistance, even forcing his troops back into Albania. Committed to Greek independence, the British sent a small contingent of men and aircraft to aid the effort. For Barnes, who had been disappointed in missing Greece during his Balkan tour, the new battlefront seemed a golden opportunity. With a number of other newspapermen, he made his way to Athens aboard a British warship. The trip passed "without molestation by Italian forces in the air, on the surface or below the surface" proving "that the sea lanes between the British Meiterranean naval bases and Greek ports are wide open for use by the British Mediterranean Fleet as well as merchant craft convoyed by its units."[36]

Along with the war correspondents who had come from Egypt, Athens was host to other reporters, including Barnes's old friend Lee Stowe. They ran up against the determination of the Greek High Command not to allow correspondents in the battle zone until the front had stabilized. Stowe wrote that Barnes, even more than the others, chafed at the restriction. He bided his time with a visit to a prison camp where he interviewed captured Italian soldiers, finding most of them little interested in fighting to expand Mussolini's empire. Even the officers conceded that there was limited enthusiasm for the war.

Ralph Barnes in Athens, November 9, 1940.

As the Greeks continued adamant, Barnes and the other reporters looked to the Royal Air Force to get them into action. They secured permission to accompany the RAF bombers on their night raids, flying from Greece to bomb sites in southern Italy and Albania that were being used to supply the forces attacking Greece. The reporters drew lots to see who would be allowed to go; Martin Agronsky and Jan Yindrich were on the first flight. The next night was Barnes's turn. He napped during the afternoon leaving a note on his door, "Important. Please do not disturb before 8:30 p.m." After a late dinner with his friends, Barnes went, bundled in warm clothing and lamenting the six hours he would face without a cigarette. He flew with three crewmen on a heavily loaded, twin-engine Blenheim bomber.

Lee Stowe wrote of waiting for Barnes's return and of the dawning realization early that morning of November 18, 1940, that something was wrong. "After nine, I went to his room, for they should all have been back by then. When he wasn't there I felt it was a crash. We spent the next two days fearing and trying to hope but I felt from the beginning what the answer would be." The plane was listed as missing, then a day later as having crashed into a mountainside in

Yugoslavia, apparently driven far off course in fog and blinding rain. Stowe discovered that Barnes had changed to that particular plane at the last minute, wanting the longer flight to Durazzo rather than to Valona. Stowe also learned that the pilot of that particular aircraft had been forced to turn back by the weather the night before. He was perhaps particularly determined to complete this mission.[37]

It was another day before the RAF command issued its communiqué: "The Air Officer Commanding the British Air Forces in Greece announces with regret that Mr. Ralph W. Barnes of the New York *Herald Tribune* has been killed in action while carrying out his duties as war correspondent in an RAF bomber aircraft. Mr. Barnes was a passenger in an RAF bomber which crashed near the Yugoslav-Albanian border, the entire crew of the aircraft being killed." Stowe wrote: "We learned then that the plane had crashed near Danilovgrad in old Montenegro, just north of the Albanian border. It had circled in rain and fog, dropping flares in a desperate effort to find a landing place. The roar of the motors had awakened the Serbian peasants. After daybreak they found the wreckage. The plane had crashed just about fifteen feet below the top of the highest peak in the vicinity. If it had been fifty or sixty yards to either side it would have missed the peak."[38]

The Commander of the Royal Air Force in Greece paid tribute:

Ralph Barnes was a firm friend of many pilots in the Middle East Command. He was extremely popular with everyone with whom he came in contact for he had a most engaging personality. He had been made an honorary member of an R.A.F. squadron—a bomber squadron in which he had many admirers. He had lived under canvas with them in the Western Desert, sharing their inconveniences and dangers, being bombed regularly and even going on a raid over enemy territory with them. That was one of the reasons he had so many admirers among the Royal Air Force—he was quite sincere in his anxiety to share their trials and dangers. He said often that he felt he was doing his bit for the sake of the democracy he valued so much.

He had that quiet, impish sense of humour that made him so liked by his younger friends of the R.A.F. He would join in any fun there was going—we all remember the night he thoroughly enjoyed a rather rough Rugger scrum in the Mess. Yet the quieter side of his character made an even greater appeal. He could and did talk well on the international situation, for he had seen history in the making and during discussions in the Mess he enthralled pilots with his experiences and opinions—opinions that were obviously founded on a wide knowledge of the situation and always absolutely impartial. No

Anglophile, but the best type of American, he felt that Britain and her Allies were fighting for the freedom of the rest of the world, and spared no effort to help in that fight.

Ralph was very anxious to go on a night raid—in fact he was quite upset when someone else was given the opportunity to make the first flight. When his turn, fated to end so tragically, came he was as keen as the most enthusiastic pilot.

He was a brave man and every R.A.F. pilot who knew him will miss his comradeship.[39]

Barnes's death shocked his friends and colleagues everywhere. In a memorial article in the *Herald Tribune*, other staffers remembered him. Sonia Tomara wrote:

He was terrific to work with and enchanting. The competition never knew what his next idea would be, for he despised routine stories but sought the most difficult, the almost impossible assignment. And when he had found it, he crashed all doors to get it. He managed to pull statesmen and diplomats out of bed and wring information out of them. And strangely enough, they did not hate him for it. … He never could write an article without surrounding himself with volumes and making a deep study of the subject he wanted to discuss. There was in him a mixture of boyish zest and profound understanding of the deep currents that were undermining Europe.[40]

Launching the Liberty ship *Ralph Barnes*.

~

When, three years later, a Liberty ship was christened in Ralph Barnes's name, his high school and college friend and fellow newspaperman, Robert Notson, spoke at its launching. He noted three characteristics that had marked Barnes's career: "his strong sense of right and wrong, his impetuous and untiring energy and his absolute devotion to duty regardless of personal convenience, comfort or fortune." Notson quoted Lee Stowe's cable after the crash: "I believe it is important for the American reading public to know about Ralph Barnes because there are few Americans abroad today, whether ambassadors, diplomats, or newspaper men, who are as irreplaceable or who have given of themselves so completely in their work."

Afterword

Along with the three members of the bomber's crew, Ralph Barnes was buried with military honors in Podgorica, Yugoslavia, following a church service by a local Anglican minister. In Oregon, the news of his death came first to Esther's mother in Portland, who telephoned to his parents in Salem. Esther was attending a Red Cross meeting when a message called her home. Joan and Suzanne learned of their father's death when they came home from school for lunch. Suzanne remembers that she insisted on going back to school after lunch that day, only to return home unable to deal with the other students' expressions of sympathy.

For Ralph's parents, the news was devastating. His father, who had for so long lived through his son's career, never really recovered from the blow. His mother increasingly retreated into dementia. Letters and telegrams of condolence poured in to the house at Chemeketa and Capitol, a testimony to the respect and affection of many colleagues and friends. In New York, Al Laney and Joe Barnes raised the money to send her friend Alice Rogers to Oregon to be with Esther for a month. A few months later, Lee Stowe visited Salem to offer what help he could.

Esther's situation was made more difficult by Ralph's parents' financial and emotional dependence on her. She worked as a librarian at the State Library and, for several years, endured a strained existence living in the Barnes home. Joan, especially, remembers those years as full of arguments and tension. Despite dire threats from her father-in-law, Esther bought a home of her own in 1945 and the next year remarried, which E.T. Barnes was never able to accept. Her new husband was Chester Downs, a Salem physician. In part out of consideration for him and in part, perhaps, because it was simply too painful for her, Esther tended to downplay the life she had led with Ralph, and the friends she had made during that time.

Mabel Baker Barnes died in the Oregon State Hospital in 1949. Her granddaughters and others have concluded that she had Alzheimer's disease. Edward T. Barnes died in 1959. Esther died on November 17, 1985, forty-five years after Ralph almost to the day. To the end of her life, she struggled with his decision to board that plane.

The fate of Barnes's paper, the *Herald Tribune*, is a sad one. Elizabeth Mills Reid, who had provided some $15 million over the years in loans to the paper, died in 1931. While the paper was a bright light in American journalism for many years, managed by Ogden and Helen Reid and later by their sons Whitelaw and Brown, it struggled financially. By 1957, the situation was desperate. The Reids were finally able to attract funding from John Hay Whitney, who left its management largely in their hands. But in 1967, having spent nearly $40 million, Whitney refused to put more money into it and the *Herald Tribune* closed. The Paris edition survives as the *International Herald Tribune*, jointly owned by the *New York Times*, the *Washington Post*, and Whitney.

~

As we have seen, Ralph Barnes came to journalism somewhat by chance. Although there was some suggestion of what the future held in the childhood newspaper and in the newspaper writing course he took in college, his letters indicate that he planned to pursue other occupations. Still, his character, his enthusiasms, and his education prepared him for the career he chose. He had grown up in a household where intellectual interests were encouraged; he had received a broad educational foundation. These served him well throughout his life. Nor can one discount the many testimonials to attractive personal qualities that made him so loved by his friends. Surely these contributed to his success.

Unquestionably, Barnes was fortunate to have pursued his career during a period of such significance. He also benefitted from the particular stage in the evolution of the field. He reported before the era of soundbites, at a time when newspapers were, if not the sole, at least the most important, source of news. Reporters were able to write at greater length and in greater depth than is generally true today. They were stationed for extended periods in particular places, and had the opportunity to become familiar with local issues. The *Herald Tribune* gave Barnes great freedom and precious little guidance in choosing his topics. He was able to pursue his interests and what he thought would be instructive to his readers. The *New York Times*, with its prestige, its larger staff and its greater financial resources, always overshadowed the *Herald Tribune*. While Barnes for the most part relished that challenge, it unquestionably took its toll. So too did the long separations from his family, the lack of financial security, and the responsibility for his parents that he so readily shouldered. The letters, and the testimony of some friends, suggest that Barnes suffered from depression. Certainly he was plagued by insecurities and driven by the competitive instincts that caused him to board that flight.

As Lee Stowe pointed out, Barnes's extended experience in the important capitals of Europe was unique among correspondents of his time. But even more unique was the way he went about his job. He brought to journalism a dogged intensity that made him pursue every lead, and an insatiable curiosity that compelled him to study in depth. He was determined to understand, and to make his readers understand, the background and the subtleties of the events he recorded. Despite his labored writing, he was able to make the occasion come alive for his readers.

Ralph Barnes's early death, the evanescent nature of reporting, and the fact that he never had the opportunity to write his book, have meant that his place in the history of his profession has received only marginal recognition. While he never garnered a Pulitzer Prize or other honors, Barnes made a distinguished contribution to journalism. His correspondence on the collectivization of agriculture in the Soviet Union revealed a process largely unknown, and for a long time ignored, in the West. Throughout his time in Russia, he studied the regime and explored the convictions, prejudices, and insecurities that governed its behavior. Subsequent events and historical scholarship have largely confirmed his observations. He identified many of the limitations that ultimately led to the collapse of the Soviet Union, while consistently believing that Communism would have no broad appeal among the American people.

Transferred to Germany, Barnes quickly grasped the centrality of antisemitism to Hitler's world view. He carefully documented the progressively more stringent restrictions on Jewish life, and recognized that the ultimate goal was the elimination of the Jews from Germany. Well ahead of other correspondents, Barnes understood the importance of the Blomberg "crisis" early in 1937 and its implications for the military establishment as the presumed last restraint on Hitler. Before the Munich Conference, he predicted that the demands of Rumania and Hungary would become an issue. He maintained that Hitler's success at Munich gave him a sense of greater freedom and less restraint, leading to the horrors of *Kristallnacht,* further action against Christian dissenters, and the final removal of Hjalmar Schacht, whose presence had reassured the financial markets at home and abroad. Barnes tried his best to convey to his readers exactly the atmosphere the Nazis created in Germany, quoting from newspapers and textbooks to illustrate the barrage of propaganda to which the German people were subjected.

From his experience in the Soviet Union, Barnes raised the possibility that Munich would make the Soviets even more suspicious of the motives of the British and French, with the result that they might look elsewhere to address their security concerns. The Nazi-Soviet Pact followed. His articles helped prepare Americans for the international responsibilities they would soon shoulder. Finally he made, and published, the prediction that the Germans would turn their military force against the Soviet Union.

These instances and others demonstrate the quality and range of Barnes's correspondence. They establish his position at the forefront of American journalism in the interwar period. One can only speculate about the contributions he might have made had he lived through the war and beyond. What would he have written about Nazi Germany's campaign against the Soviet Union? How would he have covered the formation, and the ultimate breakdown, of the great alliance that defeated Hitler? What insights would he have had about the Cold War and about the Red Scare in the United States?

It is my hope that this book has documented Barnes's contribution as an astute observer of his time, that it has demonstrated the challenges of his profession and, most of all, that it is a worthy substitute for the book Ralph might have written.

~

Notes

Part I: Oregon to Rome: June 1899—March 1931

Introduction

1. Stoneman, letter to Gary G. Newman, Eugene, Oregon.
2. Shirer, *Berlin Diary*, p. 334.
3. John Lukacs, *The Duel, 10 May-31 July, 1940: The Eighty Day Struggle Between Churchill and Hitler.* (New York: Ticknor & Fields, 1991), p. 142.

Chapter One

1. Al Laney, *The Paris Herald: The Incredible Newspaper* (New York: D. Appleton-Century Company, Inc., 1947), p. 321; *International Herald Tribune*, October 3-4, 1987.
2. Leland Stowe, *Chicago Daily News*, November 20, 1940.
3. William Stoneman, in a letter that is undated but was probably written late in 1975 or early in 1976. It is addressed to Gary Newman, a student at the University of Oregon who had learned of Barnes from George Weller. Weller, who reported from the Balkans during the 1930s for the New York *Times* and later for the Chicago *Daily News,* had spoken on the University of Oregon campus and had referred to Barnes as one of the best foreign correspondents he had ever known. Newman decided to write a term paper on Ralph Barnes and wrote Stoneman for his impressions. A contemporary carbon copy is in the Barnes papers with a note to Esther.
4. Maurice Hindus, *Hitler Cannot Conquer Russia* (Doubleday, Doran, 1941), p. 189; William Henry Chamberlin, *The Confessions of an Individualist* (New York: Macmillan, 1940), p. 155; William L. Shirer, *Berlin Diary* (New York: Knopf, 1940, Popular Library Edition), p. 334.
5. Leland Stowe, *Chicago Daily News*, November 20, 1940.
6. RWB, Moscow, December 10, 1934; *Capital Journal*, Salem, July 18, 1949.
7. James Q. Barnes, letters to his wife, November 8 and 12, 1891.
8. G. Dale Weight, "Beaver Pelt Money: Banking in Oregon—Early Years," *Willamette Journal of the Liberal Arts*, Vol. 7. Summer 1992; Nancie Fadeley, "Oregon's First Cattle Baron," *Oregon Business Magazine*, Vol. 13, No. 4: 55-56.
9. Robert Notson, longtime publisher of the Portland *Oregonian*, was Ralph's schoolmate at Salem High School and Willamette University. He has been generous in sharing his memories. This reference is from a letter to the

author, September 4, 1992. Additional information on Ralph's youth was gathered in an interview with Ruth Rhoten, August, 1993.

10. RWB, Moscow, August 17, 1932.

11. RWB, Moscow, September 2, 1931.

12. RWB, Moscow, September 2, 1931; RWB, Berlin, November 4, 1936.

13. I am invariably told by those who knew her that Esther's pictures do not do her justice. She was evidently a person of great warmth and charm to whom people were drawn.

14. The incident was recounted by Robert Notson in a letter to the author.

15. RWB, letter, July 4, 1918. Through the efforts of the Methodist leader Clarence True Wilson and his Anti-Saloon League, most of Oregon had gone dry by local option by 1908. Statewide prohibition passed in 1914. Robert Dean McNeil, *Valiant for Truth: Clarence True Wilson and Prohibition* (Portland: Oregonians Concerned about Addiction Problems, 1992), pp. 26-7.

16. The *Willamette University Bulletin*, 1917: 71.

17. Frank Bennett was a member of the fifteen-man group from Willamette. His daughter-in-law, Helen (Mrs. Frank M.) Bennett has generously shared his correspondence.

18. RWB, November 11, 1918.

19. Bennett correspondence.

20. Issues of the *Wallulah*, the Willamette University yearbook, and its newspaper, the *Collegian*, are the main source for Ralph's college career.

21. RWB, Moscow, November 21, 1931.

22. RWB, Cambridge, December 18, 1923.

23. Class of 1922 Letter for 1924.

24. Class of 1922 Letter for 1924.

25. In the early 1930s, exact date unspecified, E.T. Barnes wrote a short paper entitled "Experiences of a Foreign Correspondent," drawing from Ralph's letters and his own memories. That is the source for Ralph's early efforts to find employment.

26. Samuel T. Williamson, *Frank Gannett: A Biography* (New York: Duell, Sloan & Pearce, 1940), p. 113.

27. Journal of Esther Barnes for 1925.

28. Robert Notson, letter to the author, September 4, 1992. Ralph W. Barnes, Class of 1922 Letter for 1925, Willamette University.

29. Class of 1922 Letter for 1925, Willamette University.

30. *Brooklyn Eagle*, December 27, 1925.

31. Recommendation letters of L.M. Pasquin, dated January 20, 1926.

32. Al Laney, *Paris Herald*, pp. 105ff. Some of Laney's story may be apocryphal. He is wrong, for example, about the date of Barnes's arrival in Paris, putting it in the fall of 1925 rather than spring of 1926. Ralph's father says in *Experiences* that Ralph got the *Paris Herald* job through his Willamette friend Lawrence Davies who worked there at the time. Laney's mistakes are probably attributable to the passage of time. His affection for Barnes is reflected in the dedication of his book: "To the memory of Ralph Waldo Barnes who was the best and the most loved of all the Paris Herald's men."

33. Robert W. Desmond, *Crisis and Conflict: World News Reporting Between Two Wars 1920-1940* (Iowa: University of Iowa Press, 1982), p. 306, n 5.

34. In his definitive history, *The Paper: The Life and Death of the New York* Herald Tribune (New York: Vintage Books, 1989), p. 140, Richard Kluger observed: "But in their very availability to it, the Mills millions turned the paper into a hereditary possession to be sustained as a public duty rather than developed as a profit-making opportunity. In that loss of dynamism were planted the seeds of its doom."

Chapter Two

1. Laney, pp. 18 and 25.
2. Laney, p. 83.
3. Laney, p. 75.
4. Laney, p. 104. The period from 1926 to 1930 is not well documented in Ralph's personal papers. There are a very few surviving letters and portions of journals. Telling the story of the period is further complicated by the fact that the *Paris Herald* rarely used bylines, making it difficult to determine what articles Barnes wrote. I have relied on Laney's extensive account and on anecdotes recorded by Leland Stowe and others
5. Desmond, *Crisis and Conflict*, p. 311, mentioned the *Paris Herald's* coverage of the Lindbergh arrival and the Ederle swim as notable examples of the newspaper's improvement in the 1920s. He did not mention Ralph Barnes in connection with either story.
6. *Herald Tribune*, August 7, 1926.
7. *Herald Tribune*, August 7, 1926; Laney, p. 131.
8. Wilbur Forrest, *Behind the Front Page* (New York: D. Appleton-Century, 1934), pp. 302-8; Laney, p. 225-30; Robertson, p. 142; Kluger, pp. 234-5; *Literary Digest*, June 5, 1937, credited Barnes with the scoop on Lindbergh's first Paris flight in 1927.
9. Paris *Herald*, May 22 and 23, 1927.
10. Laney, pp. 209-211; Robertson, pp. 136-138. Robertson mentioned Ned Calmer's novel *All the Summer Days* (Boston: Little, Brown, 1961) with its character Spence, a fictionalized version of Ralph Barnes, always trying to get news of China in the paper. Edgar (Ned) Calmer worked briefly for the *Herald* after a stint with the *Chicago Tribune*. Later he was a CBS correspondent. Desmond, *Crisis and Conflict*, p. 313.
11. RWB, Class of 1922 Letter for March 8, 1927; EPB, Journal, January 30, 1927.
12. Ralph's journal is in its original form. Esther's account of the trip is a carefully typed fifty-seven page summary complete with photographs, that she prepared apparently for her parents. It incorporates parts of Ralph's journal.
13. RWB, travel journal, August 11, 1927.
14. Ralph's journal referred only to "Knauth of the United Press." I have concluded that it was Percy Knauth, who later was a correspondent in Berlin for the *New York Times* and then in Ankara, Turkey and in Europe during World War II for *Time* magazine. See Desmond, *Tides of War*, pp. 274 and 397.
15. Desmond, *Crisis and Conflict*, p. 301; Harrison Salisbury, *Without Fear or Favor: The New York Times and Its Times* (New York: Times Publishing Company, 1980), p. 31.

16. Bassow, Whitman. *The Moscow Correspondents: Reporting on Russia from the Revolution to Glasnost* (New York: Paragon House, 1989), pp. 26, 29.

17. Laney, p. 209.

18. Ironically, historical opinion has subsequently shifted back to a greater emphasis on German responsibility. See especially Fritz Fischer, *Germany's Aims in the First World War* (New York, Norton, 1967).

19. Stowe, Leland. *No Other Road to Freedom* (New York: Alfred A. Knopf, 1941), p. 247.

20. Leland Stowe, letter to Charles T. Duncan of the School of Journalism at the University of Oregon, October 23, 1975. Stowe continued: "As an example, upon joining British Forces in Cairo, immediately he read Lawrence's *Seven Pillars of Wisdom*—as education for reporting the Desert War against Rommel! Ever hear of another reporter who did things like that? (And how I wish I had emulated Ralph!) In this respect we might have emulated him, if wise and energetic enough. But to rival him in other respects, at least in their combination and top quality—impossible."

21. E.T. Barnes, "Experiences", p. 4.

22. For accounts of Barnes's role in the coverage of the Young Conference, see Stowe, pp. 248-50, Laney, p. 285, and Kluger, p. 237.

Chapter Three

1. John Lukacs, "Back from the Dead: Benito Mussolini," *The New York Times Magazine*, July 24, 1994.

2. Denis Mack Smith, *Mussolini* (New York: Alfred A. Knopf, 1982), is a good source for the Fascist regime in Italy. Our contemporary impression of Mussolini as some sort of buffoon can lead to a misapprehension about how he was perceived at the time. In fact, he was both admired and taken quite seriously. That admiration persisted for some time. John Lukacs, "Back from the Dead," reminded his readers that the 1935 version of Cole Porter's song "You're the Top" included the lines: "You're the top! You're the great Houdini! You're the top! You're Mussolini!"

3. Desmond, *Crisis and Conflict*, p. 112-17; George Seldes, *You Can't Print That* (New York: Garden City Press, 1929), p. 144.

4. Stowe, *No Other Road*, p. 248.

5. *New York Herald Tribune*, January 1930.

6. *Herald Tribune*, datelines January 25 and February 10, 1930.

7. *Herald Tribune*, datelines February 15 and March 4, 1930.

8. *Herald Tribune*, dateline January 8, 1931.

9. *Herald Tribune*, datelines June 30 and October 28, 1930.

10. RWB to his parents, November 15, 1930.

11. *Herald Tribune*, datelines May 9 and November 20, 1930.

12. RWB, Rome, November 15, 1930.

13. EPB, Rome, October 5 and December 28, 1930; RWB, Moscow, March 8, 1931.

14. *Herald Tribune*, datelines April 12, May 21, December 3, 19, and 22, 1930.

15. *Herald Tribune*, datelines February 27 and May 17, 1930.

16. *Herald Tribune* dateline May 22, 1930.

17. RWB, Rome, March 8, 1931.

18. EPB, Rome, March 14 and 17, 1931.

19. EPB, February 9, 1931.
20. *New York Times*, February 8, 1931.
21. *Herald Tribune*, February 28, 1931.
22. *New York Times*, February 9, 1930.
23. *Herald Tribune*, March 1, 1931.
24. *Herald Tribune*, March 2, 1931.
25. *Herald Tribune*, March 4, 1931.
26. *Herald Tribune*, March 5, 1931.
27. RWB, Moscow, July 14, 1931.

Part II: Moscow: March 1931—August 1935

Chapter Four

1. Richard Pipes. *Russia Under the Bolshevik Regime* (New York: Vintage Books, 1995), p. 5.
2. RWB, Rome, March 8, 1931.
3. Lippmann's decision to join the *Herald Tribune* received mixed reviews among his friends and admirers. While many cheered it as providing liberalism an important new forum, Felix Frankfurter saw it as an indication of Lippmann's steady move to the right and no cause for jubilation. Steel, *Walter Lippmann and the American Century* (New York: Vintage, 1981), p. 280; RWB, Moscow, September 23, 1931, and October 25, 1932.
4. RWB, Moscow, June 8, 1931
5. RWB, Moscow, May 21, 1931. The letters that Ralph and Esther exchanged when they were apart during the Moscow years have for the most part not survived.
6. RWB, Moscow, April 13 and May 8, 1931.
7. RWB, Moscow, April 13, 1931.
8. RWB, Moscow, June 13 and 14, 1931.
9. Whitman Bassow. *The Moscow Correspondents*: *Reporting on Russia from the Revolution to Glasnost* (New York: Paragon House, 1989), pp. 33-36, 64; "A Test of the News," *New Republic*, August 4, 1920. Constantine Oumansky, formerly foreign editor for the Soviet Tass news agency, was head of the press department and also chief censor during Ralph's time in Moscow. Later he was Soviet ambassador to Mexico where he was killed in a somewhat mysterious airplane accident in 1945. See Desmond, *Crisis and Conflict*, p. 48.
10. For descriptions of the trials of reporting from Moscow, see Bassow, p. 50 and 76; Eugene Lyons, *Assignment in Utopia* (New York: Harcourt, Brace and Company, 1937), pp. 105-6; Malcolm Muggeridge, *Chronicles of Wasted Time: The Green Stick* (New York: William Morrow & Company, 1973), p. 215; EPB, Moscow, March 12, 1935.
11. RWB, Moscow, June 8, 1931.
12. *New York Times*, May 3, 1932; RWB, Moscow, May 21, 1931. Walter Duranty is a figure of almost endless controversy. He was viewed, approvingly by liberals and disparagingly by conservatives, as a strong supporter of the Soviet regime. The truth is rather more complicated and has been the subject of a number of studies. His contemporaries in Moscow, William Henry Chamberlin and Eugene Lyons, were critical of Duranty in the specific case of reporting on the famine: Chamberlin, *Confessions*, p. 155; Lyons, *Assignment*, pp. 67 and 572.

Malcolm Muggeridge, *Chronicles*, p. 254, described Duranty's attitude toward Stalin as that of "a little browbeaten boy looking up admiringly at a big bully." Harrison Salisbury in his book on the *New York Times*, pp. 458-65, detailed a background full of occult and sexual eccentricities, presumably unknown to his bosses at the rather stuffy *Times*. Whitman Bassow discussed Duranty's career and special stature within the American journalistic community in Moscow. Duranty's coverage of the effects of collectivization was examined by Marco Carynnyk, "The Famine the *Times* Couldn't Find," *Commentary*, November, 1983. Two books, James William Crowl, *Angels in Stalin's Paradise, Western Reporters in Soviet Russia, 1917-1937: A Case Study of Louis Fischer and Walter Duranty* (Washington, D.C.: University Press of America, 1982) and S. J. Taylor, *Stalin's Apologist: Walter Duranty, the New York Times Man in Moscow* (New York: Oxford University Press, 1990), provide a complete background on the debates swirling around Duranty.

13. After a review of Duranty's reporting during the first six months of 1931, I have drawn this representative sampling from a piece entitled "Stalin: Man, Mouthpiece, Machine," published in the *New York Times Magazine* on January 18, 1931, articles dated January 5, March 8, and May 10, as well as from an eleven-part series filed from Paris during a visit there and published from June 14 through June 27.

14. The letters are full of examples. See RWB, Moscow, May 30, July 28, October 18, November 16, and December 2, 1931, October 25, 1932.

15. RWB, Moscow, May 1, 1931. In his memoirs, Lyons said that Chamberlin was "always exact and scholarly and precise" and referred to him as "the best-informed and least sensational of my American colleagues in Moscow." *Assignment in Utopia*, pp. 96 and 147. See also RWB, Moscow, February 24, 1933, and EPB, Moscow, June 14, 1933.

16. *Herald Tribune*, April 24, 1931.

17. *Herald Tribune*, May 10, 1931.

18. *Herald Tribune*, May 15, 21, 23, and 31, 1931.

19. *Herald Tribune*, May 30, 1931. According to the memoirs of the American engineer Zara Witkin, Calder changed his mind, eventually breaking with the authorities and returning to America, "angry and disgusted." Michael Gelb, ed., *An American Engineer in Stalin's Russia 1932-1934* (Berkeley: University of California Press, 1991), p. 114.

20. *Herald Tribune*, June 5, 1931.

21. *Herald Tribune*, June 18, 1931. Witkin's memoirs suggest that they never succeeded.

22. *Herald Tribune*, July 6 and 12, August 4 and 13, 1931.

23. Hélène Carrère D'Encausse, *Stalin: Order Through Terror* (New York: Longman, 1981) p. 13.

24. Lyons, *Assignment*, p. 66; Chamberlin, *Confessions*, p. 153.

25. Lyons, *Assignment*, p. 543.

26. RWB, Moscow, April 26 and April 13, 1931; Lyons, *Assignment*, p. 350.

27. Rhys Williams once chastised Lyons: "Gene, your heart is touched by the miseries of the intelligentsia, but it remains unmoved by the persecution of these monks and priests and honest believers. You're as narrow in your prejudices as any Bolshevik, only they're different prejudices." Lyons, *Assignment*, p. 356; RWB, Moscow, April 13, 1931. Typically, he suggested that

his father look up the Old Believers in the *Encyclopedia Britannica*. *Herald Tribune*, May 17, 1931.

28. RWB, Moscow, April 13, 1931.
29. See the *Herald Tribune*, June 7, 21, 28, July 2, and 12, 1931. Barnes's article on the popularity of western sports was picked up by the *Literary Digest* in its August 22, 1931, issue. In a September 2, 1931, letter to his family, Ralph referred to the piece as "one of the lesser of my products."
30. RWB, Moscow, February 24, 1933 and June 8, 1931. Letters of May 25, 1931, and September 19, 1931, also refer to these problems.
31. Muggeridge, *Chronicles*, p. 244.
32. *Herald Tribune*, July 27, 1931; RWB, Moscow, July 28, 1931.
33. *Herald Tribune*, July 24 and 28, 1931.
34. *Herald Tribune*, July 25, 1931.
35. RWB, Moscow, July 28, and August 27, 1931. The story, citing the *Herald Tribune* reporter in Moscow, appeared in *Time* magazine (August 10, 1931). Barnes noted that the Russians he met were puzzled by the interest, since "permits to go abroad are denied to a great number of Soviet private citizens. To residents of Moscow there is little to differentiate this case from many others" (*Herald Tribune*, July 28, 1931). Barnes's September 15, 1931 letter to his father talked of working four days on the Krynine case. Mme. Krynine had been refused a passport for the fourth time, but the censor refused to let him send the news to New York. The article about her exile to the provinces appeared on July 29, 1934. I find no further word as to her fate.
36. "I had to wait for the censor an hour and a half tonight—he was out. It was a terrible waste of time, and it resulted in my getting my story off later than I should have." RWB, Moscow, May 1, 1931. Muggeridge, *Chronicles*, p. 223, Bassow, *Moscow Correspondents*, p. 63.
37. Lyons, *Assignment*, p. 582; Taylor, p. 199.
38. The collectivization of Soviet agriculture has been the subject of considerable scholarship. See Robert Conquest, *Harvest of Sorrow: Soviet Collectivization and the Terror-Famine* (New York: Oxford University Press, 1986) and Hélène Carrère D'Encausse, *Stalin: Order through Terror*.
39. Conquest, *Harvest*, p. 165.
40. RWB, Moscow, April 26, June 8, July 30, August 2 and 3, 1931, November 7, 1932.
41. RWB, Moscow, August 13, 1931.
42. Hindus, *Hitler Cannot Conquer Russia*, p. 189.
43. *Herald Tribune*, August 16, 1931.
44. *Herald Tribune*, August 13, 16, and 20, 1931.
45. *Herald Tribune*, September 13, 1931.
46. *Herald Tribune*, September 23, 1931.
47. *Herald Tribune*, September 26, 27, and 29, 1931.
48. *Herald Tribune*, October 11, 1931.
49. *Herald Tribune*, September 27, October 17, 28, 30, 1931.
50. *Herald Tribune*, September 20, October 18, November 22, 1931.
51. *Herald Tribune*, December 1 and 2, 1931.
52. *Time*, December 14, 1931. RWB, letter to his parents, December 2, 1931. When, a year later, Nadia Alliluieva died, Barnes reported on the funeral. Like the rest of the press, he repeated the Soviet announcement that she had been

ill for several weeks. Her death is not mentioned in his letters and there is no way of knowing whether he questioned the official explanation. Later scholars have indicated that she committed suicide, distraught over reports of the deaths due to the collectivization of agriculture. Some have even hinted that Stalin may have been directly responsible for her death. *Herald Tribune*, November 10, 11, and 12, 1932. See also Robert Conquest, *The Great Terror: A Reassessment* (New York: Oxford University Press, 1990), p. 67, and Alan Bullock, *Hitler and Stalin*, p. 373. RWB, Paris, December 31, 1931.

Chapter Five

1. RWB, Moscow, May 30, 1931; June 14, 1931; January 14, 1933; March 20, 1933. Barnes's experience was not unique. About Joseph Barnes's time as the *Herald Tribune* Moscow correspondent from 1937 until 1939, Kluger wrote: "The hardest part of the job for him was its professional loneliness. There were never any instructions from New York or Paris about what to cover, never a rebuke when the *Times*'s veteran Moscow correspondent Walter Duranty scooped him, and only an occasional note of commendation from Wilcox or Sunday editor George Cornish. 'I got almost nothing,' he would write of his employers, 'but freedom and silence.'" *The Paper*, p. 300.

2. RWB, Moscow, October 18, 1931; Kluger, *The Paper*, pp. 251-2; RWB, Moscow, September 21, 1933; EPB, Moscow, September 30, 1933.

3. RWB, Moscow, April 26, May 21, May 30, June 8, September 2, October 13, November 21, 1931. Suzanne's birth was recorded in the *Paris Herald* on October 12, 1931.

4. RWB, Moscow, September 15, October 12, November 21, December 2 and 9, 1931.

5. RWB, Paris, December 20, 23, 25, and 28, 1931

6. RWB, Moscow, January 23 and February 3, 1932.

7. *Herald Tribune*, January 31, February 1, 9, 11, 26, March 19, 1932.

8. *Herald Tribune*, January 23 and 31, March 2 and 19, 1932; Eugene Lyons, *Assignment*, p. 517.

9. *New York Times*, January 2, 1932.

10. RWB, Moscow, February 19 and March 6, 1932.

11. RWB, Moscow, March 28 and 31, 1932.

12. *Herald Tribune*, April 17, 1932; *Literary Digest*, April 30, 1932.

13. *Herald Tribune*, April 24, 1932.

14. *Herald Tribune*, May 8, 1932.

15. RWB, Paris, June 2, 3, 1932; Moscow, June 26 and July 10, 1932.

16. *Herald Tribune*, June 5, 1932.

17. *Herald Tribune*, August 12 and 24, 1932.

18. *Herald Tribune*, September 15, 1932.

19. *Herald Tribune*, July 31 and August 25, 1932.

20. *New York Times*, August 14, 1932; *Herald Tribune*, August 29, September 18, 1932.

21. RWB, southern Russia, September 21, 1932. Barnes wrote a long mail article on travel conditions that appeared in the *Herald Tribune* on November 6.

22. RWB, Moscow, October 25, 1932.

23. *Herald Tribune*, October 7, 1932.

24. *Herald Tribune*, September 25, 1932.

25. RWB, Moscow, February 24, 1933. See also Lyons, *Assignment*, p. 424; Muggeridge, *Chronicles*, p. 255; Witkin, p. 209; and Crowl. An example of Fischer's work is his article, "Russia Moves Toward Democracy," in *Current History*, September, 1935.

26. Lyons, *Assignment*, p. 521. Malcolm Muggeridge, *Like it Was: The Diaries of Malcolm Muggeridge*. New York: Morrow, 1982, p. 58, pictured Barnes questioning Soviet Five-year Plan figures and found him "quite an exceptionally stupid man," this during Muggeridge's pro-Soviet phase. A short time later, he quoted John Cholerton of the *London Daily Telegraph* on Barnes; "The front page or the gutter as far as he's concerned" and said he (Muggeridge) was saving a remark of Barnes's on Krupskaya for his play "The Foreign Correspondent"(p. 60). Muggeridge, *Chronicles*, p. 234.

27. *Herald Tribune*, August 21, September 4, 18, October 29, 1932.

28. RWB, Moscow, August 27, 1932.

29. RWB, Moscow, October 25, 1932.

30. *Herald Tribune*, November 11, 1932.

31. RWB, Moscow, November 7, 1932.

32. RWB to EPB, Moscow, November 7, 1932.

33. Zara Witkin was a Jewish-American from Los Angeles who worked as an advisor during the Five-year Plans. Through Eugene Lyons, the correspondent for the United Press, he became involved in the social life of the American colony and considered Ralph and Esther Barnes two of his closest friends in Moscow. He collaborated with Ralph on several of his articles on the Five-year Plan. The story of Witkin's obsession with a Soviet film actress and his coming to Moscow to use his engineering expertise to build socialism and, along the way, to find her is found in Michael Gelb, ed., *An American Engineer in Stalin's Russia: The Memoirs of Zara Witkin, 1932-1934*. George F. Kennan, letter to the author, October 29, 1990.

34. Muggeridge, *Chronicles*, p. 221.

35. Witkin in Gelb, ed., *American Engineer*, p. 91 and Lyons, *Assignment*, p. 293, told of instances when they became aware of the interest of the police in their activities. Later in his book (p. 601), Lyons wrote: "Espionage and surveillance were the element in which we lived, part of the air we breathed. In the first years I continued to be surprised when Russians inadvertently showed familiarity with some phase of my private affairs that they would know only by eavesdropping on my conversation or mail, but in the end this experience became too commonplace." RWB, Moscow, June 8, 1931; August 17, 1932; July 23, 1931.

Chapter Six

1. *New York Times*, November 25 through 30, 1932.

2. RWB, on a train between Sverdlovsk and Moscow, December 5, 1932.

3. *Herald Tribune*, October 23, November 17, 20, December 29, 1932.

4. *Herald Tribune*, December 12, 1932.

5. *New York Times*, October 12, 1932. The full quote is: "'Either you are building socialism or not,' it was said, 'and why wail over broken eggs when you try to make an omelette?'"

6. *Herald Tribune*, January 1, 4, and 12, 1933.

7. *Herald Tribune*, December 18, 1932, January 13 and 21, 1933.

8. RWB, Moscow, December 28, 1932. In another letter, Barnes wrote of a sixth and a seventh article for the series. These, however, the *Herald Tribune* did not print as part of the series, but separately as two freestanding articles printed on February 19, 1933. RWB, on a train in the North Caucasus, January 26, 1933; *Herald Tribune*, January 1, 1933.

9. *Herald Tribune*, January 2, 1933.

10. *Herald Tribune*, January 8, 1933.

11. *Herald Tribune*, January 15, 1933. When he later saw this article in print, Barnes wrote his parents that the paper had "mutilated the third one pretty badly—cut out about a third of it. Guess they are short of space these days." RWB, Moscow, February 17, 1933.

12. *Herald Tribune*, January 22, 1933.

13. *Herald Tribune*, January 29, 1933. On the execution of the Czar and his family, see Richard Pipes, *The Russian Revolution* (New York: Alfred A. Knopf, 1990), p. 770.

14. *Herald Tribune*, February 6, 1933. The lead of the article indicated that it was cabled from Rostov-on-Don. It is a remarkably frank piece to have passed the Soviet censor.

15. *Herald Tribune*, February 7, 1933.

16. There is some dispute on this matter. Taylor, *Stalin's Apologist*, p. 202 wrote that Barnes and Stoneman had their articles carried out of the Soviet Union by an "obliging German Jewish fur buyer." Harrison Salisbury, *Without Fear or Favor*, p. 464, said that Barnes and Stoneman mailed the articles from Moscow to Berlin "to escape the censorship." Salisbury was wrong in placing the trip in 1932.

17. *Herald Tribune*, March 5, 1933.

18. Lyons, *Assignment in Utopia*, p. 545, Salisbury, *Without Fear*, p. 464 and Taylor, *Stalin's Apologist*, p. 216. Salisbury gave no citation for his statement; Taylor's language indicated pretty clearly that Salisbury was her source.

19. RWB, Moscow, March 8, 1933.

20. RWB, Moscow, February 24, 1933; Salisbury, *Without Fear or Favor*, p. 464. Duranty felt the need to defend himself against charges of being a correspondent friendly to the Soviet Union and thus in receipt of special favors, *New York Times*, June 11, 1933.

21. Conquest, *Harvest of Sorrow*, p. 310, said that the British Embassy in Moscow reported the travel ban to London as early as March 5, 1933.

22. RWB, Moscow, March 4, 1933.

23. RWB, Moscow, March 16, 1933.

24. *Herald Tribune*, March 13, 14, 15, 17, and 18, 1933.

25. *Herald Tribune*, March 22, 1933.

26. RWB, Moscow, March 23, 1933. The London *Daily Express* also carried the letter on March 23.

27. RWB, Moscow, August 7, 1933.

28. RWB, Moscow, February 24, 1933.

29. *Herald Tribune*, April 13, 14, 15, 16, 17, 18, and 19, 1933.

30. *Herald Tribune*, March 29 and 30, 1933; RWB, Moscow, March 27, 1933.

31. RWB, over northern France, May 4, 1933; *Oregon Statesman*, May 28, 1933.

32. EPB, Moscow, June 10, 1933.

33. EPB, Moscow, June 10 and 14, July 18, September 12, 1933.

34. EPB, Moscow, June 17, 1933.

35. RWB, Moscow, September 10, 1933.

36. Gelb, ed., *An American Engineer in Stalin's Russia*, pp. 208-210. Others, including Taylor and Salisbury, wrote that Barnes left the Soviet Union in August and cabled the article while out of the country. There is no evidence whatever that he left the Soviet Union at that time. I have concluded that Witkin's report is the most accurate. I am indebted to John McMillan for calling the Witkin memoir to my attention. Chamberlin, p. 155. When Eugene Lyons had left the Soviet Union and published his book *Assignment in Utopia*, *Time* reviewed it in the October 25, 1937, issue and referred to Barnes as the first western reporter to break the story. Conquest, *Harvest of Sorrow*, pp. 308-21, provided the most thorough account of western notice of the famine, crediting the *Herald Tribune* with "broad coverage." He is scathing in his denunciation of Duranty. See also EPB, Moscow, September 30, 1933.

37. *Herald Tribune*, August 28, 1933; *New York Times*, September 13, 1933.

38. Of this total 6.5 million died as a result of dekulakization, one million died in Kazahkstan, and seven million in the 1932 famine. The famine deaths were distributed as follows: five million in the Ukraine, one million in the North Caucasus, and one million in other parts of the Soviet Union. The total, Bullock noted, exceeded the total number of fatalities in all countries during World War I. The figures are from Conquest, *Harvest of Sorrow*, and are also cited in Bullock, *Hitler and Stalin*, p. 277.

39. Dale Carnegie Interview, Maltex Broadcast WEAF, Sunday, October 21, 1934. The typescript is among the Barnes papers.

40. *Herald Tribune*, September 20, 1933.

Chapter Seven

1. *Herald Tribune*, September 2, 20, 22, 23, 24, October 1, 1933.

2. *Herald Tribune*, October 19, 1933; *Time*, October 30, 1933.

3. RWB, Leningrad, September 21, 1933; RWB, Moscow, October 13, 1933.

4. EPB, Moscow, October 14, 1933.

5. EPB, Moscow, November 17, 1933.

6. *Herald Tribune*, October 9, 15, November 9, 1933.

7. *Herald Tribune*, October 8, 1933.

8. *Herald Tribune*, October 21, 1933.

9. EPB, Moscow, November 3, 1933.

10. *Herald Tribune*. November 18, 1933.

11. RWB, Moscow, November 26, 1933; EPB, Moscow, November 12, 1933.

12. RWB, Moscow, November 28, 1933; EPB, Moscow, December 2 and 6, 1933.

13. Frederick Jackson Turner, an American historian who taught at the University of Wisconsin and at Harvard University, read his paper "The Significance of the Frontier in American History" at the World Columbian Exposition in Chicago in 1893. His theory that the availability of free land in the west played a significant role in reinforcing democracy in the United States became very influential in the analysis of American history.

14. *Herald Tribune*, December 10 and 31, 1933. Ralph cabled a few articles during the trip then followed up with mail articles that appeared in the *Herald Tribune* over the next few months.

15. *Herald Tribune*, March 4, 1934. A second mail article on the steel complex at Kuznetz appeared on March 18.
16. *Herald Tribune*, January 14, 1934; RWB, en route between Alma Ata and Tashkent, December 17, 1933.
17. RWB, Moscow, December 29, 1933; EPB, Moscow, December 27, 1933.
18. *New York Times*, December 28, 1933.
19. James Abbe, "Men of Cablese," *New Outlook*, December 1933.
20. *Time*, June 18, 1934, based on *Herald Tribune*, June 5.
21. RWB, Moscow, January 18, 26, April 6, 1934.
22. EPB, Vienna, March 6, 1934; RWB, Moscow, March 19, April 6, 16, May 16, 1934; EPB, April 26, 1934.
23. *Herald Tribune*, April 14 and 22, 1934; EPB, Moscow, May 10; RWB, Moscow, May 16, 1934.
24. *Herald Tribune*, December 31, 1933, January 1, 5, February 8, March 25, 1934.
25. *Herald Tribune*, March 11; April 7, 8, 9, 18, and 20, 1934.
26. *Herald Tribune*, May 3 and 9, June 10 and 17, 1934.
27. *Herald Tribune*, May 20, 1934.
28. *Herald Tribune*, March 9 and July 24, 1934.
29. *Herald Tribune*, February 25, 27, March 17, April 4, 5, 25, May 10, 11, and 13, 1934.
30. *Herald Tribune*, March 8, 18, May 21, June 10, July 1, 1934.
31. *Herald Tribune*, January 23, 27, 28, April 21, 22, and 27, 1934.
32. *Herald Tribune*, June 3 and 11, July 18 and 28, 1934.
33. *Herald Tribune*, August 3, 1934.
34. EPB, Vienna, March 6, and Moscow, June 23, 1934.

Chapter Eight

1. *Herald Tribune*, August 28, 1934.
2. *Oregon Statesman*, Salem, September 5, 1934. Contact with the Roosevelt Library at Hyde Park turned up no evidence of the visit although the librarian informed me that good records of Roosevelt's Hyde Park schedule for the period do not exist.
3. *Oregon Statesman*, September 5 and 19, 1934; *Oregonian*, September 4, 1934; *Capital Journal*, September 19 and 25, 1934.
4. Duncan Aikman, *Los Angeles Daily News*, October 4, 1934.
5. *Herald Tribune*, October 17, 18, and 19, 1934.
6. RWB, on board a United Airways plane en route from Portland to New York City, October 14, 1934.
7. RWB, New York, October 29, 1934. In the end, the move was not a good one for Barnes's friend Leland Stowe. Wilbur Forrest, with whom both men had experience in Paris and who was now Ogden Reid's right hand man, did not like Stowe. When war broke out in Europe, Forrest refused Stowe's request to go overseas supposedly because Stowe, at thirty-nine, was too old. Stowe left the *Herald Tribune*, joined the Chicago *Daily News*, and saw distinguished service as a war correspondent. Kluger, *The Paper*, p. 238. See also RWB, Moscow, December 19, 1934.
8. *Herald Tribune*, October 28, 1934.
9. *Editor & Publisher*, November 24, 1934.

10. RWB, Moscow, November 30 and December 10, 1934; Bassow, *Moscow Correspondents*, p. 83.

11. *Editor & Publisher*, November 24, 1934; RWB, Moscow, December 10, 1934. Robert Conquest wrote *The Great Terror: Stalin's Purge of the Thirties* in the late sixties. His conclusions were largely confirmed by the archival material that became available after the disintegration of the Soviet Union. In 1990, he published *The Great Terror: A Reassessment* (New York: Oxford University Press) incorporating that material. Conquest is also the author of the best available analysis of the Kirov assassination, *Stalin and the Kirov Murder* (New York: Oxford University Press, 1989).

12. *Herald Tribune*, December 2, 3, 4 and 6, 1934.

13. *Herald Tribune*, December 6, 1934.

14. *Herald Tribune*, December 18 and 19, 1934.

15. *Herald Tribune*, December 22 and 23, 1934; January 16 and 18, 1935.

16. *Herald Tribune*, January 7 and 13, 1935.

17. RWB, Moscow, January 25, February 11 and 19, 1935. Kuybyshev's death has been the subject of some speculation, since he was known to have supported Kirov in some of his disputes with Stalin. However, Conquest dismissed as unproven stories that it was actually another murder. *Stalin and the Kirov Murder*, p. 77. Duranty, *New York Times Magazine*, February 17, 1935, and March 31, 1935.

18. RWB, Moscow, January 25 and February 19, 1935.

19. *Herald Tribune*, January 29, February 2 and 7, 1935.

20. *Herald Tribune*, January 31 and February 3, 1935.

21. *Herald Tribune*, February 20 and March 1, 1935.

22. *Herald Tribune*, March 2 and 10, 1935.

23. *Herald Tribune*, February 19, 1935.

24. *Herald Tribune*, March 18 and 20, 1935.

25. *Herald Tribune*, March 24, 29, 30, and 31, 1935.

26. RWB, Moscow, April 2 and 18, 1935.

27. EPB, Moscow, March 11, 17 and 30, 1935.

28. *Herald Tribune*, April 14, 1935.

29. *Herald Tribune*, April 29, May 5 and 12, 1935.

30. *Herald Tribune*, May 7, 15, and 19, 1935.

31. *Herald Tribune*, two articles which appeared on June 9, 1935.

32. RWB, Moscow, April 18, May 12 and 28, 1935; EPB, Moscow, May 6, 1935.

33. RWB, Moscow, June 10 and 12, 1935.

34. *Herald Tribune*, June 30, 1935. In a letter to his family, Barnes mentioned that an American graduate of Harvard Law School in Moscow studying Soviet law covered for him during his absence from Moscow.

35. EPB, Sochi, July 5, 1935.

36. EPB, Erevan, July 1, 1935; RWB, on a steamer from Sochi to Yalta, July 7, 1935.

37. *Herald Tribune*, July 14 and August 4, 1935; RWB, en route by air from Kharkov to Moscow, July 11, 1935.

38. *Herald Tribune*, July 25, 26 and 28, 1935.

39. *Herald Tribune*, July 29, 30, 31, and August 3, 1935.

40. *Herald Tribune*, August 5 and 11, 1935.

41. EPB, Moscow, August 22, 1935.

42. *Herald Tribune*, August 25, 1935. Nearly every subsequent study of Soviet agriculture has commented on the tremendously higher productivity of the private plots in contrast with the collective farms.

43. *Herald Tribune*, September 1, 1935.

44. *Herald Tribune*, August 25, 26, 27 and 28, 1935.

45. RWB, Berlin, September 2, 1935.

Part III. Berlin: September 1935—March 1939

Chapter Nine

1. Through the Weimar Republic, the election results reflected the economic situation:

    1924 The Nazis won 14, the Communists 45, of 493 seats.

    1928 The Nazis won 13, the Communists 54, of 491 seats.

    1930 The Nazis won 107, the Communists 77, of 517 seats.

2. See Richard Bessel, *Germany after the First World War* (Oxford: Clarendon Press, 1992) and Detlev J. K. Peukert, *The Weimar Republic* (New York: Hill and Wang, 1989) for the postwar period. So convenient was the Reichstag Fire that for a long time many maintained that the Nazis had started it themselves. Although a number of Communists were tried and convicted for the crime, it appears to have been the work of one rather unstable individual who happened to be a Communist.

3. The literature on Germany history during the 1930s is extensive. See Klaus P. Fischer, *Nazi Germany: A New History* (New York: Continuum, 1995), a comprehensive new survey. Other works of importance include William Sheridan Allen, *The Nazi Seizure of Power: The Experience of a Single German Town, 1930-1935* (New York: Franklin Watts, 1973), Daniel Goldhagen, *Hitler's Willing Executioners: Ordinary Germans and the Holocaust* (New York: Alfred A. Knopf, 1996), and Ian Kershaw's two-volume biography of Hitler, *Hitler 1889-1936: Hubris* (New York: W.W. Norton, 1999) and *Hitler 1936-1945: Nemesis* (New York: W.W. Norton, 2000). In reporting on the Third Reich, Ralph Barnes consistently stressed the centrality of Hitler's book *Mein Kampf*.

4. RWB, Berlin, September 1, 1935; EPB, Berlin, September 7, 1935.

5. RWB, Berlin, September 8, 1935; *Herald Tribune*, September 7, 1935.

6. EPB, Zurich, September 15 and 17, 1935.

7. Desmond, *Crisis and Conflict*, p. 405; Eleanor Bancroft, taped interview, February 7, 1994.

8. Deborah Lipstadt, *Beyond Belief: The American Press and the Coming of the Holocaust 1933-1945* (New York: The Free Press, 1986), p. 23 quoted Shirer and Lochner.

9. *Herald Tribune*, September 10, 11, and 12, 1935.

10. *Herald Tribune*, September 16 and 17, 1935.

11. *Herald Tribune*, September 22, 1935. The initial expulsion of the Jews from Spain took place in 1492, under Ferdinand and Isabella. The Marranos to whom Barnes refers were Jews who had converted to Christianity. Claiming to doubt the sincerity of their conversion, the Spanish government later expelled them from Spain as well.

12. Deborah Lipstadt, *Beyond Belief*, p. 28.

13. *Herald Tribune*, October 4, 11, 12, 14 and 16, 1935.

14. *Herald Tribune*, October 13 and November 11, 1935.
15. *Herald Tribune*, October 20, 1935.
16. *Herald Tribune*, October 28, 1935.
17. *Herald Tribune*, October 31, 1935.
18. *Herald Tribune*, October 21 and 30, November 2 and 4, 1935. Today the term "Confessing" is used more frequently for this element within the German Protestant Church but as Barnes used "Confessional" in his articles, I have used it also to be consistent.
19. *Herald Tribune*, November 30, December 3 and 8, 1935.
20. *Herald Tribune*, October 25 and 26, November 5 and 17, 1935.
21. EPB, Berlin, October, 1935—no exact date; RWB from Haus Schoeneck, near Berchtesgaden, November 17, 1935; EPB, Vienna, December 4, 1935.
22. *Herald Tribune*, December 23 and 24, 1935, datelines Vienna, December 9 and 10.
23. *Herald Tribune*, December 25 and 26, 1935, datelines Vienna, December 11 and 12. The Archduke Otto, the son of the last, ill-fated Emperor of Austria, waited in Belgium to be restored to the Hapsburg throne.
24. *Herald Tribune*, December 22, 1935.
25. *Herald Tribune*, December 22, 23, 25, 29, and 31, 1935.
26. EPB, Berlin, February 18, 1936.
27. *Herald Tribune*, January 6 and 7, 1936.
28. *Herald Tribune*, January 12 and 19, 1936. Unfortunately expressions of sympathy and support may have had the effect of closing Jewish eyes to the dangers ahead.
29. *Herald Tribune*, February 10, 12, 16, and 20, 1936.
30. *Herald Tribune*, February 9, 11, and 16, 1936.
31. *Herald Tribune*, January 2 and 9, 1936.
32. *Herald Tribune*, January 12, 1936.

Chapter 10

1. *Herald Tribune*, February 2, 1936. Barnes's later correspondence suggests that his main source on the German economy was an economic expert named Hoeffding, referred to in his letters as "Oleg's father." I have been unable to determine his first name. See RWB, Lancing, August 12, 1939.
2. *Herald Tribune*, February 23, 1936.
3. *Herald Tribune*, March 1 and 7, 1936.
4. *Herald Tribune*, March 8, 1936.
5. Quoted in Fischer, *Nazi Germany*, p. 411.
6. *Herald Tribune*, March 10, 13, and 16, 1936.
7. *Herald Tribune*, March 14, 16, 17 and 22, 1936.
8. EPB, Berlin, March 22, 1936.
9. *Herald Tribune*, March 29, 1936; RWB, Berlin, April 5, 1936.
10. EPB, Berlin, March 22, 1936.
11. EPB, Berlin, March 14 and 22, 1936; RWB, Berlin, April 12, 1936.
12. *Herald Tribune,* February 4, May 17, February 18, May 19 and April 8, 1936.
13. EPB, April 5, 1936.
14. *Herald Tribune*, April 3, 1936.
15. EPB, Berlin, May 17, 1936; *Herald Tribune* May 7, 9 and 10, 1936.
16. RWB, New York, May 11, 12 and 16, 1936.

17. RWB, New York, May 16, 1936.

18. RWB, on board the *Europa* crossing the Atlantic, May 22, 1936.

19. RWB, on board the *Europa*, May 22, 1936; RWB, Berlin, June 5, 1936.

20. RWB, Belin, June 5, 1936; Mary Parounagian, Berlin, June 20, 1936.

21. Mary Parounagian, Berlin, July 2, 1936; interview with Joan Barnes Kelly and Suzanne Barnes Morrison, September 25, 1992; EPB, Berlin, August 9, 1936.

22. Mary Parounagian, Berlin, July 8, 10, and 13, 1936.

23. *Herald Tribune*, July 5, 1936. An immediate illustration of Barnes's warning was provided in the Free City of Danzig. He spent several days reporting from the old Hanseatic city where local Nazis were defying the authority of the League High Commissioner, Sean Lester. *Herald Tribune*, July 6, 7, 8, and 9, 1936.

24. *Herald Tribune*, July 16 and 28, 1936. In its August 10, 1936, issue, *Time* magazine noted the *Herald Tribune*'s coup in printing the entire text of the manifesto. Barnes had obtained a copy, had it translated, and shipped it to New York on the Queen Mary, to the congratulations of his managing editor, Wilcox. RWB, Berlin, July 28, 1936.

25. *Herald Tribune*, August 2, 1936. Shirer, *Berlin Diary*, p. 52-3; Shirer, *Twentieth Century Journey: The Nightmare Years, 1930-1940* (New York, Little, Brown, 1984) p. 232-3. On Lindbergh, *Herald Tribune*, July 23, 24, and 25, 1936; RWB, Berlin, July 25, 1936. It is no doubt to this visit that Lindbergh's later very vocal opposition to United States entry into the war against Germany can be attributed. Barnes refers to the kidnapping and murder of the Lindberghs' first child in 1932.

26. *Herald Tribune*, June 28, July 12, 21, August 16, 17, and 18, 1936.

27. *Herald Tribune*, August 23 and 24, 1936.

28. *Herald Tribune*, August 29 and 30, 1936.

29. For the background and events of the Spanish Civil War, see Gabriel Jackson, *The Spanish Republic and Civil War* (Princeton: Princeton University Press, 1965); Stanley G. Payne, *The Spanish Revolution* (New York: W. W. Norton, 1970); R. A. H. Robinson, *The Origins of Franco's Spain* (Pittsburgh: University of Pittsburgh Press, 1970); Hugh Thomas, *The Spanish Civil War* (New York: Harper & Row, 1986); Burnett Bolloten, *The Spanish Civil War: Revolution and Counter-Revolution* (Chapel Hill: University of North Carolina Press, 1991).

30. *Herald Tribune*, August 30, 1936. See Franklin R. Gannon, *The British Press and Germany* (Oxford: Clarendon Press, 1971), R. Cockett, *Twilight of Truth: Chamberlain, Appeasement and the Manipulation of the Press, 1937-1940* (New York: St. Martin's Press, 1989), and Eugen Weber, *The Hollow Years: France in the 1930s* (New York: W. W. Norton, 1994).

31. *Herald Tribune*, September 14 and 15, 1936; RWB, Berlin, September 18, 1936.

32. *Herald Tribune*, September 10, 13, and 21, 1936.

33. *Herald Tribune*, September 20 and October 4, 1936.

Chapter Eleven

1. *Herald Tribune*, October 25, 26, November 1, 1936.

2. RWB, Berchtesgaden, November 5, 1936.

3. *Herald Tribune*, November 28, December 2 and 4, 1936.
4. *Herald Tribune*, December 4, 11 and 13, 1936; RWB, Berlin, December 4 and 6, 1936. The restraint of the German papers may have been due to the perception that Edward VIII was sympathetic to the Nazi regime and might be useful. See Philip Ziegler, *King Edward VIII: A Biography* (New York: Alfred A. Knopf, 1991) for the documentary evidence of Nazi interest in the Duke and Duchess of Windsor.
5. *Herald Tribune*, November 30, December 10 and 18, 1936.
6. *Herald Tribune*, December 19 and 27, 1936.
7. *Herald Tribune*, December 20, 21, and 25, 1936.
8. RWB, Berlin, December 21, 1936 and January 9, 1937; EPB, Berlin, December 18, 1936 and January 1, 1937.
9. *Herald Tribune*, December 23 and 27, 1936, January 2 and 3, 1937.
10. *Herald Tribune*, January 31, 1937; RWB, Berlin, October 19, 1936.
11. *Herald Tribune*, January 24, 1937.
12. *Herald Tribune*, January 31, 1937.
13. RWB, Berlin, January 31, 1937. His friend Joseph Barnes had recently been assigned to Moscow by the *Herald Tribune*. Ralph Barnes welcomed the assignment, pointing to Joe's fluent command of Russian, but the trials were a mystery to most.
14. *Herald Tribune*, January 23 and 27, February 3, 1937.
15. *Herald Tribune*, March 22, 23 and 26, April 8 and 9, June 21, 1937.
16. The issue is a constant in the pages of the *Herald Tribune* through the year. See for example: February 14, 28, March 3, 15, 28, April 4, June 25, and July 2, 3, and 4, 1937.
17. *Herald Tribune*, February 21 and April 1, 1937.
18. *Herald Tribune*, March 5, 6, 13, 14, 18, 21, April 3, 1937.
19. EPB, Berlin, April 6, 1937; May 9 and 18, 1937.
20. RWB, Kladow, June 2, 1937. For the staffing of the *New York Times*, see Desmond, *Crisis and Conflict*, p. 299, and *Tides of War*, p. 79.
21. EPB, Kladow, June 28, 1937; Martha Dodd, *Through Embassy Eyes* (New York: Harcourt, Brace, 1939), p. 110-11.
22. *Herald Tribune*, July 4, 15, and 18, 1937.
23. *Herald Tribune*, July 19, 1937.
24. *Herald Tribune*, July 20, August 15 and 22, 1937.
25. Shirer, *Berlin Diary*, p. 62, wrote that fifty foreign correspondents went to the train to see Ebbutt off, "despite a tip from Nazi circles that our presence would be considered an unfriendly act to Germany!" Shirer considered Ebbutt "the best correspondent here."
26. EPB, Kladow, July 8, 1937; RWB, Berlin, November 7 and December 2, 1937.
27. *Herald Tribune*, December 19, 1937.
28. EPB, Berlin, December 2, 1937.
29. Kluger, *The Paper*, pp. 295-7. Kluger's careful accounting of these events confirms Ralph and Esther's perceptions, even to the point of the problem of Ogden Reid's drinking and its relationship to the *Herald Tribune*'s difficulties.
30. EPB, Berlin, January 1, 1938; RWB, Berlin, February 27, 1938.

Chapter Twelve

1. *Herald Tribune*, January 2, 7, 9, 15, 16, 20, 25, and 30, 1938.
2. Barnes used the joke in an article, *Herald Tribune*, February 13, 1938. The best and most detailed account of this key episode in the relationship between Hitler and the German Army is Harold C. Deutsch, *Hitler and His Generals: The Hidden Crisis, January-June 1938*, (Minneapolis: University of Minnesota Press, 1974). See also Telford Taylor, *Munich: The Price of Peace* (New York: Random House, 1979), pp. 313-30.
3. Barnes reviewed the entire affair in a letter to his parents dated March 29, 1938.
4. *Herald Tribune*, January 30 and 31, 1938.
5. *Herald Tribune*, February 2, 3 and 4, 1938.
6. RWB, Berlin, February 27, 1938; *Herald Tribune*, February 5, 1938. During the following week, Barnes wrote several articles about the ongoing purge of the German army. Officers were dismissed, many resigned, a number were detained for a time; it does not appear that any were executed.
7. Deutsch, *Hitler and His Generals*, p. 267; Klaus-Jürgen Müller, "The German Military Opposition before the Second World War," in Wolfgang J. Mommsen and Lothar Kettenacker, eds., *The Fascist and the Policy of Appeasement* (London: Allen & Unwin, 1983). It should be remembered, however, that the major plot against Hitler, the assassination attempt of 1944, was essentially a plot of army officers.
8. *Herald Tribune*, February 6 and 8, 1938.
9. *Herald Tribune*, February 13 and 17, 1938. No formal account of the meeting at the Berghof was recorded. Schuschnigg made his own notes and reproduced them in his memoir *Austrian Requiem* (New York: G.P. Putnam's Sons, 1947), pp. 20-32.
10. Taylor, *Munich*, p. 352. *Herald Tribune*, March 11, 1938; RWB, Berlin, March 29, 1938. Barnes noted in his letter that Louis Lochner of the Associated Press "hit the same source shortly after midnight, and secured somewhat similar information."
11. *Herald Tribune*, March 12, 1938; Taylor, pp. 358-369.
12. *Herald Tribune*. March 13, 1938.
13. *Herald Tribune*, March 15, 1938.
14. RWB, Berlin, March 12, 1938.
15. *Herald Tribune*, February 8, 1938.
16. *Herald Tribune*, March 5, 1938. Imprisoned first at Sachsenhausen and later at Dachau, where one of his fellow prisoners was the former Austrian chancellor Kurt von Schuschnigg, Niemöller survived World War II. He was freed in 1945 by the advancing American Army.
17. RWB, Berlin, February 27, 1938, March 12, 1938.
18. RWB, Berlin, March 29, 1938.
19. RWB, Berlin, February 27, March 29, 1937.
20. EPB, Berlin, January 10, 1938.
21. RWB, Berlin, March 12, 1938; *Herald Tribune*, March 16, 1938. Barnes's prediction, based on his reading of the German press, turned out to be correct.
22. Taylor, *Munich*, p. 980.
23. Taylor, *Munich*, p. 378.
24. *Herald Tribune*, March 19, 21, 27, 29; April 1; May 15 and 17, 1938.

25. *Herald Tribune*, May 21 and 22, 1938.

26. *Herald Tribune*, May 25, 1938. Hitler responded to the suggestion that he had backed down by calling together his generals to announce that he would destroy Czechoslovakia. See Eugene Davidson, *The Unmaking of Hitler* (Columbia: University of Missouri Press, 1996) p. 198.

27. *Herald Tribune*, June 13, 1938.

28. *Herald Tribune*. May 23, 1938. EPB, Le Coq sur Mer, Belgium, letter undated but internal evidence suggests it was written about May 30, 1938.

29. EPB, Berlin, May 17, 1938. EPB, Le Coq sur Mer, undated letter, late May, 1938.

30. *Herald Tribune*, June 4 and 13, 1938.

31. *Herald Tribune*, June 8, 14, 15, 16, and 17, 1938.

32. RWB, Le Coq sur Mer, July 7, 1938; Berlin, June 19, 1938.

Chapter Thirteen

1. *Herald Tribune*, July 31, August 3,4, and 11, 1938; EPB, Berlin, August 11, 1938.

2. *Herald Tribune*, August 13, 14, 16, and 31, 1938.

3. The *Washington Post* had just begun to subscribe to the *Herald Tribune*'s foreign news service.

4. *Herald Tribune*, September 10, 11, and 13, 1938.

5. EPB, Berlin, September 13, 1938.

6. *Herald Tribune*, September 16, 1938.

7. *Herald Tribune*, September 21, 1938.

8. *Herald Tribune*, September 22, 1938.;*Freely to Pass* (New York: Thomas Y. Crowell, 1942), p. 80. Fifty years later, the British historian Donald Cameron Watt used the same quote in his history of the last year before World War II, *How War Came: Immediate Origins of the Second World War, 1938-1939* (New York: Pantheon, 1989), pp. 11 and 30. The Barnes papers include a clipping from a German newspaper picturing the German foreign minister, Ribbentrop, Chamberlain, the British ambassador, Nevile Henderson, and Ralph Barnes. There is a note on it in Barnes's handwriting: "I didn't clip this so I am not sure what paper it is from."

9. *Herald Tribune*, September 23, 1938.

10. *Herald Tribune*, September 24, 1938.

11. *Herald Tribune*, September 25, 26 and 28, 1938.

12. EPB, Berlin, September 27, 1938.

13. *Herald Tribune*, September 29, 1938.

14. *Herald Tribune*, September 30, 1938.

15. *Herald Tribune*, October 1, 1938.

16. *Herald Tribune*, October 9, 1938. See also Geoffrey Roberts, *The Soviet Union and the Origins of the Second World War* (New York: St. Martin's Press, 1995), pp. 49-91.

17. RWB, Juan-les-Pins on the French Riviera, October 10 and 21, 1938.

18. EPB, Oslo, Norway, October 9, 1938.

19. RWB, en route from Paris to Berlin, October 27, 1938. Walter B. Kerr, then a very young rookie who had left Yale because of the Depression, should not be confused with Walter F. Kerr, long the *Herald Tribune*'s theater critic. Kluger, *The Paper*, pp. 329 and 488.

20. *Herald Tribune*, November 10, 1938. The family of the young assailant, Herschel Grynszpan, was among the 13,000 Polish Jews expelled from Germany by Hitler on October 30. Richard Lamb, *The Drift to War 1922-1939* (New York: St. Martin's Press, 1989), p. 278.

21. *Herald Tribune*, November 11, 1938.

22. *Herald Tribune*, November 12, 1938.

23. *Herald Tribune*, November 13, 1938.

24. *Herald Tribune*, November 14, 1938. Days later, estimates put the number of Jews arrested at 45,000. *Herald Tribune*, November 16, 1938.

25. *Herald Tribune*, November 16 and 17, 1938.

26. *Herald Tribune*, November 18, 1938.

27. *Herald Tribune*, November 19, 1938. Dorothy Thompson was a regular contributor to the *Herald Tribune*.

28. *Herald Tribune*, November 21, 1938.

29. *Herald Tribune*, November 23, 1938.

30. *Herald Tribune*, November 29 and December 1, 2, and 4, 1938. The December 2 article about the refugee Jewish children was written by Barnes's new secretary, Tania Long. RWB, Berlin, December 9, 1938.

31. *Herald Tribune*, December 11, 16, and 20, 1938.

32. *Herald Tribune*, December 22 and 25, 1938.

33. RWB, Berlin, January 1, 1939.

34. *Herald Tribune*, December 27, 28 and 31, 1938. Barnes reported another prediction in the piece that the new year's weather would be so cold that "'one won't be able to weep over the fate of German Jews without carrying an acetylene torch, which will be used to melt the icicles formed by the tears.'" The prediction was the caption for a cartoon which showed two Catholic priests using torches on their ice-covered faces.

35. *Herald Tribune*, January 1, 3, and 6, 1939.

36. *Herald Tribune*, January 23 and 26, 1939.

37. EPB, Berlin, January 28, 1939.

38. *Herald Tribune*, January 31, 1939.

39. *Herald Tribune*, February 2 and 9, 1939.

40. EPB, Berlin, January 6, 1939; RWB, Berlin, January 31, 1939.

41. RWB, Berlin, February 14, 1939.

42. *Herald Tribune*, February 19, 23, March 5, 1939.

43. *Herald Tribune*, March 7, 1939.

44. RWB, Berlin, March 4, 1939.

Part IV. The Coming of War:
March 1939—November 1940

Chapter Fourteen

1. RWB, London, March 18, 1939.

2. EPB, Berlin, March 18, 1939.

3. EPB, Berlin, March 26, 1939.

4. EPB, London, April 6, 1939.

5. RWB, London, March 18, 1939.

6. *Herald Tribune*, March 27, 1939.

7. Watt, *How War Came*, pp. 166-7; *Herald Tribune*, March 28, 29, and 30, 1939.

8. *Herald Tribune*, March 30, 1939.

9. *Herald Tribune*, March 31 and April 1, 1939.

10. *Herald Tribune*, April 4, 1939.

11. *Herald Tribune*, April 7, 8, 9, and 10, 1939.

12. *Herald Tribune*, April 12 and 13, 1939.

13. *Herald Tribune*, April 15, 17, 19, and 23, 1939.

14. RWB, London, April 22, 1939. Kelley later served as a war correspondent for the *Herald Tribune* in the Pacific theater and reported on the liberation of the Philippines in 1945. Desmond, *Tides of War*, pp. 424, 428, and 432.

15. RWB, London, April 11 and 22, 1939. Martha Dodd, *Through Embassy Eyes* (New York: Harcourt, Brace, 1939), p. 110.

16. RWB, London, May 2, 1939. Martha Dodd was rather more complicated than Barnes imagined. Initially, she was quite impressed with the Nazis but then came to see the Soviet Union as the only hope in stopping Hitler. In the course of her relationship with Boris Vinogradov (or Winogradov, as it is spelled in the Dodd papers), a Russian diplomat who appears to have also been a spy, Martha Dodd provided the Soviet Union with embassy files and other sensitive information. Vinogradov was called back to Moscow and perished in the Stalinist purges. Dodd married Alfred K. Stern in 1938. Both fled to Mexico in 1953 because of a Justice Department investigation into their participation in Soviet espionage, a charge for which they were indicted *in absentia* in 1957. Dodd lived in Prague from 1957 until 1962 when she emigrated to Cuba. She returned to Prague in 1968 and died there in 1990. Martha Dodd papers, Library of Congress; David Fromkin, *In the Time of the Americans* (New York: Alfred A. Knopf, 1995), pp. 358-9.

17. RWB, London, May 2, 1939.

18. EPB, London, April 16 and May 10, 1939.

19. *Herald Tribune*, April 26, 1939.

20. *Herald Tribune*, April 27 and 30, 1939.

21. *Herald Tribune*, May 6, 1939.

22. *Herald Tribune*, May 9, 13, 14, 25, 28, June 1, 1939.

23. *Herald Tribune*, May 12, 1939.

24. RWB, London, May 10, 1939. *Herald Tribune*, May 28, June 4 and 11, 1939.

25. *Herald Tribune*, May and June, 1939; RWB, London, May 2, 1939.

26. RWB, London, May 10, 30, June 14, 1939.

27. EPB, Lancing, June 19, 1939.

28. *Herald Tribune*, July 5, 1939.

29. *Herald Tribune*, July 11, 12, 13, 14, and 16, 1939.

30. *Herald Tribune*, July 27, August 1 and 3, 1939.

31. *Herald Tribune*, July 30, 1939.

32. *Herald Tribune*, August 6, 1939.

33. EPB, Lancing, July 24, 1939.

34. EPB, Lancing, August 22, 1939; *Herald Tribune*, August 22, 1939.

35. *Herald Tribune*, August 23, 1939.

36. *Herald Tribune*, August 24 and 25, 1939.

37. James Reston, *Deadline: A Memoir* (New York: Random House, 1991), p. 73.

38. *Herald Tribune*, August 26 and 27, 1939.

39. Stenographic record of radio interview, National Broadcasting Company, heard on station KGW in Portland, Oregon.

40. *Herald Tribune*, August 28, 1939.

41. *Herald Tribune*, August 29, 30 and 31, 1939.

42. *Herald Tribune*, September 3, 1939.

43. *Herald Tribune*, September 4, 1939.

44. *Herald Tribune*, August 25, September 4, 5, and 6, 1939; EPB, Lancing, September 7, 1939.

45. EPB, Lancing, September 7 and 18, 1939.

46. *Herald Tribune*, September 10 and 13, 1939.

47. *Herald Tribune*, September 18, 1939.

48. RWB, Lancing, September 10, and London, September 24, 1939.

49. RWB, London, September 24, 1939; EPB, Lancing, September 24 and 30, 1939.

50. EPB, Lancing, September 30 and October 25; RWB, London, October 9, 1939.

51. *Herald Tribune*, November 11, 1939.

52. *Herald Tribune*, November 10, 16, and 17, 1939.

53. Stowe, *No Other Road to Freedom*, pp. 246-7.

54. *Herald Tribune*, November 22, 24, 25, 28, December 1 and 7, 1939.

55. EPB, Lancing, November 29 and December 10, 1939; RWB, London, December 26, 1939 and January 17, 1940.

56. RWB, London, January 21, 1940.

57. RWB, London, January 21, 1940; EPB, Lancing, January 31 and February 19, 1940; *Herald Tribune*, January 28, 1940.

58. EPB, Lancing, January 27, 1940.

59. *Herald Tribune*, January 18, 1930.

60. February 18, 19, 20 and 21, 1940.

61. RWB, Amsterdam, April 20, 1940; EPB, Lancing, April 17, 1940; *Herald Tribune*, May 12, 1940.

Chapter Fifteen

1. RWB, Amsterdam, April 20, 1940. Barnes referred to Clinton "Beach" Conger whose father, Seymour "Beach" Conger, had been Associated Press correspondent in Germany from 1911 until 1917. According to Desmond, a Conger article which appeared in the *Herald Tribune* on November 14, 1939, and in the London press on November 15, offended the German authorities apparently because it referred to plans for an invasion of the Netherlands and because it spoke of German unrest at home. While Conger was not actually expelled, his communications privileges were revoked; he could no longer attend news conferences and no one in authority would give him any information. The *Herald Tribune* reassigned him, to Rome according to Desmond, but he was in Amsterdam with Barnes, then in Paris immediately before the German occupation. Desmond, *Tides of War*, pp. 121, 127-8.

2. *Herald Tribune*, April 17, 1940.

3. *Herald Tribune*, April 18, 1940.

4. RWB, Berlin, May 3, 1940; *Herald Tribune*, April 26, 1940.

5. *Herald Tribune*, April 29, 30, May 1, 1940.

6. *Herald Tribune*, May 8 and 11, 1940.

7. *Herald Tribune*, May 11, 1940.

8. RWB, Berlin, May 10, 1940; EPB, Stratford-on-Avon, May 22, 1940. In a letter from Lancing dated August 12, 1939, Barnes wrote of a visit from Oleg Hoeffding, "son of the economic expert who was so helpful in Berlin."

9. *Herald Tribune*, May 12, 13, 14, and 15, 1940.

10. *Herald Tribune*, May 16, 1940. Barnes was correct in dismissing talk of weapons emitting special rays but wrong in his speculation attributing the German success at Eben Emael to paratroopers. The "secret weapon" was the Koch Storm Detachment, sappers who landed on top of the fort in gliders in an operation that especially delighted Hitler. See Alistair Horne, *To Lose a Battle: France 1940* (London: Macmillan, 1990), pp. 267-71.

11. *Herald Tribune*, May 15, 1940. This is one case in which the awkwardness of Ralph's translation may suggest the awkwardness of the original.

12. *Herald Tribune*, May 18, 19, 20, and 21, 1940.

13. *Herald Tribune*, May 22, 1940.

14. *Herald Tribune*, May 23, 1940. In *The Ordeal of Total War: 1939-1945* (New York: Harper, 1968), page 27, Gordon Wright spoke of "mild panic at Hitler's headquarters," in response to the Allied initiative; but when the Allied advance slowed, Guderian renewed the advance of his tank corps on May 22. Of Dunkirk, he wrote: "The eight-day naval operation that followed was astonishingly successful; 200,000 British and 130,000 French soldiers were taken off the beaches, though all of their equipment was lost. While German dive bombers harassed the embarking troops, German tank forces along the perimeter of the Dunkirk beachhead failed to move in for the *coup de grâce*. A legend later materialized that Hitler had overruled his generals on this point, and had intentionally spared the escaping British in an effort to arrive at an early peace settlement with London. In fact, the German high command was sharply divided over the wisdom of risking its tanks in the difficult terrain around Dunkirk; Hitler took the side of the cautious faction, partly because he believed that the Luftwaffe could do the job alone." In the second volume of his history of the war, *Their Finest Hour* (New York: Houghton Mifflin, 1949), p. 68, Winston Churchill discussed the German decision, which he attributed to Rundstedt's uneasiness about putting tank forces in jeopardy.

15. *Herald Tribune*, May 25 and 26, 1940.

16. RWB, Berlin, May 25 and following, 1940.

17. *Herald Tribune*, May 31, June 1, 2, 3, and 10, 1940; EPB, New York, June 13, 1940; *Oregonian*, August 5, 1940.

18. *Herald Tribune*, May 29, 30, 31, June 1, 1940.

19. RWB, Berlin and en route to Dunkirk, May 30 and June 1, 1940. In his reporting and his personal correspondence, Barnes used the French spelling "Dunkerque;" I have used the more common English spelling.

20. Barnes's dispatch, datelined June 2, was delayed and did not appear in the *Herald Tribune* until June 5, 1940.

21. *Herald Tribune*, June 6 and 7, 1940. Both articles are datelined June 4. In her book *No Ordinary Time* (New York: Touchstone, 1994), p. 63, Doris Kearns Goodwin quoted Barnes's description of Dunkirk from the June 7 *Herald Tribune*.

22. *Herald Tribune*, June 8, 1940.

23. *Herald Tribune*, June 11 and 12, 1940.

24. *Herald Tribune*, June 14, 1940.

25. *Herald Tribune*, June 15, 1940.

26. *Herald Tribune*, June 18, 1940.

27. *Herald Tribune*, June 19, 1940.

28. The background of the Fall of France and the Vichy regime has been the subject of a number of works. Two worth consulting are Weber, *The Hollow Years: France in the 1930s.* (New York: Pantheon, 1989) and Alistair Horne, *To Lose a Battle: France, 1940* (London: Macmillan, 1990).

Chapter Sixteen

1. EPB to her family, Bronxville, June 17, 1940; RWB, Berlin, June 26, 1940.

2. *Herald Tribune*, June 20, 1940.

3. *Herald Tribune*, June 23, 1940. On June 20, Barnes had filed one last dispatch from Berlin, detailing reports he was hearing of the German plans for the French surrender. Supposedly it would take place in the forest of Compiègne, in the location and in the very railcar in which Marshal Ferdinand Foch had in November, 1918, imposed the terms for the armistice on the defeated Germans. Ralph further reported on the terms expected to be imposed including the annexation of Alsace and possibly Lorraine. The German High Command also announced the beginning of bombing raids on Britain, in reprisal, they maintained, for British bombing of non-military targets in Germany. *Herald Tribune*, June 21, 1940.

4. RWB, Budapest, June 28, 1940.

5. EPB, Bronxville, June 24, 1940.

6. Shirer, *Berlin Diary* , p. 334, and *The Nightmare Years*, p. 550. As a broadcast rather than a print journalist, Shirer was more constrained, in that his scripts had to be approved by the censor prior to his broadcast.

7. Howard K. Smith, *Last Train from Berlin* (New York: Alfred A. Knopf, 1942), p. 148.

8. Robert W. Desmond, *Tides of War*, p. 122. Desmond is, of course, in error is saying that Barnes had also been expelled from Germany in 1939. His transfer to London was at his own and his paper's initiative.

9. RWB, Bucharest, July 15, 1940.

10. *Herald Tribune*, July 2, 4, 5, 7, 10, and 12, 1940.

11. *Herald Tribune*, July 15 and 19, 1940.

12. *Herald Tribune*, July 22, 1940; RWB, Sofia, Bulgaria, July 19, 1940.

13. *Herald Tribune*, July 26 and August 1, 1940.

14. RWB, Ankara, August 4, 1940.

15. RWB, Jerusalem, August 16, 1940; *Herald Tribune*, August 11, 1940.

16. *Herald Tribune*, August 27, 1940.

17. *Herald Tribune*, August 31, 1940.

18. *Herald Tribune*, September 1, 1940.

19. RWB, Cairo, September 6, 1940.

20. *Herald Tribune*, September 10 and 12, 1940.

21. RWB, Alexandria, September 11, 1940.

22. RWB, Cairo, September 15, 1940.

23. *Herald Tribune*, September 17, 1940.

24. *Herald Tribune*, September 21 and 25, 1940.

25. *Herald Tribune*, September 29, 1940.

26. *Herald Tribune*, September 30, 1940.

27. *Herald Tribune*, October 5 and 9, 1940; *Time*, October 14, 1940.

28. *Herald Tribune*, October 10, 1940.

29. *Herald Tribune*, October 21 and 22, 1940.

30. *Herald Tribune*, October 5, 1940; *Time*, October 13, 1940; Stowe, *No Other Road*, p. 245.

31. Stowe, *No Other Road*, p. 252.

32. *Herald Tribune*, October 30, 1940.

33. RWB, Cairo, September 19, 1940.

34. EPB, Salem, October 14, 1940. Two copies of this letter are in the Barnes papers. One has a stamp on the back of the letter "American Legation December 12, 1940 Cairo"—it is not clear that Ralph ever received it. There is a second copy of the letter apparently sent through the Pacific route.

35. RWB, Cairo, October 6 and 9, 1940. Cable, Cairo, October 10, 1940.

36. *Herald Tribune*, November 10, 1940.

37. Stowe, *No Other Road*, p. 258-59.

38. Stowe, *No Other Road*, p. 263.

39. *Herald Tribune*, November 21, 1940.

40. *Herald Tribune*, November 20, 1940.

Bibliography

Newspapers and Periodicals

Eagle, Brooklyn, New York
Capitol Journal, Salem, Oregon
Clarion, Salem High School, Salem, Oregon
Collegian, Willamette University, Salem, Oregon
Herald Tribune, New York
International Herald Tribune, Paris, France
New York Times
Oregon Statesman, Salem, Oregon
Oregonian, Portland, Oregon
Paris Herald, Paris, France
The Oregon Journal, Portland
Wallulah, Willamette University, Salem, Oregon
Willamette University Bulletin, 1917

Books and Articles

Abbe, James. "Men of Cablese," *New Outlook* 162 (December, 1933).

Abrams, Alan E., ed. *Journalist Biographies Master Index: A Guide to 90,000 References to Historical and Contemporary Journalists in 200 Biographical Directories and Other Sources*. Detroit, 1979.

Allen, William Sheridan. *The Nazi Seizure of Power: The Experience of a Single German Town, 1930-1935*. New York: Franklin Watts, 1973.

Alsop, Joseph W., with Adam Platt. *I've Seen the Best of Times*. New York: W. W. Norton, 1992.

Bassow, Whitman. *The Moscow Correspondents: Reporting on Russia from the Revolution to Glasnost*. New York: Paragon House, 1989.

Bauer, Yehuda. *American Jewry and the Holocaust*. Detroit: Wayne State University Press, 1981.

Beattie, Edward W., Jr. *"Freely to Pass"*, New York: Thomas Y. Crowell, 1942.

"Berlin Correspondents Have 'Harrowing, Nervewracking Job.'" *World Press News*, July 13, 1939.

Bessel, Richard. *Germany after the First World War*. Oxford: Clarendon Press, 1993.

Bohlen, Charles E. *Witness to History: 1929-1969*. New York: W.W. Norton & Company, 1973.

Bolloten, Burnett. *The Spanish Civil War: Revolution and Counter-Revolution.* Chapel Hill: University of North Carolina Press, 1991.

Bullock, Alan. *Hitler: A Study in Tyranny.* New York: Harper and Row, 1962.

———. *Hitler and Stalin: Parallel Lives.* New York: Alfred A. Knopf, 1992.

Calmer, Ned. *All the Summer Days.* Boston: Little, Brown, 1961.

Carrère D'Encausse, Hélène. *Stalin: Order Through Terror.* New York: Longman, 1981.

Carynnyk, Marco. "The Famine the *Times* Couldn't Find," *Commentary* 76, November, 1983.

Chamberlin, William Henry. *The Confessions of an Individualist.* New York: Macmillan, 1940.

———. "Soviet Taboos," *Foreign Affairs* April, 1935.

Churchill, Winston. *Their Finest Hour.* New York: Houghton, Mifflin, 1949.

Cockett, R. *Twilight of Truth: Chamberlain, Appeasement and the Manipulation of the Press, 1937-1940.* New York: St. Martin's Press, 1989.

Conquest, Robert. *The Great Terror: A Reassessment.* New York: Oxford University Press, 1990.

———. *Harvest of Sorrow: Soviet Collectivization and the Terror-Famine.* New York: Oxford University Press, 1986.

———. *Stalin and the Kirov Murder.* New York: Oxford University Press, 1989.

Crowl, James William. *Angels in Stalin's Paradise, Western Reporters in Soviet Russia, 1917-1937: A Case. Study of Louis Fischer and Walter Duranty.* Washington, D.C.: University Press of America, 1982.

Cull, Nicholas John. *Selling War: The British Propaganda Campaign against American "Neutrality" in World War II.* New York: Oxford University Press, 1995.

Davidson, Eugene. *The Unmaking of Hitler.* Columbia: University of Missouri Press, 1996.

Denny, Harold. *Behind Both Lines.* London: Michael Joseph, 1943.

Desmond, Robert W. *Crisis and Conflict: World News Reporting between Two Wars, 1920-1940.* University of Iowa Press, 1982.

———. *Tides of War: World News Reporting 1931-1945.* University of Iowa Press, 1984.

Deutsch, Harold C. *Hitler and his Generals The Hidden Crisis: January-June 1938.* University of Minnesota Press, 1974.

Dodd, Martha. *Through Embassy Eyes.* New York: Harcourt, Brace, 1939.

Duranty, Walter. *I Write as I Please.* New York: Simon & Schuster, 1935.

Eddy, Sherwood. *Russia Today: What We Can Learn From It.* New York, 1934.

Emery, Edwin and Michael C. Emery. *The Press and America: An Interpretative History of the Mass Media.* 4th ed. Englewood Cliffs, N.J., 1978.

Fadeley, Nancie, "Oregon's First Cattle Baron," *Oregon Business Magazine,* Vol. 13, No. 4, April 1990.

Fest, Joachim. *Hitler.* New York: Harcourt, Brace, Jovanovich, 1973.

Feuchtwanger, E. J. *From Weimar to Hitler: Germany 1918-1933.* New York: St. Martin's Press, 1995.

Fischer, Fritz. *Germany's Aims in the First World War.* New York: W. W. Norton, 1967.

Fischer, Klaus B. *Nazi Germany: A New History.* New York: Continuum, 1995.

Fischer, Louis. *Men and Politics: An Autobiography.* New York: Duell, Stone and Pearce, 1941.

———. "Russia Moves Toward Democracy," *Current History*, September, 1935.

Forrest, Wilbur. *Behind the Front Page*. New York: D. Appleton-Century, 1934.

François-Poncet, André. *The Fateful Years*. NY: Howard Fertig, 1972.

Fromkin, David. *In the Time of the Americans*. New York: Knopf, 1995.

Gannon, Franklin. *The British Press and Germany 1936-1939*. Oxford: Clarendon Press, 1971.

Gelb, Michael, ed. *An American Engineer in Stalin's Russia: The Memoirs of Zara Witkin, 1932-1934*. Berkeley: University of California Press, 1991.

Goldhagen, Daniel. *Hitler's Willing Executioners: Ordinary Germans and the Holocaust*. New York: Alfred A. Knopf, 1996.

Goodwin, Doris Kearns. *No Ordinary Time*. New York: Touchstone, 1994.

Halperin, William. *Germany Tried Democracy*. New York: W. W. Norton, 1965.

Harsch, Joseph C. *Pattern of Conquest*. Garden City, New York: Doubleday Doran, 1941.

Heald, Morrell. *Transatlantic Vistas: American Journalists in Europe, 1900-1940*. Kent, Ohio: The Kent State University Press, 1988.

Henderson, Loy W. *A Question of Trust*. Palo Alto: Stanford University Press, 1980.

Hindus, Maurice. *Hitler Cannot Conquer Russia*. New York: Doubleday Doran, 1941.

Hohenberg, J. *Foreign Correspondents: The Great Reporters and Their Times*. New York: Columbia University Press, 1964.

Horne, Alistair. *To Lose a Battle: France, 1940*. London: Macmillan, 1990.

Jackson, Gabriel *The Spanish Republic and Civil War*. Princeton: Princeton University Press, 1965.

Kennan, George F. *Memoirs 1925-1950*. New York: Bantam, 1969.

Kerr, Walter. "Berlin Men Got Break When Nazis Took Paris." *Editor and Publisher*, August 3, 1940.

Kershaw, Ian. *Hitler 1889-1936: Hubris*. New York, W.W. Norton, 1999.

———. *Hitler 1936-1945: Nemesis*. New York, W.W. Norton, 2000.

Kluger, Richard. *The Paper: The Life and Death of the New York Herald Tribune*. New York, Vintage Books, 1989.

Knightley, Philip. *The First Casualty: From the Crimea to Vietnam: The War Correspondent as Hero, Propagandist and Myth Maker*. New York and London: Harcourt Brace Jovanovich, 1975.

Lamb, Richard. *The Drift To War 1922-1939*. New York: St. Martin's Press, 1989.

Laney, Al. *Paris Herald: The Incredible Newspaper*. New York: D. Appleton-Century, 1947.

Lansing, Bernard. "A Reporter at Large: *Kopfwashen* at the Adlon." *New Yorker*, February 15, 1941.

Larson, Cedric. "The German Press Chamber." *Public Opinion Quarterly*, October 1937: 53-70.

Liddell Hart, B. H. *History of the Second World War*. New York: Putnam, 1982.

Lippman, Walter and Charles Merz. "A Test of the News," *New Republic*, August 4, 1920.

Lipstadt, Deborah. *Beyond Belief: The American Press and the Coming of the Holocaust 1933-1945*. New York: The Free Press, 1986.

Lochner, Louis. *Always the Unexpected: A Book of Reminiscences*. New York: Macmillan, 1956.

———. "News-Gathering in Nazi Germany." *Quill*, August 1939: 5-6, 14.

———. *What about Germany?* New York: Dodd and Mead, 1942.

Lukacs, John. "Back from the Dead: Benito Mussolini," *The New York Times Magazine*, July 24, 1994.

———. *The Duel, 10 May-31 July 1940: The Eighty Day Struggle between Churchill and Hitler.* New York: Ticknor & Fields, 1991.

Lyons, Eugene. *Assignment in Utopia.* New York: Harcourt, Brace and Company, 1937.

———. *Moscow Carrousel.* New York: Alfred A. Knopf, 1935.

———. "The 'Purging' of Russia's Communists," *Literary Digest* 117, March 17, 1934.

MacKenzie, DeWill. "Understanding the Problems of the Foreign Correspondent." *Journalism Quarterly*, March 1941: 23-28.

Mack Smith, Denis. *Mussolini.* New York: Alfred A. Knopf, 1982.

McCormick, Anne O'Hare. *The World at Home: Selections from the Writings of Anne O'Hare McCormick.* Ed. Marion Turner Sheehan. Introd. James B. Reston, New York: Alfred A. Knopf, 1956.

McDonough, Frank. "*The Times*, Norman Ebbut and the Nazis, 1927-1937," *Journal of Contemporary History*, Vol. 27, 1992.

McNeil, *Valiant for Truth: Clarence True Wilson and Prohibition.* Portland: Oregonians Concerned about Addiction Problems, 1992.

Miller, Webb. *I Found No Peace: The Journal of a Foreign Correspondent.* London: Victor Gollancz, 1937.

Mommsen, Wolfgang J. and Lothar Kettenacker, eds. *The Fascist Challenge and the Policy of Appeasement.* London: Allen and Unwin, 1983.

"The Moscow Correspondent —A Symposium," *Survey, A Journal of Soviet and East European Studies,* July 1967.

Muggeridge, Malcolm. *Chronicles of Wasted Time. Vol. 1, The Green Stick.* New York: William Morrow & Company, 1973.

———. *Like It Was: The Diaries of Malcolm Muggeridge.* New York: William Morrow & Company, 1982.

Norden, Margaret K. "American Editorial Response to the Rise of Adolf Hitler: A Preliminary Consideration," *American Jewish Historical Quarterly.* October, 1968: 290-301.

Oeschner, Frederick. *This is the Enemy.* Boston: Little, Brown, 1942.

Payne, Stanley G. *The Spanish Revolution.* New York: W. W. Norton, 1970.

Peukert, Detlev. *The Weimar Republic: The Crisis of Classical Modernity.* Trans. Richard Deveson. New York: Hill and Wang, 1992.

Pipes, Richard. *Russia Under the Bolshevik Regime.* New York: Vintage Books, 1995.

———. *The Russian Revolution.* New York: Alfred A. Knopf, 1990.

Reporting World War II Part One: American Journalism 1938-1944. New York: Literary Classics, 1995.

Reston, James. *Deadline: A Memoir.* New York: Random House, 1991.

Roberts, Geoffrey. *The Soviet Union and the Origins of the Second World War.* New York: St. Martin's Press, 1995.

Robertson, Charles, L. *The International Herald Tribune: The First Hundred Years.* New York: Columbia University Press, 1987.

Robinson, R. A. H. *The Origins of Franco's Spain.* Pittsburgh: University of Pittsburgh Press, 1970.

Salisbury, Harrison. *Without Fear or Favor: The New York Times and Its Times*. New York: Times Publishing Co., 1980.

Sanders, Marion K. *Dorothy Thompson: A Legend in her Time*. Boston: Houghton Mifflin, 1973.

Schuschnigg, Kurt Von. *Austrian Requiem*. New York: G.P. Putnam's Sons, 1947.

Seldes, George. *You Can't Print That!* New York: Garden City Press, 1929.

———. *Sawdust Caesar: The Untold Story of Mussolini and Fascism*. New York: Harper and Brothers, 1935.

Sheean, Vincent. *Personal History*. New York: The Literary Guild of America, 1935.

Shirer, William L. *Berlin Diary: The Journal of a Foreign Correspondent, 1934-1941*. New York: Alfred A. Knopf, 1942.

———. *Twentieth Century Journey: The Nightmare Years, 1930-1940*. Boston: Little, Brown, 1984.

Smith, Howard K. *Last Train from Berlin*. New York: Alfred A. Knopf, 1942.

Steel, Ronald. *Walter Lippmann and the American Century*. New York: Vintage Books, 1981.

Stowe, Leland. *No Other Road to Freedom*. New York: Alfred A. Knopf, 1941.

Taylor, S. J. *Stalin's Apologist: Walter Duranty, the New York Times Man in Moscow*. New York: Oxford University Press, 1990.

Taylor, Telford. *Munich: The Price of Peace*. New York: Random House, 1979.

Thomas, Hugh. *The Spanish Civil War*. New York: Harper & Row, 1986.

Thompson. Dorothy. *Let the Record Speak*. New York: Reynal & Hitchcock, 1939.

Tolischus, Otto. *They Wanted War*. New York: Reynal & Hitchcock, 1940.

Victor, Walther. "Journalism Under Hitler's Heel." *Quill*, June, 1943.

Watt, Donald Cameron. *How War Came: Immediate Origins of the Second World War, 1938-1939*. New York: Pantheon, 1989.

Weber, Eugen. *The Hollow Years: France in the 1930s*. New York: W. W. Norton, 1994.

Wells, Linton. *Blood on the Moon*. Boston and New York: Houghton Mifflin, 1937.

Wright, Gordon. *The Ordeal of Total War: 1939-1945* New York: Harper, 1968.

Ziegler, Philip. *King Edward VIII: A Biography*. New York: Knopf, 1991.

Index